GOA

DEVELOPMENT REPORT

सत्यमेव जयते

PLANNING COMMISSION

GOVERNMENT OF INDIA

Goa
Development Report

सत्यमेव जयते

PLANNING COMMISSION
GOVERNMENT OF INDIA
NEW DELHI

Published by

ACADEMIC FOUNDATION
NEW DELHI

First Published in 2011 by

Academic Foundation

4772-73 / 23 Bharat Ram Road, (23 Ansari Road), Darya Ganj, New Delhi - 110 002 (India).
Phones : 23245001 / 02 / 03 / 04. Fax : +91-11-23245005. E-mail : books@academicfoundation.com
www.academicfoundation.com

Published under arrangement with :

Planning Commission,
Government of India,
New Delhi.

Cataloging in Publication Data--DK
Courtesy: D.K. Agencies (P) Ltd. <docinfo@dkagencies.com>

Goa development report / Planning Commission, Government of India.
p. cm.
ISBN 13: 9788171887880
ISBN 10: 8171887880

1. Economic development--India--Goa (State). 2. Human services--India--Goa (State). 3. Goa (India : State)--Economic policy. 4. Goa (India : State)--Social policy. I. India. Planning Commission.

DDC 330.954799005 22

Designed and typeset by Italics India, New Delhi
Printed and bound in India.

Core Committee

The Composition of the Core Committee for preparation of Goa State Development Report is as follows:

Prof. V.L. Chopra *Member* *Planning Commission, Government of India*	**Chairman**
Shri Uddipta Ray *Secretary (Planning)* *Government of Goa*	**Member**
Dr. Anupam Saraph *Director* *Institute for Change Research, Goa*	**Member**
Shri Ravi Mital *Adviser (SP-Goa)* *Planning Commission*	**Member Secretary**

एम. एस. आहलुवालिया
MONTEK SINGH AHLUWALIA

सत्यमेव जयते

उपाध्यक्ष
योजना आयोग
भारत
DEPUTY CHAIRMAN
PLANNING COMMISSION
INDIA

FOREWORD

One of the important initiatives of the Planning Commission was to sponsor the preparation of the State Development Reports which would serve as critical documents to help set the agenda for the economic growth of the states. This exercise was undertaken in recognition of the fact that economic circumstances and performance of the individual states varied and it was necessary to examine development challenges for individual states in the light of State specific constraints. The basic idea is to produce quality reference documents on development profiles of individual States and to suggest possible strategies for accelerating growth, and reducing poverty and inequality.

The Goa State Development Report has been prepared in collaboration with the Institute for Change Research, Panaji. The report has reviewed Goa's experience in development and highlighted issues critical for the State in the years ahead. I hope its publication will stimulate debate on growth strategies appropriate for Goa. I am sure the roadmap indicated in the report will stimulate a broader awareness of the critical policy issues facing the State and will assist the State to move to a higher growth path and achieve all round human and economic development.

(Montek Singh Ahluwalia)

योजना भवन, संसद मार्ग, नई दिल्ली – 110001 दूरभाष : 23096677, 23096688 फैक्स : 23096699
Yojana Bhawan, Parliament Street, New Delhi : 110001 Phones: 23096677, 23096688 Fax : 23096699, E-mail : dch@.nic.in

DIGAMBAR V. KAMAT
Chief Minister, Goa

सत्यमेव जयते

Secretariat, Porvorim, Goa
Tel.: (O) 0832-241 9504
241 9843

MESSAGE

I am very glad to know that Planning Commission (State Plan Division) Government of India, has prepared Goa State Development Report.

Evolving plans is of utmost importance to undertake systematic development of any state. Through the publication of Goa Development Report the Planning Commission has done a remarkable job which I am confident will go a long way in disseminating information and acquaint the people of the State of the plans and vision set by the Goa Government for a progressive and prosperous State.

I am sure, the endeavour of the Planning Commission will help the State to take it further on the path of progress and prosperity.

I extend my best wishes.

D Kamat

(DIGAMBAR V. KAMAT)
CHIEF MINISTER

DR. NARENDRA JADHAV
MEMBER
PLANNING COMMISSION
GOVERNMENT OF INDIA

सत्यमेव जयते

YOJANA BHAWAN
PARLIAMENT STREET
NEW DELHI-110 001
Tel.: 011-2309 6566
Fax: 011-2309 6567
E-mail: dr.ndj@nic.in
drnarendra.jadhav@gmail.com

MESSAGE

In keeping with the Central Plan Scheme of the "50th Year Initiative for Planning", the Planning Commission has been preparing Development Report of each state. These SDRs are an attempt to compile quality reference documents on the profile and strategy for accelerating the pace of development in the respective State. The report will be of immense help to both Centre and State machineries engaged in steering the Plan process of the State on a higher and equitable growth plan.

The State of Goa is poised as one of the most advanced States with highest per capita income and with best socio-economic indicators in the country. I hope that the Report which analyses the potential sectors of the State economy and suggests policy action would prove useful to the State. This Report will be an important document and will impart value for development practitioners interested in the State.

I would like to place on record Planning Commission's appreciation to all those who have worked in preparing the Report. I am thankful to the Government of Goa for their constant support and cooperation to the team members in preparing this Report. The efforts made by the officers of the State Plans Division, Planning Commission in liaising with the State Government agencies are commendable.

Narendra Jadhav

Contents

List of Tables and Figures

Tables

Figures

Acknowledgements

This Report would not be possible without the strong guidance, unflinching support, faith and contributions of many people who have made this report.

Planning Commission of India

Shri Montek Singh Ahluwalia, Deputy Chairman, Prof. V.L. Chopra, Member, Smt. Adarsh Misra, then Principal Adviser, Shri V.K. Bhatia, then Adviser, Shri Ravi Mital, Adviser, Shri N.D. George, then Director, Smt. Preeti Madan, then Director, Shri H.K. Hajong, Director, Shri Saji Thomas, Consultant and many of the subject experts and Advisers of the Planning Commission of India.

Government of Goa

Mr. Pratapsingh Raoji Rane, the than Hon. Chief Minister, Goa, Mr. Manohar Parrikar, Hon. Leader of Opposition, Ms. Kiran Dhingra, Chief Secretary, Government of Goa, Mr. Dharmendra Sharma, Secretary Planning and Secretaries and Directors to the Government of Goa.

Advisory Committee

Chairman of the Advisory Committee, Dr. V.A. Pai Panandikar, Former Adviser to Prime Minister of India, Founder President of Centre for Policy Research, Dr. Arvind Kudchadkar, Former Vice Chancellor of the Dhirubhai Ambani Institute of Computer Technology and IIT Mumbai and Dr. Satish Shetye, Director of National Institute of Oceanography.

Principal Researchers

Dr. Bala Murali Krishna, UNI, Mr. Jayant Chayya, ICG, Ms. Shaila D'Souza, Goa University, Mr. O.L da Lapa-Soares, ICR, Dr. Dayanand M.S., Goa University, Dr. Narayan B. Desai, Educationist, Mr. Durairaj, RSPL, Mr. Yatin G. Kakodkar, CII, Mr. Nitin Kuncolienkar, GCCI, Dr. Prita Mallya, Damodar College, Dr. Pranab Mukhopadhyaya, Goa University, Mr. Mark Rodrigues, GCCI, Dr. Anupam Saraph, ICR, Prof. Ranjini Swamy, Goa Institute of Management.

Research/Data Assistants

Ms. Gitanjali Borkar, Mr. Arjun Harlarnkar, Ms. Shilpa Netravalkar, Ms. Reetika Syal and Ms. Vilma Fernandes.

Edited by

Dr. V. SriRanjani, Goa University.

Organisations

Business associations, NGOs, industrial houses and citizens' associations and hundreds of stakeholders.

Executive Summary

This Goa State Development Report documents: issues and their fiscal implications, the institutions and governance, the infrastructure, the development and growth areas, the carrying capacity and sustainable activity, the strengths, weakness, opportunities and threats, the outlook: possible scenarios in the short, medium and long term and recommendations and development strategies for different sectors of the Goan economy.

Having sought participation of more than 250 groups and individual stakeholders from across the State the report incorporates many of the issues raised by stakeholders.

The report covers socio-economic and demographic profile, natural resources: water, energy and environmental security, agro economy, mining, manufacturing, industry and value added trading, infrastructure and integrated development, transportation and logistics, health and wellness, employment and security, education and human resource development, tourism and entertainment, information, banking and risk management services, governance: institutions and public private partnerships, governance: reforms, urbanisation and growth nuclei, and economic growth and fiscal policy in the State.

The economy of the 3,700 square kilometre State with its 1.3 million population has a real CAGR of 3.6 per cent between 1998-99 and 2002-03 or on a per-capita basis at a CAGR of 2.1 per cent. In the same period, in real terms, the secondary sector, which is 39.7 per cent of the economy, has grown at a CAGR of 7.7 per cent the tertiary, which is 55.4 per cent, at 2.4 and primary sector, which is 12.9 per cent of the economy at 1.2 per cent.

The report looks at the key infrastructure requirements for growth and services: the sea and airports, the connecting of these to the railways and roadways, the water, sewage and waste management augmentation. It covers the key parameters for governance reforms: measures of performance, composition and representation, tenure, accountability, role, scope and jurisdiction. It highlights the gaps in governance and infrastructure in different sectors, particularly pointing out the quality gaps in education and human resources.

The report summarises key indicators in a table at a glance to serve as a ready reference of numbers available and as a means to evolve standards for collecting data in the future.

The report outlines a development strategy for Goa that will enable Goa to sustain a growth of its per capita NSDP yet ensures sustainable development. The strategy focuses on infrastructure driven growth and education and governance driven development. The report recommends mission based governance boards with broad participation of stakeholders to develop policy and audit the progress and a common shared registry of citizen, business, project, asset, receipts and expenditure to ensure successful implementation of the development strategy.

Chapter 1

Socio-Economic and Demographic Profile

Issues

Location and Size

1. With the Arabian Sea on the west of its 100 km coastline, the State of Goa today stretches over an area of 3,702 sq. km, 1,736 sq. km in North Goa and 1,966 sq. km in South Goa.

2. Goa served as a transit point for trade from the east during the Portuguese colonisation because of its strategic location on the west coast of India.

Administrative Units

3. Goa was liberated from Portuguese colonial rule in 1961, but remained a Union Territory up till 1987 when Goa was declared the 25th State in India.

4. For administrative purposes, Goa is currently divided into two districts, North and South Goa District. There are 6 *talukas* or CD blocks in North Goa and 5 in South Goa. There are a total of 347 inhabited villages with 209 in North Goa and 138 in the South. Of the 188 *panchayats* in the State, 119 are in North Goa and 69 in the South. There are 14 municipal towns with 7 each in North and South Goa and 30 census towns with 20 in North Goa and 10 in South Goa.

Growth

5. Since liberation in 1961, the rate of decadal growth has continuously declined till 2001. In the 1991-2001 decade, the population has grown by 15 per cent which was driven by a whopping 40 per cent growth of urban population while the rural population has declined by 2 per cent in the same period.

6. According to the 2001 Census, the total population of Goa is 757,407 in North Goa and 586,591 in South Goa. Bardez is the most populated, followed by Salcete and then Mormugao. The population in Mormugao has grown the fastest, followed by Bardez and Salcete. Bicholim has seen the slowest growth followed by Pernem and Sanguem.

TABLE 1.1

Decadal Growth of Population 1961-2001

	1961	*1971*	*1981*	*1991*	*2001*
Total population	589,997	795,120	1,007,749	1,169,793	1,347,668
Rural population	502,668	591,877	684,964	690,041	677,091
Urban population	87,329	203,243	322,785	479,752	670,577
Decadal growth in total population		34.77	26.74	16.08	15.21

Source: Census of India.

7. All *talukas* show growth of their urban population with Ponda registering the highest growth, followed by Pernem, Bicholim and Sanguem.

8. Bardez, Bicholim, Ponda and Sanguem show a decline in rural population. Rural population in Bicholim has shrunk the fastest, followed by Ponda and Bardez. Rural population has grown the fastest in Satari, followed by Quepem.

9. This demographic data indicates increasing urbanisation of the State as a whole and a possible relocation of the rural population to urban centres within each *taluka*.

10. The poverty ratio in the State according to Planning Commission estimates for the year 1999-2000 is 4.4 per cent, which is the second lowest in the country next only to Jammu & Kashmir. Poverty in rural Goa is 1.35 per cent and 7.52 per cent in the urban areas. These figures are much lower than the national average of 26.10 per cent (27.09 per cent in rural areas and 23.62 per cent in urban areas and inverse of the national trend where

TABLE 1.2

Growth of Population from 1991 to 2001 in Different *Talukas* in Goa

		1991				2001			
		Area	*Total*	*M*	*F*	*Total*	*M*	*F*	*Growth*
Urban	Bardez	59	84,315	43,220	41,095	133,445	69,189	64,256	58.27%
	Bicholim	28	20,200	10,532	9,668	37,087	19,140	17,947	83.60%
	Canacona	19	10,447	5,381	5,066	11,901	6,196	5,705	13.92%
	Mormugao	48	96,727	52,095	44,632	120,362	64,435	55,927	24.43%
	Pernem	3	4,578	2,296	2,282	9,613	4,950	4,663	109.98%
	Ponda	5	14,661	8,149	6,512	48,615	25,675	22,940	231.59%
	Quepem	37	29,481	14,977	14,504	33,980	17,248	16,732	15.26%
	Salcete	85	111,295	55,640	55,655	151,579	76,307	75,272	36.20%
	Sanguem	5	6,198	3,181	3,017	11,006	5,558	5,448	77.57%
	Satari	12	6,825	3,486	3,339	7,917	4,031	3,886	16.00%
	Tiswadi	85	95,025	49,664	45,361	105,072	53,974	51,098	10.57%
	Urban total	385	479,752	248,621	231,131	670,577	346,703	323,874	39.78%
Rural	Bardez	20,470	105,068	51,768	53,300	94,250	47,216	47,034	-10.30%
	Bicholim	21,073	64,332	32,912	31,420	53,647	27,567	26,080	-16.61%
	Canacona	33,335	30,269	15,241	15,028	32,096	16,080	16,016	6.04%
	Mormugao	6,124	23,776	12,070	11,706	24,587	12,135	12,452	3.41%
	Pernem	24,917	62,111	31,176	30,935	62,386	32,114	30,272	0.44%
	Ponda	28,756	113,566	58,083	55,483	100,826	51,460	49,366	-11.22%
	Quepem	28,156	35,037	17,822	17,215	40,054	20,279	19,775	14.32%
	Salcete	20,782	108,602	52,631	55,971	110,456	53,491	56,965	1.71%
	Sanguem	86,883	53,157	27,132	26,025	53,074	27,017	26,057	-0.16%
	Satari	48,341	42,705	21,567	21,138	50,696	25,849	24,847	18.71%
	Tiswadi	12,901	51,418	25,767	25,651	55,019	27,337	27,682	7.00%
	Rural total	331,737	690,041	346,169	343,872	677,091	340,545	336,546	-1.88%
State	Bardez	20,529	189,383	94,988	94,395	227,695	116,405	111,290	20.23%
	Bicholim	21,101	84,532	43,444	41,088	90,734	46,707	44,027	7.34%
	Canacona	33,354	40,716	20,622	20,094	43,997	22,276	21,721	8.06%
	Mormugao	6,172	120,503	64,165	56,338	144,949	76,570	68,379	20.29%
	Pernem	24,919	66,689	33,472	33,217	71,999	37,064	34,935	7.96%
	Ponda	28,762	128,227	66,232	61,995	149,441	77,135	72,306	16.54%
	Quepem	28,193	64,518	32,799	31,719	74,034	37,527	36,507	14.75%
	Salcete	20,867	219,897	108,271	111,626	262,035	129,798	132,237	19.16%
	Sanguem	86,888	59,355	30,313	29,042	64,080	32,575	31,505	7.96%
	Satari	48,352	49,530	25,053	24,477	58,613	29,880	28,733	18.34%
	Tiswadi	12,985	146,443	75,431	71,012	160,091	81,311	78,780	9.32%
	State total	332,122	1,169,793	594,790	575,003	1,347,668	687,248	660,420	15.21%
	Urban percentage	0.12	41.01	41.80	40.20	49.76	50.45	49.04	
	Rural percentage	99.88	58.99	58.20	59.80	50.24	49.55	50.96	

Source: Census of India, 1991, 2001.

rural poverty is greater than urban poverty). The scenario according to the 2004-05 estimates of the Planning Commission are, however, rather bleak. While the percentage of poverty in rural Goa is only 5.4, in the urban areas it has gone up to 21.3 per cent which makes Goa, the State with the 13th highest percentage of poverty out of 35 States/Union Territories. According to the same data source, 1.9 per cent of the rural population and 20.9 per cent of the urban population are below the poverty line.

Women and Children

11. On most demographic indicators, like the literacy rate, maternal mortality rate, female mortality rate, Goa is

way ahead of most other states in India. Similarly, the average age at marriage for a woman in Goa is 25 years. As the NFHS 3 (National Family Health Survey—III) indicates, Goa also ranks high on maternity care indicators like antenatal checkups, iron and folic acid supplementation, tetanus toxoid injections, delivery at medical facility, assistance at delivery from a trained health professional, checkups after delivery, etc.

Sex Ratio

TABLE 1.3

Sex Ratio, 1900-2001

Year	*Sex Ratio (No. of Females to 1000 Males)*
1900	1091
1910	1108
1921	1120
1931	1088
1940	1084
1950	1128
1960	1066
1971	981
1981	975
1991	967
2001	960

Source: Economic Survey 2003-04, Directorate of Planning, Statistics and Evaluation, Government of Goa.

12. The sex ratio is an indicator of the status that women enjoy in any society (i.e., the number of females to every 1,000 males). There is now a clear evidence that in Goa, like the rest of the country, there is a male child preference among eligible couples (NFHS 3). This is despite the high literacy rate and per capita income that Goa enjoys. This probably explains the declining sex ratio in the state over the last 50 years. Of greater concern however, is the fact that juvenile (0-6 years) sex ratio in 2001 (at 933) was lower than that of the adult sex ratio (960) implying that in the years to come, there will be even lesser female adults to male adults.

13. A low TFR (total fertility rate) is seen as a positive developmental outcome of greater awareness. In Goa, the TFR is as low as 1.79 children per woman (NFHS III), 1.77 in urban areas and 1.81 in rural areas, which is below the replacement rate of population. Another positive statistic worth noting here is that there exists universal knowledge of contraception in the state among women of childbearing age. However, the use of contraception in the State is as low as 48 per cent which is the same as the national average of current contraceptive prevalence. This leads to suspicions that the family size is being controlled by means other than contraception. Given the evidence that there is a male child preference and the low fertility rate is leading to a falling family size, it is not unlikely that the choice of children (both number and sex) is not happening randomly but by means of sex selective techniques and abortions/female foeticide.

14. The size of family among other things is determined by economic well-being of the family. It is worth investigating whether increase in tourism plays any role in the decline in sex ratio, as large tourist inflows have scaled up the cost of living in the State.

TABLE 1.4

Sex Ratio (0-6 years)

Indicator	*Year*	*India*	*Goa*
Sex ratio (0-6 years)	2001	927	933

Source: Census of India.

15. Ponda and Sanguem are the only two *talukas* where the juvenile (0-6) sex ratio is greater than the adult sex ratio. Salcete is the only *taluka* where the number of women is greater than men (for adults) and equal for juveniles. South Goa as a district has larger number of women than men in rural areas. This is, however, pushed by two dominant *talukas* of Salcete and Mormugao. In North Goa, only Tiswadi has a similar showing in the rural areas but is not matched by the juvenile figures. Contrarily, in none of the urban areas is the sex ratio favourable to women. In fact, Ponda and Mormugao show up with the lowest adult sex ratio in the State's urban areas.

Workforce

16. The sex bias may be driven by economic considerations accentuated by the state's workforce profile. The gender gap in Goa's workforce is very striking—men constitute 72 per cent of the registered workforce while women are only 28 per cent. This gap is higher than the national average (*Economic Survey 2003-2004*). It is, however, well accepted that these kinds of statistics are unable to account for "unpaid" work that women do at home. Given that the educational profile of men and women in Goa are similar, this gap in workforce profile is, therefore, difficult to fathom and needs serious policy redressal.

17. The current "world best practice" of affirmative action, where organisations actively promote equal opportunity in education and employment with no

TABLE 1.5

Sex Ratio in Different *Talukas* in Goa (Census 2001)

State/District/Taluka	*Sex Ratio*					
	Total Population			*Age Group 0-6 Years*		
	Rural	*Urban*	*Total*	*Rural*	*Urban*	*Total*
Goa	988	934	961	952	924	938
N. Goa Dist.	970	931	953	939	935	938
Pernem	943	942	943	921	827	907
Bardez	996	929	956	926	924	925
Tiswadi	1013	947	969	932	972	958
Bicholim	946	938	943	939	914	928
Satari	961	964	962	935	980	941
Ponda	959	893	937	970	921	953
S. Goa Dist.	1018	937	972	972	913	937
Mormugao	1026	868	893	917	889	893
Salcete	1065	986	1019	1000	928	957
Quepem	975	970	973	937	909	924
Sanguem	964	980	967	997	911	981
Canacona	996	921	975	925	998	944

Source: Economic Survey 2004-05, Directorate of Planning, Statistics and Evaluation, Government of Goa.

discrimination on grounds of caste, creed, religion, sex or nationality, is not practiced in Goa. There is a need for such intervention by the State by establishing an equal opportunity commission to deal with discrimination. It should promote affirmative action on behalf of segments of the population that feel deprived in the current framework.

TABLE 1.6

Sex-wise Composition of the Workforce

Sex	*Goa* 1991	*Goa* 2001	*India* 2001
Male	71.4	72.00	68.4
Female	28.6	28.00	31.6
Total	100.00	100.00	100.00

Source: Economic Survey 2003-04, Directorate of Planning, Statistics and Evaluation, Government of Goa.

TABLE 1.7

Distribution of Total Worker by Category in Percentage

State/ District	*Area*	*Total Workers*			*Cultivators (%)*			*Agricultural Labourers (%)*			*Workers in Household Industries (%)*			*Other Workers (%)*		
		Total	*M*	*F*	*Total*	*M*	*F*	*Total*	*M*	*F*	*Total*	*M*	*F*	*Total*	*M*	*F*
Goa	T	522,855	375,218	147,637	9.6	6.9	16.7	6.8	4.3	13.4	2.8	2.4	3.9	80.7	86.5	65.9
	R	274,452	185,648	88,804	16.7	12.7	25.2	11.3	7.3	19.7	3.2	2.7	4.1	68.8	77.2	51.1
	U	248,403	189,570	58,833	1.8	1.1	4.0	1.9	1.3	4.0	2.4	2.1	3.6	93.9	95.6	88.4
N. Goa	T	307,628	217,255	90,373	10.2	7.0	18.0	7.2	4.5	13.8	3.0	2.5	4.2	79.5	86.0	64.0
	R	175,509	118,605	56,904	16.3	11.8	25.7	11.1	7.1	19.6	3.5	2.9	4.8	69.1	78.3	49.9
	U	132,119	98,650	33,469	2.2	1.4	4.9	2.0	1.4	3.8	2.3	2.0	3.3	93.4	95.3	88.0
S. Goa	T	215,227	157,963	57,264	8.8	6.6	14.8	6.3	3.9	12.9	2.6	2.3	3.3	82.3	87.2	69.0
	R	98,943	67,043	31,900	17.5	14.3	24.2	11.6	7.7	19.8	2.6	2.5	2.8	68.2	75.4	53.1
	U	116,284	90,920	25,364	1.3	0.9	2.9	1.8	1.1	4.2	2.5	2.1	4.0	94.3	95.9	88.9

Source: Census of India, 2001.

Social Stratification

18. Information from Census sources lists data on distribution of SCs and STs (scheduled castes and scheduled tribes) in Goa for the year 2001. The SC population is 1.8 per cent of Goa's total population while the ST constitute 2.4 per cent. A larger proportion of both SCs and STs are located in urban areas rather rural areas in Goa.

19. In terms of sex-wise distribution of the SCs and STs, the sex ratio for SCs is above the State average while that of the STs is below it. The sex ratio of STs in rural areas is alarmingly low at 827 which goes against the state trend where this ratio in rural areas has been higher than in urban areas.

TABLE 1.8

Sex Ratio of SC/ST

	Sex Ratio (Social Stratification)		
	All Goa	*SC*	*ST*
Total	961	975	893
Rural	988	994	827
Urban	934	959	928

Source: Census 2001.

Age Structure and Dependency

20. The workforce structure of Goa in the near future can be predicted from the age profile of its current population. An analysis of the age profile would also help in determining the proportion of the population that belongs to the working age group and the proportion that is dependent on the earlier group.

21. Tables 1.9 and 1.10 indicate that the dependency ratio (proportion of those who are not working *vis-à-vis* those who are in the working age group) has been decreasing steadily from 45.3 (1961) to 35.7 (1991) and 32.9 (2001) respectively. The working age group (which is the total population minus the children from 0-14 years and the persons above 60) has been expanding from 3,42,648 in 1961 to 8,97,157 in the year 2001.

22. Since there are various measures of dependency, we will quickly look at some of these figures in the Goan context. What is significant to note here is that despite an overall declining sex ratio, the proportion of female senior citizens is far more than male senior citizens. This probably is the only age group where women outnumber men. This number too has been declining. The proportion of senior citizens (above 60 years of age) in the total population has remained steady—it was 8.1 per cent of the total population in 1961, to 7.1 per cent in 1991 and 8.3 per cent in 2001.

FIGURE 1.1

Age Structure of Population from 1961-2001

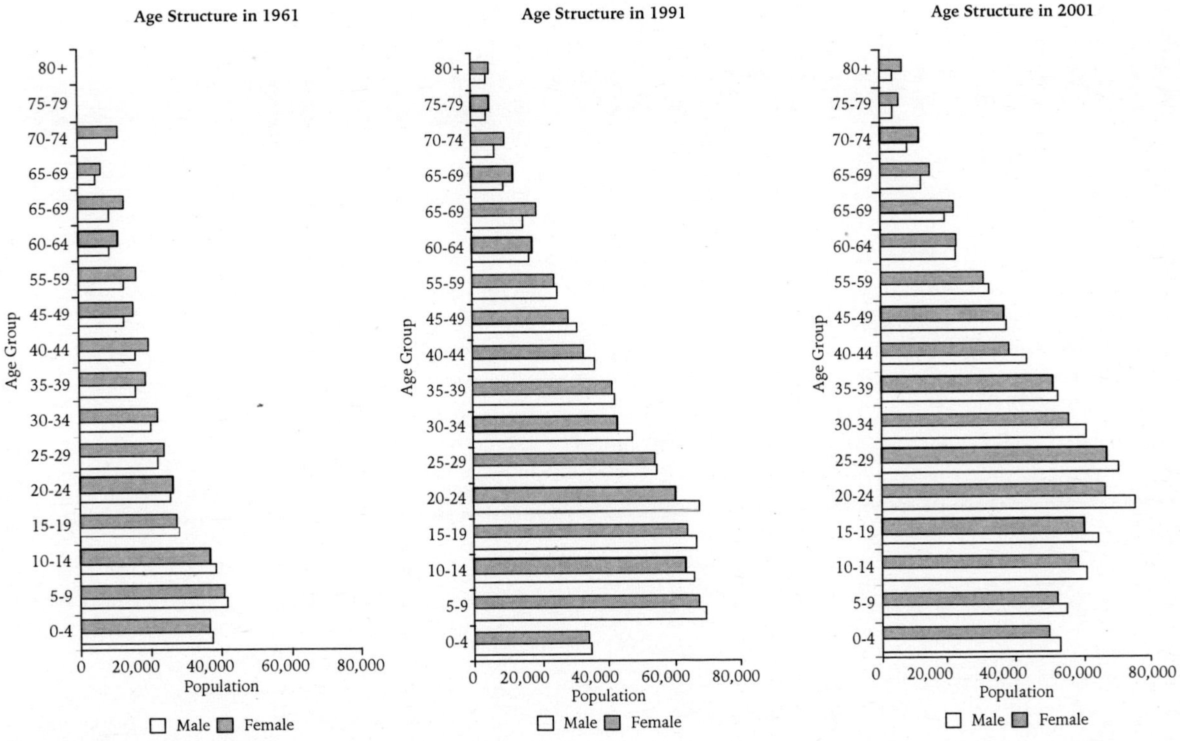

Source: Census of India, 1961 to 2001.

TABLE 1.9

Age Structure of Population from 1961 to 2001

	Total			Male			Female		
	1961	*1991*	*2001*	*1961*	*1991*	*2001*	*1961*	*1991*	*2001*
0-4	74629	205165	103,823	37605	104161	53,624	37024	101004	50,199
5-9	83182	...	107,390	42270	...	54,996	40912	...	52,394
10-14	75641	128932	120,013	38805	66051	61,304	36836	62881	58,709
15-19	55198	130846	125,031	28180	66676	64,970	27018	64170	60,061
20-24	52535	128114	142,016	25992	67394	75,652	26543	60720	66,364
25-29	46480	108529	138,614	22579	54983	70,745	23901	53546	67,869
30-34	41879	90678	117,544	20084	47583	61,304	21795	43095	56,240
35-39	34795	82547	104,565	16344	41929	53,245	18451	40618	51,320
40-44	35179	68611	82,539	15914	36253	44,065	19265	32358	38,474
45-49	28341	59712	75,632	13106	31234	38,066	15235	28478	37,566
50-54	28835	48005	64,311	12459	24893	32,882	16376	23112	31,429
55-59	19406	32904	46,905	8739	16187	23,063	10667	16717	23,842
60-64	21357	32899	42,394	8462	14800	19,972	12895	18099	22,422
65-69	10441	19897	28,168	4421	8592	12,501	6020	11305	15,667
70-74	18768	15257	20,484	7574	6343	8,650	11194	8914	11,834
75-79	N.A	6995	10,315	N.A	3035	4,279	N.A	3960	6,036
80+	N.A	7459	10,912	N.A	2967	4,274	N.A	4492	6,638
Age not stated	1	N.A	7,012	N.A	N.A	3,656	1	N.A	3,356

Source: Census of India, 1961 to 2001.

TABLE 1.10

Indicators of Dependency

Indicator	*Total*			*Male*			*Female*		
	1961	*1991*	*2001*	*1961*	*1991*	*2001*	*1961*	*1991*	*2001*
Children (0-14)	233452	334097	331226	118680	170212	169924	114772	163885	161302
Senior citizen 60+	50566	82507	112273	20457	35737	49676	30109	46770	62597
Total dependent persons	284018	416604	443499	139137	205949	219600	144881	210655	223899
Working age group	342648	749946	897157	163397	387132	463992	179251	362814	433165
Total population	626667	1166550	1347668	302534	593081	687248	324133	573469	660420
Proportion of working to dep. population	120.6	180.0	202.3	117.4	188.0	211.3	123.7	172.2	193.5
Proportion of working to total population	54.7	64.3	66.6	54.0	65.3	67.5	55.3	63.3	65.6
Proportion of dep. pop. to total population	45.3	35.7	32.9	46.0	34.7	32.0	44.7	36.7	33.9
Proportion of 60+ to total population	8.1	7.1	8.3	6.8	6.0	7.2	9.3	8.2	9.5
Proportion of 60+ F to 60+ M				147.2	130.9	126.0			
Total workers/dependent population		99.1	117.8						

Note: Calculated from the table above.

Institutions and Governance

Uniform Family Law

23. One aspect of policy that clearly provides for equal treatment is the Uniform Family Law, which already exists in Goa due to its Portuguese colonial legacy, though many are unaware. While the rest of the country debates the pros and cons of a Common Civil Code, the *Codigo Civil Portugues* or the Portuguese Civil Code (PCC) of 1867, (often referred to as the Common Civil Code), based on the French Civil Code (Code Napoleon) has been in effect in Goa since 1870. The PCC includes laws of marriage, divorce, inheritance and succession, children and adoption, etc.

24. Under the Uniform Family Law, registration of births, deaths and marriages is mandatory. The process of registration is supposed to ensure a share of family assets to the girl child as well as the wife (in her husband's assets).

25. Although registration is mandatory for all communities in Goa, there are drawbacks—sometimes the procedures are long drawn, they do not apply uniformly to all communities and are cumbersome. However, in Goa there is a high level of legal awareness. One of the contributing factors is the tax benefit that couples can avail of on the registration of marriage under the Civil Code. Income from all sources is considered joint property and taxed likewise, that is each partner is taxed on only half of the total amount of assets owned. All children have a share in the family property and sons and daughters are treated alike.

Commission for Women and Children

26. In order to redress some of the problems that women face in the state, a State Commission for Women was set up in 1995. It receives complaints on property inheritance, sexual abuse, violence against women, bigamy, mental health, infrastructure for women, social security for single women and single parenthood, placement in intermediate homes, polygamy and other relevant issues.

27. There is also a State Commission for Children that has recently been set up to look into the concerns of children in the State. Goa was the first state to enact the Children's Act. This Act of 2003 aims to protect the rights of children at home, in educational institutions, by the health care system, etc., and also attempts to address issues of trafficking and child labour. The Act makes possible the setting up of children's courts, which aims to make the process of law and justice child-friendly.

28. Since the arrest of Freddy Peats in the 90s in connection with a child sexual abuse racket that he was running under the guise of a rescue home, several NGOs have begun working towards addressing the plight of the less privileged children and the growing number of street children in Goa. While the State has free education till class X, it does not have a social security policy to provide shelter and nutrition (beyond the mid-day meal) at schools for less privileged children.

29. However, with the recent cases of paedophilia in Goa and the instances of child abuse even in shelter homes, there is need for a system of screening of the various charities and homes that have sprung up around the State.

Comunidade System of Common Property Management

30. A unique feature of Goa, which sets it apart from the rest of the country is the system of local self-governance or common property resource management called the Comunidades, which have been in existence even prior to the institution of *panchayats*. This institution continues to exist parallel to the *panchayats*, although the role played by the Comunidade has been modified considerably since the *panchayat* system came into existence. The origins of this system are not clear. According to the Report of the Goa Land Reform Commission (1964: 22) brought out by the Government of Goa Printing Press, a large number of families from across the Western Ghats settled in Goa due to reasons such as war, disease, poverty, etc., in those regions. These settlers, formed cooperative associations under the leadership of the male members of the family who came to be known as *gaunkars*. The *gaunkars* with the help of their dependents and others, reclaimed and cultivated the wastelands. They then appropriated this land collectively and divided its produce amongst themselves. Even today male descendents of *gaunkars* can register themselves with the Comunidade as *zonekars* (sons of the soil) and can claim their share of Comunidade land or produce.

31. This system had no place for daughters, wives or mothers in its management or in terms of share entitlements. The Comunidades carried out several functions including the construction of roads, irrigation systems, the upkeep of religious places, schools and even health care particularly at the time of epidemics. Today several of these jobs managed earlier by the Comunidades have been taken over by the municipalities and *panchayats*. The *gaunkars*, particularly the elders (*vodils*), settled disputes and even discharged punishments for minor offences in the village. The membership to the Comunidade included apart from male descendents, also shareholders who were also always male. There were some instances, however, where the surplus of the annual income of the Comunidade was given to widows and children of members. Here, voting was by *vangod* or family aggregate and every decision had to be unanimous. Even one negative vote would imply the rejection of the proposed matter.

Infrastructure

32. Public amenities need to be sensitive to the needs of women, children, the aged and handicapped. There are no reserved parking areas or mandatory ramp accesses to buildings for wheelchairs. Public conveniences such as accessible, clean toilets are also largely non-existent.

33. Mobility infrastructure, particularly affordable public transport needs to be strengthened especially because of rising fuel prices, shrinking road space and acute lack of urban parking spaces. More people now commute between towns than ever before on a daily basis for work, which places demands on better linking of towns.

Housing

34. With the growing urbanisation of Goa and nuclearisation of families, there will be large demand for housing by local residents in the years to come. This demand for living space would be additional to the "holiday homes" that people from outside Goa are purchasing in the state.

35. This has led to a surge in land prices affecting local residents and their plans to purchase new homes. The effort of the government to curb illegal purchases of land by foreigners has been a step in the right direction.

36. Urban community housing schemes for the poor needs to be implemented. The existing rule of compulsory provision of parking by new houses has to be stringently implemented, otherwise it will further aggravate traffic congestion.

Water

37. The growing population and increasing number of urban settlements has resulted in an increase in demand for water. Not only has there been a rise in the number of permanent residents but also of the mobile population of tourists especially along the coastal belt which is going to stress the current groundwater levels as well as the water supply system. A combination of market-based and command-control mechanisms have to be brought in to ensure a rational water-use policy.

Electricity

38. A rising per capita income in the state with rising urbanisation and tourist inflow, has caused various lifestyle changes in Goa making it more energy-intensive. There is an urgent need to increase supply sources.

Sewage and Solid Waste Management

39. There is a growing burden of sewage collection and treatment as Goa urbanises. The need for new dumping areas and sewage treatment plants is the need of the hour. In the coastal belt there have been reports of contamination of groundwater from overloaded septic tanks. In urban areas, the pressure on existing infrastructure has led to cases of piped water contamination. Garbage sorting has to be more thoroughly implemented not only in urban areas but also rural areas where the amount of non-biodegradable solid waste being disposed has increased substantially.

Carrying Capacity and Sustainable Activity

40. The Ecological Footprint[1] of Goa is 1.48 ha per person against an Indian average of 1.8 ha per person. However, with the population of Goa in 2001 and an area of 370,000 ha, Goa already has a deficit of 1,429 ha.

41. The carrying capacity, or number of people that can be supported by the economy of Goa, however, depends on its ability to support economically viable activity within its own region. Given that all of Goa's energy is imported, its economic activity is sustained by this supply. Its carrying capacity would be determined by the amount of economic activity and therefore, people with a given material standard of living, that the energy imports could support.[2] To increase the carrying capacity, the policy makers need to make judicious choices about the nature of economic activity for which the energy is made available.

42. As a corollary, sustainable development activity is a socio-ecological process characterised by the fulfilment of human needs while maintaining the quality of the natural environment indefinitely. As defined by the Brundtland Commission set up by the United Nations General Assembly, in its report of 1987, sustainable development is development that "meets the needs of the present generation without compromising the ability of future generations to meet their own needs".

Strengths, Weaknesses, Opportunities and Threats

Strengths

43. Goa's biggest strength is the high literacy rate in the State. Its medical infrastructure also puts it way ahead of most other States in India as reflected in the health achievements of the population.

---

1. The concept of Footprint was developed by Wackernagel and Rees and is a UN method for quick estimation of the ecological sustainability of the region. It assesses the ability of the existing landmass to support the economic and ecological needs of the community. A deficit implies it needs services from the hinterlands beyond its own land to carry out economic or ecological activity vital for its own existence.

2. Malcolm Slesser, the father of the Carrying Capacity Concept, has been using this mechanism to compute the carrying capacity of dozens of regions across the world and estimating the rates at which the economies can perform.

44. The small size of the State makes it possible for Goa to become a model state of the country. The high political participation and involvement in local affairs can increase self-regulation in the community and make devolution and decentralisation effective.

Weaknesses

45. The growing population and an unregulated tourism growth has placed unsustainable demands on the natural resources of the State.

46. Mining which has had its positive economic effects has also placed large costs on the environment and health of the local population.

47. The rising cost of living has also disturbed the staple diet and nutrition basket of the local population.

Opportunities

48. Goa has a large educated manpower with the ability to read and write in English. This is a big asset that would help it to integrate into the global knowledge economy.

49. The clean environment, presence of few non-polluting industries and a large medical infrastructure provides potential for health tourism which needs to be tapped carefully without overdrawing on the natural resources.

Threats

50. Economic growth has also seen a number of structural changes in Goa. There has been a growing inequality in the State and this needs long-term policy solutions. The decline in nutritional status both due to higher prices during some peak tourist season and lifestyle changes also needs to be taken note of.

52. The declining sex ratio is a matter of grave concern. There is growing incidence of suicides, violence and crime especially against women, senior citizens and children which needs to be addressed.

53. As incomes in the State have grown, so has vehicular traffic. Inadequate traffic supervision of vehicles and road rage is leading to a large number of casualties and fatal accidents on Goa's roads.

54. Most importantly, the lack of strict enforcement of rules and regulations is the largest threat to Goa.

Recommendations and Development Strategies

54. The following suggestions may be considered:

a. With a shifting of age structure to a larger workforce, urgent measures are required to create jobs for entrants to the workforce. A special effort needs to be made to accommodate women into the workforce as they have a very low representation right now.

b. This would go a long way towards addressing the declining sex ratio in the State. Another factor that would help in this is a strict enforcement of the PNDT (Post Natal Diagnostic Test) Act in order to avoid female foeticide and sex selection of children in the State.

c. Innovative social security plans to address the needs of the senior citizens, old-aged workers need to be initiated as a large proportion of the population will age in the coming 20-30 years.

d. There is an urgent need to increase the proportion of persons who have technical and university education to allow Goa to integrate into the knowledge economy.

e. Tourism which has emerged as the largest sector needs to be made sustainable by appropriate regulation that would disallow unscrupulous over-exploitation of resources.

f. Mining has been an important contributor to the state's GDP. However, there should be better provision of health and other social infrastructure in mining areas where damage to the environment has been quite extensive affecting local residents. Ecological regeneration of these areas is also an urgent need.

g. A tighter watch must be kept on land transaction in the state because of rising land prices triggered by illegal use of foreign funds and unscrupulous land dealers.

h. There is an urgent need to improve urban amenities due to growing urbanisation in the state and stress on existing urban infrastructure.

Chapter 2

Natural Resources

Energy/Water Environmental Security

ENERGY AND ENVIRONMENTAL SECURITY

Introduction

1. "Success Stories and Strategy for Development in Goa" would have been an appropriate heading for this chapter on energy. Forecasting demand for long term in this knowledge era cannot be based on conventional time series exploration. A simple example is in the growth of domestic electricity consumption, which during the last three years, has deviated from conventional growth rates by very large extent. This is especially true of the domestic electricity consumption that has shown higher rate of growth. In any society, saturation, slowdown, strangulations to growth would inevitably occur. In addition to carrying capacity calculations, the growth enablers, saturation levels and possible impediments to growth have also to be considered.

2. Energy also includes power, renewable energy, oil and gas. A separate section is also devoted to emerging technologies in order to address the ways to quickly adopt them as and when they become commercially viable. Water as a resource has been considered in a separate section. This has been followed by environmental security discussions.

3. Each of the development indicators has a story to tell, whether successful or otherwise, and these indicators are the result of a road travelled over the years. The discussions on various development indicators, in this chapter reveals that the energy sector in Goa as financially very healthy with innovative, pioneering and sound policies.

4. Prudent management desires that this is the time to conserve, improve efficiency and enhance quality of delivery in addition to ensuring security so that the leadership position in the sector can be maintained. The State has to continue to be out of box thinking solution provider in this sector so as to remain in forefront.

5. The Electricity Act 2003, Government of India Electricity Policy 2005, formation of Bureau of Energy Efficiency under Energy Efficiency and Conservation Act and Central Scheme of APDRP (Accelerated Power Development and Reform Programme) are nascent governing paradigm for the sector. The emerging technologies cannot be ignored in a knowledge society.

6. Ultimately the future success of the sector will depend upon meeting the consumer needs in the knowledge society in terms of energy security, reliability, quality and service at a reasonable rate. In addition, since inefficient use of energy is a depletion of natural resources, the efficiency in energy use is an important criteria to be fulfilled.

7. The poor ought to have a voice in policy-making and implementation so that service will improve. As Dominque Kon Son Tack of Macao Water Supply says, "After twenty years of ensuring water security, now the focus is on ensuring user satisfaction."

Power: Road Travelled

8. This section on energy covers the energy needs of the State and meeting them. The section also looks at various policies that were adopted by the State till date. For the convenience of discussion, the section is arranged into subsections. The present indicators on power are a result of various policy roads that the State travelled after liberation from Portuguese rule in December 1961. At the time of liberation, power supply was only available in five major towns in Goa. Each of this town had a diesel generating station supplying power for predetermined hours in the towns. The aggregate installed capacity was less than 2.5 MW.

9. The Government of Goa constituted the Electricity Department (GED) in 1963 with the objective of making grid power available to the State. GED also was conferred with licensee status under the now repealed 1910 Electricity Act.

10. Today the State demand exceeds 350 MW and the State even can claim 100 per cent not only village electrification but also 100 per cent household electrification. A brief background on the policies will help in understanding this achievement.

Decade: 1961-1971

11. Soon after formation of the GED in 1963, a decade scheme covering the period 1963-64 to 1973-74 was prepared. The decade scheme focused on obtaining cheap hydropower from Karnataka and a second source, costly thermal power from Maharashtra. A contract of 10 years 50 MW power at Re. 0.0575 per kWh was entered with Karnataka State Electricity Board in 1967 while a 4 MW demand-based contract was entered at the then prevailing H.T (high tension) consumer rate of about Re. 0.22 per kWh. During this period a 110 KV D/C Transmission link was established with Karnataka. A 33 KV D/C link was established with Maharashtra. The feasibility of a hydroelectric scheme was investigated at Dudhsagar and found to be unviable as a storage scheme. A network of 33 KV was laid across to all major towns and the diesel generating stations in the towns were closed down. The last operating diesel generating station at Mormugao was closed down in November 1970, by making available grid power. At the end of 1971, the power demand of Goa rose to 11 MW.

Decade: 1971-1981

12. The Fifth Five Year Plan, with two years of plan holiday covered the period of 1971-1981. The 110 KV receiving station at Ponda was commissioned in January 1972. Village electrification was given utmost priority. In a single year 1975-76, 56 villages were electrified. The sub-transmission and distribution system was laid covering the entire State during this decade. Transmission links of 220 KV were established with Maharashtra and Karnataka grids under centrally sponsored schemes. The substation at Ponda was upgraded from 110 KV to 220 KV in 1981.

13. After expiry of 10 years contract with Karnataka Electricity Board for 50 MW power supply, both Karnataka and Maharashtra Electricity Boards treated Goa as a H.T. consumer with tariff hikes (Re. 0.58 per kWh and Re. 0.82 kWh) and Goa was subject to demand cuts and energy quota. The power demand at this time rose to 70 MW.

Decade: 1981-1991

14. The period 1981-1991 was covered by the Sixth and Seventh Five Year Plans. Under the Low-Income Group (L.I.G) scheme the State concentrated on intensive electrification and formulated schemes to electrify those wadas (houses with five or more households) that had earlier been left out. Under this scheme, a house was provided with two light points with lamps. These schemes pioneered centrally sponsored schemes of hamlet electrification and Kutir Jyoti schemes.

15. This decade was devoted to exploring renewable energy within the State. Anemometers to measure wind speeds were imported and installed at test sites. Two wind energy generators of 55 KW were installed at pilot sites. Micro hydroelectric plant of 40 KW was designed including turbine and installed on experimental basis. The hydro schemes at Salaulim, Anjunem and Dudhsagar were re-looked at for feasibility.

16. Government of India allocated power from centrally owned National Thermal Power Corporation Power (NTPC). It was from Ramagundam in Andhra Pradesh that 100 MW was allocated and another 110 MW was allocated from Korba in Madhya Pradesh. Goa with 210 MW of allocation in 1985 became a power surplus state.

17. Within the State 110 KV lines were laid and major 110 KV substations were set up at Kadamba, Tivim and Xeldem. Lighting of streets for the entire State was taken over by GED from local bodies by levying a surcharge of Re. 0.02 per kWh on the consumer, with a view to take advantage of bulk purchase of fittings and spares. This is also a pioneering scheme by the State.

18. A scheme for power subsidy of 25 per cent to industrial consumers was introduced to attract industries. Power subsidy to consumers other than small-scale industries is again a pioneering scheme in India. At the end of 1991, the demand for Goa was nearly 130 MW.

Decade: 1991-2001

19. The power subsidy and surplus power availability had also resulted in power guzzler (steel scrap melting) industries setting shops in Goa. The power demand rose to 201 MW. The end of 1995 also witnessed stress on interstate transmission system. The upstream transmission systems outside Goa were not upgraded to deliver the increased demand and the voltage plunged to 165 KV at 220 KV in Goa.

20. To cater to the need for having local generation of at least 15-20 per cent for system stability and to take advantages of the economic liberation policy of the Government of India, Goa was one of the few pioneering States to invite tariff-based bids (not project cost-based) for setting up IPP (independent power producers), after zeroing on pollution-free Naphtha as fuel. A 48 MW combined cycle power plant was commissioned in August 1999. The government also formulated a policy of allowing third party sale by Captive Generation through the distribution licensee (Electricity Department,

Government of Goa) wires. There was, however, not a single taker for this policy.

21. The State engaged various consultants like PricewaterCooper, SBI Caps, Goa Institute of Management for studying the structural changes and suggestions for the reorganisation GED.

Period: 2001-2005

22. During this decade, the government allowed the 48 MW, IPP to provide quality power to industries through the own wires of IPP. This policy brought in healthier cooperative competition at the distribution level. These policies were introduced much before Electricity Act 2003 was passed in Lok Sabha.

23. Goa's transmission link with Western Grid was upgraded through 400 KV grid line. The State was also engaged in trading of surplus power through PSU (public sector undertakings) as well as private trading companies. After introduction of availability based tariff (ABT), Government found that ABT mechanism itself is a better alternative to trading.

24. The government did appoint a single member State Electricity Regulatory Commission, but the Commission resigned before it even began to function. Thereafter, the Government did adopt a role of self-regulation. It announced reduction in industrial tariff by about 10 per cent in February 2002 and also froze the tariff for the next three years.

25. The State is engaged in implementing APDRP for upgrading the distribution infrastructure through Power Grid Corporation. The demand of Goa is around 350 MW.

26. The State had appointed National Hydro Power Corporation (NHPC) as consultant through Water Resources Department (WRD) to explore the feasibility of setting up small hydropower generating stations. NHPC is said to have identified about six such projects totaling about 15 MW.

27. During the four and half decades, 1961-2005, the State has been responsive and has come out with pioneering innovative policies to ensure growth and to solve the power-related problem.

Indicators

28. The State development indicators for power are the per capita consumption in kWh (units), the ratios of different category of consumers, distribution network density, transmission network density and the availability of power and their sources.

29. These indicators are being compared with the neighbouring states of Maharashtra, Karnataka, Pondicherry and all-India average.

Per Capita Consumption in kWh

30. A perusal to the year-wise per capita consumption chart indicates that in the base year 1986-87, the per capita consumption of Pondicherry, Maharashtra and Goa were 345, 327 and 339 kWh respectively. These three states were nearly equal. The all-India average and Karnataka were almost equal at 191 and 197 kWh respectively. The all-India average and Karnataka had shown an almost similar growth rate in the period 1986-1999. Interestingly, Pondicherry had a high rate of growth in the period 1986 to 1993.

31. With regard to the growth rate of Goa:

- Goa had a steady growth during the period 1986-1991 at 6.7 per cent.
- During the period 1991-1996, growth rate was 6.6 per cent.
- Growth during 1996-1999 was slightly less due to power unavailability and quality problems. The commissioning of IPP in August 1999 in Goa accelerated the growth thereafter.
- The period 2001-2004 saw a growth rate of 8.22 per cent due to increase in domestic consumption coupled with availability of quality power selected industrial estates, Maharashtra and Karnataka have been chosen for being neighbouring states. Pondicherry has been chosen as it is also a small state.

32. Figure 2.2 compares per capita consumption of various categories of consumers in Goa with western region and all-India average in the year 2003-04. Per capita consumption of Goa is higher than not only all India but also western region in domestic, commercial and industrial categories.

FIGURE 2.1

Per Capita Consumption in kWh

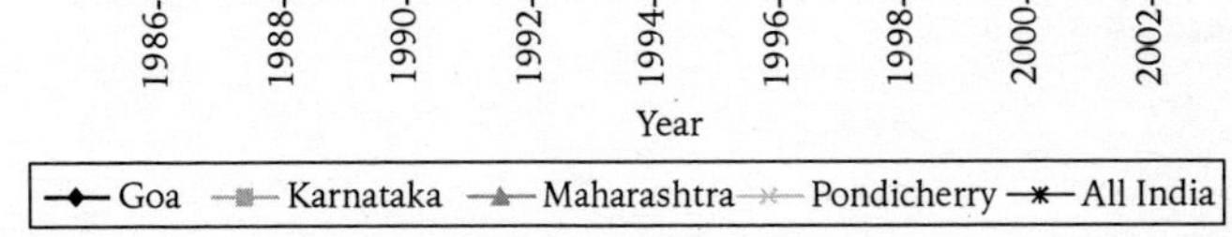

Source: CEA and TEDDY, a TERI publication.

FIGURE 2.2

Category-wise Per Capita Consumption in kWh

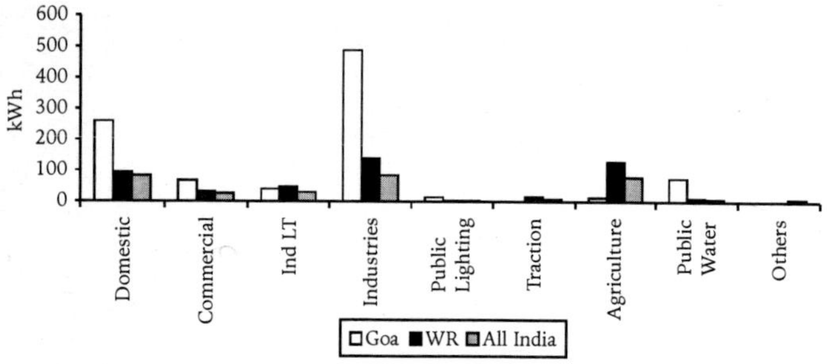

Source: CEA and TEDDY, a TERI publication.

33. Figure 2.3 shows Thailand's per capita energy consumption. The per capita energy consumption in year 1996-97 was 1355 kWh and grown to 1728 kWh in 2003-04. The overall growth rate was 4 per cent but the growth during period 1999 to 2003-04 has been at 7.1 per cent.

34. Goa appears to have overtaken Thailand in the growth rate of per capita consumption. Thailand has been chosen for international comparison as like Goa, it also has less of agriculture and is a growing economy as well.

Ratio of Category Consumers

35. The ratio of various categories of consumers is tabulated in Table 2.1 for the neighbouring states and Thailand. The categories in per cent of total have been limited to domestic, commercial, industrial, agriculture and others for the year 2003-04.

36. The ratios read with per capita consumption indicate that Goa has high domestic consumption. This is because of high per capita income the State enjoys. Thailand has higher ratio of commercial consumption. The power demand for agriculture is not likely to increase. The scope therefore, continues to remain for increase in domestic, commercial and industrial sectors in Goa.

FIGURE 2.3

Growth of Per Capita Consumption in Thailand in kWh

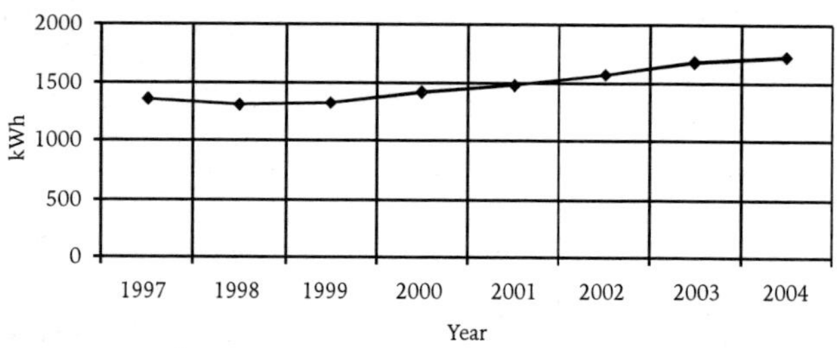

Source: Government of Thailand.

TABLE 2.1

Ratio of Category of Consumer: 2003-04

	Goa	*Karnataka*	*Maharashtra*	*Pondicherry*	*All India*	*Thailand*
Domestic	27.06	19.28	24.04	14.92	24.86	22.83
Commercial	7.04	6.98	9.53	4.14	7.81	31.71
Industrial	55.12	26.22	38.52	66.19	34.51	45.42
Agriculture	1.33	38.86	20.40	6.56	24.13	.02
Others	9.45	8.66	7.51	8.19	5.69	.02

Source: CEA.

Transmission and Distribution Network and their Density

37. The absolute number in kilometres of length of lines for transmission and distribution does not reveal the adequacy or inadequacy of the system. The density of lines per sq km area reveals the spatial spread to some extent. However, the carrying capacity and the throughout sustainability can be understood only when it is coupled with the load density. The following table gives the relevant data. This data has also been used to determine the carrying capacity of the system and its sustainability.

TABLE 2.2

Transmission and Distribution Line Density

	Ckt Length in km	*Spatial Density km/Sq.km*	*Load Density km/MW*
220 KV lines	744	0.30	2.19
110 KV lines	795	0.30	2.34
33 KV lines	1131	0.45	4.04
11 KV lines	3164	1.22	11.30
L.T lines	8440	3.26	30.14

Source: All India Statistics for Year 2003-04: CEA.

38. While computing load density for distribution lines, industrial loads that are supplied at 110 KV and to forest land have been deducted.

ATC Losses

39. A review of aggregate of technical and commercial losses (ATC) in the system indicate that though at an average these losses over the years are less than 21 per cent, there are no indications to state that the losses are being effectively controlled. Over the years the losses did not show a steady trend of neither increasing nor decreasing. It goes as low as 18 per cent and then rises again to 22 per cent or higher levels.

FIGURE 2.4

Year-wise ATC Loss in Per cent

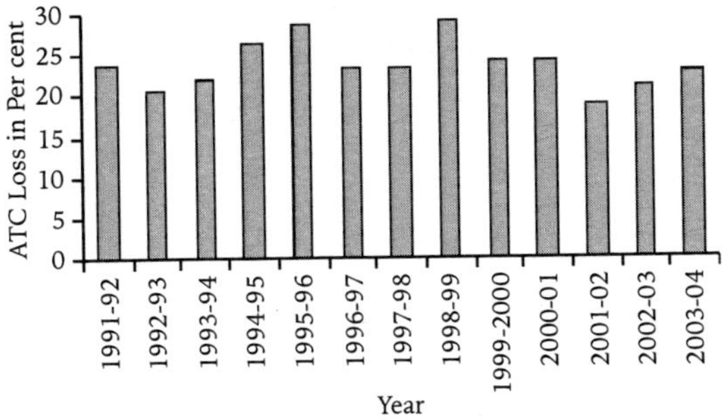

Source: TEDDY upto year 2000-01.

Power Demand

40. Peak power demand of any State comprises peak demand that has been met by the State owned utility and met by others including standby, IPP and captive plants. There is always migration between these sources on the basis of availability, grid quality and cost of fuel. For example, a demand, which is being met by standby generation due to grid constraint, will move from standby to grid, as soon as the grid constraint is removed. Ignoring these factors will lead to improper planning and incorrect conclusions in a small state where such migration can be significant.

41. The peak demand during the summer of 2005 was as below:

TABLE 2.3

Assessed Power Demand in MW during May 2005

	Demand in MW
Demand met from Western Region grid	256
Demand met from Southern Region grid	70
Demand met by REL purchased power	16
Sub-total (officially reported demand)	340
Demand met by REL by direct sale to consumers	24
Demand met by standby generation due to Tivim grid constraint	6
Demand met by standby generation due to Xeldem grid constraints	3
Demand met by standby generation due to quality problems like beneficiation plants at Binani, Amona and Costi	14
Demand curtailed due to Xeldem grid constraints and remain curtailed—steel melting units	12
Demand met by Captive units Zuari Fertiliser	11
Total	412

Source: Statistical Handbook of the Government of Goa for the relevant years.

42. The above calculations indicate a demand of 412 MW as against 340 MW officially reported as power demand.

Generation Sources

43. The generation sources and their fuel are indicated in Table 2.4. The Government of India has allocated for Goa power from NTPC sources, which are located outside the State. The same has been considered.

TABLE 2.4

Generation Sources as on 2005

Source	*Allocation/Installed MW*	*Fuel*
NTPC – Korba	210	Coal
NTPC – Vindhyachal	35	Coal
NTPC- Ramgundam	75*	Coal
NPC-Kakrapar	15	Nuclear
NTPC – Sipat	12	Coal
Sub-total of allocation	347	
Additional PPA with NPC-TAPP	11	Nuclear
Reliance Energy –CCPP	48	Naphtha
Zuari – CPP 1&2	7+4	FO
Stand by plants – MRF, Binani, MPL	18	FO
Stand by plants others	185	HSD

Note: *Allocation from NTPC Ramagundam reduced from 100 MW to 75 MW. Typical availability against allocation at the State has to be considered as 90 per cent of allocation.

Source: Statistical Handbook of the Government of Goa for the relevant years.

FIGURE 2.5

Fuel-wise Generation Sources (Per cent)

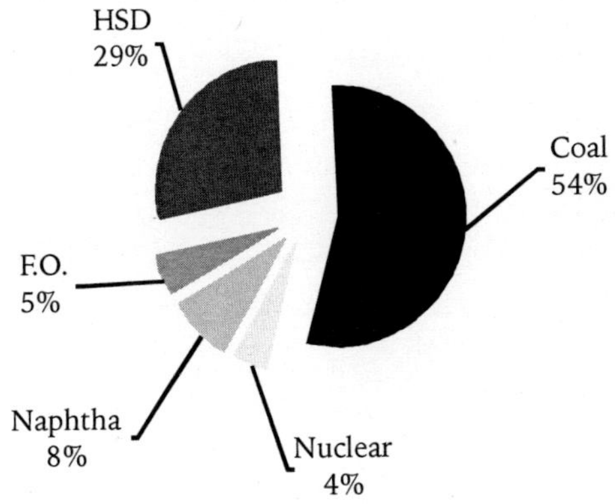

Source: Statistical Handbook of the Government of Goa for the relevant years.

44. The source-wise installed capacity indicates that coal and HSD (high speed diesel) (standby generation) are predominant over other fuels. Both these fuels are polluting in nature. All coal-based plants are situated outside the State while all HSD-based plants are located within the State.

Daily Load Curve

45. Daily load curve varies and is sensitive to many factors like weather, holiday, season etc. A typical summer

day has been considered and given in Figure 2.6 as representative of a curve for the purpose of understanding the system operation. The data refers to only the demand that is being met by the utility. For simplicity the day has been divided into eight time zones.

46. A perusal of daily load curve will indicate that the State has surplus of power for about 20 hours in a day and over draws for about 4 hours a day. The State has net surplus under ABT regime.

FIGURE 2.6

Typical Assessed Daily Load Curve in MW

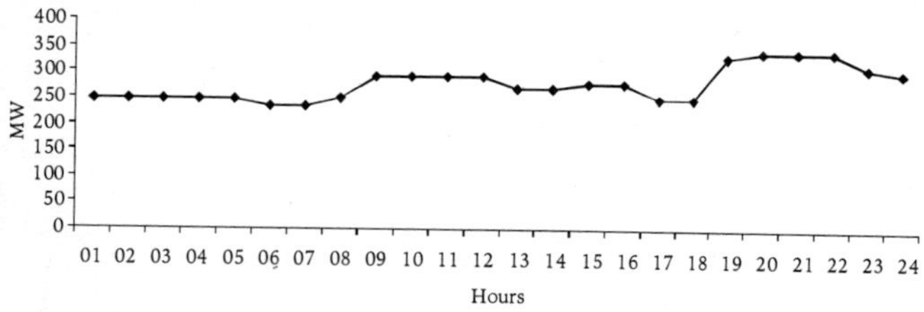

Source: Statistical Handbook of the Government of Goa for the relevant years.

Financial Health of Utility

47. The Electricity Department of Government of Goa (GED) had made an operating surplus of Rs. 158 crore during the financial year 2004-05 on a revenue of Rs. 635 crore. The operational surplus of 24 per cent is very healthy for any business.

Current Issues and their Fiscal Implications

48. The intention is to identify and highlight the current issues. Wherever it is possible to guestimate the fiscal impact, the same has been provided. The possible approach to solution is indicated. It is not the intention of this report to be techno-economic feasibility study.

49. The current issues that arise from this objective are:

- Energy Security
- Power Reliability
- Power Quality
- Demand Side Management
- Capacity Building, and
- IPP, CPP and Co-Generation

Energy Security and Fiscal Implications

50. Energy is the basis of not only economic activity but also for quality of life. No power (non-availability of power) is costlier than power that can be directly quantified. The fiscal implication of ignoring energy security will be not only negative growth in GDP, increase in health-related problems due to increased pollution but also social unrest on account of lack of employment opportunities.

National Electricity Policy, 2005

51. The targets of the Policy to be achieved by year 2012, like 100 per cent village electrification, 100 per cent metering and per capita consumption of 1000 kWh have already been achieved by Goa. The policy aims at use of IT in administrating the system. GED needs to implement a road map for effective use of ICT for administration and technical operation of the system.

Long-Term Contracts

52. Goa has relied on long-term contracts with NTPC or neighbouring boards and IPP for its energy security. With limited and at times non-availability of any fuel within Goa, the creation of power generation capacity within the State had not been possible. Though currently Goa has surplus power for 20 hours a day, this situation is not likely to be valid beyond the next two years. The exponential increase in domestic air conditioners (estimate of addition of 20 MW demand in summer night per annum) will change the scene even if there is no appreciable industrial growth.

53. Further, the Government of India may reallocate NTPC power to other States as 25 MW of power from Goa was reallocated to Daman. During the late seventies and early eighties, Goa went through a crisis on account of absence of proper long-term contract.

54. In order not to be trapped again in perpetual low voltage, power cuts and energy quota, it is suggested that the first and foremost step is to use the lessons that are learnt from success. When demand was only 5 MW in 1967, contract was made for purchase of 50 MW of power. When demand was only 70 MW, 210 MW of allocation was secured in 1983. Therefore, now when the State is notionally surplus, it should enter into long-term future contracts.

Interstate Transmission

55. Similarly the period 1995-1999 witnessed problems of low voltage in absence of upstream improvement in the transmission system bringing power to Goa. The public does not want electric power lines strewn over the countryside, particularly over their own backyards. Real or imagined, there is a general belief that the electromagnetic waves emitted by electric power lines are harmful. Increasingly, it will be difficult to lay interstate as well as

intrastate transmission lines. The second lesson that was learnt was that automatic upgradation of upstream transmission lines will not take place. Therefore, it is necessary to have generation within the State for grid stability. At the least, 25 per cent or more of the demand should be generated within the State.

Coal-based Power Plants

56. The electric Gigawatt power plants are attractive terrorist targets and may even be vulnerable to cyber terrorism. It will be difficult in future to add coal-based large power plants outside the state to supply cheap power to Goa. In addition under ABT, the rate for unscheduled interchange (UI) has also increased to Rs. 5.70 per unit.

Enabling Factors for Generation within Goa

57. In this regard there are three main enabling factors that have emerged. One is that Dabhol LNG terminal will get commissioned soon. This will facilitate availability of clean and cheap fuel in Goa. Goa should make all efforts to get LNG pipeline laid into Goa from Dabhol, so as to bring in clean fuel into Goa.

58. The second enabling factor is maturity of distributed generation technology in the world. Smaller capacity plants are as efficient as larger power plants.

59. The third most important lesson is that Goa has the knowledge of effectively using surplus power by taking advantage of ABT and/or trading in power. The surplus power if any, due to contracting of additional power in 2006-07, can be gainfully used.

60. Goa has an option of setting up of a 500 MW power plant or adds 50 MW to meet incremental power needs.

Options to Meet Power Peak Demand

61. While discussing energy security, the need to meet peak demand for five hours every day during the night cannot be ignored. The cost of meeting this need is also increasing. Under ABT regime, the peak power can cost as high as Rs. 5 per unit in summer.

62. Goa can also explore the feasibility of pumped storage hydro-electric scheme in Dudhsagar or at any other suitable site of capacity of about 30 MW or more. The feasibility of NHPC identified projects as pumped storage schemes may also be explored.

63. In addition, the possibility of rain harvesting tanks on high grounds coupled with small dams at lower tailrace level should be explored. Such an arrangement will serve the twin purpose of meeting peak power and rainwater harvesting. (Please refer to section on water.) This will help in meeting the four hours peak requirements at night.

Power Reliability and Fiscal Implications

64. Reliability is a major issue in Goa in areas supplied by GED. Reliability refers to unscheduled interruption in power supply. Presently official data is not available in this regard from GED. Data collected from a H.T. consumer located within two kilometres of a 33/11KV substation in an urban area indicated number and duration of power failures as below:

TABLE 2.5

Unscheduled Outages at a Typical Urban H.T. Consumer

Month	*< 15 min*	*15 Min to 30 Min*	*30 Min to 1 Hr*	*> 1 Hr*	*Total*
Jan.	22	0	1	2	25
Feb.	22	1	3	2	28
Mar.	33	1	1	1	36
Apr.	32	0	3	4	39
May	41	9	7	6	63
June	68	5	0	7	80
Total					271

Source: Statistical Handbook of the Government of Goa for the relevant years.

65. If the above data is extrapolated for a year, then the number of outage per year will work out to 536 per year.

Efforts to Improve Reliability under APDRP

66. The urban area has peak power demand of about 21 MW. This area was compared with a similar area in Vietnam.

Nam Dinh in 1998	
Peak Load (MW)	21.00
Energy Sales (gWh)	285.00
Distribution Losses (%)	7.77
MV Outages	163

67. By implementing reliability improvement measures, specially formulated by ADB, in Nam Dinh in Vietnam, the MV outages were reduced from 163 in 1998 to 91 in 2003 and losses were reduced to 4.4 per cent. The reliability of power supply in Goa is six times less than a third tier area like Nam Dinh in a country like Vietnam.

68. For improving reliability and through-put capacity, GED is implementing APDRP schemes in Goa. Power Grid Corporation, the scheme implementer, has executed schemes costing about Rs. 27 crore and Rs. 26 crore. In the absence of published data on interruptions, enquiry with local residents revealed that in their perception, there has been marked improvement than the previous years.

69. However, a visit to one of the renovated substations under APDRP scheme also indicated that the outdated electro mechanical relays instead of digital relays are still employed for protection scheme.

70. Under APDP (Accelerated Power Development Plan), GED is converting overhead system into underground system in urban areas. For example, an amount of Rs. 36 crore is proposed to be invested in Margao, one of the major towns. The work is in progress. Similar work in Panaji is yet to be taken up.

71. The base data with regard to power reliability, improvement expected, the method of measuring the same and related metric are not in public domain. Publishing the relevant data will go a long way in identifying the effectiveness of APDRP scheme. What is not measured cannot be managed is a best-known paradigm.

Fiscal and Environment Impact of Power Reliability

72. Most of the industries in Goa have standby HSD fuelled diesel generation sets. Similarly domestic consumers have resorted to invertors to run fans and lights. Every PC (personal computer) has an UPS (uninterrupted power supply) associated with it. Apart from the capital cost, the energy wasted due to start and stop operation or in the efficiency of UPS or inverter is estimated to be 9 per cent of industrial energy consumption. The impact on productivity for every interruption is said to be 12 minutes.

Power Quality and Fiscal Implications

73. Power quality and reliability, which is delivered to the consumer depends on not only the generation, transmission but also the last mile connectivity. Power quality refers to surges, sags, swells and harmonics in the power supply. Published data in this regard is not available. One of the 33 KV industrial consumer reported THD (total harmonic distortion) as 7 per cent as against acceptable 3 per cent.

74. However, every installation has one or two power conditioning devices such as stabilisers, AVRS, surge arrestors etc., indicating that improvement in this area is also needed.

75. Every refrigerator, air conditioner, is associated with a voltage stabiliser. The capital cost of these equipments and energy efficiency of these equipments are the fiscal impacts. Normally the energy efficiency for these equipments is 97 per cent. The loss on account of power quality may be therefore, estimated as 3 per cent of cost of power purchased.

Demand Side Management and Fiscal Implication

76. Normally demand side management (DSM) is a term that is loosely referred to flattening of daily load curve. But DSM also refers to adopting policies that will promote the right kind of growth and restrict unwanted growth. DSM is a tool to ensure also energy security.

77. Experience has shown that announcement of 25 per cent subsidy to industries in November 1990, brought in power guzzlers into the State. Similarly, rising LPG prices may force domestic consumers to change to electricity for cooking from LPG, if domestic electricity tariff continues to be subsidised. Presently solar water heating system is an unattractive commercial proposal due to low electricity tariff. Energy conservation and energy efficiency are kissed goodbye in the absence of awareness and education.

78. DSM projects involve a combination of both energy efficiency and energy conservation measures that can result in low and even no cost air pollution mitigation options. The level (and cost) of reduction is dependent on the source of electricity. If the electricity is generated by fossil fuels (e.g., coal, oil, natural gas), then the reduced demand shall translate into less generation and reduced level of emissions.

79. Demand side management is, therefore, a mix of right kind of tariff policy, subsidy and education programme.

Energy Efficiency by Ultimate Consumer

80. Macroeconomic policies sometimes discourage the undertaking of energy efficiency measures. Environmentally, harmful subsidies reduce the private costs of producers and consumers resulting in overutilisation of natural resources. Energy subsidies and low tariff, for example, lead to energy-intensive economic structures and technologies, and wasteful management practices. It has been estimated that the elimination of energy subsidies worldwide would reduce global carbon emission by 9.5 per cent.

81. The energy efficiency by user is an issue that needs to be addressed. The issue of replacing motors with energy efficient motors is not a very popular programme in the State. The State may encourage formation of awareness clubs in schools regarding energy efficiency.

Energy Audit and Energy Conservation

82. The State may also formulate schemes to promote energy audit and ESCO (energy service companies) that provide performance-based services. Policies may also be made to coopt NGOs and institution of engineers in promoting energy use in an efficient manner.

83. Energy conservation and efficiency improvement in the Indian power sector requires special attention since the sector has been suffering from a chronic supply shortage, lack of capital investment for new capacity addition and environmental problems associated with coal-based power plants. High auxiliary consumption and T&D loss further aggravate the problem.

84. In the electricity sector, there is no incentive to encourage conservation, as a minimum charge is required to be paid by the consumers. The government should review the minimum charge concept levied by power utilities and the consumer should be charged for the actual consumption of power.

Energy Savings Integrated Rural Energy Programme (IREP)

85. Goa Energy Development Agency (GEDA) is implementing IREP programme. Under this programme cash subsidy is being provided for energy saving devices such as pressure cookers, kerosene stoves with ISI marks, CFL lamps (compact fluroscent lamps), improved *chulas* in selected rural blocks. These blocks are Sangem, Quepem, Canacona, Satari and Pernem. In these blocks, the entire cost of obtaining electricity connection from GED by low income group is borne by GEDA. Subsidy for CFL is available for all *talukas*.

IPP (Independent Power Producer), CPP (Captive Power Plant) and Co-Generation

Independent Power Producer

86. Through a tariff-based global bidding route, 48 MW CCPP (Combined Cycle Power Plant) using Naphtha as fuel was selected as an IPP. The plant was commissioned in August 1999 and connected to sub-transmission system at 33 KV. As a result, the voltage profile improved, losses reduced and the transformer loading reduced.

87. Further the IPP was allowed to supply directly to consumer through its own wires by reducing the supply to grid. The consumers who are connected to IPP network in Goa experience less than two interruptions in a year. The consumers receiving power supply directly from IPP reported that the quality is in confirmation with IEEE standards.

88. High cost of Naphtha and the resultant cost of power supplied by the IPP is another issue that needs to be addressed. The cheap power from NTPC is an allocation to the entire State and not to any particular set of consumers. The State may consider revival of the November 1990 subsidy scheme to the affected industrial consumers.

Co-Generation and Captive Generation

89. Currently 11 MW generation at Zuari and 4 MW at Binani operate as captive generation. 12 MW power plants at Mandovi Pellets, 4 MW at MRF are operating at standby power plants. Sanjivini sugar mills has 0.6 MW of co-generation plant. The Sesa Goa group is setting up with third party a 30 MW capacity waste heat recovery power plant.

90. The policy announced in 1998 on granting open access to co-generation and captive generation has not yielded any results. So, there is need to have a re-look at these policies with a view to improve energy efficiency.

Development and Growth Areas

91. The demand growth is dependant upon overall growth of economy and policies in addition to an excellent power infrastructure. The average growth rate of per capita consumption over the previous 20 years has been at 6.7 per cent resulting in doubling of consumption in 10 years. However, during the past 5 years the economy was growing at 8 per cent and per capita consumption growth rate during last 5 years also is 8.2 per cent.

Limiting Factor for Demand Growth

92. Goa presently has only a handful of industries, which demand power more than 5 MW. There is scope for setting up such many industries considering the availability of non-agriculture land in Pernem *taluka* or at other places.

93. The State encourages only clean industries. There are no tax incentives for setting up of industries in Goa, the state has neither raw materials nor market for finished goods. The railway will limit the flow of goods into and out of Goa to rest of India. Power-intensive industries are not expected.

94. One question which planners ask is that when will the power demand in Goa get saturated. Considering the per capita consumption of Macau, a similar Portuguese colony and per capita consumption of Silvassa, erstwhile Portugal colony, saturation in per capita consumption is not expected to occur before 4000 kWh.

95. A demand forecast for the next 15 years is made considering that the demand will double in 15 years instead of the present projection of 10 years due to prudent demand side management policies. Based on the said assumption, the following scenarios are considered.

Scenario-1: Base Case

96. In the next five years the demand growth will be three per cent since no major industries, hotel projects etc., are expected. Subsequent five years will have demand growth of six per cent followed by demand growth of four per cent in the next five years.

Scenario-2: High Growth

97. In the next five years the demand growth will be four per cent since no major industries, hotel projects etc., are expected. Subsequent five years will have demand growth of eight per cent followed by demand growth of six per cent in next five years.

Scenario-3: Slow Growth

98. In the next five years the demand growth will be two per cent since no major industries, hotel projects etc., are expected. Subsequent five years will have demand growth of four per cent, followed by demand growth of two per cent in next five years.

Demand Growth Projections

99. The projections in peak demand in MW have been carried out and tabulated below for the three scenarios.

TABLE 2.6

Demand Forecast in MW

Year	*2011*	*2016*	*2021*
Base case	435	582	708
High growth	456	611	807
Very slow growth	414	504	556

Source: Statistical Handbook of the Government of Goa for the relevant years.

Impact of SEZ on Power Demand

100. The Special Economic Zone (SEZ) act has fuelled a lot of interest in Goa for setting up of SEZ. Five SEZ projects have been approved by the State and three are under consideration. The area covered by these SEZ is estimated to be 10 million sq.m. Considering that these will be developed with a minimum load density of 15 W per sq.m, the load on account of SEZ would alone be 150 MW in five years. The demand growth projections considering SEZ will be as below:

TABLE 2.7

Demand Growth Projections Considering SEZ

Year	*2011*	*2016*	*2021*
Base case	585	783	952
High growth	606	890	1152
Slow growth	564	686	758

Source: Statistical Handbook of the Government of Goa for the relevant years.

Energy Projections

101. Corresponding to the above, the energy requirement is calculated and given below in MU.

Year	*2011*	*2016*	*2021*
Base case	3126	4184	5087
High growth	3291	4834	6257
Slow growth	3113	3786	4183

Infrastructure and Carrying Capacity

102. There is great amount of concern for the electric power carrying capacity and reliability of the electric grid beyond 500 MW. The carrying capacity of existing infrastructure including that are already under construction is considered and further investments have been arrived at accordingly. The investment required for meeting base case is worked out.

Generation or Import of Power

103. Goa is connected to Western grid with 400 KV D/C line with 2×315 KVA transformers. This system has a sustainable through-put capacity of 500 MW to be brought into the State. This system can also be used to send out in reverse manner 500 MW of power outside the State.

104. In addition, 220 KV D/C lines with western region and southern region have through put capacity of 100 MW each. Hence, upto 700 MW can be brought into the State.

Transmission System

105. Though the present transmission system in Ponda, Tivim and Xeldem including those planned at Amona have aggregate through-put capacity of 500 MW, there is not sufficient matching 110 KV system in the downstream side. To meet base case demand of 706 MW, investment needed in transmission system will be Rs. 400 crore at current costs.

Distribution System

106. The carrying capacity of distribution system is only 280 MW. To upgrade the same to meet the base case, the investment needed will be Rs. 680 crore.

Sustainability of Power System

Generation or Import of Power

107. The limiting factor on sustainability will be the load development on the upstream side of these grid lines. For sustainability generating station like Dabhol, which are situated on the upstream, has to be of sufficient capacity. But this will be outside the control of the State. Therefore, bringing in fuel into the State is a preferable energy security option.

Transmission System

108. Concentration of transmission system at few load centres is not sustainable. These need to be spread spatially on the basis of load growth.

Distribution System

109. Sustainability of distribution system will solely depend upon technology adoption. Automation and remote operation will be of major importance. The capability and capacity for technology adoption has to be built in.

Tariff Sustainability

110. Any discussion on sustainability cannot exclude the discussion on financial sustainability.

The cost functions generally are

Generation cost	=	f (t, fc, a, u)
Transmission cost	=	f (t,l,n,a,r,sc,u)
Distribution cost	=	f (t,l,n,a,r,sc,x)

where

t	means technology employed
fc	means fuel cost
a	means the age of the system
u	utilisation
n	efficiency
l	means land use cost
r	redundancy
sc	means spare capacity
x	means cross subsidy

111. The above simply means that the cost of a nascent coal-based power plant will be higher than an age-old inefficient coal-based power plant itself.

112. Within the sector unless every player makes comfortable margin on a level playing field, there will be tensions and the system will not be sustainable. For example, expecting load dispatcher as a non-profit organisation to be a mere service provider will cause tensions.

113. Tariff is sustainable only if costs are pooled and social needs are taken care of. Attempts to corner profits by a section of the sector like generator or trader or distributor have not yielded sustainable results.

114. Further sustainable tariff has to attract investment in distribution in addition to generation. The tariff has to reflect the cost of service. Subsidies in tariff has to be transparent for an understanding and knowledgeable consumer. As the society tends to be information-oriented and quality conscientious, it is imperative to structure tariff in a transparent manner.

Distributed Generation for Sustainability of Power System

115. Large power plants are feeding the grid at present. Under distributed generation there will be multiple generating sources of small, medium and large size connected to the grid. The advantages include voltage support, stability and reliability of the system. Distributed electric power is already more economic than centralised power generation in areas where an electric power grid does not reach. It also provides much needed security for factories and facilities that must have a reliable power supply.

116. In view of these considerations, the best solution to the problem may be a combination of expanding purchasing power from national grid and reducing grid demand by removing electric power loads through incentives for installation of distributed generating units. These should include besides conventional power plants, renewable energy also. Someday we will be able to generate all of the electric power that Goa needs with emerging technologies like fuel cells.

Renewable Energy

117. Renewable energy is an important component of energy security in addition to environment conservation. The green house gas emissions and depletion and deterioration of natural resources are a major concern worldwide. The strategy is that of developing and promoting appropriate technologies using natural resources such as biomass, water, wind and solar energy. Kyoto protocol and the clean development mechanism (CDM) are expected to provide new impetus for the growth in renewable energy.

Road Travelled

118. In 1982, Department of Non-Conventional Energy Sources (DNES) was formed in Government of India. GED was appointed as nodal agency for the promotion of renewable energy in 1985.

Period 1981-1991

119. GED took initiative in promoting solar hot water systems by installing demonstration plants and a 1000 litre system was installed at the canteen of Ciba-Geigy (now Syngenta) at Old Goa.

120. GED also took initiative to carry out wind surveys and installed two 55 KW pilot wind generation units, one each at Farmagudi and Canaquinim. These did not yield desired results due to turbulent winds and unreliable grid. GED also appointed National Aeronautical Laboratory, which recommended wind generation at a height above 150M due to high turbulence at lower heights.

121. An experimental micro hydel project of 40 KW using 17M head of water at Harvalem was designed and installed. Tata Consultants recommended installation of 2 MW generation unit at Salaulim by tunneling the dam which the dam safety panel did not agree. Wapcos were appointed to explore hydro potential at Anjunem and preliminary site work was also carried out.

122. Two villages *viz.*, Tudou and Gaodonrem were electrified by installing centralised solar PV system.

123. IREDA (Indian Renewable Energy Development Agency) was established as a financing agency for renewable energy as a public sector enterprise in 1987.

Period 1991-2001

124. In 1992, Government of India upgraded DNES as Ministry of Non-Conventional Energy Sources (MNES). Then Goa Energy Development Agency (GEDA) was formed under the Department of Science & Technology. GED was relieved of this responsibility relating to renewable sources of energy.

125. MNES provides various types of fiscal incentives for the renewable energy sector, which include: accelerated depreciation in the first year of the installation of the project; exemption/reduction in excise duty; exemption from the central sales tax; and customs duty concessions on the import of material, components and equipment used in renewable energy projects.

126. For creation of an attractive environment for evaluation and purchase, wheeling and banking of electrical energy generated from renewable energy sources, the MNES has issued a set of guidelines to all the states. It has suggested that states should announce general policies for purchase, wheeling and banking of electrical energy generated from all renewable energy sources. Fourteen states have so far announced such policies in respect to various renewable energy sources. Goa has not announced any such scheme.

127. GEDA is the facilitator in implementation of MNES schemes and IREDA is the channel partner. GEDA has successfully promoted many solar water-heating projects. A success story is 2000 litre project for Hotel Mandovi. GEDA is also planning for a wind farm in Goa.

Period 2001-2005

128. GEDA continues to effectively implement solar thermal and solar PV programmes. Wind energy survey is being conducted in Loliem in South Goa. Similar survey programme will commence in Pernem *taluka* also shortly. GEDA is also promoting an energy plantation programme in the State.

129. The State had also engaged National Hydro Power Corporation to identify small hydro power plants.

Indicators for Renewable Energy

130. The indicators for renewable energy are tabulated below:

TABLE 2.8

Renewable Energy Indicators

Description	*Unit*	*Quantity*
Wind generator	mw	0.11
Solar hot water – industrial	KL	Not available
Solar PV systems	KW	2 villages
Biomass – steam generation	kw	600
Mini and micro hydel	MW	0.04

Source: Statistical Handbook of the Government of Goa for the relevant years.

131. The installed capacity wind generator system is comparatively low considering the installed capacity worldwide and the share of India in such systems.

Worldwide Wind Power (January 21, 2004)

Installed Capacity:	39,294MW
Germany:	14,609MW
USA:	6,374MW
Spain:	6,202MW
Denmark:	3,110MW
India:	1,815MW

Italy:	904MW
Canada:	312MW

Issues and their Fiscal Implications

132. There appear to be possibilities in improving the targets for utilising renewable energy. The issues connected with the same are:

- Perceptions
- Technology costs
- Supply chain
- Market value
- Monitoring mechanism and
- Enabling CDM

Perceptions

133. Before 1991, because of subsidies on power, agriculture and domestic sectors and also on middle distillates like kerosene and diesel, the consumer preferences were away from using renewable technologies because of the high initial investment cost. This is slowly changing in case of industrial solar hot water systems, which are being installed without subsidy.

134. However, there are various general perceptions among people that impede the growth of renewable systems. Some of them are listed below:

They are too diffuse.

That can be a good thing but they can never meet a significant portion of our energy needs.

Depends on their end-use and they cost too much.

Consider all costs and especially life-cycle costing.

It takes more energy to make renewable energy hardware than it ever produces.

We have lots of fossil fuel.

135. The best way is to educate the value of renewable energy among the children to provide correct perceptions to the society. Tamil Nadu has pioneered eco-clubs in schools. These students participate in worldwide similar programme. The fiscal implication of forming eco-clubs and sustaining them through literature, competition and rewards, besides encouraging them to participate in international programme will be one crore rupees per year.

Technology Costs

136. Most of the energy produced from renewable sources like wind, water, solar are classified as infirm power (power is produced when wind is available). Further wind generation needs to draw reactive power from grid to generate power. A robust connectivity to the grid is another cost. Monsoon is associated with high wind but also associated with poor reliability of local grid. Therefore, considerable investment is needed in making robust connectivity at 110 KV or above. Such connectivity will cost Rs. 12 crore and above and depends upon the location in Goa. The policy on renewable energy should consider sharing this cost.

Supply Chain

137. For biomass based systems, supply chain is an important issue. Small-scale cow dung-based biomass gasified units were readily accepted but subsequent maintenance of them is a problem. Any commercially viable biomass-based programme needs establishment of robust supply chain management programme. For example, the biowastes from hotels can be gainfully used in a commercial biogas programme. In order to achieve the same, instead of transporting as solid waste and incurring high transportation costs, it may be better to partially digest it at the hotel, and transport partially digested slurry to the viable gasification unit. Such coordinated efforts will need to be initially supported. Such arrangement will require initially subsidising transport cost through capital subsidy.

Market Value

138. Whether a real estate property is provided with solar water heater or not has no impact on market value. Installing individual residential water heaters is costlier than having electric power operated water heater due to subsidised domestic tariff. Large-scale solar water heating systems will be economical. A modification in building code or law will be necessary to make it compulsory for the developers to do it. This will enhance the market value of the solar systems and will not have fiscal impact on the public exchequer.

Monitoring the Programme

139. For effective monitoring of renewable programme, many countries, even States implement eco star programme. The programme is similar to hotels being graded as five stars, four stars on the basis of services. Each institution is given eco stars on the basis of their eco friendliness. For example, hotels, schools, municipalities, industries can be awarded five eco star hotel, four eco star school, three eco star municipality etc. Such awards will help to monitor the programme.

Enabling CDM

140. The transaction cost of obtaining benefit from CDM is one of the major issues for investors in renewable technologies. Investments can be attracted into the growth of renewable energy provided an enabling mechanism for CDM is established. Financial institutions may consider this opportunity.

Development and Growth Areas

141. While growth in power is driven by the consumer demand, renewable energy development is driven by vision. A 20 to 30-year vision, bold and measurable targets, and clear policy incentives are critical. There is a role for visionary goals in directing policy and implementation. Ties of policies to economic development are to focus on positives and potential rather than dwelling only on the negative uncertainties.

142. Europe has actively used tax policy to achieve and direct targeted activities. Status of some of the European states is given below for reference.

Netherlands

143. Netherlands has prepared a National Energy Vision and Scenarios for 2030 and 2050. Their policy combines industrial, agricultural, transportation, land use, housing and fiscal measures. They propose transition projects exploring a number of technology pathways. The Dutch industry is targeting a 22 per cent reduction in energy use by 2050. Major efforts will be in wind, biomass and hydrogen. The goal is to draw 30 per cent of energy from biomass by 2040.

Denmark

144. Denmark is building a global renewable energy industry by integrating renewable energy onto their grid. Presently nearly 20 per cent of electricity is from wind. Up to 25 per cent of energy will be coming from renewables this year—wind, biogas and biomass. The goal is of stabilising energy consumption during the long-term economic growth. Danish manufacturers have half of global wind turbine market and employ 14,000 people.

Germany

145. Schleswig-Holstein has achieved some of the world's highest levels of wind energy development and grid penetration. Germany has bold targets for GHG reductions, aggressively implementing wind and other renewables and pursuing hydrogen and fuel cell development. By 2010, Schleswig-Holstein expects 50 per cent of their electric power to be supplied by wind. 25,000 MW of new wind was identified for offshore development. Wind energy directly employs 40,000 people in Germany. German wind industry's use of steel is exceeded only by automobile manufacturing.

Iceland

146. Iceland is dedicated to transitioning to a renewable-based hydrogen economy. Iceland has already converted more than 97 per cent of its electricity and residential heating to renewable sources. Over the next 50 years, Iceland expects to convert its bus fleet, its 1,80,000 cars and 2,500 fishing vessels to hydrogen power.

Suggested Growth Areas

147. Renewable energy is an important component of energy security. For the purpose energy security in addition to having generation within the state, it is necessary to have a target that at least 10 per cent of demand shall be met by renewable sources by next 15 years. Such a commitment by the State will be necessary.

Solar Hot Water and Thermal Systems

148. Medium solar thermal system technology has matured and is commercially viable. To enable its growth it may be necessary to change building bye-laws in developments exceeding 20 dwellings that provision of solar thermal systems as compulsory.

Solar PV Systems

149. Tudou village, which was electrified by centralised solar PV cell in 1988 has now been connected to electricity gird. Promotion of solar PV cell programme may be restricted to remote and inaccessible areas only.

Biomass Programme

150. Biomass steam generation programme is presently adopted by Sanjivini Sugar Mills. Pilot energy plantation is being promoted by GEDA. Energy plantation will depend upon the profitability of land use. Further being a high rainfall region, the moisture in the plant will be high. So energy will be required to dry the plantation before feeding to the burner of bio steam producer. This will reduce the overall thermal efficiency. This in turn will depend upon the profitability of the power generator. Present power purchase tariffs will not promote this programme.

151. Biomass gasification projects will be a necessity for Goa in view of presence of the hotel industry. Out of

85,000 star rooms in India, Goa has 25,000 star rooms. The tourist inflow is 2 million in a year. This generates kitchen waste. The biomass can be semi-digested in the hotel and transported as slurry to a centralised location. At this location it can be gasified and gainfully utilised.

Wind Energy

152. Wind map as published by MNES, does not indicate Goa as a potential State to harness wind energy. Studies which are being undertaken by GEDA may throw light on particular sites in Goa.

153. Cost of power generated using wind energy has been decreasing over the years. Cost of wind energy which was Rs. 120 per kWh in 1979 has come down to Rs. 3.50 per kWh in high wind zones in 2005 due to technological advancements. The cost of wind energy is likely to reduce as years go. Presently Goa obtains bulk power from NTPC sources at Rs. 1.50 per kWh. According to projections based on reduction in wind energy costs and rise in power purchase cost, wind power may become economical only by the year 2020. Till that time there should be conscious decision to buy conventional power.

FIGURE 2.7

Year-wise Generation Cost in Rs/kWh

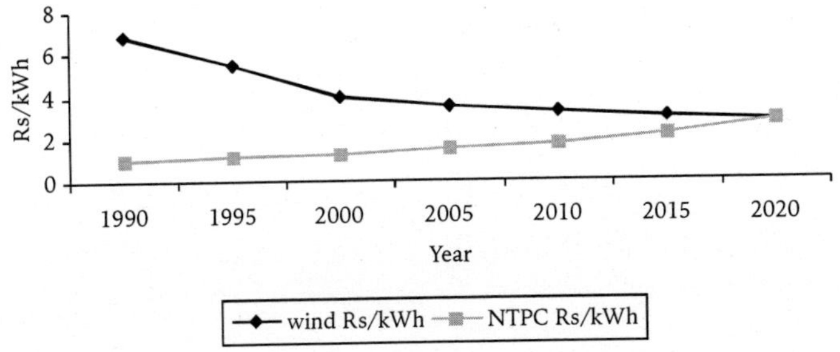

Source: Statistical Handbook of the Government of Goa for the relevant years.

154. Wind farm size has to be a minimum of 15 MW considering the grid connectivity costs. This calls for lands in few hectares. The land in Goa has high costs. Some suggestions were also made for offshore wind farm. Denmark has installed offshore wind generation units.

155. Growth of wind generation in Goa will be therefore, limited by need for subsidising land costs and need for considerable investigation on environment impact due to slowing down of the downstream wind, noise, bird hits and other reported effects.

Micro, Mini and Small Hydro Power Programme

156. The 40 KW demonstration micro hydel project at Harvelm was in operation for a period of four years after it was decommissioned. During this period it had successfully demonstrated viability as well as environmental friendliness. But the capacity is too low for Goa which has a high per capita consumption.

157. Private participation in development of individual projects of size 2 MW or a cluster of hydro projects aggregating to 2 MW and above may be invited.

Sustainability of Renewable Energy Development Programme

158. Though Goa took pioneering steps in early years in promotion of wind energy and micro hydel, these were not sustained due to following reasons:

Micro hydel station due to very low capacity.

Wind due to non-availability of spares since the supplier BONUS – Thermax closed down their operation in India. Besides the energy generated was also less than estimated due to turbulence in wind and low grid reliability.

Sustainable renewable energy and its development depend upon the same becoming commercially sustainable in the long run. Initial subsidies may attract some investments in the beginning years.

Oil and Gas Indicators

159. The use of petrol and HSD has been primarily for transport of goods and people. A portion of HSD is being used for standby power generation. Industrial use of F.O. is limited to steam generation for process and partly for power generation. LPG is the fuel for cooking used by domestic as well as hotels. Naphtha is being used as feedstock for fertiliser industry. Naphtha is also being used by the 48 MW CCPP for generation of power.

TABLE 2.9

Fuel Consumption during 2004-05

Fuel Type	*Thousand Metric Tonnes (TMT)*
HSD	265.50
Petrol	59.70
F.O	144.00
Naphtha	245.00

Source: IOC, Vasco.

Issues and Fiscal Impact

Environment Impact

160. Naphtha usage for fertiliser is 70 per cent while power is 30 per cent. Naphtha being clean fuel for power generation, has no adverse impact on environment. Use of

F.O for steam and power generation has an adverse impact. This can be eliminated only by making available LNG and by improving grid quality power supply. Use of HSD for standby power generation can be also limited by improving grid quality.

161. Transportation of goods includes fishing vessels beside trucks. The improvement of technology will continue to lessen the environment impact.

High Cost of Fuel

162. High cost of fuel is a major concern. Cheaper fuel like LNG should be made available. Non-availability of cheaper fuel is a drain on the economy. Even if LNG is available at an international price of $5 per MMBTU, then the saving expected is Rs. 500 crore per annum, which will be available to the economy.

Development and Growth Areas

163. Since the State has a policy of promoting only clean industries, there will not be any accelerated growth in consumption of oil and gas. In addition, the rising cost of fuel abnormally will in itself encourage conservation and efficiency mechanism to be in place.

Sustainability of Oil Cost

164. The high cost of oil itself is an impediment for sustainability of the economy.

Emerging Alternatives and Technologies

165. There are emerging fuels like bio-diesel, hydrogen etc. Besides fuel, alternative technologies are also rapidly emerging for electric power generation. We will have choices in energy and their usage soon. This section will neither discuss the merits or demerits, nor evaluate these emerging alternatives and technologies. These are beyond the scope of the development report. We will limit this discussion to the following:

Any unique potential in Goa, which can be further investigated;

Feasibility of piloting any emerging technology and

Preparedness to adopt these technologies as and when they become affordable.

Road Travelled

166. Historically Goa has pioneered technology of producing wine known as feni from cashew fruits and coconuts. Goa has also technology to extract oil from the kernel of cashew nut. Goa has also indigenously mastered the technology of houses with mud walls, which can withstand 3000 mm of annual rainfall. It has blended Portuguese architecture with Indian architecture and created a unique brand value for itself.

Period 1961-1971

167. The Government of India under CSIR had established National Institute of Oceanography (NIO) in Dona Paula for ocean research. ICAR had established a Research Station at Old Goa for Agriculture Research.

Period 1971-1981

168. NIO and ICAR centres grew as prime research units. Goa University was also established as a separate entity from Bombay University.

Period 1981-1991

169. Goa piloted many programmes connected with renewable energy sources like wind, micro hydel, centralised solar system etc., as explained in the previous section under renewable energy.

170. TERI established a branch in Goa to carry out policy research.

Period 1991-2001

171. Goa has prepared itself to accept gas as and when it becomes available, by installing a 48 MW CCPP in 1000 and operating it using naphtha. The first private research centre in process Panandikar Research Lab was estabilished.

172. Sesa Goa applied for patent for its clean technology for Coke production in USA.

Period 2001-2005

173. Ciba Specialty Chemicals converted its operations in Goa as a global research centre for the group. Ratiopharm, has also selected Goa for its R&D activities. Konkan Railway chose Goa to carry out its Sky Bus development project.

Indicators

174. If we consider the number of patents in energy and environmentally clean technologies as indicators, then the application of patent by Sesa Goa will fall in this category.

Issues and Fiscal Implications

175. Goa is also exposed to Japan, Korea, Taiwan and China through strong trade links in mining and IT sector. People of Goa travelled and settled in erstwhile Portuguese colonies in Africa and South America. The present

generation also has strong links with Australia, USA and Canada. Goa also receives two million tourists every year from all over the world with majority from Europe.

176. Such wide exposure to outside world enables Goa to adopt any new technology that is globally available. In creativity, ingenuity and adopting new technologies, Goa is one of the best forerunners in the world.

177. The patent laws and IP rights will enable and accelerate many technologies to emerge from Goa.

Energy for Public Transport

178. Monsoon in Goa is very active from June to September. The average number of rainy days in a year is 100. Under such climate, the convenience of getting into a vehicle at home and getting down at the destination without getting wet is a necessity and not a luxury.

179. Worldwide experience in countries both developed and developing is that massive investments in improving public transport system, has not yielded any result in reducing personal vehicles and consequently in improving energy efficiency and/or reducing pollution. Countries like Bogoda have successfully tried bus rapid transport system, which provide access to a bus within 500 metres of residence and hence attracted 4 per cent of personalised vehicle to bus transport.

180. At present spatial disbursement of houses and the climatic conditions in Goa may encourage only personalised vehicles. The transport problem in Goa had been solved by a unique method of having motorcycle taxis with pilots. Later on, hiring out of motorcycle itself was introduced.

Development and Growth Areas

Bio-diesel

181. The possibility of refining oil from cashew kernel for bio-diesel or using it for bio-medical purpose will be a major development area.

Energy Efficiency Improvement

182. Improving energy efficiency in areas of production process of mining, power guzzlers, distillation process for feni, beneficiation process of iron ore and pharmaceutical process (clean room and air conditioning) will be another area of growth for emerging technologies.

Offshore or Hill Top Wind Energy

183. The surface of Goa is undulated and hence, the surface wind is turbulent and not recommended for harnessing energy. Offshore wind energy or wind farms on top of identified hilltops with tall towers will be a potential that can be explored. Hubs of wind generators shall be located preferably 150M above sea level.

Ocean Energy

184. Ocean energy may be a source for Goa. The chair in NIO has to be strengthened in this area.

Natural Gas

185. There seems to be no other alternative than to get either LNG or NG into the state immediately.

Sustainability of Emerging Technology Programme

186. Normally, state funded programmes are focused and time bound. For example, obtaining NG or LNG into the State is a need for sustainability in energy but this is not in the agenda of the State. The need may vary from time to time, but the policy mechanisms should sustain emerging technology programme. This issue will be discussed under governance.

Institutions and Governance

Governing Structure

187. Presently departments and institutions concerned with natural resources are as below:

- Electricity Department (GED) carries out all functions of a power utility as well as policy framework.
- Goa Energy Development Agency (GEDA) carries out functions relating to promotion of renewable sources of energy and implements subsidy schemes relating to Integrated Rural Energy Programme.

188. Power Advisory Committee and CADA provide stakeholders inputs on all policy and tariff issues.

189. Fundamentally, the electricity department is a government-owned distribution utility. There is no government-owned generating station or a major network of transmission lines. The governing structure has to be viewed from providing service to the ultimate consumer at reasonable costs. While pursuing the policy of privatisation, the experience of Delhi or Orissa cannot be neglected. It should also be taken into account the fact that the present institutional structure has served well in its objective. It has also encouraged investment in generation from private sector. The investments in generation or distribution will flow automatically as there is a financially strong distribution sector at present. Any

attempt to rock the existing system may not yield results unless such system improves the distribution/delivery system.

Public-Private Participation

> When Government out sources management of water distribution to the private sector, it shifts its role from the management of water supply to management of contract for water supply. And it is usually as competent or not at both. Private sector will deliver only if effectively regulated, enforceable consumer safe guards, monitoring mechanisms, performance incentives service standards, clear channels of accountability through engagement of consumer exist. The poor should have a voice in policy-making and only then implementation service will improve.
>
> — D. Narasimha Rao,
> Visiting Faculty, IIM, Bangalore.

Alternatives for Distribution from a Government-Owned Entity

Alternative-1: Distribution Corporation

190. The Government of Goa had appointed several agencies to study the issue of public-private participation since 1996. The State had appointed an international consulting firm in 1996, followed it with Goa Institute of Management, BSES and Bajaj Institute of Management at regular intervals. These reports revolved around privatisation or converting GED into corporation. In smaller states the government is within the reach of the common man. Creation of corporation only creates a layer between the Government and the common man. This is the major reason for not implementing the cabinet decision. GED already maintains corporate financial discipline and publishes, profit and loss account and balance sheet. No specific advantage is expected by making into a corporation. On the other hand, distribution through local bodies will not only empower local bodies and also reduce layer in decision-making and provide much better access to common man

Alternative-2: Privately Owned Distribution Company/Corporation

191. Whatever may be the need or advantages, there is generally strong resentment on privatisation of power distribution among the public in general. Secondly, the present electricity department is a cash cow to the government. Though it is possible for the government to carry out the role of a power trader and privatise the distribution system, such a move will not be politically advisable. Any discussion on this will be in vain till there is a political will.

Alternative-3: Ushering Private/Public Competitions in Distribution

192. Goa is the only State in India, which experimented with a novel idea. The private IPP was allowed to lay distribution cables in the same industrial area, where the government was distributing power. Under this scheme, an industrial consumer has a choice of: (i) Getting power from government from electricity department wires, or (ii) Getting power from IPP directly from the said IPP's own cables, or (iii) by setting up their own generation plants, or (iv) Purchase of power from group captive power plants through government-owned wires.

193. The model is successfully working for the last five years or more. The drawback is that there is uneven playing field since the government enjoys the benefit of pooled cost of cheaper power, which is not available to the IPP. This model can be extended, provided IPP is also allowed access to cheap source of power.

Alternative-4: Franchisee Alternative for Power Distribution

194. The current issues that were highlighted in previous paragraphs on power quality and reliability refer to service levels in delivery of power to the customer. The State has allowed an IPP to supply power directly to consumers using their own wires. Thus, a consumer has a choice to get his works connected to GED network or the IPP network. There is also mutual cooperation between IPP and GED in this regard. This arrangement has resulted A-Class quality power available to consumer. The arrangement is an example of a healthy distributed generation.

195. Replication of this arrangement to other areas is difficult mainly because having more than one set of wires is not a practical solution in many places.

196. The same sets of problems (interruption, low voltage, surges, energy security, performance below desired service levels) have been with us for several years. It seems we have been busy using the same set of non-solutions all over again. We propose a franchisee alternative.

197. GED is operationally a cash surplus organisation. Hence, investment by it may not be a problem. The immediate and foremost need is therefore, to improve the power reliability, power quality and service in delivery of power to the consumer. The fiscal on GDP and pollution on environment due to running of DG sets are high. GED being also service provider as well as regulator, there are inherent conflicts. Service deficiencies have also

encouraged formation of interest groups like DG set supplier, UPS supplier etc. The governing mechanism should therefore, address this issue.

198. Under Franchise operation scheme, the licensee provides all the technical and managerial support. The licensee sets the quality and service standards and monitors the service levels. Franchisee being in local area, serves the community well and responds to its needs faster than a remotely controlled entity.

199. The question that arises is, in case of power who is the best franchise operator. Success stories in India has shown that local municipality like BEST, NDMC are best operators. Even private operators when confined to a municipal limit like Ahmedabad Electricity Supply, CESC or Surat Electricity Supply deliver better.

Suggestion for Distribution

200. Therefore, suggestion is to initially consider every municipality and municipal corporation as franchisee of GED. In addition to organisations like Chamber of commerce or Industrial Associations in relevant industrial area can be a franchisee.

Regulation—SERC

201. Considering that SERC for smaller states is not a viable proposition, GoI has introduced the concept of common SERC for a group of smaller States and UTs. Such appointments will make the SERC functional.

Generation

(a) Framework for Meeting Growth in Power Demand

202. By the year 2011, the demand will be close to 600 MW. The electric power distribution grid and gigawatt power plants are attractive terrorist targets and may even be vulnerable to cyber terrorism.

203. The discussion on framework for generation has to examine the following alternatives in addition to maximising internal resources:

- Purchase of power from generating stations located outside Goa: Presently GED purchases power from Central government owned generating sources located outside the State. Goa is the only State, which is connected to both southern and western regional grid. The transmission network of 400 KV D/C connecting Goa with western grid has capacity for bringing in 800 MW. The 220 kv D/C line connecting Southern Grid has capacity of 400 MW. Under E.A. 2003, purchase of power from generating stations outside the State either directly or through traders is possible.
- Setting up of large generating station within Goa: The question of setting up large coal-based thermal power plant is repeatedly raised over the time; 2 × 60 MW in the early 1970s, 2 × 120 MW in the late 80s and now 2 × 250 MW. Every time this crops up, the same two questions are raised. One is about pollution and second is about the capacity utilisation of such a power plant because when such a capacity is added there will be power surplus within the State in the initial years till corresponding load growth takes place. While pollution can be controlled within limits by technology, capacity utilisation is an issue. If the plant is allowed to sell power outside the State in the initial years of operation, in future years the power may not be available for the State. This means that the State should be willing to pay for idle capacity known as deemed generation. Then the power cost will be over Rs. 3.25 per unit.
- Distributed Generation: The alternative to large power plants lies in distributed generation (DG) of moderate capacity, say 25-100 MW.

  Goa has already successfully implemented DG. In addition to 48 MW CCPP at Sancoale, 30 MW waste heat recovery power plant is being installed in Amona by Goa Energy Private Limited. Allowing generators to lay dedicated lines and sell power to third party directly has enabled DG. The policy also enables group captive and sale of surplus power to GED.

  Goa is also the first state to introduce successfully retail level competition in power. An industrial consumer has option to buy from licensee, generator or group captive generator.

  Under SEZ act, the developer of SEZ is free to source and if needed free to develop generation. The Development Commissioner of SEZ will enable and facilitate the same.

  Major advantages of such DG are that it reduces ATC losses, brings in efficiency and ensures incremental growth in generation capacity. The IPP in Goa though distributes power over 42 km length has ATC loss less than 2 per cent, and 100 per cent revenue recovery.
- Maximise internal resources

(b) Development of LNG or CNG Terminal

204. The basic issue is whether to bring into Goa fuel for generation of power or bring in power through wires from power plants that are situated outside Goa. In India as per Kirti Parikh report, coal-based generation will remain as the major backbone of power industry. Being sensitive to environmental concerns, setting up of large-scale coal-based power plant within the state is remote. Goa has to therefore, continue to explore all the avenues.

205. SEZ developers will drive the economics of setting up of LNG or CNG terminal.

(c) Development of Hydro Generation

206. Goa government has appointed NHPC as consultants and identified 60 MW small and medium hydropower sources. Projects like Dudhsagar, in addition, offers excellent opportunity for pumped storage schemes to meet peak load of the State. The State is in the process of appointing consultants for implementation of hydro projects.

207. Goa has already invited expression of interest from bidders for development on BOOT basis the Anjunem Project. Under this model, the developer will be required to supply 12 per cent of generated power free of cost to the State towards royalty. The balance power will be sold to grid at the bid rate. The lowest bidder gets the right to develop the project. To sum up successfully, Goa has employed policy measures and used consultants (central sectors like Power Grid, NHPC) to implement the development schemes. This appears to be the right approach considering that for a small state, capacity building in these specialised areas is not only difficult but retaining the human resources also extremely difficult.

208. But it is a fact that the State lagged in development of hydro potential. The solid example is that even though the Planning Commission allotted funds in 1988-89 for a small hydro project at Anjunem, it remained undeveloped till date in 2005-06 after 18 long years. The present GED or WRD has no significant institutional framework to develop this potential. GED focuses only on distribution and WRD only on irrigation.

209. Therefore, it is proposed to fill in the vacuum of institutional arrangement for development of hydro power plants. Instead of creating an additional institution it is proposed that the Goa Energy Development Agency (GEDA), an agency dedicated to development of renewable energy, should take over the development of hydro energy.

210. Further any development of hydro potential involves interaction with traditional users of water and land. It is also proposed that the unique institution of Goa 'the Comunidade" be involved in the same.

TABLE 2.10

Strengths, Weaknesses, Opportunities and Threats

	Strengths	*Weaknesses*	*Opportunities*	*Threats*
Power	Financially strong utility. Healthy cooperation with IPP Innovative policies	Reliability and quality of GED supplied power High cost of naphtha-based power	LNG or NG Public and private participation through Franchisee For energy service companies	High cost of fuel Absence of future power allocations
Renewable energy	Piloting various schemes and excellent rural network	Financial status Renewable energy owners and users participation	Promotion of biofuels, Hydro electric schemes Pumped Storage Schemes Energy plantations Wind mapping and wind energy schemes	Misconception on hydro and other renewable energy schemes
Oil & Gas	Clean fuel used for power generation Inland water barge transport for iron ore transport	Increase use of personalised vehicle	LNG or NG or CNG	High cost of fuel
Emerging technology	Ability to pilot and absorb new technologies	Absence of institutional mechanism	Biodiesel, offshore wind farm	Rapid increase in conventional technology

Source: Statistical Handbook of the Government of Goa for the relevant years.

Outlook: Possible Scenarios in the Short, Medium and Long Term

Business-As-Usual

211. Power will be imported and power distribution quality will continue to have problems. The population of standby DG sets will increase. There will not be any appreciable contribution from renewable sources of energy. The hydroelectric potential will remain be a long drawn process.

Utopia

212. LNG or NG will be available in Goa. Goa will generate power and export to neighbouring states. There will be offshore and hill top wind farms to generate power. Peak load will be met by pumped storage hydroelectric schemes. Renewable sources will meet 15 per cent of energy requirements.

213. Franchisee will ensure quality power distribution. Water will be available to users 24×7. Non-revenue water will be a history. The poor will have say in policy.

Dystopia

214. Power will be rationed and cuts imposed. DG sets will pollute the State. Battery fumes because of large population of invertors will cause serious health hazards.

215. Use of inefficient technology will continue. Power quality will be a major problem. Renewable energy will be wasted away.

Recommendations and Development Strategies

216. The following recommendations may be considered:

1. *Policy for Quality Power:* Distribution will continue to remain the focus area. Policy framework to allow franchisee with industrial associations, municipalities should be introduced to achieve consumer satisfaction. This will address power quality problems on priority.
2. *Policy for Encouraging Distributed Generation:* Policy of allowing generating companies to supply directly to industries or group of industrial units by constructing own lines has to be extended to all generating companies. Such companies should be allowed to buy power from other generating companies or traders in order to serve such consumers with reliability and also economically. This will encourage distributed generation within the State.
3. *Continuation of Long Term Power Purchase Policy:* GED has entered into long-term contracts with PSU generating companies through allocation route. GED also similarly has long-term PPA with IPP through tariff-based bidding route. GED should continue entering into long-term contracts with IPPs by global tariff bidding route and Central PSUs will ensure energy security.
4. *Hydro Power Development:* The institution of Goa Energy Development Agency should be strengthened for development of hydropower rather than being entrusted to GED or WRD. Concerned community has to be involved through the comunidade institution.
5. *Continuation of Existing Policy on Transmission:* Transmission backbone will have to remain within the control of GED and shall be strengthened.
6. *Policy to Encourage Energy Efficiency:* There is no institution or policy to encourage energy efficiency. ESCOs will be promoted to enhance energy use efficiency. Eco star programmes will be introduced in schools to promote energy and water conservation measures.
7. *Policy for Renewable Energy:* Mandatory purchase of power from renewable energy with a target at 5 per cent of energy portfolio should be introduced.
8. *Policy on Regulation:* Regulatory framework as per E.A 2003 should be put in place.
9. *Policy on Fuel:* Policy framework to attract LNG or CNG or NG fuel has to be strengthened for making available within the State.

WATER AND ENVIRONMENTAL SECURITY

Introduction

217. The gainful utilisation of natural resources in an efficient and sustainable manner is primary for economic welfare and quality of life for any society. Any under or overexploitation of natural resources will inflict long-term injuries to the society that may be too difficult to be corrected in future. In a given geographical area, not all the required natural resources are available in plenty and some of the resources will even be in deficit. While the deficit has to be imported, the surplus has to be shared in economically gainful manner for all the stakeholders including future generations.

218. The natural resources—water, energy and environment are so interlinked and complex, that organisation of this report is in itself a challenge. Traditional conventional wisdom of ordering of resource-based development plan i.e., resource and its uses has been modified so as to include utilisation point of view. For example conventionally one looks at available groundwater resources first, then its use and the potential for future use. While resource-based planning has its own advantages, the linkages for meeting the needs through alternate means efficiently are normally overlooked in this approach. To meet the drinking water needs, the resource may be a major river project or groundwater project or seawater de-salination project etc. This section is therefore, designed as far as possible from the demand point of view rather than the resource availability point of view.

219. The emerging technology and economic growth will have a larger impact than till now experienced on natural resources. Water as a resource has been considered in a separate section. This has been followed by environmental security discussions.

220. Prudent management desires that this is the time to conserve, improve efficiency and enhance quality of delivery in addition to ensuring security so that the leadership position in the sector can be maintained. The State has to continue to be out of box thinking solution provider in this sector so as to remain in forefront.

221. Forest management groups, River Basin Organisation and Water User Association will be guiding posts in development of water resources.

222. The poor will have a voice in policy-making and implementation so that service will improve.

223. The institution and governance section deals with the present structure of governance. The last section on summary and conclusion contains SWOT (Strength, Weakness, Opportunity, Threat) analysis, outlook and the recommendation for development strategies.

224. Water is life and blood of our environment and without water no living being can survive. It plays a unique role in traditional and modern economy and is mandatory in all daily chores of mankind including drinking, domestic, agriculture and industry. Water is a finite resource and cannot be replaced and/or duplicated and produced on commercial scale. Only 2.7 per cent of the water on earth is fresh. Clean and fresh water is a unique commodity, therefore, to be valued and safeguarded.

TABLE 2.11

Water Resources in World

Total water resources in world	1460 Million
Saline water	97.30%
Fresh water	2.70%
Fresh water distribution	
Polar ice caps	77.20%
Groundwater & soil moisture	22.40%
Lakes, swamp & reservoirs	0.35%
Atmosphere	0.04%
Rivers & streams	0.01%

Source: Water Resources Ministry, Government of India.

225. The Table 2.12 provides data on available, utilisable and presently being used water in India in BCM.

TABLE 2.12

Water Resources in India

Total water from precipitation/yr	– 4000 BCM
Total water availability/yr	- 1869 BCM
Total water utilisable/yr	- 1122 BCM
Surface water utilisable/yr	- 690 BCM
Groundwater utilisable/yr	- 432 BCM
Present water utilisation	- 630 BCM
Surface water utilisation/yr	- 400 BCM
Groundwater utilisation/yr	- 230 BCM

Source: Statistical Handbook of the Government of Goa for the relevant years.

226. Utilisable surface and groundwater are 17.25 per cent and 10.8 per cent respectively of total water from rainfall in India. Out of utilisable water, the actual utilisation of surface and groundwater in India is 57.97 per cent and 53.24 per cent respectively.

227. This report is concerned with water as a resource and hence will not address resources such as inland waterways transportation, water sports or entertainment and use of water bodies for fish culture or any other related activity. The report is limited to water use for irrigation, domestic, industrial and generation of power. Similarly, the change and growth in demand of water for irrigation, cropping pattern, etc., are related to agriculture and hence not included scope of this document.

228. The State of Goa is located on the west coast of the country and receives copious rainfall by the southwest

monsoons. The entire precipitation is however, limited to the monsoon period of just four months from June to September. The State possesses a vast potential of assured water. As per the study conducted by N.I.O (National Institute of Oceanography), about 80 per cent of rainwater gets drained to the Arabian Sea during the monsoon period of just four months. Goa possesses nine river basins namely, Terekhol, Chapora, Baga, Mandovi, Zuari, Sal, Saleri, Talpona and Galgibag.

229. The estimated annual water availability is computed from the recorded rainfall for the year 2005 as recorded in Goa observatory as below:

TABLE 2.13

Rainfall Recorded in 2005

	Centre	*Rainfall in mm*
1	Panaji	3345.1
2	Mormugao	2751.4
3	Pernem	3341.2
4	Valpoi	4628.3
5	Margao	3002.3
6	Mapusa	3216.0
7	Canacona	3369.5
8	Sanguem	3590.7
9	Ponda	3640.4
10	Quepem	3329.5

Source: Statistical Handbook of the Government of Goa for the relevant years.

230. The annual water after draining into available for utilisation is estimated as 2.55 BCM.

Road Travelled

Period 1961-1971

231. A primary task undertaken by Central Water and Power Commission (CWPC), immediately after liberation was to set up gauging stations and collect data of flow in the rivers. CWPC had set up a division office for this purpose and after collecting data closed this office in the year 1970.

232. This period also was a period of investigation, identification, survey and formulation of projects.

Period 1971-1981

233. Major irrigation schemes Salaulim and Anjunem were implemented. Drinking water system upgraded from 1.5 MLD to 12.5 MLD. A number of minor irrigation schemes were developed.

Period 1981-1991

234. Salaulim water supply scheme of 16 MLD was implemented. Command Area Development Agency (CADA) for development of Salaulim and Anjunem areas was institutionalised.

Period 1991-2005

235. Anjunem medium irrigation project was completed. Salali estimated to cost Rs. 160 crore. Rs. 157.18 crore is utilised. Tillari is another ongoing interstate scheme with Maharashtra. The cost of project is Rs. 952.44 crore while Goa's share is Rs. 698.97 crore. Goa's portion expenditure is Rs. 344.43 crore upto March 2004.

236. A consolidated data from 1961 onwards till date, plan-wise on the capacity created and the amount invested was not available despite efforts to obtain and collate the same.

Indicators

Success Story—Equitable Distribution of Water

237. Out of 395 rural habitats, 388 are fully covered with regard to water supply. The balance 7, which are situated in remote and inaccessible areas are partially covered. Before looking into details, Goa is a success story in addressing the water needs of rich and poor, urban and rural, coastal and interior areas in equitable manner. The State has successfully handled and avoided any conflict arising out of water between all the stakeholders.

Potential Created

238. The cumulative potential created for use of water in India and Goa is furnished below:

TABLE 2.14

Potential for Water Use in India and Goa

(in thousand ha)

Sector	*India*		*Goa*	
	Ultimate Irrigation Potential	*Cumulative Potential*	*Ultimate Irrigation Potential*	*Cumulative Potential*
Major & medium	58460	36910.43	62	21.17
Minor irrigation	81430	56900.02	54	19
Ground	17380	13611.00	29	4
Surface	64090	43289.00	25	15
Total	139890	93810.45	116	40.17

Source: Water Resource Ministry, Government of India.

239. As against all India creation of potential of 71.32 per cent, Goa has created a potential of 41 per cent.

Groundwater Resources of Goa

240. Groundwater forms about 38 per cent of the 112 MHAM utilisable water of the country catering to 60 per cent of irrigation and more than 90 per cent of domestic needs of rural population. There is increasing demand of groundwater due to increasing population, irrigation, industrialisation and urbanisation. This has put tremendous pressure on groundwater system by way on indiscriminate sinking of bore wells and dug wells resulting in lowering of water levels and deterioration of quality in different parts of the country. Hence, there is a need to assess groundwater resources for its sustainable management. This report is an effort in this direction.

241. Groundwater occurs mainly in weathered and fractured hard rocks formation in the State. Though the average rainfall in the State is up to about 3700 mm, summer months face drying up of dug wells and scarcity of groundwater. This is because of high surface and sub-surface run off due to hilly topography and laterite nature of aquifer.

242. The groundwater resources of the State has been estimated by Central Ground Water Board, SWR, Bangalore and Water Resources Deptt. of Goa based on the recommendations of 'Ground Water Resources Estimation Methodology—97'. As per the estimates of the *talukas* are falling in safe category for groundwater development with 27 per cent stage of groundwater development in the State. Greater stress has been noticed in Tiswadi, Bardez *talukas* in North Goa and Canacona and Salcete *talukas* in South Goa districts. It is hoped that the report will be of immense use to agencies involved in development and management of groundwater resources.

243. The total annual recharge is 28471 ham, 80 per cent of which is contributed by rainfall and rest through other sources. The net groundwater availability is 26712.42 ham and the stage of groundwater development is 27 per cent. The entire State is 'safe' from groundwater development point of view.

Projected Groundwater Resources as on March 2004

244. Groundwater resources are computed as on March 2001 and the same is projected for the March 2004. For the purpose of computing the resource for 2004, draft has been projected by taking projected population and groundwater abstraction structures. Computation of population and draft for domestic purposes is done using rate of growth of population.

TABLE 2.15

Groundwater Resources of Goa—Salient Features

Sl. No.	*Particulars*	*Description*		
1.	Geographical area of the State	370198		
2.	Total number of districts	2		
3.	Total number of *talukas*	11		
4.	Type of assessment units	*Talukas*		
5.	Base-year	2001		
6.	Year of projection of draft data	2004		
7.	Number of wells (MI Census 2001)	North Goa	South Goa	State
7.1	Dug wells	3359	1261	4620
7.2	Bore wells	71	19	90
7.3	Total wells	3430	1280	4710
7.4	Annual growth rate of wells	10/8%	9.6%	10.2%
8.	Net water availability of the State (HAM)	26712.42		
9.	Groundwater draft (HAM)			
9.1	Irrigation draft (HAM)	3943.83		
9.2	Domestic and industrial draft (HAM)	3266.87		
9.3	Total draft (HAM)	7210.7		
10	Net groundwater availability for future irrigation development (HAM)	18480.2		
11.	Balance groundwater irrigation potential available (HA)	35379.12		
12.	Stage of GW development (%)	27		
13.	Categorisation	Safe (all *Talukas*)		
14.	Norms used			
			Alluvium	10-12
			Laterites	3
			Basalts	1-2
			Dolomitic limestone	3
	Sp. Yield (%)		Granite/ Schist/Gnesis	3
			Greywacke with conglomerate	3
			Metabasalt	3
15.			Alluvium	10
			Laterites	6-8
			Basalts	6
			Dolomitic limestone	6
	Sp. Yield (%)		Granite/ Schist/Gnesis	6-9
			Greywacke with conglomerate	6
			Metabasalt	6

contd...

...contd...

16 Canal seepage factor	3 hectare per day per million sq. m of wetted area		
17. Return flow surface irrigation (4815 ham)	Type of crop	DTW range (mbgl)	Return flow factor
	Paddy	<10	0.50
	Paddy	10-25	0.40
	Paddy	>25	0.25
	Non-paddy	<10	0.30
	Non-paddy	10-25	0.20
	Non-paddy	>25	0.10
18. Return flow groundwater irrigation (739 ham)	Type of crop	DTW range (mbgl)	Return flow factor
	Paddy	<10	0.45
	Paddy	10-25	0.35
	Paddy	>25	0.20
	Non-paddy	<10	0.25
	Non-paddy	10-25	0.15
	Non-paddy	>25	0.05
19. Recharge factor water bodies	0.00144 m/day/hectare		
20. Unit draft			
20.1 Domestic	60 lpcd		
20.2 Dependency	1		
20.3 Irrigation	Dug well : 0.6 ham/year BW : 1.1 ham/year DCB : 1.1 ham/year		
21. Comparison	GEC84 (1992)	GEM97 (2004)	
21.1 Total annual recharge (ham)	22000	28471.53	
21.2 Total draft for all uses (ham)	2000	7210	
21.3 Stage of groundwater development (%)	9	27	

Source: Statistical Handbook of the Government of Goa for the relevant years.

Groundwater Resources of Goa

245. The summary of groundwater resources of Goa State as on March 2004 is as follows:

1. Net annual groundwater availability — 26712.42 ham
2. Existing groundwater draft for irrigation — 3943.83 ham
3. Existing gross groundwater draft for domestic and industrialwater supply — 3266.87 ham
4. Allocation for domestic and industrial water supply for next 25 years — 4288.39 ham
5. Net groundwater availability for future irrigation development — 18480.2 ham
6. Existing stage of groundwater development in the State — 27%
7. Categorisation — Safe

Comparison of the Resources as on 2004 with 1992

246. The groundwater resources estimated by GEM-97 methodology as on March 2004 was compared with the resources of 1992 assessed by GEC84 methodology. The total annual recharge as on 1992 was 22000 ham as against 28471.53 ham as on 2004. This may be due to additional recharge from water bodies like dams, ponds and tanks. Total draft groundwater for all uses has considerably increased, during the period from 2000, to 7210 ham. This steep growth is attributed to several factors of which the easy loan to farmers to go in for bore well, the free power supply, the availability and awareness of bore well technology even in remote villages and the quick returns from investments on bore wells played a major role. In addition to this, the change in lifestyle and urbanisation with piped water supply and maintaining gardens and law using groundwater created a stress on the groundwater regime. The stage of groundwater development has increased from 9 to 27 per cent.

Groundwater Development

247. Goa has been prudent in not exploiting its groundwater resources. States like Delhi, Haryana, Punjab and Rajasthan have exploited more than 70 per cent and Gujarat, Tamil Nadu have exploited 50-70 per cent of groundwater potential. Out of 14 lakh habitations in India, 14 per cent of area is having poor quality of groundwater. The status of development of various states in India is given below:

TABLE 2.16

Groundwater Development in India and Goa

Stages of Groundwater Development			
States	*[%]*	*States*	*[%]*
Andhra Pradesh	28.56	Maharashtra	37.04
Arunachal Pradesh	-	Manipur	Neg.
Assam	8.75	Meghalaya	3.97
Bihar	26.99	Mizoram	Neg.
Chhattisgarh	5.93	Nagaland	Neg.
Goa	27	Orissa	21.23
Gujarat	55.16	Punjab	97.66
Haryana	112.18	Rajasthan	86.42
Himachal Pradesh	10.72	Sikkim	Neg.
Jammu & Kashmir	0.81	Tamil Nadu	64.43
Jharkhand	33.13	Tripura	33.43
Karnataka	34.6	Uttar Pradesh	46.89
Kerala	22.17	Uttarakhand	37.78
Madhya Pradesh	27.09	West Bengal	38.19

Source: Water Resource Ministry, Government of India.

248. Since the utilisation of surface water itself is not only sufficient but also efficiently and equitably distributed to meet the needs, groundwater development appears not on priority.

Table 2.16 indicates very high level of utilisation of available water in India in some states. Goa has used only 8.2 per cent of its groundwater and hence there is growth potential.

249. The groundwater development is less than 10 per cent in smaller and hilly states as compared with other larger states. The states like Meghalaya, Mizoram, Nagaland, Assam, Sikkim etc., are less than 10 per cent. In comparison with these hilly and high rainfall states, Goa has performed better in groundwater development.

250. The groundwater potential of Goa has been identified by the Central Groundwater Board. But the drawal is required to be limited for the fear of saline water intrusion in the coastal areas. Various irrigation projects one way are beneficial to keep the water table higher to minimise the intrusion of salinity while at the same time meeting the demands of the population for domestic, irrigation and industrial use etc.

251. Goa has steep western gradient permitting fast drainage with lesser scope for groundwater discharge near the coast. Natural fresh water springing in the bottom of hillocks is locally known as *zorim*. Such springs exit along the coast in Palolem (Canacona *taluka*), Sancoale (Mormugao *taluka*) and Vagator (Bardez *taluka*). In the absence of adequate data, a sample survey was conducted in the month of April to know whether the springs become dry and also whether the wells near coastal areas have any indication of not getting replenished. Nothing adverse was found. This means that the groundwater is not overexploited.

252. Kavaloshi in Sindhudurg district of Maharashtra has successfully implemented aquifers recharging programme by constructing appropriate bunds. Repeating similar technology will help to improve the situation.

253. As Brian J. Skinner, a geologist from Yale noted, "More than any other factor, availability of water determines the ultimate population capacity of a geographic province." (1969). The effect of social imbalance and resultant influx of migration into Goa on account of water availability from states that have overexploited their water resource will be a future reality.

Issues and Fiscal Implication

Irrigation Water

254. No major issue has been reported with respect to availability for irrigation till date. Rotational water distribution system (*warabandi*) is introduced. Farmers who are beneficiaries are involved in water distribution process and also given a role to own the irrigation system for maintenance and repairs and are encouraged to form water users associations (WUAs) to facilitate in bridging the gap between potential created and potential utilised. Thus, the equitable distribution of water is ensured and the disputes are minimised. Thus, the irrigation projects with the proper water management while meeting the demands of increasing population help to recharge groundwater and in turn help in avoiding/minimising the intrusion of salinity into fresh water.

FIGURE 2.8

Water Use Pattern

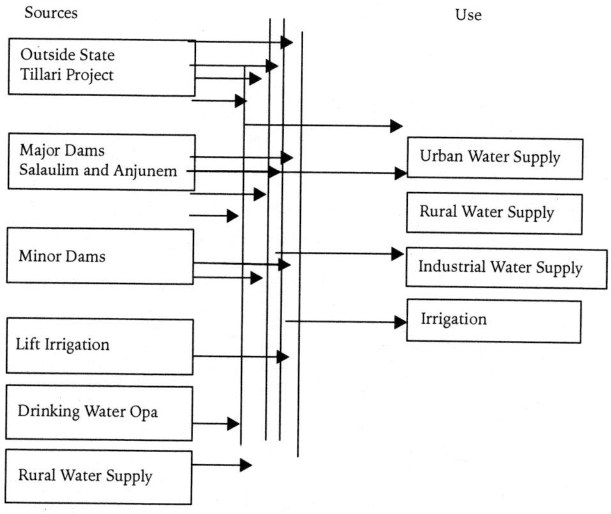

Source: Statistical Handbook of the Government of Goa for the relevant years.

Tillari Irrigation Project

255. The Tillari irrigation project is a joint venture of Government of Goa and Government of Maharashtra. It envisages the construction of an earthen dam across river Tillari, a west flowing river originating from Sayahadri Mountains in Chandgad *taluka* of Kolhapur district of Maharashtra state, crosses Maharashtra state near village Maneri to enter Goa state where it is popularly known as Chapora. The main components of the project are as under:

An earthen dam across river Tillari to impound 462.17 MCM of water having a length of 88 m and maximum height of 72.50 m from the deepest point of the river bed.

A saddle masonary dam of 278.50 m length with 4 numbers of radial gates of size 12 m × 6.5 m to pass out the design flood of 7,270 cumes.

Irrigation-cum-power outlet tunnel has been proposed on the left side of the saddle spillway for releasing the water into left bank canal through the power house with 10 MW installed capacity.

A pick up weir across Kharari *Nallah* to utilise the trail race discharge of 2.89 cumecs with a micro Hydel project 1,200 KW capacity at the feet of this weir.

Canal system: Left bank main canal takes off from ICPO tunnel and runs 18.379 kms in Maharashtra state and 37.40 kms in Goa state. It carries a discharge of 32.56 cumecs at head. It commands an area of 1698 ha in Maharashtra and 19971 ha in Goa. Right bank main canal takes off from the Terwanmedhe pick up weir and runs 24.692 kms in Maharashtra and 23.75 kms in the Goa state. The discharge capacity at the head is 2.89 cumecs and it is further augmented to 14.50 cumecs through the link canal at 14.775 kms in Maharashtra. It commands an area of 4978 ha in Maharashtra and 5007 ha in Goa. Link canal takes off from LMBC at 13 kms and runs 3.53 kms to join with RBMC near village Parma, after crossing over the Perma river through the Aqueduct. It carries a discharge of 12 cumecs for augmenting the discharge of RMBC. Banda branch takes off from RBMC at Ch 6.02 kms (Goa portion) and runs for a length of 57 kms in the Maharashtra state with a designed capacity of 6.5 cumecs to cater to the needs of Maharashtra. Sanquelim branch canal takes off from LMBC at Ch 1.700 kms (Goa portion) and runs for a length of 14.00 kms with a design capacity of 4.46 cumecs.

Delay in Execution of Major Irrigation Projects

256. The Tillari and the Saulalim irrigation projects are under construction for a period more than two decades. Such long delay in projects of this size and magnitude is definitely a matter of concern. The delay results in increase in project cost and also the opportunity to reap benefits is lost. Such long delay calls for auditing of the project and its benefits.

Drinking and Industrial Water

257. Every urban household receives water in an underground sump and pumps to overhead tank. Thus, every household stores water for daily requirement. Though drinking water is not available for 24 hours, and in some areas supply is only on alternate days during summer, general satisfaction level is high.

258. Though there is general satisfaction, the objective of having 24 hours water supply with appropriate pressure should be aimed at.

Quality and Reliability

259. Water samples which were analysed indicated that the quality of water as very good. No disease outbreak like in Manila has been reported. The reliability of water supply is over 98 per cent.

260. The various contaminants found in other states of India is given below:

Arsenic – parts of West Bengal, UP, Chhattisgarh.

Fluoride – parts of Andhra Pradesh, Assam, Bihar, Gujarat, Haryana, Karnataka, Kerala, MP, Chhattisgarh, Maharashtra, Orissa, Punjab, Rajasthan, Tamil Nadu, UP, WB.

Salinity – parts of Andhra Pradesh, Bihar, Gujarat, Haryana, Karnataka, Kerala, MP, Chhattisgarh, Maharashtra, Orissa, Punjab, Rajasthan, Tamil Nadu, UP, NCT Delhi.

Iron – Assam, Bihar, Orissa, Rajasthan, Tripura, WB.

Efforts of SPCB (State Pollution Control Board) on Monitoring of Water Quality

261. In the year 1991, the Goa State Pollution Control Board (GSPCB), in collaboration with the CPCB (Centre Pollution Control Board) took up the responsibility of regular monitoring of water quality of the two major estuaries of Goa, the Mandovi and Zuari, under MINARS. Four stations (two each in Mandovi and Zuari) were established in the estuarine regions of these rivers. While the stations Panjim in Mandovi and Cortalim in Zuari represented the seawater-end, the stations Tonca and Panchwaddi were situated towards the freshwater-end of Mandovi and Zuari respectively. Monitoring of water quality at these stations is being carried out regularly on a monthly basis since 1991.

262. The parameters measured are: water temperature, pH, Dissolved Oxygen (DO), Biological Oxygen Demand (BOD), Chemical Oxygen Demand (COD), turbidity, nitrate-N, nitrite-N, total coliform and faecal coliform. Analysis of the results of monitoring at the four estuarine stations, during the past six years (1999-2000 to 2004-2005), indicates that: The average annual pH was relatively higher (7.4-7.8) at the Panjim and Cortalim stations which are closer to the mouth of Mandovi and Zuari, respectively, as compared to the stations towards the freshwater side, namely, Tonca and Panchwaddi where the average annual pH varied between 6.4 and 7.3. On an annual basis, the average pH at individual station however, did not show much variation, except at station Panchwaddi where the pH varied between 6.4 and 6.8.

263. The DO concentrations showed a general trend of increase between the years 2001-02 and 2004-05 at all stations. The most noticeable change however, was observed in case of faecal coliforms, which steadily increased from a 2-3 MPN/100ml in 1999-2000 to 12-13 MPN/100ml in 2004-05. The reasons for this rapid rise over a period of 5-6 years need to be investigated.

264. The CPCB adopted the Water Quality Criteria for the designated best use in respect of freshwaters and coastal/estuarine waters, and communicated the same to the various states in 1978-79. The water quality parameters for each of these classes were established. A comparison of the data of the 4 estuarine stations and the 7 freshwater stations with the corresponding Primary Water Quality Criteria for class "C" and "SW-II" of fresh and estuarine waters, respectively, indicates that the water quality of both the categories of water is generally good and meets the water quality requirements for the designated best use for the respective category of waters.

Water Conservation and Efficiency

265. Depletion of water resources degrades natural environment, which can necessitate costly and habitat destroying water projects. About 100 districts in 14 states of India experience recurring droughts. The number of blocks in the country that are 'overexploited' where groundwater draft is more than replenishable limits is 673. The blocks that fall in 'Dark' category where draft is nearly equal to replenishable limits number 425. Groundwater levels have declined by more than 4 metres in the last 10 years in more than 249 districts of 16 states. Excessive development led to decline in groundwater level resulting in water scarcity and deterioration in groundwater quality in some areas in India.

266. Presently as indicated in Table 2.16, groundwater use in Goa is less than 10 per cent. Though Goa appears to have no problem, conservation of water shall help in preventing pollution of surface and groundwater resources. In addition to water conservation, water use efficiency measures can reduce water consumption. Water conservation and efficiency practices can reduce water consumption by as much as one-third.

267. The benefits include energy savings by using less energy for pumping and treating water. Financial savings to the user from reduced water use include less sewer and effluent service costs due to reduction in use. Various environmental benefits such as increased water availability in streams, sustainable groundwater availability, protection from pollution etc., also accrue. It also reduces necessity of government regulations on abstraction of groundwater.

Success Story

268. Water conservation and efficiency in use has to be promoted through school children. This is a success story in educating school children on water conservation and efficiency in use. An international school in Bangalore commissioned its students in Vth standard to survey how their domestic servants obtained water and met their needs. The survey led the students to realise the hardships in obtaining water and its use. These students are very active in spreading the message of water conservation and efficiency after their first hand knowledge.

Development and Growth Areas

269. The policy in water development till date is to develop available potential for irrigation and follow it by command area development. Such a policy needs to be continued in case of irrigation schemes. Unlike other commodities whose demand depends market forces, water demand depends upon its availability.

270. Further for a farmer to have a level playing field, it is necessary that water is available to him in his field, whether through his own well, or through an irrigation scheme, at a cost that is comparable elsewhere.

Demand Growth

271. Demand growth as anticipated for India and Goa are furnished below:

TABLE 2.17

Estimated Sectoral Water Requirement (BCM)

	Year 2010		*Year 2025*		*Year 2050*	
Uses	*Goa*	*India*	*Goa*	*India*	*Goa*	*India*
Irrigation	2.56	557	3.08	561	3.20	807
Domestic	0.16	43	0.21	55	0.25	111
Industries	0.41	37	0.54	67	0.78	81
Energy		19		31		70
Inland navigation		7		10		15
Ecology		5		10		20
Evaporation		42		50		76
Total	3.13	710	3.83	796	4.23	1180

Source: Statistical Handbook of the Government of Goa for the relevant years.

Rainwater Harvesting

272. Demand side management *viz.*, regulation is difficult to implement and not popular. Supply side management has positive impact and is the best option. Rainwater harvesting through simple techniques utilising non-committed surplus monsoon runoff is technically feasible and an economically viable option. The entire precipitation takes place within a span of four months and the number of rainy days is nearly 45 in a year.

273. Rainwater harvesting is the process to capture and store rainfall where it falls and to reduce runoff, evaporation and seepage for its efficient utilisation.

Rainwater harvesting is an effective tool to utilise a large quantity of high quality water which otherwise goes as waste creating several problems on the way.

274. There are two main techniques of rainwater harvesting—Storage of rainwater on surface for future use, recharge groundwater. The storage of rainwater on surface is a traditional technique and structures used were tanks, ponds, check dams, weirs, etc.

Traditional Tanks

275. Ponds, tanks and other natural water bodies were created by our ancestors and were maintained by people participation. The water bodies were annually desilted and the clay was even used as plastering material for the *kachha* houses. The silt in big tanks is used as natural manure for fields. Initiative in revival of traditional water bodies such as tanks and ponds and techniques of recharging groundwater are the need of the hour. To meet the water requirement throughout the year, revival of traditional tanks is unavoidable.

276. There is at least one water body in each habitation. These are not numbered and documented. These structures are also attached to temples or mosques. There is need to repair, renovate and restore the structures to facilitate water conservation and augment groundwater recharge. A guestimate is that there are at least 100 such structures that need immediate attention.

Artificial Ground Charging

277. Artificial recharge method is controlled by several factors in the Indian context and the cost estimates as published by Ministry of Water Resources excluding cost of land for each method is as below:

TABLE 2.18

Artificial Recharge Methods

Artificial Recharge Methods	*Tentative Cost in Rs.*
Percolation tanks	10000 per (TCM)
Recharge shaft (Depth, 10-15m, Dia- 2-3 m)	60,000 to 85,000
Recharge pit (2X2×3)m	5000
Check dams	10000 per TCM
Recharge trench	5000-10000
Recharge through H. pump	1500-2500
Recharge through dug well	5000-8000

Source: Statistical Handbook of the Government of Goa for the relevant years.

278. These estimates are very low since in Goa, the excavation in rocky soils will be about Rs. 400 per sq.m as against Rs. 40 per sq.m in a normal soil and minimum wage of a worker is Rs. 80 per day.

279. Funding, operation and maintenance of these artificial recharge mechanisms are issues that needs to be addressed. Though in Goa groundwater is not being over exploited, it is considered necessary to create awareness and promote these methods.

Rainwater Tanks in Private Sector—Success Stories

280. Companies like Zuari Agro Chemicals, Meta Strips and Syngenta have successfully developed storage tanks for rainwater and are gainfully using them throughout the year. Syngenta has mastered the technique of containing the evaporation losses.

Hydroelectric Schemes

281. As indicated in previous sections, it is necessary to harness all available hydro potential in the State.

Comunidade Percolation Tanks

282. The major reason for failure of traditional tanks is said to be lack of people's participation in its maintenance. Goa has a well-woven Comunidade system. It is proposed that the percolation tanks will be owned, operated and maintained by them.

283. Goa has many numbers of small hillocks with an elevation of 70m or above mean sea level (MSL), and habitats live at the foot of such hillocks. Typical examples are villages like Madcaim, Kundaim, Lutlim etc. This opens up potential for multipurpose tanks. A water percolation tank can be established on top of the hillock, while a tailrace pond can be constructed at the bottom of the hillock. Such a combination will also serve as hydro generation during monsoon and peak hour generation during non-monsoon period.

284. In addition the hillock slope may be explored for cultivating crops like cashew, which can yield bio-diesel besides the nut and feni.

285. This multipurpose project may qualify under CDM (clean development mechanism) for carbon credit. The earning will meet the operational cost with some surplus for the community. This will also promote local employment and there will be incentive for the Comunidade to maintain the system.

286. The rate of evaporation in Goa is 150 cms as against more than 300 cms per year in some places in India. Thus, proper care is to be exercised if the harvesting structure is to store water on the surface.

287. The feasibility of setting up such multipurpose schemes of 250 KW and above need to be investigated further. This may be a tall order but worth investigating as it will lead to an integrated development.

Dedicated Industrial Water Supply

288. Future bulk water requirement for industries should be met by allowing directly the industry or group of industries owning the pipeline from raw water source. Such an arrangement will result in following benefits:

There will be addition to through-put capacity of bulk supply of water.

Domestic and public water supply system will not get loaded with industrial demand. The through-put capacity of bulk delivery of water to habitats will not become a constraint.

Water supplied to these industries can be metered and billed at source itself. The non-revenue water on account of leakage, theft etc., will become the responsibility of concerned industrial users.

Pollution, waste water etc., if any caused by industrial consumers can be easily monitored.

Export of Water

289. By using surplus off peak power and the water potential, export of water gainfully to water deficit tier II city like Coimbatore in Tamil Nadu may be an option for growth.

State Water Policy and Schemes

290. The state water policy for optimum utilisation of water resources was formulated in the year 2000. The nine river basins in the state are:

- Terekhol 71 sq.km
- Chapora 255 sq.km
- Baga 50 sq.km
- Mandovi 1580 sq.km
- Zuari 973 sq.km
- Sal 301 sq.km
- Saleri 149 sq.km
- Talpona 233 sq.km
- Galgibag 90 sq.km

291. Long term water management strategy of the State includes:

- Optimum utilisation of available water developing all possible sites for maximum storage.
- Massive *in situ* soil and water conservation measures.
- Minimisation of conversion of agriculture land for non-agricultural purposes.
- Encouraging afforestration programne in the river catchment areas.
- Linking irrigation and hydel reservoirs with urban and rural water supply schemes.
- Maintain water quality of fresh water lakes and integrate with drinking water schemes.
- Optimum utilisation of fresh water lakes, springs etc., for water supply and irrigation.
- Encouraging conversion of marshy land and water logged areas into sweet water lakes.
- Selective and judicious groundwater development.
- Working towards permanent solution for areas frequently affected by drought.

292. Short term water management strategies adopted by the State are:

- Encourage drip irrigation and other water saving technology.
- Desliting of tanks, pond, deepening of community wells and construction of contour check dams.
- Training programme for public to maintain and upkeep of wells and installation of hand pumps for bore wells.
- Plugging leakages in existing distribution pipes and replacing non-functional pumps in bore wells.
- The above strategies are being implemented by the state from 2000. These cover the immediate needs of the State and also ensure that in long term the water resources protected and maintained without affecting ecology.

293. The Schemes the state is executing currently and their review is as under:

- Interlinking of river and post-monsoon water harvesting

  The state has completed two river linking programmes: (a) Chapora river at Sal with Assonora river, and (b) Salaulim to Khandepar river. Both these projects have immensely helped the public by ensuring adequate drinking water supply to North Goa and Panaji town.

The state has completed 18 *bhandharas* by creating 354.68 lakh cu.m of storage capacity in Madei basin, 25.18 lakh cu.m in Assonara river basin, 8.66 lakh cu.m in Kushavati river enabling post-monsoon rainwater harvesting. These projects have helped in maintaining groundwater level.

Proposals under implementation are 14 *bhandharas* in the Talpona river basin and creation of 443.84 lakh cu.m in the Kushavati river and 87.41 lakh cu.m in the Madei river basin.

- Salaulim Project and Tillari Project

  These projects are unduly delayed and need to be looked into.

- Command area development programmes

  Presently the State is training the farmers and implementing *warabandi* schedule. This has been well accepted and received by the farmers.

- Flood control, drainage and anti-sea erosion

  It is reported that the State has cumulatively constructed 55,765 kms of embankment for flood control and drainage programme. This appears to be high for a small state like Goa.

- Augmentation of regional water supply programme

  The works covered under the scheme are, laying of 700 mm CI pipeline from Opa to Panaji, 15 MLD scheme for Pernem and augmentation of Sanquelim water supply scheme. The scheme on implementation will benefit Pernem *taluka* on completion.

- Rural water supply and urban water supply

  Dhargal area which is in remote area will be benefited by this scheme.

- Rural sanitation and sewarage

  Under this scheme extension of sewerage system is being carried in Taleigao, a suburb of Panaji. Sewage line laying work is also under progress in Margao.

Sustainability of Water System

294. Sustainability in water system depends upon creation of potential and bulk supply capacity ahead of demand increase. There should be continuous capacity building.

295. The water cycle has to be efficient. The whole cycle refers to rainwater harvesting, storage pumping treatment, conveying, distribution, storage at user site, pumping at user site and efficiency of use and disposal of wastewater. Study on total efficiency on water cycle is recommended.

296. Sustainability has to also address revenue from water system. Subsidies are inevitable in water-related tariff. Innovative pricing similar to newspaper pricing has to be found. Newspaper is actually paid by the advertiser than the newspaper reader.

297. Sustainability of water system should also address metering system. Only measured quantities can be managed better. Bulk metering and sub-metering will help in understanding the system. A transparent uniform metering policy with public understanding will help in improving the system.

Environment Sustainability and Security

298. Environment sustainability is a function of carrying capacity and the footprint. Any activity consumes energy and some activities also use materials. Some processes also need water. These activities produce value added product and/or service. In addition, waste material is generated, wastewater is released and there are emissions to atmosphere. Some of these wastes are recycled and used.

FIGURE 2.9

Typical Process Flow

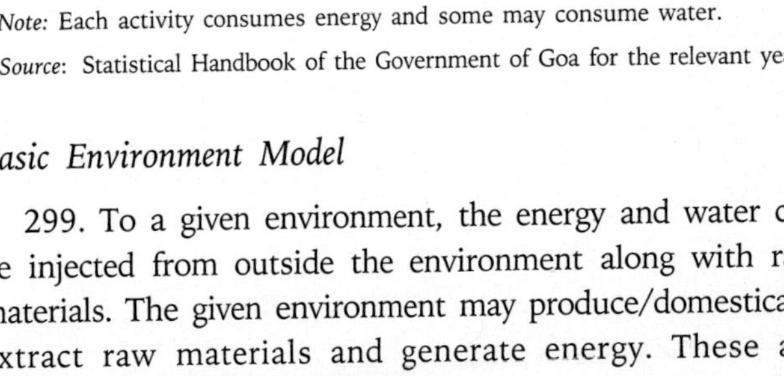

Note: Each activity consumes energy and some may consume water.

Source: Statistical Handbook of the Government of Goa for the relevant years.

Basic Environment Model

299. To a given environment, the energy and water can be injected from outside the environment along with raw materials. The given environment may produce/domestically extract raw materials and generate energy. These are consumed by stocks (human and animals) and also used in economic activity to produce goods and services.

300. The environment exports water, energy and the products. This model is given below:

FIGURE 2.10

Basic Environmental Model

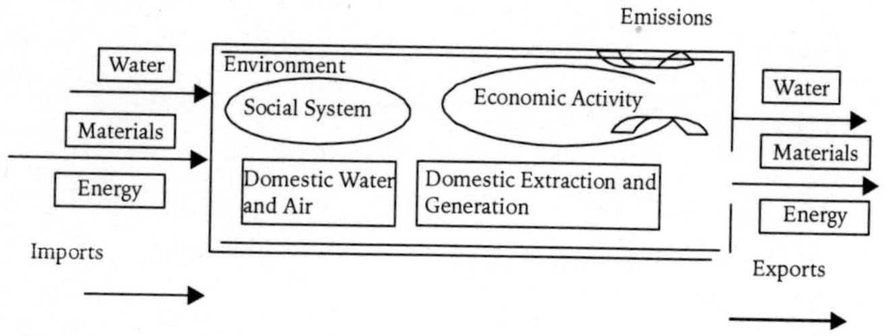

Source: Statistical Handbook of the Government of Goa for the relevant years.

Sustainability

301. An environment's carrying capacity is its maximum persistently supportable load (Catton, 1986).[1]

302. The "inverted-U" theory (environmental "Kuznets Curve") states that as income increases, environmental degradation occurs upto a peak level, then at higher income the degradation decreases. This simply means that higher per capita income need not necessarily mean increased environmental degradation.

Footprint

303. Ecological footprint, with multiple constraints such as food, fuel, water, housing and waste disposal, is used to calculate current demand on resources by each country in hectares of land per person. The total world ecological footprint is 2.7 global hectares per person. With a world-average biocapacity of 2.1 global hectares per person, this leads to an ecological deficit of 0.6 global hectares per person. If a country does not have an ecological deficit, it has an ecological remainder—it is called an ecological creditor country. In contrast, a country with an ecological deficit is called ecological debtor country.

TABLE 2.19

Consumption Characteristics and Ecological Footprints of Various Countries and World Average

Consumption Per Person	*Canada*	*USA*	*India*	*World*	*Goa*
CO_2 emissions (tonnes/year)	15.2	19.5	0.81	4.2	
Purchasing power ($US/year)	19,320	22,130	1,150	3,800	
Vehicles per 100 people	47	57	0.2	10	
Paper consumption (kg/year)	247	317	2	44	
Fossil energy use (gigajoules/year)	250	287	5	56	
Fresh water withdrawals (m3/year)	1,688	1,868	612	644	
Ecological footprint hectares/ person	7.1	9.4	0.9	2.7	1.48

Source: Wackernagel and Rees, 1996.

Impacts on Environment

304. Goa, situated between Arabian Sea and the Western Ghat, is environmentally very fragile. The factors which primarily attribute to the environmental sensitivity of the entire geographical area of the State include high slope, extended coastline and beaches, forests, estuaries and mangroves and finally, marshes and swamps. The erosion rate is severe in coastal and midland *talukas*, primarily on account of deforestation and improper land use practices. In the *taluka*-wise estimate of severe erosion, the percentage of degraded areas to total geographical area is 69.3 per cent for Mormugao, 50.2 per cent for Pernem, 42.6 per cent for Canacona and 40 per cent for Bicholim.

305. The State of Goa has 1224.38 sq.km (33 per cent) of land under forest and a 120 km long coastline. Environment degradation is always a major concern. The economic activity and the society revolve around mining, tourism, fishing and pharmaceutical industry. The impacts of these economic activities on environment are inevitable. The economic survey of Goa indicates that Goa has highest per capita income in India. It has also highest per capita energy consumption and water consumption in India. These can be termed as positive or negative in the way one looks at it. Therefore, the management to minimise these impacts and steps taken to optimally utilise the resources are of prime importance. The State and the society has been successful in this regard.

Land Use

306. Goa has an area of 361113 ha and the land use pattern in the State is as below:

TABLE 2.20

Land Use Pattern in Goa

Forest	*Not Available for Cultivation*	*Cultivable Waste Fallow Land*	*Pasture and Tree Crops*	*Gross Cropped Area*
34.75%	10.28%	15.21%	0.52%	46.86%

Source: Statistical Handbook of the Government of Goa for the relevant years.

307. The category I, II, and III CRZ (Coastal Regulation Zone) restrictions are enforced in Goa. There are 2500 cases of CRZ violations pending in various courts of law. These indicate that the State machinery and the NGOs are active watchdogs and are not allowing any violation to go unnoticed. The society is well educated not to allow such violations.

308. Two sponge iron plants have been set up in orchard region. Goa has laterite rocky strata. In the

1. Catton, W. (1986). "Carrying capacity and the limits to freedom", Paper prepared for *Social Ecology Session 1: XI World Congress of Sociology*. 18 August. New Delhi, India.

plateau on the top of hills, there is exposed laterite rock that is quarried and used for construction. There is no vegetation on them even though they are situated in orchard regions. High and medium slope areas in the State lack adequate vegetation cover. A classic example is the village of Kerim in Pernem *taluka* which has 3.6 sq.km of barren rocky plateau adjacent to orchard and within 500 m along the coast. Such a place is suitable for only an industrial activity, though situated among orchard and seashore. The State has set up a High Powered Coordination Committee, which approves the location of industries in a transparent manner. SPCB also approves after public hearing the location of industry.

309. Agriculture land is found being not cultivated in coastal areas. The coastal area agricultural activity is limited to coconut farming and paddy growing during monsoon. Traditionally agriculture activity is not a fulltime year around activity, because paddy needs sweet water that is available only during monsoon months. Therefore tourism, which is greatly higher during non-monsoon, blends well with agriculture activity.

310. A major concern is that due to recent trend in increase in price of land, the land will be abandoned for speculation from agriculture. The conversion land use from agriculture to non-agriculture process is transparent through public notification, which restricts unrestrained conversion of land use.

Impact of Large Influx of Tourists

311. Till the year 2000, the months of November, December and January were only considered as tourism months. The occupancy rate in the months of June to September used to be less than 21 per cent. After 2000, there has been steady increase in arrival of tourists during the monsoon months also. Some hotels report occupancy rate as high as 82 per cent during the monsoon. Such steady flow of tourists has ensured that the infrastructure is not under utilised during the monsoon.

FIGURE 2.11

The General Trend is Indicated

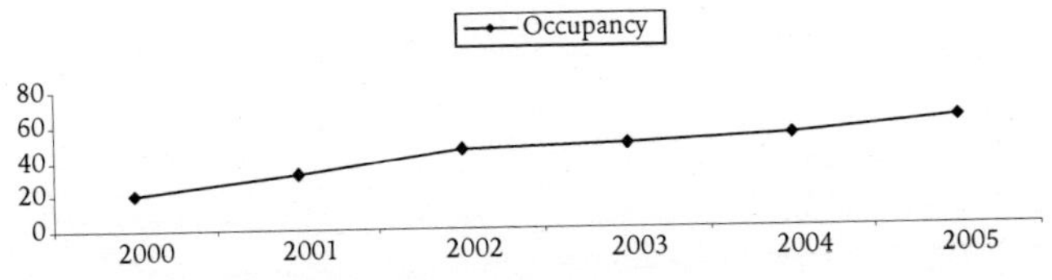

Source: Statistical Handbook of the Government of Goa for the relevant years.

312. The Calangute belt has a population density of 1,017 as against sustainable density of 3,000, reported by Goa vision 2020. The population density is still within sustainable limits.

313. There is increase in the demography of tourists who arrive in Goa especially from Scandinavian countries and England. Unlike the early seventies when tourists were back packers of age less than 30, the tourists who arrive in the age bracket of more than 60 are high. These tourists of age 60 and above, have purchased homes, rent back facilities and live in Goa from November to March to avoid winter in their country. There is an absence of authentic data on the impact of such population migration on social and environment.

314. Shifting of work from agriculture to service sector is an economically forward looking positive activity. This, in turn, helps modernisation of agriculture since the earning from service, flows back into agriculture sector. This is evident from reduced agriculture lending in the State.

Pollution Monitoring

315. SPCB monitors the air quality of major cities at locations where vehicle density is high. Online monitoring electronic display boards have been installed in Panaji at the bus-stand so that awareness is created in addition to monitoring.

Sewage System

316. Except in major cities, the septic tank system is prevalent in whole of Goa. Sulab international has carried out excellent work and covered entire Goa with toilet facilities. Goa being porous laterite strata, the increase in pollution level in groundwater is natural in Baga-Nerul watershed area as reported. Since treated drinking water is available in all villages, this has not turned into a major health problem. But long term collection of waste, disposal of sewage etc., through a self-supporting BOOT system is vital.

Impact of Mining Industries

317. Mining industry in Goa is to be considered as a traditional industry. It started as SME (Small and Medium Enterprises), was mechanised more than 60 years ago, before Goa was liberated from Portuguese rule and brought in valuable foreign exchange during the last six decades. The following measures have been taken by the mining industry:

- Mineral Ore Exporters Association, Government and the local bodies have formed a co-ordination committee to look into and solve any problem relating to mining.

- Trucks are covered with tarpaulin so that materials do not spill during the transit.
- In critical areas, roads have been improved and bridges have been built.

318. As regards the problem of ore from Karnataka being exported through Murmogao Port, the following impacts can be observed:

- Creation of mining dumps en-route.
- Over-loading of transport system—roads, railway and water ways, and
- Loading of Murmogao Port facilities.

319. Historically, Karnataka's iron ore was moved through Goa in the early nineties but due to slump in markets the same was stopped in the mid-eighties. Some mines in adjoining area of Goa in Anmod were also closed. The phenomenon of export from Karnataka has occurred from 2002 in a large scale, due to increase in demand from China for iron ore. Iron ore mines in Anmod region have been re-opened. Whether this demand will last for next 20 years or will it come to a standstill as it happened in the mid-eighties—remains to be seen. Reports from Hong Kong Trade development council suggest as below:

> China's steel output in 2004, at 272.79 million tons, rose 22.7 percent over the previous year. Judging from the newly added capacity, China can produce an additional 43 million tons or more. Iron and steel enterprises are now facing price pressures from products of upper stream enterprises. Some iron ore providers want to raise prices for their products, a demand the iron and steel enterprises say they are unable to meet. Hard negotiations have been going on over international iron ore prices. The talks, involving Japan, Europe, China and other countries, have so far yielded no results. The relationship between demand and supply is expected to ease markedly this year as compared with the previous year. On the international front, no major iron smelting equipment will be put into use except in China, so the demand for iron ore will only surge moderately. Furthermore, around 20 million tons of iron ore remain stranded at warehouses at ports or enterprises due to the lack of transport resources.

320. The stress on environment in Goa due to iron ore from Karnataka is likely to remain and the solution lies in strengthening the railway from Londa to Goa by doubling the track so that ore can move through rails than through road.

Forest

321. The state of Goa has under forest and tree cover over 56.6 per cent of the geographic area including 33 per cent under Government Forest. The protected area under Wildlife Sanctuaries Act is 62 per cent of forest area. In addition to The Indian Forest Act 1927, The Forest Conservation Act 1980, the Preservation of Tree Act 1984, is enforced strictly. It is evident from the Revised Regional Plan-2011, in the *taluka*-wise estimate of forest degradation, that the degradation is limited to three *talukas* only. The percentage of degraded areas to total geographical area is 22.6 per cent for Canacona, 14 per cent for Ponda and 13.7 per cent for Quepem. The Bicholim *taluka* has only 4.20 per cent of degraded areas to its total geographical area as far as the forest degradation is concerned. For Tiswadi and Mormugao *talukas*, this percentage is zero. This is inspite of mining being very active in Bicholim and Sanquem *talukas*.

322. The major reason for non-invasion of forest by the increase in population, is the easy access to high yielding, value added economic activity coupled with high level of general awareness about environmental issues.

Mangroves

323. Mangroves are situated along the Zuari river, the Mandovi, Mapusa and Cumbarjua canals. The high quality of life and easy availability of cooking gas, prevented felling of mangroves, for fuel woods. MoEF and SPCB strictly monitor the mangroves and also ensure additional trees are planted. Bund breakage cause damage to mangroves and hence bund maintenance is also given priority.

Khajan Lands

324. The *khajan* lands, which account for about 17,200 hectares of area are protected by embankments, which are prone to frequent breaches resulting in intrusion of saline water into fertile alluvium lands, mostly used for agriculture in the Salcete, Bardez, Tiswadi, Ponda, Bicholim and Pernem *talukas*. Hence, bunds and sluice gates need to be strengthened to protect the fertile *khajan* lands in the coastal plains.

Marshes and Swamps

325. Marshes and swamps in Goa are existing in two *talukas*, *viz.*, Pernem and Salcete. These are freshwater areas, next to the river courses of the Chapora, Terekhol and Zuari. The major threats these areas are exposed to are pollution and destruction of biodiversity due to high pressure of development along the waterfront.

Promotion of Electronic Industries

326. Goa has supported only environmentally friendly

industries. The culture is also found to be suitable for service industries and pharma industries. Both mining and tourism industries provide employment opportunities to all sections of society. The opportunities are for unskilled, skilled, well educated, experts, entrepreneur etc., unlike other industries. No other industry can provide such opportunity. Further in globalisation, electronic industries have to be of global size. Development of SEZ will help in further promotion of clean industries.

Urban Environment

327. All the major municipalities in Goa have banned the use of plastic carry bags. Panaji has introduced separation of biodegradable and non-biodegradable waste. The Forest Department has taken the onus of developing and maintaining the parks. In collaboration with corporate sector, urban areas are maintained fairly well.

328. The environmental issues of domestic waste, sewage, solid waste management are yet to be fully addressed.

Capacity Building and Institutional Framework Requirement

329. Capacity building and institutional framework are needed in the following areas:

- Formation of Private Forest Board for promoting, developing and managing trees outside forest.
- Formation of sewage Board for collection, disposal and treatment of sewage, solid waste etc.

Institutions and Governance

Governing Structure

330. Presently departments and institutions concerned with natural resources are as below:

- Water Resources Department (WRD) carries out all functions related meeting irrigation needs.
- Public Works Department (PWD) carries out functions of distribution of drinking water supply.
- Power Advisory Committee and CADA provides stakeholders inputs on all policy and tariff issues.

Public-Private Participation

331. As stated by D. Narasimha Rao, visiting faculty IIM, Bangalore:

> When Government out sources management of water distribution to the private sector, it shifts its role from the management of water supply to management of contract for water supply. And it is usually as competent or not at both. Private sector will deliver only if effectively regulated, enforceable consumer safe guards, monitoring mechanisms, performance incentives service standards, clear channels of accountability through engagement of consumer. Poor have a voice in policymaking and implementation service will improve.

Community Participation in Water and Renewable Resources

332. People's participation is reducing in maintaining water bodies, and Government is unable to provide funds for maintenance of these structures. Immediate action is required to repair, renovate and restore the traditional water bodies to mitigate water crisis. People's participation and awareness can bring the past glory back. In addition to restoring traditional water bodies, development of rain water harvesting percolation tanks, identifying peak power hydro power stations etc., need full participation of community in the development. Comunidade and GEDA, WRD, PWD and GED can work together.

333. Participatory approaches aim to achieve the following:

- Local support for programme including the involvement of local leadership.
- Voluntary generation of ideas and interventions by community members. Ownership of programmes by community members.
- Community organisational structures from the management of interventions.
- Removal of obstacles to collaboration—attitudes, beliefs and behaviours, training of local animators.

334. Participatory approach has to involve Comunidade from the concept stage itself.

At the planning process itself: Basic parameters can be explained to the community representatives, so that they understand the options available and their advantages and disadvantages.

At the implementation stage: The community can take charge of the material transportation to the site, and to the extent possible be involved in actual execution of the project. This will ensure a shared sense of ownership of the project in the community members.

Operation and maintenance: Routine operation and maintenance must be taken over by the communities themselves.

Sharing of harvested water: This is crucial, since this is an area which has the potential for serious conflict.

TABLE 2.21

Strength, Weakness, Opportunity and Threat

	Strength	*Weakness*	*Opportunity*	*Threat*
Water	Equitable distribution	Absence of people participation in development	Potential creation	Migration of population into Goa
	Quality of water		Groundwater use	
	High availability		Direct conveying for industrial use	Madai river diversion by Karnataka
			Possibility of water export	

Source: Statistical Handbook of the Government of Goa for the relevant years.

Following the agreed norms for abstraction and discipline by each and every member of the community is absolutely essential, and this is possible only if the community is involved.

Evaluation and modification of design: Once the benefits are realised, the community should develop the capability to reflect critically and improve upon the design.

335. In case of hydroelectric and/or pumped storage schemes, private investments are needed. Comunidade too has to be involved in the organisation and management.

Outlook: Possible Scenarios in the Short, Medium and Long Term

Business-as-Usual

336. Drinking water will continue to be restricted. There will not be any addition in capacity creation for irrigation. The hydroelectric potential will remain only on paper.

Utopia

337. Rainwater harvesting, percolation tanks, biomass and bio-diesel units will be set up with comunidade and private participation. Water will be gainfully exported.

Dystopia

338. Drinking water will be available only once a week. Forest cover will be destroyed to cut wood for fuel. Rainfall will decrease. Use of inefficient technology will continue. Power and water quality will be a major problem. Barren landscape will increase. Renewable energy will be wasted away.

Recommendations and Development Strategies

339. Drinking water will be made available 24 hours a day and user participation mechanisms shall be institutionalised to curtail non-revenue water.

340. GEDA and Comunidade will be joined to promote hydroelectric schemes along with private participation.

341. Renewal of traditional tanks, rainwater harvesting along with biofuels will be accorded priority.

342. Forest cover should be ensured to all Comunidade lands on plateau region to avoid further misuse of such lands.

343. Need to introduce cooperative farming by using the methods of the Comunidade system to conserve arable land. At present, tenants who have acquired comunidade land under the Tenancy Act, appear to have failed to maintain the agricultural infrastructure required for such lands.

Chapter 3

Agro Economy

1. The contribution of agriculture to the net state domestic product (NSDP) of Goa has been steadily declining over time. In 1993-94, agriculture contributed to 11.27 per cent of the NSDP; in 2002-03, its contribution was only 8.18 per cent of the NSDP. Again, agriculture was the source of employment for 60 per cent of the state's workforce at the time of the state's formation in 1987. Today, it offers employment to about 16 per cent of the workforce. In the last two census surveys it appears that there has been a negative growth in the number of cultivators.[1]

Agriculture Trends and Indicators in Goa

2. About 54 per cent of total geographical area of Goa is available for cultivation purposes. More than 80 per cent of the total cropped area is used for the cultivation of rice, coconut and cashew crops.[2] About 18 per cent of the land is used for growing fruits, cereals and vegetables. A very small but growing proportion of the land is being used for the cultivation of arecanut, pepper and oil palm. This trend has persisted over time with marginal changes.

3. The area being used for agriculture is declining. This is evident in the increased per cent of net cultivated area that is currently fallow.

4. It is also evident that there is a decline in the area of holdings (of different sizes) being cultivated. The decline is especially steep in the case of landholdings larger than 10 hectares. An increasing proportion of land that is cultivated comprises landholdings of less than 2 ha.

TABLE 3.1

Per cent of Total Cropped Area used for Cultivation of Various Crops during the Period 1999-2004

Crop	*1999-2000*	*2000-01*	*2003-04*	*2004-05*
Rice	33	33.4	31.3	30.9
Cereals (others)	7.4	7.3	8.1	8.44
Vegetables	4	4.4	4.6	4.6
Fruits	7.2	6.1	6.06	6.09
Sugarcane	0.77	0.729	0.717	0.715
Cashew	32	31	32.4	32.4
Arecanuts	0.9	0.93	0.95	0.945
Coconut	14.5	14.6	14.9	14.86
Oil palm	0.399	0.416	0.477	0.484
Pepper	0.16	0.28	0.35	0.35

Source: Directorate of Agriculture, Goa.

TABLE 3.2

Fallow Land as a Per cent of Net Cultivated Area

Land	*1995-96*	*2003-04*
Current fallow (ha)	1004	8173
Net cultivated area (ha)	56488	136170
Per cent of net cultivated area that is fallow	1.77	6

Source: Agricultural Census: Report on main Census, Goa. Directorate of Planning, Statistics and Evaluation, Goa. State Focus Paper, 2002-03, NABARD.

1. *Source: Economic Survey, 2004-05*. Government of Goa publication.
2. Most of the rice is grown for personal consumption. However, cashew and coconut are mainly grown for commercial purposes.

TABLE 3.3

Area Cultivated (in hectares), in Each Landholding Size

Landholding Size (ha)	*1980-81 Area*	*1985-86 Area*	*1990-91 Area*	*1995-96 Area*
<1 ha	23998	21864	18591	19623
1-2 ha	15464	14299	10967	10760
2-4 ha	11755	12529	09279	09181
4-10 ha	11481	11699	09165	08188
>10 ha	32489	20291	18527	11270
Total area cultivated	95187	80682	66529	59022
% of total cult. area in landholdings of less than 2 ha	41%	44%	44%	51%

Source: *Agricultural Census: Report on the main Census*, Goa. Directorate of Planning, Statistics and Evaluation, Goa. Later data not available.

5. Production of many crops has largely stagnated at 1990-91 levels. The aggregate food production index and the crop-wise production index illustrate this. The cashew and arecanut crops are the sole exceptions.

TABLE 3.4

Crop Production Index (1991-92=100)[3]

Year	*Rice*	*Ragi*	*Cashew*	*Coconut*	*Arecanut*	*Sugarcane*
1999-2000	102	25.5	141	110.5	128.8	77.8
2000-01	103.6	11.9	174	113.7	171.2	82.7
2001-02	103.6	7.5	187.6	113.7	171.2	80.2
2002-03	103.57	7.18	187.6	113.7	171.2	70.4
2003-04	124.4	9.4	189.7	110.9	181.5	65.5
2004-05	105.8	8.04	208.6	112.3	170.9	68.8

Source: Directorate of Agriculture; Accessed "Goa: Economy in Figures". Directorate of Planning Statistics and Evaluation, Government of Goa publication, for production figures of 1991-92.

TABLE 3.5

Food Production Index (1991-92=100)

Year	*Food Grain Production (tonnes)*	*FPI (1991-92=100)*
1991-92	147133	100
1999-2000	150801	102.5
2000-01	153074	104.04
2001-02	153074	104.04
2002-03	149941	101.9
2003-04	181002	123
2004-05	155703	105.8

Source: "Goa: Economy in Figures". Directorate of Planning Statistics and Evaluation, Government of Goa publication.

6. Since 1999, there has been a significant rise in the productivity of fruits (54%), cashew (43%), arecanut (28%) and *kharif* rice (22%). Productivity of coconut and vegetables has increased marginally by 7 per cent and 6 per cent respectively. The productivity of other crops has either declined or stagnated.

Institutions and Governance

7. The State and Centre independently and in collaboration, facilitate the agricultural activities of the State.

(a) Farmers receive information from the Directorate of Agriculture about the various government schemes (eg., subsidies available on agricultural inputs). They also receive information about newer varieties of crops available and better farming practices needed for enhancing productivity. In case of animal husbandry, information is available from the Department of Animal Husbandry.

TABLE 3.6

Average Yield of Some Food and Non-food Crops Over Time

Year	*Rice kharif Kg/ha*	*Rice rabi Kg/ha*	*Ragi Kg/ha*	*Cashew Kg/ha*	*Coconuts/ha*	*Arecanut Kg/ha*	*Sugarcane Kg/ha*	*Veg.*	*Fruits*
1990-91	2413	2716	1029	534.5	11984	943	60958		
1995-96	2746	2727	972	732	15822	1005.9	37444		
1999-2000	2323	2610	1104	324	4868	1213	51266	9272	24905
2001-02	2358	2724	887	425	4368	1213	58560	9272	26541
2002-03	2633	2584	891	425	4868	1213	55109	9272	38820
2003-04	3270	3154	897	425	4867	1656	47609	9034	36292
2004-05	2852	2597	855	466	4909	1559	50069	9854	38532

Source: 1990-1995 figures have been procured from "Goa: Economy in Figures". Directorate of Planning and Statistics, Government of Goa publication. Productivity of non-food crops for 1990-91 and 1995-96 was calculated using data on land area under cultivation of different crops from the Agricultural Census of those years.

3. Data on vegetable production for 1991-92 were not available. Therefore, vegetable crop production index could not be calculated.

(b) Farmers can also avail of seedlings from the Directorate of Agriculture. (The seedlings alone are procured from government agencies across the country and provided to the farmers.)

(c) Credit is available to the farmers through the cooperative and commercial banks that are refinanced by the NABARD.

(d) Water/irrigation and power are the responsibility of the respective state departments.

(e) Training and information is available from the State Agriculture Department, the Department of Animal Husbandry and the ICAR, Goa, a Central government organisation devoted to doing research on agriculture and allied activities.

(f) Marketing support is provided by Central government institutions like the APMC, the horticultural division of the state government and some agricultural cooperatives.

8. The APMC provides sellers with: (a) information on the price they can realise, (b) facilities such as market yards, godowns, betelnut treatment facility and grading facility at the yard.

9. The agricultural cooperatives like the Goa Bagayatdar Sahakari Kharedi Vikri Saunstha Maryadit and Adarsh Cooperative Society provide farmers with: (a) a ready market, (b) price information on a daily basis for some agricultural produce, and (c) access to agricultural inputs.

10. In case the price of some goods is unremunerative, the Directorate of Agriculture pays the differential between the sale price and its estimate of the minimum support price needed by the farmers to cover their costs. Besides these agencies, the indirect support of other state/Central organisations such as the Forest Department, Land Records Department, etc., is critical.

Analysing the Decline in Land Devoted to Agriculture

11. In this section three factors that could explain the decline in land utilisation for agriculture are discussed. These are: (a) returns from agriculture, (b) the financial sustainability of processing units, and (c) emerging alternatives to agriculture as an occupation.

12. Returns from agriculture: An examination of the major cost elements incurred by the farmer and the prices realised on the crop produce indicates that the farmers are experiencing declining returns from farming.

13. Fertiliser prices and pesticide prices have risen by an average of about 8 per cent and 108 per cent respectively between 1998 and 2005. Labour costs have also risen by about 18 per cent in the period between 1998 and 2002. (More recent data on ages were not available.) The following tables give the details.

TABLE 3.7

A Comparison of the Average Daily Wages Earned (in Rupees) by Agricultural Workers, 1998-2002

Type of Labour	*1998-99*	*2001-02*
Agriculture plantation	108.54	128
Agriculture field crops	105.6	124.9

Source: Rural Wages. Directorate of Planning, Statistics and Evaluation, Govt. of Goa.

14. Not documented is the increasing difficulty in obtaining skilled labour for agricultural operations. This could be indirectly inferred from the fact that agricultural wages have been increasing more rapidly in Goa than the wages for other skilled occupations over the last decade.

TABLE 3.8

Prices of Pesticides (Rupees/kg) Sold at Goa Bagayatdar Co-op Society for the Period 1999-2005

Pesticide/Type	*1998-99*	*1999-2000*	*2000-01*	*2001-02*	*2002-03*	*2003-04*	*2004-05*	*2005-06*	*2006*
Copper sulphate	45	48	46	46	43	41	52	54	125
Grammozone	235	240	260	290	276	268	278	280	274
Fytolon	148	162	168	170	184	173	175	190	390
Organic manure (neem cake)	3.6	5.1	4.5	4.8	4.0	5.0	6.0	6.3	6.3

Source: Goa Bagayatdar Sahakari Kharedi Vikri Saunstha Maryadit.

TABLE 3.9

Prices of Different Fertilisers (Rupees per kg) at Goa Bagayatdar Cooperative Society for the Period 1999-2005

Fertiliser Type	*1998-99*	*1999-2000*	*2000-01*	*2001-02*	*2002-03*	*2003-04*	*2004-05*	*2005-06*	*2006*
Sampurna	7.5	7.5	8.0	8.15	8.15	8.65	8.65	8.65	8.65
Urea	3.75	4.1	4.7	4.8	5.0	5.0	5.0	4.8	5.0
10-26-26	7.5	7.5	7.5	8.2	8.7	8.7	8.65	8.3	8.6
18-46-0	8.5	8.5	9.1	9.25	9.75	9.75	9.75	9.35	9.75
MOP	3.75	3.75	4.35	4.4	4.65	4.65	4.65	4.45	4.65
Steranil	5.7	5.9	5.8	5.7	6.2	6.5	6.2	6.7	7.2
20-20-0	6.65	6.65	7.0	7.15	7.6	banned			
Single super phosphate	3.4	3.4	3.2	3.5	3.6	4.0	3.8	4.0	4.0
Uniphose	2.8	2.8	3.0	3.2	3.4	3.8	3.8	3.95	4.6
Bio-Phos	42	42	42	42	42	42	46	49	49

Source: Goa Bagayatdar Sahakari Kharedi Vikri Saunstha Maryadit.

TABLE 3.10

A Comparison of the Average Daily Wages Earned (in Rupees) by Agricultural Workers, Non-agricultural Skilled Labour and Non-agricultural Casual Labour, 1995-2002

Type of Labour	*1995-96*	*1998-99*	*2001-02*
Agriculture plantation	75.9	108.54	128
Agriculture field crops	72	105.6	124.9
Non-agriculture, skilled	90.57	116.4	128.7

Source: *Rural Wages*. Directorate of Planning, Statistics and Evaluation, Govt. of Goa.

15. Water does not seem to be available in required quantities. The rainfall has been declining over time in Goa. In 1998, Goa received 3079 mm of rainfall; in 2003 it received 2682 mm of rainfall. Moreover, the rainfall in the intervening years has been steadily declining.[4] Irrigation is thus becoming increasingly essential for watering of crops. However, only 25 per cent of the total cropped area gets irrigation. Even in areas getting irrigated, there are increasing complaints about: (a) inadequate water discharge, (b) breakdown of the irrigation channels, and (c) mechanical breakdowns which either cut off water to the fields or provide inadequate water.

16. Access to crop and term loans can help farmers tide over rising input prices and make needed investments. Agricultural credit has increased from about 6 per cent of the total credit disbursed by banks in 2001 to about 8 per cent of the total credit disbursed in 2004.[5] Commercial banks are the largest lenders of agricultural credit. They lend about 80 per cent of the value of crop and term loans to farmers.[6] However, NABARD officials indicate that these loans are largely finding their way to farmers with clear title to their land.

TABLE 3.11

Number of Complaints Regarding the Use of Minor Irrigation Schemes Over the Period, 1993-2000

Type of Constraints	*Irrigation Census 1993 (Nos.)*	*Irrigation Census 2000-01 (draft)*
Inadequate power	227	217
Mechanical breakdown	30	130
Less water discharge	402	636
No filling of storage	219	150
Siltation	198	53
Breakdown of channel	51	103
Miscellaneous	6755	2021

Source: *Minor Irrigation Census*. Directorate of Planning, Statistics and Evaluation, Govt. of Goa.

17. In sum, prices of agricultural inputs like fertilisers, labour and pesticides have increased by 18-108 per cent in the period 1998-2004. The three inputs account for a significant proportion of the cost of production of many crops. The cost of production of many of the crops was not available. Data on the cost of production of rice and arecanut was available. In the case of rice for instance, the three inputs constitute about 73 per cent of the costs.[7] In case of arecanut, they account for about 60 per cent of the

4. *Economic Survey 2001-02*.
5. *Source*: State Focus Paper, *Goa: Potential linked state credit plan 2005-06, 2006-07*. NABARD, Goa Regional Office, Panaji.
6. Ibid.
7. *Source*: Directorate of Agriculture, Government of Goa.

cost of production.[8] However, some crops like cashew and coconut may incur lesser costs on these three inputs as the seedlings are not planted every year, pesticide and fertiliser requirements are not used much and labour requirement is not as intensive as in the case of rice.[9]

18. The prices realised by the farmers for various crops in the Goa Bagayatdar Kharedi Vikri Saunstha, a large cooperative, are detailed below.

TABLE 3.12

Prices (Rupees/Kg) Realised by Farmers on Sale of their Produce to the Goa Bagayatdar Kharedi Vikri Saunstha, 1999-2005

Crops	*1999-2000*	*2000-01*	*2001-02*	*2002-03*	*2003-04*	*2004-05*
Arecanut	126.02	69.75	42.68	41.25	50.67	50.46
Cashew	47.83	44.2	32.95	34.91	37.21	37.28
Coconut (price per nut)	4.76	2.2	2.79	3.8	5.28	5.55
Black pepper	202	130	68	84.12	75.05	67.53

Source: Goa Bagayatdar Sahakari Kharedi Vikri Saunstha Maryadit.

19. Over the five-year period from 1999-2004, the price of arecanut has decreased by 60 per cent; the price of cashew has decreased by 33 per cent; the price of pepper has reduced by 67 per cent. The price of coconut had declined for three years before recovering and even improving over earlier levels. Prices of vegetables were not available for comparison. In the case of arecanut, there is clear evidence that the price realised by the farmers in the period 2001-2005 was less than the cost of production as calculated by the Directorate of Agriculture.[10]

20. Banks do not offer any insurance against price declines. In 2001, the state government stepped in with the scheme of Minimum Support Price for arecanut, coconut, oil palm and sugarcane. However, farmers do avail of the minimum support price mainly in the case of arecanut and sugarcane. The support price is revised every 4-5 years, based on an estimate of the cost of cultivation. Unfortunately the prices of inputs do not remain stable in the interim period. This could lead to a situation where the minimum support price does not truly reflect the input costs of the farmers. The farmer thus may not get adequate relief.

TABLE 3.13

Number of Beneficiaries of Minimum Support Price and Amount Disbursed (in Rupees) for the Years 2001-02 and 2002-03

Minimum Support Price Scheme	*Year 2001-02*	*Year 2002-03*
No. of beneficiaries		
Arecanut	1315	1781
Coconut	102	1
Oil palm	178	-
Sugarcane	1486	1538
Amount disbursed (Rs)		
Arecanut	3090935	4749855
Coconut	284891	8415
Oil palm	235450	-
Sugarcane	13225679	6543732

Source: Directorate of Agriculture, Panaji, Goa.

21. The viability of local agro-processing units: The presence and effective functioning of processing units in Goa could help stabilise prices of some agricultural commodities that serve as their inputs. Senior functionaries of one processing unit for each of two crops, namely sugarcane (a failed crop) and cashew (a successful crop) were interviewed to get an understanding of the industry and the unit.

22. There is only one sugarcane processing cooperative in Goa and farmers have to sell their sugarcane produce to the unit. The supply of sugarcane from local farmers is less than what is required, prompting the cooperative to seek additional sugarcane from neighbouring states. The cooperative gives the sugarcane farmer the statutory minimum price fixed by the Central government. (Sugarcane farmers also approach the state government for assistance under the minimum support price.)

23. The unit is able to meet the obligations to the farmer only after receiving continued financial support from the state government. Central government restrictions on the amount of sugar that can be sold, where it can be sold, and (in case of 45 per cent of the sugar sold) the prices at which the sugar can be sold have resulted in rising finished goods inventory and increasing debts in the cooperative. The cooperative had an accumulated loss of about Rs. 22.8 crore in 2003-04.

8. *Source*: Directorate of Agriculture, Government of Goa.

9. *Source*: ICAR scientist.

10. The cost of production of arecanut was Rs. 71.97 in 2001 and about Rs. 74 per kg in 2004. The cost of production in the interim period ranged between these two amounts.

TABLE 3.14

Number of Farmers availing Support Price for Sugarcane, the Price given by the Directorate of Agriculture to the Growers

Year	*No. of Beneficiaries*	*Quantity (MT)*	*Amount Paid (Rs)*	*Support Price/ MT (Rs) to Growers*
2001-02	1486	64515.51	13225679	100
2002-03	1536	65436.64	6543732	100
2003-04	1483	60583.79	6058444	100
2004-05	1446	55202.75	5520320	100
2004-05	1344	58253.9	5825451	100

Source: Directorate of Agriculture, Panaji.

24. The story is different in case of cashew processing. Cashew farmers can sell their produce to a variety of buyers including cooperatives, private/registered traders and agents of the privately owned cashew processing units. About 50 per cent of the total cashew produced in Goa is sold within Goa.[11] The local cashew sold in Goa meets about 80 per cent of the cashew kernels required by processing units. There are about 75 cashew processing units, of which about 25 are large/medium scale units, competing for the cashew crop. Competition for the local cashew is largely from the large and medium scale units.

25. Larger cashew processing units engage agents to ensure a regular supply of cashew kernels for their units. The agents: (a) pay the contract price on behalf of farmers, to the institutions/landholders who give the land on contract to the farmer, (b) provide free cashew seedlings[12] (high-yielding varieties) on behalf of the processing units which buy their produce, (c) take possession of the cashew kernels and arrange for the transportation to the processing unit (on behalf of the processing unit which engages them), and (d) pay the farmer for the kernels purchased. The farmer weeds the land, plucks and crushes the cashew fruit and extracts the cashew kernel.[13] Small farmers apparently engage their own families as labour; larger farmers engage outside labour. The cashew crop is reaped once a year. For the rest of the year, women from the farmers' families work in the processing units.

26. Larger cashew processing units compete in the local, national and export markets. Government intervention is minimal. They achieve price stability in exports through forward sales, wherein the seller undertakes to sell cashew throughout a year to an international buyer at a specific price that is negotiated at the beginning of the year. If the returns from export consignments are lower than the market price during the year, the prices of cashew sold in the national markets are adjusted for better returns.

27. In sum, the sugarcane processing unit is a monopoly and its functioning is extensively controlled by the government; the cashew processing units are many and privately owned (therefore, not subject to such extensive government intervention). Government intervention in the functioning of sugarcane processing unit provides stability of prices to the farmer but has adversely affected the cooperative's financial viability. Under these circumstances, the ability of the processing units to pay attractive prices to sugarcane farmers is compromised, unless the state government provides the unit with financial support.

28. Emerging alternatives to agriculture: The following developments of the past decade have opened out new options to the people of Goa. First, there has been an increase in the demand for non-agricultural use of land partly due to increasing population density. Immigration from neighbouring Indian states in response to job opportunities has increased over time. There is also an increasing interest among expatriate Goans and foreigners to invest in property at Goa.

TABLE 3.15

Population Density in Goa Over Time

	1993	*1997-98*	*2000-01*	*2003-04*
Persons/sq km	316	316	363	364

Source: "Goa: Economy in Figures", Directorate of Planning Statistics and Evaluation, Government of Goa publication.

28. This has led to increasing land prices. In 1997, house prices in Goa reportedly rose by around 40 per cent in 12 months. The trend has continued,[14] making it attractive for Goan farmers to sell their land. Most of the conversions of agricultural land into non-agricultural land seem to be taking place in the coastal areas of Tiswadi, Bardez, Salcete, Mormugao and Quepem. Reports indicate that in non-industrial belts, much of the land initially used for agriculture is being used for developing residential spaces. In industrial belts, most of the land that is converted is being used for commercial purposes.[15]

11. *Source*: Officer of the Goa Bagayatdar Saunstha.

12. The government also supplies cashew seedlings at subsidised rates to the farmers.

13. Larger farmers get the rate of cashew from the cooperatives/APMC which guides the price they charge the agent.

14. Wall, Barbara (1997). "Far flung adventures in real estate", *International Herald Tribune*. At *http://www.iht.com/articles/1997/01/11/mprop.t.php*

15. Source: *http://www.goacom.org/news/news2000/apr/msg00035.html*

30. Second, rural youth have more career options besides agriculture. Two developments are contributing to this: (a) Increasing literacy among the rural and urban youth have widened horizons and created some capability to obtain opportunities in other areas of the economy. Literacy rates have improved more in the rural areas between 1997 and 2004.

TABLE 3.16

Literacy Rates between 1997-2004

	1997-98	*2003-04*
Urban		
Male	86.33	90.06
Female	73.38	79.65
Rural		
Male	81.71	87.69
Female	62.87	71.6

Source: "Goa: Economy in Figures", Directorate of Planning Statistics and Evaluation, Government of Goa publication.

31. (b) There has been an expansion in the number of units in the manufacturing and tourism sector. Clearly the growth in the tourism sector is much higher than in the manufacturing sector. We presume that the increase in the number of units would imply increased job opportunities for youth with education. As a result, more rural youth are seeking and obtaining jobs in other sectors of the economy.

TABLE 3.17

Increase in Units in the Manufacturing and Tourism Sector across Time

Sector	*1992-93*	*1997-98*	*2003-04*
Hotels/Lodging houses	360	485	2027
Manufacturing (SSI)	5201	5488	6852
Mfng. (medium/large scale units)	52	113	154

Source: "Goa: Economy in Figures", Directorate of Planning Statistics and Evaluation, Government of Goa publication.

32. In sum, declining margins from agriculture (due to rising costs of production and declining prices) have contributed to reduced farming, evident in increasing fallow land. Simultaneously, the rising land prices, greater education and greater employment opportunities in the tourism/manufacturing sector have made the movement away from agriculture easy and attractive.

Analysing Agricultural Productivity of Crops

33. The cashew, arecanut and fruit crops have registered substantial increases in productivity over time. Some other crops like coconut and vegetables have registered marginal increases in productivity. The rest have registered declining/stagnating productivity. This section explores some reasons for the declining/stagnating productivity of crops.

34. Declining land quality (increasing salinity). A study of six villages in Goa found that land salinity has increased over time, making agricultural activities unproductive. The increased salinity appears to be the result of a neglect of soil conservation and productivity-enhancing activities, including maintenance of embankments, de-silting of rivulets, etc. The neglect followed a shift in power from the comunidade system to the *panchayat* and tenant associations.

35. Earlier, Goan villages were administered by comunidades. The comunidades owned the village land and auctioned the cultivation rights to farmers annually. The profits earned this way were used to oversee and undertake a variety of soil conservation and agricultural productivity enhancing activities. In case farmers did not manage the land properly, they ran the risk of not receiving any land on contract the next year. With the introduction of the Tenancy Act of Goa (1964): (a) the management of village affairs was transferred from the Comunidades to two local-level bodies—the *panchayats* (local government) and a tenants' association, (b) comunidades could not auction land; instead, tenant farmers were allowed to claim ownership of land they tilled in return for a fixed price, (c) the responsibility for maintenance of embankments, soil conservation initiatives, etc., was transferred to the tenants and their associations.

36. The new institutions however, did not give adequate attention to the state of embankments and other infrastructure, crucial for enhanced and sustained productivity. Their lack of experience in managing such activities, the lack of strictures against improper management of the land and possibly their lack of awareness of the importance of such productivity enhancing measures could explain the neglect. The result has been increased salinity of land in some areas of Goa and reduced agricultural productivity.[16]

16. *Source*: *http://72.14.235.104/search?q=cache:b5Z2wAHVVzgJ:www.sandeeonline.org/publications/policy_brief/policy_brief_13.pdf+tenancy+act,+goa&hl=en&gl=in&ct =clnk&cd=7*

37. Inadequate inter-agency cooperation for improving agriculture infrastructure. The new tenants depend increasingly on the state to take up the responsibility for maintenance of local infrastructure. Besides the Directorate of Agriculture, cooperation is required from other state and central agencies in providing such infrastructure to the farmers. However, these other agencies report to different administrative heads and have different objectives and priorities. As a result, priorities are not commonly agreed upon by all the agencies. Concerted efforts towards development of agriculture infrastructure are thus, lacking despite the presence of coordination mechanisms. There is no statistical evidence for this. However, this was mentioned by a few officers of the government who were interviewed.

38. Usage of fertilisers and pesticides respectively. It is clear that farmers are reducing their consumption of fertilisers and pesticides, despite evidence of increasing land salinity and use of newer/improved variety of seeds. Crop-wise and region-wise distribution of the use of fertilisers and pesticides would have been more revealing. Increased salinity of land/use of improved varieties of seeds require more and timely application of one or more such inputs for higher productivity.[17] Lacking this, agricultural productivity can decline.

TABLE 3.18

Fertiliser used Per Hectare (Metric tonne/ha) of Total Cropped Area, Over Time

Year	*Total Cropped Area (ha)*	*Total Fertiliser Consumed (metrictons)*	*Fertiliser Used/Total Cropped Area MT/ha*
1999-2000	171455	7279	0.0424
2000-01	171356	5843	0.034
2001-02	161907	5861	0.036
2002-03	171455	4085	0.0238
2003-04	168634	4380	0.026

Source: Directorate of Agriculture, Panaji.

39. One possible reason could be the rising prices of these inputs (Tables 3.8 and 3.9 illustrate this). Another possible reason could be the scarcity of labour. Application of the fertilisers or pesticides requires labour which seems to be in short supply and very expensive (Table 3.10 on labour rates is self-explanatory).

TABLE 3.19

Pesticide Consumption Per Hectare Over Time

Year	*Tot Cropped Area (ha)*	*Pesticide Consumption (metre tonnes)*	*Pestcd. consmp./ha*
2001-02	161907	4.9	0.03 tonnes/ha
2002-03	171455	4.79	0.028
2003-04	168634	4.6	0.027
2004-05	NA	5.2	

Source: Directorate of Agriculture, Goa.

40. The consequence for productivity is illustrated in the case of coconuts. For 2-3 years, the coconut crop across the State was affected by a pest called red palm weevil. Treatment was available but required application of the insecticide to each nut, a highly labour-intensive process. Many farmers preferred allowing the crop to heal naturally to finding and paying for the requisite labour.[18] The quality and yield of coconuts suffered as did the price realised.

Allied Activities: Agro-industry in Goa

41. The agro-industry absorbs the produce of agriculture and allied activities (like crops, poultry and fisheries). We have described earlier, the status of agro-processing units for some agricultural crops. This section explores the poultry, fisheries and the dairy industry in Goa.

42. Poultry industry: The population of poultry per thousand people has declined over the last five years as of 2003. Data on the number of layers and number of eggs laid indicates stagnation in numbers over the period 1999-2002[19] despite increasing density of human population. More than 70 per cent of eggs are being obtained from the neighbouring states.[20] There is no data on the per cent of broilers obtained from neighbouring states.

TABLE 3.20

Number of Livestock/1000 Human Population from 1992-2003

Livestock	*1992 Census*	*1997 Census*	*2003 Census*
Total poultry (numbers)	730317	789504	560906
Total human population (lakhs)	11.7	11.7	13.48
Poultry/1000 population	624	674	416

Source: Livestock Census, Fisheries Department, Government of Goa.

17. *Source*: Agricultural officers in the Directorate of Agriculture.

18. *Sources*: (a) *http://icargoa.res.in/red-palm-weevil.htm;* (b) Interview with ICAR scientist.

19. *Source*: *Integrated Sample Survey for Estimation of Milk, Eggs and Meat Production*. Directorate of Animal Husbandry and Veterinary Services, Panaji.

20. *Source*: A large poultry farmer.

43. The poultry industry in Goa is now dominated by a few private large-scale poultry farmers. Smaller poultry farmers (with about 5-10,000 birds at most) appear to have suffered losses following the bird flu epidemic among poultry. It appears that they are no longer in the business.

44. Margins in the business are small and particularly sensitive to the prices of poultry feed.[21] Attempts at growing the feed in Goa have been unsuccessful, apparently because of unsuitable climate/soil conditions. Importing the feed from neighbouring states would make the price of local poultry unremunerative.

45. A few of the successful large poultry farmers in Goa have responded in the following ways to the nature of this business: First, they have set up their own feed production farms (this does not include maize, which needs to be purchased) in Karnataka. Feed mixing is done within the unit at Goa. Second, they have expanded volumes. Third, they invest in many experiments to reduce the costs of production.[22] Fourth, they have integrated forward into processed foods (this also enables the units to increase the returns from their business) such as cakes/pastries, semi-cooked food items. Lastly, they largely cater to the retail (not institutional) market because sale proceeds are immediately realised and the margins are higher.

46. They get the necessary financial support from banks. They would like more cold storage facilities so that the perishable items like eggs can be stored and sold when prices are more remunerative.

47. Marine industry: Table 3.21 indicates the quantity of fish production over time. Fish production was higher prior to 1999. Subsequently, fish production fell until 2003. However, the rupee value realised has increased over time. The value realised per tonne of fish sold has been steadily increasing, with occasional peaks. For instance, the value realised on sale of marine fish in 2003 has increased by 41 per cent since 1999.

48. Fish production is now done by a few large scale fishermen, who not only have a large fleet of mechanised boats but also have branched into processing of the fish. Traditional fishermen are small players in the market. About 85-90 per cent of the fish obtained in Goa finds its way to the local markets (institutional and retail) and the markets of neighbouring states. Fish is auctioned every morning to the highest bidder.[23] Only about 10-15 per cent of the fish produced in Goa is exported. The number of export units has declined over time.[24] Exporters attribute this decline to: (a) increased price of fish and diesel which increases the cost of inputs,[25] (b) price sensitive customers who would prefer to buy elsewhere than pay more for fish, and (c) irregular supply/non-availability of many desired/ high-value species like shrimps.

TABLE 3.21

Marine Fish Production (in tonnes) and Value of the Production (in Rupees) between 1992-2003

Type of fish	*1992*	*1996*	*1999*	*2000*	*2001*	*2002*	*2003*
Marine fish (Tonnes)	97014	93,760	62,113	67,328	69,386	67,563	83756
Value (Rs.,Lakhs)	3546	10,280	8126	15002	16123	13318	15530
Value (Rs.)/tonne	3655	10964	13082	22281	23236	19711	18541

Source: "Goa: Economy in Figures", Directorate of Planning, Statistics and Evaluation, Panaji, Goa.

TABLE 3.22

Marine Exports (in tonnes) from Goa Over Time

Marine species	*1999*	*2000*	*2001*	*2002*	*2003*
Shrimps	99	33	55	0	0
Fish	7594	10350	6679	15668	9730
Ribbon	1931	6108	865	10292	5323
Mackerel	2034	3453	3166	2804	2042
Reef cod	831	266	2072	1620	1501
Cuttlefish	1159	687	193	2300	265
Squid	537	147	593	20	0
Crabs	0	33	0	38	104

Source: Statistics of marine products and exports. The marine products export development authority, Kochi, Kerala.

49. The export units that survive are vertically integrated. They have presence in all operations right from fishing, trading in local fish markets and exporting fish. Perhaps most important is their control on the fish catch by having their own fleet of mechanised boats. Some survivors are planning to add more value to the fish by processing them further (e.g., making surami paste out of cheaper fish) for the export market. Others are

21. Poultry feed comprises 75-80 per cent of the production cost of a bird.

22. For instance they are exploring: (a) alternative food supplements for their ability to quickly increase weight of the chicks, (b) ways of enhancing poultry weight gain in as little time as possible, (c) reducing the mortality among the chicks.

23. *Source*: Fishing industry insider; owner of fishing boats and fish processing unit in Goa.

24. Interview with an experienced fish-exporter in Goa.

25. Prices of the fish have been increased by about 34 per cent between 2000-2004.

diversifying to meet domestic (local and national) institutional demands for fish.

50. Sustained increase in fish production is constrained by the current practice of overfishing. At least two factors appear to contribute to overfishing in Goa.

51. Greater mechanisation of boats. In 1982, 21 per cent of the boats were mechanised. In 1997, mechanised boats constituted 60 per cent of all boats in use. Again, until 1997, about 30 per cent of the mechanised fishing boats had more than 25 hp. As of 2003, about 85 per cent of the mechanised boats have more than 25 hp.[26] Thus, a larger proportion of boats are not only mechanised but have larger horsepower and capable of going deep into the seas. Mechanisation thus allowed fishermen to venture more frequently and deeper into the sea. Many species such as prawns[27] that were available nearer the coast have become extinct, at least partly due to overfishing. Fishing deeper in the sea and for longer durations is now not an option. It is a necessity to even obtain modest catches.

52. Ineffective implementation of the fishing ban. In the May-August period of every year, the state government imposes a ban on fishing, to ensure bigger catches later. A report by scientists of the National Institute of Oceanography has suggested that if the ban period is respected, the fish production can increase substantially. However, the big boat-owners do not adhere to the ban period in its entirety because: (a) fishermen from other states do not respect the ban, and (b) there are short-run economic gains for anyone fishing before the expiry of the ban period (especially when other fishermen are largely adhering to the ban). Patrolling the sea and ensuring adherence of the ban is not apparently implemented effectively. Neither the boat-owners' unions nor the Fisheries department is willing to take responsibility for enforcing the ban by policing the seas. It appears that there is no penalty enforced on those who violate the ban.[28]

53. Animal husbandry and dairy industry: The population and health of livestock and cattle in Goa is important for ensuring an adequate and wholesome quantity of meat, milk and milk products for the rising human population in the State. Table 3.23 indicates the number of animals in the State over time. It is evident that the absolute number of cattle and buffaloes as well as the proportion of cattle and buffaloes in the total livestock has been declining steadily.

54. During this period, the population of pigs as a proportion of livestock has remained stable. Given the increasing density of human population, this trend indicates a likely shortfall of meat, milk and milk products.

TABLE 3.23

Number of Livestock, Cattle, Buffaloes and Pigs in Goa Over Time

	1998-99	*2001-02*	*2004-05*
Livestock	3,10,340	3,25,715	2,92.053
Cattle	97,598	87,978	75,775
Buffaloes	44,674	40,222	37,409
Pigs	89,852	105,402	91,445

Source: "Goa: Economy in Figures", Directorate of Planning, Statistics and Evaluation, Panaji, Goa.

55. Table 3.24 indicates the number of milch animals in milk. Over the period 1998-2002, crossbred cows (in milk) constituted about 12 per cent of all milch animals (in milk) while *desi* cows and buffaloes, each constituted about 40 per cent of milch animals in milk. The number of crossbred cows in milk has declined marginally while the number of *desi* cows and buffaloes in milk has increased by about 15 per cent and 15.5 per cent respectively.

TABLE 3.24

Number of Animals in Milk (Average across Seasons) in Goa Across Time

Cattle Type	*1998-99*	*1999-2000*	*2000-01*	*2001-02*
Crossbred cows (in milk)	5094	5405	5174	4922
Desi cows (in milk)	16362	19627	18802	18860
Buffaloes (in milk)	16380	18965	18589	18920
Total bovine animals in milk	37836	43997	42565	42702

Source: Integrated Sample Survey for Estimation of Milk, Eggs and Meat Production. Directorate of Animal Husbandry and Veterinary Services, Panaji.

56. Table 3.25 gives the average milk yield/day/animal for each type of milch animal. It is clear that the productivity of crossbred cows is highest and is steadily increasing over the period 1998-2002. The productivity of buffaloes has stagnated and that of *desi* cows has declined from 1998-99 levels.

26. *Source*: *Livestock Census*, Department of Animal Husbandry, Goa

27. A few attempts have been made to grow prawns in farms. Industry experts say that only tiger-prawn farming would be economical. The experience of prawn-farming is that the yield is good for three years after which, the size of the prawns decreases and the time taken to grow into adults, increases. This decreases the returns on the investment.

28. *Source*: Fishing industry insider; owner of fishing boats and fish processing unit in Goa.

TABLE 3.25

Average Milk Yield/Day/Animal in Milk

	1998-99	*1999-2000*	*2000-01*	*2001-02*
Crossbred cows (in kgs)	5.413	5.923	6.213	6.603
Desi cows (in kgs)	1.849	1.359	1.433	1.44
Buffaloes (in kgs)	3.292	3.176	3.369	3.33

Source: Integrated Sample Survey for Estimation of Milk, Eggs and Meat Production. Directorate of Animal Husbandry and Veterinary Services, Panaji.

57. It appears that increases in milk production from the existing stock of cattle would require more attention to the health and nutrition of the *desi* cows and buffaloes. This in turn is a function of the quality of food given to the animal and the availability of prompt and high quality veterinary care for the animals. In the long term, the population of crossbred cows needs to increase.

58. The health and nutrition of cattle is affected by the status of the cattle owners, which is described in Table 3.26. Bovine animals are largely owned by cultivators who have less than an acre of land. About 80 per cent of these owners concentrate on dairying (not agriculture or service/business) as an occupation.[29]

TABLE 3.26

Percentage of Bovine Owners having Different Sizes of Landholdings in Goa Over Time

Landholding(ha)	*1998-99*	*1999-2000*	*2000-01*	*2001-02*
0-0.5 ha	48%	45	50	50
0.5-1 ha	35	31	27	31
1-2 ha	11	17	17	13
2-5 ha	6	5	5	6
>5 ha	-	2	1	-

Source: Integrated Sample Survey for Estimation of Milk, Eggs and Meat Production. Directorate of Animal Husbandry and Veterinary Services, Panaji.

59. Most cattle owners appear to own small herds of animals. Among the 17,750 members of the Goa State Cooperative Milk Producers Union Ltd. (hereinafter referred to as Goa Dairy) for instance, 7565 members supply milk on a regular basis and the rest supply milk only in season. Among the 7565 regular milk suppliers, about 48 per cent supply between 1-10 litres per day and only 1.6 per cent supply more than 51 litres per day.[30] About 40 per cent of the cow owners and 48 per cent of the buffalo owners are illiterate. The level of illiteracy is more among owners of small herds (1-4 animals).[31]

60. Feeding practices: About half of the cows tend to be stall-fed, with little or no grazing. (Crossbred cows are rarely grazed.) Most buffaloes however, tend to be grazed and stall-fed.[32] Buffalo owners tend to allow the buffaloes to graze in the day and keep them tied in the stall only at night.[33] Only a small proportion of the land owned by the cattle owners (ranging from 10-13 per cent) is used for growing green fodder.[34]

61. The farmers feed their milch animals a combination of green fodder, dry fodder and concentrates. The mixture of the feed is done by the farmer and is not standardised. *Desi* cows are apparently seen as religious symbols by the largely Hindu cattle owners. They are not viewed as a business proposition, unlike in the case of buffaloes and crossbred cows. Thus, not much is expected of them and not much is invested in their health/nutrition.[35]

62. Farmers in Goa experience difficulty in getting green and dry fodder of nutritive value. There is not enough green fodder cultivation at Goa. At the state-level, only about 7300 acres of land is used for fodder cultivation.[36] The dry fodder available is largely straw, which is low on nutritive value. Much of the nutrition for the milch animals thus comes from the concentrate alone. Goa Dairy is the largest supplier of concentrate until date. It manufactures cattle-feed concentrate and sells it to farmers at state controlled prices.

63. Animal health care services are being provided largely by the veterinary doctors employed by the Goa Dairy and the Department of Animal Husbandry. Table 3.27 indicates that the number of animals treated for diseases or vaccinated at the government-run dispensaries/hospitals has decreased significantly in the period 1996-2004.[37]

29. Murali, P. (2007). "An economic analysis of production and marketed surplus of milk in Goa State." Ph.D thesis submitted to the National Dairy Research Institute (ICAR), Bangalore.
30. Dr. Dhuri, Manager, Goa Dairy.
31. Murali, P. (2007). "An economic analysis of production and marketed surplus of milk in Goa State." Ph.D thesis submitted to the National Dairy Research Institute (ICAR), Bangalore.
32. Animal Husbandry Department reports.
33. Dr. Dhuri from Goa Dairy.
34. Ibid.
35. Interview with a few owners of small herds of *desi* cows.
36. Goa Dairy reports.
37. The number of animals treated by Goa dairy doctors appears to be increasing, but the numbers are too small to contradict the larger trend in government dispensaries.

TABLE 3.27

Number of Animals (in lakhs) Treated by Government-Run Dispensaries and Hospitals

	1996-97	*1999-2000*	*2000-01*	*2001-02*	*2002-03*	*2003-04*
Animals treated (lakhs)	10.53	2.63	2.42	2.59	1.58	1.18
Animals vaccinated (lakhs)	12.39	6.67	6.73	3.2	2.18	1.44

Source: State of Goa: Indicators of Socio-Economic Development. Directorate of Planning Statistics and Evaluation. Govt. of Goa.

64. In sum, the number of cattle and buffaloes together as a proportion of livestock has been declining despite an increasing human population. This decline could be due to: (a) lack of availability of good green and dry fodder, (b) inadequate health care provided to the animals.

65. Diary industry: The demand for milk in Goa has been steadily increasing. Local supply is not able to cater to this demand. An indication of the shortfall is evident in Table 3.28. Demand for milk has more than doubled during the period 1998-2005 but the local milk production has just increased by about 24 per cent. Again, the per capita milk production is only about 91 gm per person against the recommended 200-300 gm/person.

66. As a result, the production of the sole milk cooperative, Goa State Cooperative Milk Producers Union Ltd (referred to as Goa Dairy), is supplemented by milk from about 30 private sector/cooperative milk suppliers from neighbouring states. The Goa Dairy procures milk from local farmers and also from neighbouring states, to fully utilise its production capacity of 1,00,000 litres/day. Milk from the 18,000 strong members of this cooperative is procured through 174 village milk societies.[38] The percentage of milk procured from other states is declining, though it continues to be in a significant proportion (45 per cent) of milk procured. Table 3.29 gives the details.

67. Despite procuring milk from other states, the Goa Dairy is not able to meet the demand for milk and milk products. To better meet the demand for milk and milk products in the state, Goa Dairy has implemented many schemes. For instance, the Goa Dairy provides: (a) a collection point (village milk society) quite near the production point; (b) subsidy and support money to the farmers to help them tide over the rising cost of animal procurement, medicine and fodder; (b) incentives for increased buffalo milk production and for the best quality milk produced; (c) veterinary services (including artificial insemination) at nominal rates to the farmers, often at their doorstep (a mobile van is available for this purpose); (d) cattle-feed concentrate at state-determined prices. These facilities have ensured that about 80 per cent of the milk available for sale at the farms is sold to the Goa Dairy,[39] even though private parties offer a more attractive

TABLE 3.28

Milk Demand Production (in tonnes) and Per Capita Milk Availability in Goa across Time

	1998-99	*1999-2000*	*2000-01*	*2001-02*	*2002-03*	*2004-05*
Milk demand (lakh litres/day)	0.75-1 Avg 0.87		1-1.25 Avg		1.125 1.25-1.75 Avg 1.5	1.75-2.5 Avg 2.125
Milk demand (tonnes) %	31,000		40000		53000	75000
Milk prodn. (tonnes)	39000	43000	44000	45000	46000	48600
Per capita milk production Gm/person	79 gm	86 gm	91 gm	91 gm	NA	NA

Source: "Goa: Economy in Figures", Directorate of Planning Statistics & Evaluation, Govt. of Goa; %: figures are approximations, based on conversion of lakh litres/day into annual demand in tonnes.

TABLE 3.29

Milk Procurement from Local Village Societies and from Neighbouring States Over Time

	1998-99	*1999-2000*	*2001-02*	*2002-03*	*2003-04*	*2004-05*	*2005-06*
Local milk procured (lakh litres)	98.42	103.39	139.55	146.67	156.44	181.29	184.26
Procurement: neighbouring states (lakh litres)	178.09	191.82	175.46	177.64	178.50	160.82	152.87
Total procurement	276.51	295.21	315.01	324.31	334.94	342.11	337.13

Source: Internal Report of Goa Dairy, 2006.

38. NDDB Annual Report, 2000-01.

39. Murali, P. (2007). "An economic analysis of production and marketed surplus of milk in Goa State." Ph.D thesis submitted to the National Dairy Research Institute (ICAR), Bangalore.

price for the milk. Further increase in milk supply to Goa Diary hinges on increasing the milk production in local farms. (External suppliers are not as reliable in their supply.[40])

68. Greater local milk production is possible if: (a) milk production is economically viable for the farmer and (b) the stock of crossbred cows is increased. Table 3.30 indicates the cost of production and net returns earned on crossbred cows and buffaloes in 2005/06. The cost of production in Goa is apparently higher than in neighbouring states.[41] However, the farmer is a net earner from milk production.

TABLE 3.30

Cost of Production and Returns (Rs./day/animal) from Crossbred Cows and Buffaloes

	Crossbred Cows	*Buffaloes*
Total fixed costs	9.08	7.01
Variable costs:		
Concentrate	30.52	16.57
Green+dry fodder	9.87	6.785
Medicine+vet	1.44	0.92
Family labour	15.8	11.09
Hired labour	4.43	1.15
Miscellaneous	1.21	0.65
Total variable costs	63.27	37.16
Total cost of production	72.33	44.17
Returns from sales	82.68	65.7
Net returns	10.35	21.53

Source: Murali, P. (2007). "An economic analysis of production and marketed surplus of milk in Goa State," Ph.D thesis submitted to the National Dairy Research Institute (ICAR), Bangalore.

69. It must be noted, however, that the gains are after considerable support through subsidies on medicines/ purchase of animals, access to nominally-charged veterinary services and state control over the pricing of cattle-feed concentrate. These subsidies increase the earnings of the farmer but at the cost of profitability of the Goa Dairy. The recent reports of the Goa Dairy indicate that it is selling milk and cattle-feed concentrate at retail prices lower than the costs it incurs.

70. Table 3.31 gives the details of the cost of production per litre of milk produced and the average price realised by farmers on milk supplied to Goa Dairy. Over the period 1995-2007, the cost of production has roughly doubled; however, the prices that local farmers realise at Goa Dairy for cow milk has increased 72 per cent and that for buffalo's milk has increased just 35 per cent in the same period. Despite subsidies, the costs incurred in milk production are increasing at a faster pace than the price realised.

71. There is evidence that efficiency is higher among owners of large (greater than eight cattle) than among small cattle herds.[42] If the farmer has to earn more, efficiency of milk production may need improvement.

72. Milk production can also be increased if the stock of crossbred cows and buffaloes is increased. External procurement of full-grown crossbred cows appears to be risky, with a good chance of diseased or defective crossbreds being put up for sale in neighbouring states. Therefore, it maybe more appropriate to ensure more calving of crossbreds in the state. The population of cross bred cows below a year has registered a 72 per cent increase from 1997 to 2007. In the same period, the number of buffaloes below a year has increased about 10 per cent.[43]

73. In sum, the poultry, marine and dairy industry indicate some similarities. Local players in poultry,

TABLE 3.31

Cost of Production of Milk Produced and the Price Paid to the Farmers (Rs./litre) for Cow and Buffalo Milk Respectively

Cost and Price/Year	*1995*	*1998-99*	*2000-01*	*2003-04*	*2005-06*	*2007-08*
Avg. cost of production (Rs/litre)	4-5	5-6.5	6.5-7	7.5-8	8-8.5	>9
Avg. price for cow milk (Rs/litre) to locals	8.61	9.97	10.88	12.41	14.44	14.88
Avg. price for buffalo milk (Rs/litre) to locals	11.6	11.6	12.88	13.47	14.93	15.73

Source: Internal reports of Goa State Cooperative Milk Producers' Union Ltd.

40. Dr. Dhuri, Manager, Goa Dairy.

41. *Source*: Dr. Dhuri, Manager, Goa Dairy.

42. *Source*: Murali, P. (2007) "An economic analysis of production and marketed surplus of milk in Goa State." Ph.D thesis submitted to the National Dairy Research Institute (ICAR), Bangalore.

43. *Source*: 1997 data from Department of Animal Husbandry's annual reports. 2007 data from Goa Dairy's internal reports.

fisheries and dairy industries are not able to meet the demand because the local supply of necessary inputs such as eggs/birds, some varieties of fish and crossbred cattle is not adequate. The factors contributing to the lack of supply across these industries are different. Research and extension services need to address these concerns.

Research and Extension Services in Goa

74. The ICAR, Goa, was established in 1989, to cater to the research and technology needs of Goa in the fields of horticulture, crop science, animal sciences and fisheries and to extend the benefits of this research/technology to farmers.

75. ICAR, Goa, has 19 scientists (out of a sanctioned 21), 10 of whom are working in the area of crop sciences, 4 in the area of animal husbandry, 2 in the area of soil and water conservation and 2 in the area of fisheries. One scientist has been assigned administrative duties and so is unavailable to do science. Among the scientists, only 10 are PhDs.[44]

76. Scientists in crop sciences are conducting investigative studies on: (a) the viability of different varieties of rice, sugarcane, groundnut, coconut and fodder, (b) the viability of different varieties of cashew, mango, oil-palm and arecanut, (c) how intercropping and better pest management can improve the productivity of crops. Scientists in animal husbandry are exploring ways of improving the productivity of poultry, pigs and rabbits by introducing viable hybrids, experimenting with different living conditions and nutrients/feeds.

77. The institute conducts many programmes (largely of one-day duration) for farmers through the Krishi Vigyan Kendra, the State Agriculture Department or the State Animal Husbandry Department, to disseminate the knowledge they develop. Over the decade 1989-2000, the institute has conducted 923 programmes through the Krishi Vigyan Kendra, for 15,140 trainees. Of these programmes, 57 per cent were on crop sciences and horticulture, 25 per cent were on home science-related issues such as nutritive recipes, child care etc., 10 per cent were on animal sciences, 4 per cent on plant protection and 1 per cent on fisheries. Programmes on agricultural extension were less than 1 per cent of the programmes conducted.[45]

78. Besides these programmes, the ICAR, Goa, also organised exhibitions, 34 *melas*, 19 field days (where lectures are arranged for farmers in community halls and there are demonstrations of techniques) and demonstrations over the decade. The institute had started a lab-to-land programme in which a few farmer families were adopted, given inputs and practical guidance on the field to increase appropriate usage of technologies. However, the programme was discontinued in 1992.[46] The adoption rate of practices suggested in training programmes ranges from 5-60 per cent.[47]

79. It appears that ICAR, Goa is giving more attention to crop sciences than to other agricultural sciences in the development and dissemination of knowledge. Research seems to be primarily focused on fodder/poultry feed and on improving the fertility of buffaloes need a lot of attention but the lack of scientists in these areas could be constraining the amount of research being done in these areas. With regard to impact on farming practices, adoption rates vary considerably across programmes. Most programmes conducted for farmers are one-day programmes. Moreover, the more effective lab-to-land programme has been discontinued. On the positive side, the cashew hybrids developed in ICAR are apparently disseminated by the Department of Agriculture to farmers.[48] However, on the negative side, some larger poultry farmers and cattle owners appear to be unaware of the research developments in ICAR, Goa.

Recommendations for the Future

80. People in Goa are veering away from agriculture for many reasons. First, increasing literacy and education on the one hand and increased employment opportunities in the tourism/manufacturing sector on the other have opened out more options. Second, declining margins from agricultural activities make the continuance of agricultural activity less appealing economically.

81. The few crops that appear to be doing well are cashew, arecanut and fruits. However, even there, government subsidy on seedlings/government support through the minimum support price scheme seems necessary. We recommend the following steps to make agriculture attractive to the existing growers.

44. ICA report, Goa.

45. ICAR report on achievements of the decade 1989-2000.

46. Interview with scientist, ICAR, Goa.

47. ICAR report.

48. *Source*: Dept. of Agriculture officials and a large producer of processed cashews.

82. Focus attention on permanent crops that require less intensive labour inputs and are less perishable. The success of cashew and arecanut are indicative of the need to focus on such produce.

83. Help tenant farmers (with no clear title to the land they cultivate) also access bank loans. Introduce some insurance against price fluctuations. A stronger derivates market for agricultural commodities may help reduce the dependence on government subsidies.

84. Encourage many avenues for sale (such as private traders, processing units, cooperatives, etc.) of the agricultural produce. Minimise governmental intervention in the functioning of processing units. Competition across these avenues must be encouraged.

85. Introduce contract farming or its variant, as in the case of cashew, especially in circumstances where there are many competing buyers of the farmer's produce and the farmers are organised.

86. Strengthen local/village-level institutions. As the comunidades are being replaced by other, newer institutions, it is important to ensure that the management of these institutions are aware of the importance of managing the local agricultural infrastructure and are trained in the skills needed. There must be rewards for farmers adopting soil conservation/long-term productivity enhancing measures.

87. Examine the extent and type of intervention by the State/Centre that is needed to promote higher productivity in the agricultural and allied activities sectors. What structural mechanisms may be more effective in reaching information/knowledge/benefits to the farmer? Are so many state and central agencies needed to promote agricultural activity? How can they be made responsible and accountable for common goals in each state?

88. In case of poultry, the margins recovered are small. Farmers who have survived are large-scale, and have more integrated operations (forward and backward). Given fluctuating prices and a perishable product, they need more infrastructure support such as cold storage units, to store their produce if needed. Applied research on cost-effective poultry management practices need to be done in collaboration with poultry farmers so that the results can benefit practice.

89. In the case of marine fisheries, the key to sustenance seems to be ensuring adequate fish supply and protecting many species of high value fish. This requires careful management of the number of mechanised boats and stringent monitoring and enforcement of the fishing ban.

90. In case of dairy industry, the keys to sustenance are: (a) increasing the population of crossbred cows and buffaloes and reducing dependence on *desi* cows, (b) improving access to good quality green and dry fodder at reasonable rates, and (c) spreading better dairy management practices especially among owners of small herds, so that efficiency can be improved. Training and research efforts need to be synchronised with these concerns.

Chapter 4

Mining

Issues and their Fiscal Implications

1. The mining sector's stakeholders are essentially the government, the industry and the community. The government is essentially focused on revenue, employment and foreign exchange earnings, they are also responsible for safeguarding the environment, the safety and the welfare of the community and the progressive expansion of the industry. The industry is essentially focused on generating adequate returns from their capital investment. The community looks for employment and an improved quality of life.

Scope

2. Goa has a number of mineral deposits like iron ore, manganese ore, bauxite, high magnesia, silica sands, limestone and clay. Iron ore however, available in abundant quantities, estimated by IBM in 2000 at about 745 million tonnes and has a ready market.

TABLE 4.1

Mineral Resources of Goa (As on 1-4-2000)

(in '000 tonnes)

Mineral	*Proved*	*Probable*	*Possible*	*Total*
Bauxite	37872.00	16187.00	10223.00	64282.00
China clay	-	16.00	-	16.00
Iron ore (Hematite)	461013.90	149372.41	119460.79	729847.10
Iron ore (Magnetite)	67358.00	5416.00	115218.00	187992.00
Manganese ore	6253.64	23875.77	17037.04	47166.45
Quartz/Silica sand	20.00	1736.00	18248.00	20004.00

Source: Indian Mineral Year Book-2003.

3. With the conclusion of World War II and the beginning of the reconstruction in Europe and Japan, generated a great demand for steel, hence the world iron ore trade expanded rapidly as iron is a major input for steel production. It roughly takes about 1.6 tonnes of iron ore to produce 1 tonne of steel.

4. It was at this point of time that Goa entered the iron ore world market in the late 1940s with a small consignment of one hundred tonnes to Europe. This interestingly was the first iron ore export from the sub continent in the modern times.

5. Exploitation was initially done by traditional methods of pick and shovel and transportation by bullock cart and river transportation to the port of Mormugao by canoe and country craft. Progressively, machinery was introduced in the mining operation, and trucks and self propelled barges were used for transportation. At the port a mechanical ore handling plant was installed for basic loading at berth and uptopping done in midstream by transshippers. By 2004-05, Goa produced 21.7 mt. and exported 23.4 mt of iron ore valued at Rs. 2,200 crore. Goa's export worked out to over 40 per cent of the country's total export of 793 million tonnes.

Growth

6. The iron ore production has increased about 4 per cent over 2003-04, a slowdown of about 6 per cent over the previous year. The production of other mineral groups like manganese and bauxite are not significant and are presently not exported. The production is indicated as under:

TABLE 4.2

Production of Minerals in Goa: 2000 to 2005

Ore Type	*2000-01*	*2001-02*	*2002-03*	*2003-04*	*2004-05*
Iron ore	N.A.	16,698,000	20,689,000*	22,095,000	23,308,000
Manganese ore groups	95,515	95,141	32,451	49,050	19,786
Bauxite	30,000	—	43,557	—	—

Source: GMOEA.

TABLE 4.3

Iron Ore Export from Goa (in '000 tonnes)

Year	*Tonnes*
1961–62	6345
1971–72	7641
1981–82	9925
1991–92	11650
2001–02	16698
*2002–03	20689
2003–04	22095
2004–05	23308

Note: *includes 1,729,219 tonnes of non-Goan ores blended with Goan ore.
Source: GMOEA.

Expanse

7. At present, out of the State's total surface area of 365,563 ha, about 30,000 ha, i.e., about 8 per cent of the land area is covered by mining leases numbering 274, out of these only 81 are operating covering an area of 5804 ha. Hence, the actual area under mining i.e., the broken up area would be about 2,500 ha, about 2 per cent of the total surface area of Goa.

TABLE 4.4

Land under Mining (in ha/per cent)

Land	*Area*	*Per cent*
Total surface area	365563	100
Mining land	70000	19
Leased out	30000	8
Operating leases	5804	2
Broken up	2500	1

Source: Department of Mines, Government of Goa.

8. The iron ore is transported across the State for loading and eventual export. A fleet of about 3,000 trucks are used by the industry, processed ore is then transported to the river side jetties totaling about 45 on the River Mandovi and Zuari and mechanically loaded onto self-propelled barges (fleet of 232 in 2004) for delivery to the port of Mormugao and the Panjim outer harbour, where ore is loaded vide the Mechanical Ore Handling Plant (MOHP) or transshippers respectively onto vessels for onward dispatch to destination ports in China, Japan, Europe etc.

Environment

9. It is a well-accepted fact that open cast mining has adverse effects on the environment, impacting the quality of land, air, water and forest resources. Mining damages and alters the skyline, degrades the soil in surrounding areas especially during the monsoons when the run off from stockpiles, overburdened dumps find their way into the neighbouring agricultural fields. Every tonne of iron ore mined generates rejects of approximately 2-3 tonnes. These dumps are located inside and outside the lease area creating artificial hills. Mining is done on hilltops, on the sides of hills as well as on ground level depending on where the deposits are located—being a location-based activity. Stacking sites at the river loading points also pose problems of material being washed into the river during the monsoon.

10. Further at ground level, mining progressively goes below the water table. Mining is then continued by pumping out the water. This water finds its way into streams and the surrounding agricultural fields creating damage and siltation problems besides the loss of water in the nearby wells.

11. Explosives and drilling operations cause noise pollution. Vehicular transportation by road creates noise and dust pollution.

12. Action has been taken by the industry to reduce these problems. Retaining walls are built around dumps as per IBM guidelines and dump surfaces are planted with grasses and other suitable planting material. Ripper dozers have been introduced eliminating the use of explosives and drilling.

13. In the case of below the water table operations, the affected parties are supplied with water through pipes by the sector operators. Rainwater from the pits created by mining is released to the surrounding areas during the lean season for agricultural operations.

14. Out of 11 *talukas* of Goa, 5 are affected by mining. There is severe air pollution (SPM/RPM) problem at Sanvordem town and Colem and Usgaon village of Sanguem district. The current level of monitoring and execution by the State Pollution Control Board is inadequate.

15. A large number of trucks (more than 5,000) runs daily from Bellary region of North Karnataka, carrying iron ores. This causes large-scale air pollution (SPM/RPM) on the highway (Karnataka-Goa National Highway No. 17) as well as the villages on the side of the highway, up to Mormugao Port Trust (MPT); these fine iron dust release, during the transportation, exceeds the stipulated norm of the Pollution Control Board.

16. Another matter of concern is the mushrooming of iron ores dumps (intermittent stock yards) haphazardly at

Darbandora region, which includes protected forests and even wildlife sanctuaries. Several times these dumps even choke the upstream *nallas*, streams and tributaries of the Mandovi.

17. Three sponge iron plants have been built in the orchid-rich Colem region of the Western Ghats. Stricter land-use regulation that could have prevented it, is not implemented by the Government.

Local Economy

18. Revenue collected from the sector include royalties, dead rent (on non-operating mines), surface rent (areas opened up), road tax, barge tax, sales tax, octroi, forest cess, port charges and vessel related charges in case of MPT and Panjim Port, etc.

19. Well over Rs. 100 crore accrues to the state authorities. Panjim Port, which provides no facilities as all loading is done midstream at its outer harbour, collected over Rs. 10 crore in the financial year 2004-05.

20. The contribution to the revenues of the Central government is not available but taxes etc., are paid in the form of income tax, corporate tax, central excise duties on spares, service tax on port-related charges, on outsourced jobs at the mines and elsewhere. In the case of Mormugao Port the sector paid about Rs. 240 crore in 2004–05 in charges and about Rs. 20 crore in service tax at 10.2 per cent on port-related charges.

21. Serious consideration ought to be given to reducing taxes etc., to this sector which is 100 per cent export-oriented. A case in point: the export sector was in the past exempted from service tax, however, vide a circular effective 16-08-2002—10 new services were covered one of which "cargo handling service" includes ports.

Employment

22. The mining sector employs a workforce of 35,000 i.e., a dependant population of about 1.5 lakh. Of these, 8,000 work directly at the mines, 25,000 indirectly and the rest comprise workers at the ports. It must be noted that 85 per cent of the cargo handled at the port of Mormugao is iron ore export. Hence, it is imperative for the port to upgrade its efficiency and improve its functioning efficiency.

Institutions and Governance

23. The present structure of governance is complex and cumbersome. The sector is governed by multiple ministries, acts and rules, both Central and State—about 10 Central and 6 State agencies are involved. To list a few:

Central	*State*
Ministry of Mines and Minerals	Department of Mines
Indian Bureau of Mines	
Ministry of Environment & Forests	Conservator of Forests
Ministry of Labour	Directorate of Science Tech. and Environment
Directorate of Mines Safety	State Pollution Control Board
Ministry of Finance Customs	Capt. of Ports Jetties
RBI	Inland Waterways Rules
DGFT	
Ministry of Surface Transport	Panjim Port Authority
Ministry of Commerce & Industries	

24. The Central and State agencies involved are the State Collector for land conversion, the State Directorate of Mines, the Central Ministries of Mines, Indian Bureau of Mines, the Central Directorate of Mines Safety. With regard to pollution, we have the Ministry of Forests & Mines and the State Pollution Control Board in the event of deforestation operations, the Forest Conservation Act comes into play requiring permission from the State Conservator of Forests who must get clearance from the Central government.

25. At the beneficiation stage we have the appropriate licencing authority and the State Pollution Control Board.

26. Transportation is regulated on the roads by the Regional Transport Authority under MV Act (Motor Vehicles Act), the State Pollution Control Board and with regard to using waterways for transport, by the State Captain of Ports. Jetties come under CRZ regulation controlled by the State Directorate of Science, Technology and Environment, the State Captain of Ports and the State Pollution Control Board.

27. At the point of export at the port we have unloading and loading operations under the control of the Port Authorities of the Mormugao Port Trust, the Central Ministry of Surface Transport and the Customs.

28. The State Department of Mines, the State Licensing authority, enforces the Mining Concession Rules and are responsible for carrying out inspections to enforce the fulfilment of Lease Deed Conditions. The Department of Mines is also responsible for the collection of dues in the form of royalties, dead rent and surface rent.

29. The Central ministries' Mines Labour Welfare Commissioner collects a cess and looks after the safety and welfare of workmen.

30. IBM of the Central Ministry of Mines implements the Mineral Conservation Rules and is the approving authority for "Mining Plans" and "Mine Closure Plans" as well as the environmental aspects in the 'Mining Plan' details. IBM is also responsible for the economic exploitation of minerals.

31. Goa Mineral Ore Exporters Association (GMOEA) is the Trade Association of the Mineral Exporters of Goa. The Goa Mining Association (GMA) covers both exporters and non-exporters. The Association plays a vital role in the affairs of the mineral trade and operations. The Mineral Foundation of Goa (MFG) was set up in 2001 by the industry to address environmental and social development issues and contribute to the economic and social development of the communities in the mining belt.

32. The Foundation provides need based services in water conservation, women's development and infrastructure development.

33. With regard to water conservation, the Foundation works towards revival of traditional water harvesting systems, watershed development, desilting of water ways, streams, *nallas* etc., and construction of settling ponds.

34. The Foundation enables women to equip themselves with skills in alternate income generation activities i.e., stitching and tailoring, computer education, *masala* making and other related cottage industries.

35. With regard to education, they have made school books available free of cost, instituted scholarships to needy students for professional education that covers tuition, boarding and lodging.

36. The Foundation also conducts health camps and provides financial assistance for surgery within and outside Goa.

37. It also helps in the development of physical infrastructure improvement for schools—for buildings, extensions, compound walls, etc. It also provides furniture, books for library, laboratories and clean drinking water.

38. In its contribution towards the community it has provided crematoriums, repair roads, setting up of truck washing systems and the like.

39. In the field of environment, the Foundation has introduced Nature Clubs, Natural Resource Conservation and the like.

40. The foundation has also initiated research in soil reclamation and organised seminars and workshops on mining legislation, environmental restoration, etc.

41. Since its inception in 2001, the Foundation has already spent Rs. 7 crore on its various activities.

Infrastructure

42. The mining industry uses the roads, bridges, rivers, ports.

Roads

43. The average distance between the mines and the river loading points, numbering about 45, averages about 30 km and carry approximately 18 mt. of ore per year. These public roads pass through habitations creating hazards of air, noise and dust pollution besides endangering the safety of the inhabitants.

44. In many cases, the roads are narrow and require widening, straightening and better maintenance.

45. In order to avoid these problems, the industry has requested that dedicated roads be designated for the exclusive use of the industry. This would help speed up the movement of ore and reduce pollution to habitations by bypassing them.

46. Existing bridges along the route require to be strengthened. The bridge at Usgaon over the river Mhadei has particularly been identified as a problem point which disrupts the smooth flow of traffic. A new or an additional bridge may be the solution.

Rivers

47. The rivers Mandovi and Zuari link the mines to the port of Mormugao and the Panjim outer harbour. About 232 self-propelled barges transport the ore from the river loading points to the ports. The rivers require regular dredging due to the heavy monsoon precipitation and siltation. With about 30 new modernised large capacity barges of plus 3000 DWT joining the river fleet, major dredging will have to be undertaken and river navigational aids modernised. It has been the long pending demand of the industry that the rivers Mandovi and Zuari be declared as national waterways, which could then be financed through centrally sponsored schemes.

TABLE 4.5

Growth of Barge Fleet

Year	Tonnage	Year	Tonnage
1974-75	13225	1990-91	13289
1975-76	11884	1991-92	12330
1976-77	12633	1992-93	13452
1977-78	10464	1993-94	15973
1978-79	8926	1994-95	15576
1979-80	13242	1995-96	15277
1980-81	12829	1996-97	14962
1981-82	13740	1997-98	18896
1982-83	11403	1998-99	14969
1983-84	11885	1999-2000	13811
1984-85	12589	2000-01	15713
1985-86	14282	2001-02	17576
1986-87	14025	2002-03	18718
1987-88	11701	2003-04	22631
1988-89	13660	2004-05	24609
1989-90	12512		

Source: GMOEA.

Ports

TABLE 4.6

Commodity-wise Traffic Handled from Mormugao Port Trust

	2000-01	2001-02	2002-03	2003-04	2004-05
Total iron ore/ iron ore pellets	15457028	17910867	18664316	22942146	24716783
Other cargo	481064	397971	605219	463985	311205
Total exports	15938092	18308838	19269535	23406131	25027988
Total imports	3573293	4599655	4379780	4467779	5631475

Source: MPT

49. The Port of Mormugao situated at the mouth of the river Zuari handled nearly 25 mt. of iron ore for exports in 2004-05—about 19 mt. of Goan ore and about 5 mt. of non-Goan ore mainly from Karnataka's Bellary—Hospet Mining Belt.

50. Vessels at the Port are loaded either in midstream, by transshipper, floating crane, or at the Berth Nos. 6, 9 and 11. Berth No. 6 and 9 are equipped with Mechanical Ore Handling Plants. Berth No. 6 has a handling capacity of 1000 tonnes per hour while Berth No. 9 has a capacity of 8,000 tpa.

51. The year 2004-05 saw record levels of loading by the following; Berth No. 9 handled 12.4 mt, Berth No. 6 handled 2 lakh tonnes, midstream plus 3 mt and transshippers around 8.9 mt. All this totals upto 24.6 mt. These record levels may not be sustainable as the Port is already overloaded. The port has experienced bunching of vessels leading to high demurrage charges. The port needs to invest urgently in loaders/unloaders of higher capacity and higher speed. This will lead to speedier clearance of ships in port, there is also need for a new berth with superior infrastructure.

52. The ageing 8,000 tph MOHP at Berth No. 9 installed to handle Panamax vessels of 50 to 70,000 DWT needs to be upgraded to service the huge bulk carriers that call at the port. The MOHP loads vessels up to one lakh tones alongside the berth, the vessels then go midstream and are uptopped by the transshippers, 6 of which operate at the MPT and POH, owned by the exporters. The transshippers in service have a loading rate varying from 17 to 24,000 tpd. Two new transshippers that now come into operation have a capacity of up to 65,000 tpd. The Panjim Port handles 8 mt of iron. The Port has only midstream facilities owned and operated by the same private sector exporters.

53. Ore exported from these two ports work out to 32 mt that is about 40 per cent of India's total exports of iron ore of 79 mt.

Water

54. The industry uses saline water or water from the mined out pits in its beneficiation process and 80 per cent of the used water is recycled for future use.

Power

55. Most of the heavy machinery used in operation are wheel-based and diesel powered. Beneficiation plants are run by gensets using diesel. Electricity used from the power grid is estimated at about 10-12 MW pa which is adequate.

Development and Growth Areas

56. The increasing world demand for iron ore offers scope for further development of this sector. As seen from the preceding sections the mining sector has performed well showing incremental growth and technological development in terms of quantum, value additions, technologies and transportation and handling technologies. However, the limitations are many and can be listed in various areas:

1) Multiplicity of controlling agencies.
2) Very limited lease period and area with their accompanying problems.

TABLE 4.7

Mode of Loading

	Berth no. 9	*Berth no. 6*	*Midstream*	*Transhipper*	*Berth no. 11*	*Floating Crane*	*Total*
1989-90	7835390	118374	392614	4002286	N.A	N.A	12348664
1990-91	8812934	32605	281685	4044531	N.A	N.A	13171755
1991-92	8466145	48775	546731	3138518	N.A	N.A	12200169
1992-93	8923651	N.A	640553	3782691	N.A	N.A	13346895
1993-94	9474712	N.A	787366	5492397	N.A	N.A	15754475
1994-95	8702001	N.A	917555	5674903	N.A	N.A	15294459
1995-96	8442212	N.A	637961	6047022	N.A	N.A	15127195
1996-97	8458869	N.A	442427	5856295	N.A	N.A	14757591
1997-98	9717768	N.A	618675	8341328	N.A	N.A	18677771
1998-99	9209490	N.A	346004	5413163	N.A	N.A	14968657
1999-2000	9127462	N.A	317609	4365609	N.A	N.A	13810680
2000-01	10829437	N.A	115700	4767520	N.A	N.A	15712657
2001-02	10688862	N.A	313649	5867146	15210	691853	17576720
2002-03	10988598	N.A	308250	7179192	N.A	242467	18718507
2003-04	11730700	N.A	2635070	8265455	N.A	N.A	22631225
2004-05	12427638	208801	3049012	8924230	N.A	N.A	24609681

Source: GMOEA

3) Urgent need to device economies of scale in mining areas, lease period in transportation i.e., size of barges and trucks which are limited by the lack of wide roads—need for major dredging of the rivers.

4) At the mines, trucks of 25 tonnes capacity must be introduced.

5) Hostile activities of NGOs and some mining communities against environmental hazards must be minimized by educating them on the conditionality of the mining lease. Agreements covering the environmental hazards and controls and also of the IBM's guidelines in this regard which are being observed by the operators and supervised by the appropriate authority at every stage of the mining operations. Environmental safeguards are built into the lease deed agreement, the mining plans and the mine closure plans at the outset and enforced by both IBM of the Government of Goa and the department of the government of Goa. These licences are issued under predetermined conditionality to minimise environmental hazards during operations and eventually restore the environment after the closure of mines.

6) Establishment of dedicated roads exclusively for the use of the mining sector for transportation of ore by trucks from the mines to the river loading points with no habitats permitted on this route. This will help speed up the movement of ore and ensure safety all around.

7) At the mines, more mechanisation for excavation and loading will be necessary using the state of art moving equipment. Large trucks of 25-tonne capacity will need to be put into service.

8) Beneficiation process will need to be upgraded by all mines to improve the quality of the ore utilising the low grade ores by introducing improved technologies like log washers, magnetic separators of both high and low intensity. These magnetic separators are capable of upgrading ores with 40 per cent iron content up to about 65 per cent. Further technologies for recoveries from tailing must also be encouraged.

9) Modernisation of barge fleet to +3000 DWT, which is underway, needs major dredging of the rivers.

10) The number of jetties would need to be increased in number and modern handling capacity. In this case, Coastal Regulation Zone (CRZ) regulations would have to be relaxed.

11) Modernisation of transshippers with higher speeds and high handling capacity.

12) Facilities at the port of Mormugao need to be modernised urgently, like the earlier mentioned MOHP with high capacity loaders and unloaders.

Better management at the port, would reduce bunching of vessels and reduce vessels time in port.

13) Cluster development at the mines in the form of joint operations would generate better economies of scale so also would shared logistics in the form of transport and handling facilities.

Strengths, Weaknesses, Opportunities and Threats

Strengths

57. Goa has an abundant variety of minerals and a variety of grades of ore available virtually on the surface. Goan iron ore is a well established brand name in the world iron trade over the past half century and is well received in world markets. The industry has established long term strategic alliances with major buyers in Japan, China, Korea and have proved to be reliable suppliers.

58. The geography of Goa favours the industry—the mines located in Goa's mid and highlands are connected by navigable rivers to the port with a well developed inter modal transport system of roads and rivers from the mine head to the natural deep water Port of Mormugao and the Panjim Outer Harbour. The industry has a good value addition transforming low grade ores to marketable grades aided by washeries, benefication and metallic separators etc.

59. Adequate technical manpower, latest technology and machinery are available for future development. The demand situation assures the industry favourable cost/price conditions over the next five years. Another advantage is that Goan ores are blendable with those of major suppliers like Australia and Brazil.

Weaknesses

60. As per the Mines and Minerals (Development and Regulation) Act, 1957, the maximum limit of mining lease in a state is 10 sq.km. and the maximum period for which a mining lease may be granted shall not exceed 30 years, provided that minimum period for which any mining lease may be granted shall not be less than 20 years, mining lease may be renewed for a period not exceeding 20 years. The primary weakness of the industry in Goa is largely the availability low grade ores of different types, mainly haematite and magnetite. Added to this is the problem of small sized leases. Furthermore the lease periods are for very short durations of 10 years only, this naturally acts as a deterrent to investment in sophisticated technologies and expensive machinery.

61. The benefication process technologies also need to be upgraded to be able to compete with the big players like Australia and Brazil.

62. Earthmoving equipment, trucks and barges are presently just about adequate for current operations.

63. Infrastructure constraints in the form of narrow roads restrict the size of trucks, these roads also pass through habitations endangering their safety and contributes to dust and noise pollution.

Opportunities

64. Currently international demand forecasts indicate a growing demand for crude steel over the next five years—Chinese demand being the main driver over the past few years. In 2004, Chinese crude steel growth rate was 23 per cent compared to world crude steel growth rate of 9 per cent. In the first quarter of 2005, Chinese crude steel production registered at above 25 per cent on a per year basis. The Chinese growth rate is expected to continue for sometime in the future with a projected growth rate of above 10 per cent in 2006 over the base figure of 272 mt in 2004.

65. The present high demand leads to price increase in FOBT contracts offering greater profitability to the industry.

66. Improved machinery and technology is now available and invention, development and discovery of new and cheaper technologies for extraction and processes for benefication help market very low-grade ores.

67. Dredging of the river Mandovi and Zuari need major and urgent dredging to allow easy passage for the larger capacity (+3000t) barges coming into service. River navigation aids are poor.

68. The Port of Mormugao is experiencing bunching of vessels due to poor planning and an inadequate number of berths added to low speed loading of vessels and unloading of incoming barges from the rivers.

Threats

69. Competition from countries like Australia and Brazil with high grade ores and who enjoy economies of scale plus state of the art technology and infrastructure pose a threat to the Goan iron ore industry with its low grade ore coupled with small scale mining operations.

70. Rising oil prices and new expensive technologies are a detriment due to our small scale restrictive operations.

71. Restrictive environment legislation including a ban on mining in forest areas where most of the proven reserves lie pose a problem to the future of the industry in Goa.

72. Further regulatory restrictions lie in the area of the riverine transport infrastructure in the expansion of construction of existing and new jetties, maintenance of ore dumps sited on the riverbanks under the CRZ legislation.

Recommendations and Developmental Strategies

Need for a Comprehensive State Mining Policy

73. Since the iron ore mining sector is exclusively into exports, the lease area could be given Export Oriented Unit (EOU) status. This would bring costs down by making all inputs tax free including VAT and service tax.

Land Use

74. Mining lease areas may be declared as mining zones as done in the case of industrial areas. This would avoid hassles of going through land conversion procedures etc. This would not only reflect the activity of the area but also automatically bestow the right to mine. Existing mining area should not be suddenly declared as sanctuaries by Forest Department. Development of habitats in the mining area should be discouraged e.g., Bicholim village which was developed into a full fledged town over a period of time.

Environment

75. Introduction of an environment audit and long term mining leases will encourage ploughing back of profits/earnings. R&D on rejects should be encouraged as these dumps pose a problem and also the skyline should be changed. Mine closure plan should be strictly followed for reclamation of land in the State.

Roads

76. Existing roads need to be widened, improved and should bypass habitats. Also, there is a need for dedicated roads from mines to river loading points as mining road corridors. Existing jetties should be upgraded and new jetties should be built with larger capacities as large barges come into operation. There is a need to minimise CRZ regulations for construction and maintenance of river loading points.

There should be an increase in investment for loading and unloading facilities at jetties. Also, new bridges are needed to take higher capacity trucks.

Rivers Navigation

77. Declaration of the rivers Mandovi and Zuari as National Waterways—as centrally sponsored schemes of the Inland Waterways Authority are then available for maintenance and dredging.

78. Major dredging of these rivers to accommodate the larger capacity barges, 30 in number, of plus 3000 DWT coming into operation. Dredging will allow easy and quicker transit time. Navigation aids need to be upgraded and this can be done by the industry.

Port

79. Mormugao Port urgently needs new berths with superior infrastructure. Current loader/unloader need to be replaced with higher capacity and higher speed equipment. This will lead to quicker turn around of vessels. Port-related charges need to be reduced to bring them abreast with rates in similar ports abroad for similar services.

Technical Guidance

80. For the best use of mineral resources available in the state it is imperative to provide the following:

(a) Need for undertaking scientific studies for the possibilities of setting up mineral-based industry in the State.

(b) Need to reduce the procedure delays in granting mining leases particularly from the angle of forest and environment.

(c) Bulk of the export of iron ore is in the form of fines for which adequate sintering or pelletisation capacities need to be created.

(d) Of the total export of about 78 million tonnes of iron ore from India, 31.42 million tonnes was exported from Goa port in 2004-05, which is around 40 per cent of the total export.

References

AEQM Plan for the Mining Belt – DPSE - TERI.

Census of India – various issues.

Economic Survey - GoG.

Goa Mineral Ore Exports, Selected Statistics – Goa Mineral Exporters Assoc.

Goan Iron Ore Industry - GMOEA.

Handbook of Statistics – DPSE, Goa –various issues.

Index of Industrial Production – DPSE, GoG various issues.

India's Trade and Export Prospects in Minerals, Metals & Alloys – IBM 2000.

Iron Ore Manual, Tex Report Co. Ltd.(Japan) - various issues.

Mineral Foundation of Goa – Annual Reports.

NCAER (2002). *Role of Mineral Ore in the Economic Development of Goa.*

Regional Plan for Goa 2011 – T&CPO, GoG.

Sesa Goa Ltd., Annual Reports.

Suryanareyan & Sudarsen. Andaman and Nicobar Islands.

Chapter 5

Manufacturing and Value Added Trading

Issues

Spread

1. For a small State of 3,700 square kilometres, there are 20 locations for industrial estates in Goa. This increases the burden on the transportation, logistics and results in a spread rather than containment of hazardous waste and pollution.

TABLE 5.1

Industrial Estates in Goa

Estate	*Plots Allotted*	*Plots Vacant*	*Sheds Allotted*	*Units Functioning*
Corlim	79	-	76	58
Margao	37	1	98	80
Sancoale	160	-	101	81
Mapusa	17	-	30	37
Tivim	64	-	89	95
Bicholim	82	-	72	70
Honda	26	7	31	24
Bethora	86	-	41	80
Kundaim	339	1	72	172
Canacona	68	-	27	24
Tuem	62	-	22	29
Kakoda	65	41	45	39
Verna	433	14	6	184
Cuncolim	218	-	6	57
Pilerne	130	-	-	46
Marcaim	116	8	-	43
Shiroda	-	17	-	-
Colvale	24	-	-	5
Pissurlem	43	58	-	5
Sanguem	1	3	-	-
Total	2050	150	716	1129

Source: Economic Survey, 2004-05.

Growth

2. The state of Goa does not have a long history of industrialisation. Prior to liberation in 1961, the State had predominantly agriculture and trading economy with few natural resources-based industries like agro-processing and mining. Since liberation, the State has steadily switched over to a manufacturing-based and service economy. The share of manufacturing sector in Goa's net state domestic product has increased from 7 per cent in 1960 to 40 per cent in 2002-03.

Small Scale Industries

3. Small scale units form a significant part of industrial growth in Goa. Post-statehood, the trend in registration, employment generation and investment is depicted in Table 5.3. During the period 1-4-2000 to 31-3-2005, the number of small scale industries has registered a growth of 16.9 per cent. The highest growth was in other manufacturing industries (130.6 per cent), followed by manufacture of rubber, plastic, petroleum and coal products (24.7 per cent), beverages, tobacco (22.2 per cent), electrical machinery apparatus appliances and supplier parts (18.8 per cent), food product (14.8 per cent) and non-metallic mineral products (13.1 per cent).

4. As on 31-10-07, Goa has 7119 small scale industrial units providing employment to 49201 persons. Beginning from a few small scale natural resource-based industries like cashew, rice and flour mills, matches, ice, coconut oil, iron ore processing units, etc., the industrial base has gradually diversified into a wide range of products.

5. The small scale sector comprises food processing, fruit processing, metal products, wood products, paper products and printing, rubber, plastics and petroleum products, non-metallic mineral products, other chemical products, electrical machinery and appliances, textile

TABLE 5.2

Industrial Registrations in Goa

Year	*1987-88*	*1988-89*	*1989-90*	*1990-91*	*1991-92*	*1992-93*	*1993-94*	*1994-95*	*1995-96*	*1996-97*	*1997-98*	*1998-99*	*1999-2000*	*2000-01*	*2001-02*	*2002-03*	*2003-04*	*2004-05*
Total no. of industries	3305	3643	3966	4165	4393	4617	4851	5063	5195	5368	5579	5902	6,089	6,299	6,607	6,868	6,969	7,099
Increase in industrial registration (%)	-	10.23	8.87	5.02	5.47	5.1	5.07	4.37	2.61	3.33	3.93	5.79	3.17	3.45	4.89	3.95	1.47	1.87
SSI	3271	3602	3924	4120	4344	4558	4787	4995	5118	5278	5,488	5765	5949	6157	6469	6714	6852	6954
Increase in SSI registration (%)	-	10.12	8.94	4.99	5.44	4.93	5.02	4.35	2.46	3.13	3.98	5.05	3.19	3.5	5.07	3.79	1.5	1.91
LMS	34	41	42	45	49	59	64	68	77	90	91	137	140	142	138	154	154	154
Increase in LMS registration (%)	-	20.59	2.44	7.14	8.89	20.41	8.47	6.25	13.24	16.88	1.11	50.55	2.19	1.43	-2.82	11.59	0	0

Source: Directorate of Industries, Goa.

TABLE 5.3

SSI Units in Different Industry Categories in Goa

S.No.	*Year*	*No. of Units*	*Employment*	*Fixed Investment (Rs. in crore)*
1	1987-88	3271	22657	50.8
2	1988-89	3602	24438	60.3
3	1989-90	3924	26136	71.9
4	1990-91	4120	27328	80.7
5	1991-92	4344	28459	90.0
6	1992-93	4558	29672	99.9
7	1993-94	4787	30918	112.6
8	1994-95	4995	32042	122.4
9	1995-96	5118	33136	134.4
10	1996-97	5278	34472	157.6
11	1997-98	5488	36734	184.2
12	1998-99	5765	39432	219.1
13	1999-2000	5949	40797	221.5
14	2000-01	6157	42312	223.5
15	2001-02	6469	44222	285.6
16	2002-03	6714	46163	302.7
17	2003-04	6852	47055	313.0
18	2004-05	6954	47815	327.6
19	2005-06	7060	49125	340.6
20	2006-07 (upto Dec. '06)	7095	49257	350.0

Source: Directorate of Industries, Goa.

TABLE 5.4

Electricity Demand and Supply in Goa

Type of Industry	*No. of SSI*	*Units % to Total*
Food product	1280	17.98
Beverages, tobacco & tobacco products	471	6.62
Jute, hemp and mesta textile	13	0.18
Textile products (including wearing apparel other than footwear)	229	3.22
Wood and wood products, furniture & fixtures	521	7.32
Paper & paper products and printing, publishing and allied industries	619	8.69
Leather and leather fur products (except repairs)	34	0.48
Rubber, plastic, petroleum and coal products	571	8.02
Chemical & chemical products (except products of petroleum and coal)	430	6.04
Non-metallic mineral products	462	6.49
Basic metal and alloy industries	185	2.60
Metal products and parts (except machinery and transport equipment)	938	13.17
Machinery tools & parts	75	1.05
Electrical machinery apparatus appliances & supplier parts	454	6.38
Transport equipments & parts	113	1.59
Other manufacturing industries	269	3.78
Repairs service	455	6.39

Source: Electricity Dept., Goa.

products, basic metals and alloy units, transport equipments, machinery tools and parts, leather and jute products, etc.

Large and Medium Industries

6. As on 31-10-2007, Goa has 209 medium and large scale industrial units. The large and medium scale sector comprises food products and beverages, soya processing, breweries, agro-oils, flour mills, slaughter houses and meat processing units, sugar mills, chemical units like cement plants, fertilisers, industrial gases, mineral-based industries, ore beneficiation plants, potassium permanganate, insecticides, pharmaceutical formulations, ophthalmic lenses, basic metal and alloy units like pig iron plants, steel ingots and rolled products, ferrous and non-ferrous alloys, aluminum tubes, various types of petroleum-based industries like plastic products, PVC bottles, laminated products, films, automobile components, fibre-glass-based products, rubber products, electrical machinery and

TABLE 5.5

Large and Medium Industry Units Registered in Goa: 1987-2005

S.No.	*Year*	*No. of Units*	*Employment*	*Fixed Investment (Rs. in crore)*
1	1987-88	32	7906	804.28
2	1988-89	38	8367	820.36
3	1989-90	39	8456	826.01
4	1990-91	42	9080	903.99
5	1991-92	45	9515	933.81
6	1992-93	53	10821	1229.25
7	1993-94	61	11476	1298.54
8	1994-95	66	12328	1384.15
9	1995-96	93	16420	2301.64
10	1996-97	107	17525	2502.9
11	1997-98	141	20292	3682.31
12	1998-99	147	20718	3760.63
13	1999-2000	153	21470	4325.89
14	2000-01	156	21609	4367.25
15	2001-02	174	23547	5061.2
16	2002-03	178	23858	5162.52
17	2003-04	192	24767	5439.72
18	2004-05	195	24817	5446.16

Source: Directorate of Industries, Govt. of Goa.

appliances like fans, motors, generators, washing machines, resistors, batteries, PCBs, telecom products like electronic exchanges, lamps, wire communication systems, floppy discs, building materials, cotton spinning, ship building, repairing and general engineering, high precision activities like jewel bearing, diamond drilling, etc.

7. Rubber, plastics, petroleum and coal products are concentrated in Verna and Kundaim, iron and steel-based units in Bicholim, pharmaceuticals in Verna as well as the estates of Ponda *taluka*, the electronics & telecommunication industries in Verna and ship building and repairs in Mormugao, Vasco.

Industrial Production

8. The Quick Estimates of the Index of Industrial Production (IIP) for the period 1994-95 to 2001-02 (P) are provided in Table 5.6. As seen in the Table below, the manufacturing index has been rising steadily throughout the period covered. Whereas, the mining index has been sluggish and stagnant, except the last two years of the period covered. The growth over the period 1994-95 to 2003-04 (P) was 20 per cent for mining, 204 per cent for manufacturing and 189 per cent for general index. The corresponding growth figures for all India during the same period were 34 per cent, 80 per cent and 73 per cent.

9. Among the industry groups, as many as 4 out of 11 groups have shown a negative growth during the period 1994-95 to 2001-02. These include food products, beverages, tobacco and related products, non-metallic mineral products and transport equipment and parts. Among these, transport equipment and parts has shown the highest negative growth of 83 per cent.

TABLE 5.6

Index of Industrial Production by Industry Group (Base 1993-94 = 100)

Industry Group	*1994-95*	*1995-96*	*1996-97*	*1997-98*	*1998-99*	*1999-2000*	*2000-01*	*2001-02*	*2002-03*	*2003-04*	*2004-05*
Food products	121.41	88.85	102.69	116.10	127.48	156.19	129.34	107.67	180	152	125
Beverages, tobacco and related products	206.88	233.26	183.55	202.75	148.38	182.35	154.50	178.03	227	218	236
Textile products	133.93	165.64	274.88	272.11	278.47	525.68	237.74	245.97	209	195	197
Paper & paper products	201.33	212.15	236.76	502.43	502.65	610.36	361.75	446.63	429	525	501
Basic chemicals & chemical products	124.41	134.88	202.90	233.48	189.13	166.94	167.55	179.46	192	202	231
Rubber, plastic, petroleum and coal products	96.76	104.34	108.82	114.95	116.86	122.15	119.63	103.37	161	178	191
Non-metallic mineral products	34.19	41.64	42.51	21.93	15.31	11.06	13.40	14.28	13	5	6
Basic metal and alloy industries	181.49	250.08	327.12	332.68	394.93	966.81	1065.74	1357.58	1416	1432	1409
Machinery and equipment other than transport equipment	288.16	673.66	521.99	906.00	1348.94	1378.72	1875.83	2214.08	2395	2678	2734
Transport equipment and parts	130.38	89.87	102.11	108.78	85.23	49.07	54.50	22.21	38	39	48
Other manufacturing industries	114.83	157.13	185.87	169.93	192.86	185.49	161.65	184.69	119	146	45

Source: Central Statistical Organisation.

10. Among the industry groups with positive growth, machinery and equipment other than transport equipment has shown the highest growth of 668 per cent during the above period. This is closely followed by basic metal and alloy industries with a growth of 648 per cent. Paper and paper products had a growth of 122 per cent and textile products had a growth of 84 per cent. The Index of Industrial Production by Industry Groups is shown in Table 5.6.

Composition of Net Value Added

11. Chemical industries add to the maximum net value added amongst the major industry categories for the period 1999-2000 to 2002-03.

TABLE 5.7

Net Value Added amongst the Major Industry Categories for the Period 1999-2000 to 2002-03

Industry Division	*Net Value Added (Rs. in lakh)*					
	1999-2000	*2000-01*	*2001-02*	*2002-03(Q.E.)*	*2003-04*	*2004-05*
Food products	15963	22419	22870	20520	21399	17557
Textiles		6159	4981	4460	8042	7970
Basic chemicals & chemical products	59027	60690	87609	134181	111413	151491
Rubber, plastic, petroleum and coal products	21378	20286	8201	14403	16077	15859
Basic metal and alloy industries	9516	4512	7078	12784	15948	18592
Machinery and equipment other than transport equipment	6354	3299				
Structural metal products					3107	3762
Office accounting and computing machinery	4531	4787	6589	5590	8959	8457
Electrical machinery and apparatus	1411	6163	6625	4761	11204	5485
Other transport equipment			2124	2267		1324
Other industries	9452	18733	14073	-3281	32569	44756
All industries	127632	147048	160150	195685	228718	275253

Source: Directorate of Planning, Statistics & Evaluation, Govt. of Goa.

TABLE 5.9

Details of IEMs Implemented from August 1991-2007 based on Part B of IEM Form Filed by Entrepreneurs

State	*No.of IEMs*	*Investment (Rs.Crore)*	*Employment (Numbers)*
Goa	101	819	13236
All India	6925	258253	1108195

Source: Directorate of Industries, Govt. of Goa.

Employment

12. As per the Annual Survey of Industries conducted by the Directorate of Planning, Statistics and Evaluation, Government of Goa, during the year 2001-02, the top four industry groups with respect to total persons engaged were chemical and chemical products (27.80%), food products and beverages (14.07%), basic metals (10.72%) and rubber and plastic products (7.26%).

Subsidies

13. State Investment Subsidy Scheme, 1990 which was initiated after attaining statehood in 1987, envisaged providing capital investment subsidy to industrial units. The units claiming the benefits of subsidy under this scheme have to employ at least 80 per cent of locals. This measure has been effective in providing employment to locals to the maximum extent possible. Only in exceptional cases of non-availability of required technical expertise, the units are exempted and that too after ascertaining the shortfall of this technical manpower from the Regional Employment Exchange and notifying the vacancies in the local dailies. The Scheme is discontinued w.e.f. 31.03.2003.

14. Under Goa Industrial Policy, 2003, the incentives/ subsidy schemes were envisaged with the objective of promoting local entrepreneurship, local employment opportunities, consumption of local raw materials and improving export markets have not proved to have long term sustainability. The industrial policy will be more effective if it sets enabling conditions and strictly fixing sunset clauses for validity of subsidies. Subsidies which

TABLE 5.8

Industrial Investment Proposals August 1991-2007

	IEM+LOI+DIL		*Industrial Entrepreneur Memorandum (IEMs)*						*Letters of Intent (LOIs)+Direct Industrial Licences (DILs)*					
Name of the State	*Total Investment (Rs.Crore)*	*Percentage*	*Numbers Filed*	*Percentage*	*Proposed Investment (Rs.Cr)*	*Percentage*	*Proposed Emp.(Nos)*	*Percentage*	*Numbers granted*	*Percentage Investment (Rs.Cr)*	*Proposed Emp.(Nos)*	*Percentage*	*Proposed*	*Percentage*
Goa	8294	0.28	602	0.84	8126	0.28	66047	0.47	37	0.87	168	0.13	3526	0.39
All India	3009303	100.00	71271	100.00	2884643	100.00	14145906	100.00	4270	100.00	124660	100.00	914453	100.00

Source: Directorate of Industries, Govt. of Goa.

are having an overlapping scope and nature should be combined.

Industrial Areas/Clusters

15. All the industrial estates developed by the State government till date have been multi-industry and managed exclusively through state sponsored infrastructure facilities. The budgetary constraint of the government has resulted in inadequate facilities in most of the industrial estates. A sustainable effort will be to introduce a cluster development method wherein the management of infrastructure facilities should be augmented through user charges or through public-private partnerships method. In addition to private investment, public support by way of viability gap funding can be envisaged. The State government should come out with a white paper on adequacy of infrastructure facilities and accordingly enact an infrastructure law which will facilitate private participation in development of economic activities in the State.

Industrial Sickness

16. Several internal and external factors have put considerable pressure on the performance of the industries, resulting in a number of them becoming sick units. Recognising the urgent need to support sick units, the State government has formulated the Goa Sick Industrial Units Revival and Rehabilitation Schemes, 2008. Warning signals have been laid down for identification of sickness and eligibility criteria have been set for availing assistance for revival. A rehabilitation package is envisaged to be formed after the scrutiny by the Appraisal Committee.

Institutions and Governance

Following organisations facilitate and regulate industry and trade in Goa:

Directorate of Industries

17. The Department of Industries, Trade and Commerce is concerned with the promotion, development and regulation of industries in the State of Goa. It handles the registration of industrial units. The department gives provisional registration for a period of five years. Once the unit starts its production, it can apply for permanent registration.

High Powered Co-ordination Committee (HPCC)

18. The Government has set up a High Powered Co-ordination Committee to cater to the infrastructure requirement of industrial units, particularly in the medium and large-scale sector.

19. All medium and large scale units, including industrial units requiring release of substantial power, water, land and infrastructure facilities and those prone to cause pollution have to seek specific approval of HPCC, by providing the required information in the prescribed format.

20. The entrepreneurs intending to set up medium and large scale industrial projects in the state of Goa have to submit 16 sets of HPCC formats duly filled in. These applications are thereafter circulated among all the HPCC members for obtaining their comments.

21. Generally, the meeting is held in consultation with the Hon'ble Chief Minister and Hon'ble Minister for Industries being the Chairman and Vice Chairman of HPCC, respectively. Once the meeting is fixed, the Director of Industries, Trade and Commerce, prepares the agenda notes highlighting briefly the comments and observations made by HPCC members. Thereafter, if there is enough time, the agenda notes are forwarded to the HPCC members; otherwise, such agenda notes are circulated among HPCC members on the date of meeting itself. If for some or other reasons comments are not received from any of the above HPCC members, the same is recorded in the agenda notes and the issues are sorted out with the HPCC members in the meeting.

22. After deliberating and discussing each of the case/ application among the HPCC members during the meeting held under the Chairmanship of Hon'ble Chief Minister, the setting up of the projects coming up before HPCC are either approved, rejected or deferred in the HPCC meeting, depending upon various factors such as requirement of water, land, power, employment potential, extent of pollution, if any, likely to be caused, etc.

23. The draft minutes of the HPCC meeting are then drawn by the Directorate which are subsequently forwarded to the Hon'ble Chief Minister and Hon'ble Minister for Industries for their approval through the Secretary (industries).

24. Once the draft minutes are approved by the Chairman of HPCC, the same are referred back to the Director of Industries, Trade and Commerce, who in turn communicate the relevant and operative part of the minutes of HPCC as applicable to the concerned entrepreneur/applicant, and a mention is made that the applicant shall obtain all the permissions and licences as required under the law for setting up and for the operation of the unit. Also, the unit whose project is

approved should take effective steps to implement the project within a period of one year and should furnish regularly, quarterly progress reports in regard to the implementation of the project.

25. Medium and large scale units which are exempted from the compulsory industrial licencing have to file an Industrial Entrepreneurs Memorandum (IEM) in terms of Notification No.477 dated 25/7/1991 with Government of India, Ministry of Industry, Department of Industrial Policy and Promotion, Secretariat for Industrial Assistance (Industrial information, Memorandum Section), New Delhi, in the prescribed format, before setting up their unit. And those units in respect of which industrial licensing is compulsory, they have to apply for industrial licence to Government of India, Ministry of Industry, New Delhi, for the unit to be set up and the product proposed to be manufactured.

Industrial Development Corporation

26. The Goa Industrial Development Corporation was established by the government with the aims and objectives of securing and assisting in the rapid and orderly establishment of industries in industrial areas and industrial estates in Goa. One of the important activities of the Corporation is setting up of industrial estates and offer developed plots to industrial units.

27. Locating an unit in the industrial units can accrue several advantages to the investor—no separate permission for conversion of land for non-agricultural use is required. Clear title of land is assured.

28. Speedy clearance/issue of construction licence, occupancy certificate, etc. Industrial estates have been declared as notified areas. The land is owned by the Corporation and allotted initially for 30 years on lease, extendable upto 95 years, on easy instalments.

29. Water supply is provided and distributed to the units directly by GOA-IDC without charging additional cost. Alternative arrangements are made when necessary.

30. Ample power supply is easily available from the Electricity Department of Government of Goa and from private sector companies.

31. Plots are carved out to accommodate small, medium and large scale industrial units with various amenities, in a well planned layout and congenial atmosphere and as per the needs of the units.

Goa State Pollution Control Board

32. The Goa State Pollution Control Board had been constituted on 01/07/1988 by the State government under the Water (Prevention and Control of Pollution) Act, 1974.

33. This is the competent body entrusted with the functions relevant to control pollution of water, air and hazardous waste. The specific objective of the Board is to maintain quality of water and air within the State. In pursuance to these functions, the Pollution Control Board scrutinises every industrial proposal within the State, from the point of view of minimising environmental pollution due to liquid, effluent solid waste or gaseous emissions. Though the Board is not a licencing authority, its clearance is essential for every industrial proposal at two stages.

34. The Board as a prescribed authority issues authorisations/registrations under various Rules framed under the Environment (Protection) Act, 1986. The Rules under which authorisations are issued are stated below:

1) Bio-Medical Waste (Management and Handling) Rules, 1998.
2) Hazardous Wastes (Management and Handling) Rules, 1989.
3) Municipal Solid Wastes (Management and Handling) Rules, 2000.
4) Batteries (Management and Handling) Rules, 2001.
5) Plastics Manufacture Sale and Usage Rules, 1999.

Economic Development Corporation

35. The EDC Limited, originally known as the Economic Development Corporation of Goa, Daman & Diu Limited (EDC), incorporated on 12th March, 1975 as a public limited company under the Companies Act, 1956, has been the state financial institution set up by the Government of Goa with the prime objective to promote industrial development.

36. Originally EDC had been operating in the Union Territory of Goa, Daman & Diu and thereafter, the State of Goa, besides Union territory of Daman & Diu and lately Dadra and Nagar Haveli. The territorial area of operation has now been extended over the entire Union of India with amendment of Memorandum & Articles of Association.

37. EDC has been acting as a State Industrial Development Corporation (SIDC), besides, being accorded the twin status of State Financial Corporation (SFC) by IDBI/SIDBI.

The main objectives of the company are:

- To carry on the business of an investment company for providing financial assistance to industrial enterprises and for enterprises like hotel and tourism-related services, hospital and medical aid services and to professional enterprises for starting, running, expanding, modernising their professional activities etc.

- To extend financial assistance in various types of instruments as fund-based and provide guarantees, securities etc., as non-fund-based activities, and to provide fee-based financial services.
- To establish companies in subsidiary or joint sector for starting, taking over or conducting industrial enterprises and other economic activities of any description.
- To encourage and promote participation of capital in various forms like equity, preference or debentures in industrial enterprises and other economic activities.
- To identify and motivate entrepreneurs to set up industries and assist them in the spade work by conducting various forms of Entrepreneur Development programmes.
- To offer and act as an agent for the disbursement of various incentives and concessions and benefits on behalf of the Government to units and enterprises assisted by EDC Ltd.

38. Besides EDC Ltd., Maharashtra State Financial Corporation Ltd., also extends term loan facilities to industry. GHRSSIDC Ltd. caters to the raw materials as well as marketing needs of the SSI Units of the State. KVIB is also functioning in the State extending financial assistance to village and cottage industries.

39. Almost all the national level industrial promotional agencies are functioning in the State. SIDBI, SISI, NSIC, KVIC, IFCI, IDBI, ET&DC and CIPET have offices in the State. Goa has an UNDP assisted tool room and training centre. Further the State has a network of more than 330 branches of various commercial banks and cooperative banks supplementing the efforts of EDC and MSFC in extending financial assistance to trade industry, tourism and service sectors.

Role of Institutions

40. Econometric research at the World Bank suggests that the influence of high quality public institutions may exceed the impact of good economic policies.

41. Effective state institutions are likely to be critical in mediating the impact of globalisation in small states. A well-working bureaucracy is important for formulating and implementing economic and social policies. Such policies enable states to upgrade their skill bases, manage their interactions with foreign investors and sources of technology and devise ways to cushion their populations from the instability that accompanies openness.

42. High quality institutions in small states matter more in terms of managing already high levels of globalisation (i.e., helping to sustain high growth rates and low growth volatility) than in attaining additional levels of global integration.

43. Two kinds of political institutions seem particularly important—those that reflect higher levels of state capacity and those that manage social conflicts. The quality of state intervention is more relevant than merely whether the state intervened or not.

Role of Government

44. Over the years, development was seen as simply increasing GDP. Today, there is a broader set of objectives, including democratic development, egalitarian development, sustainable development and higher living standards.

The role of the government should encompass the following areas:

- Promoting institutional development.
- Investment in infrastructure, human capital and industry.
- Trade policies—interstate trade expansion.
- Promoting technological dynamism, industrial policy and in increasing productivity in both industry and agriculture.
- Setting goals of economic policy.
- Institutional and policy malleability—adapting to economic change.

45. The thrust of the government should not only cover economic institutions and primary policy but its major functions should shift as development proceeds. The Government needs to establish its credibility for successful long term economic growth. A strong government is needed to initiate economic development.

46. The Government must increase its own capacity by raising the training and professionalism of its civil service, the efficiency of its public administration and reduce the level of corruption of its bureaucrats.

47. The role of government is actually being re-defined rather than reduced. The state needs to play a decisive role in education, training, research and development and the flow of information.

48. The Government should introduce varied mechanisms for mobilising local and regional stakeholders so as to ensure concerted support for local economic development. In this regard, networks, economic watch and knowledge transfer are often identified as the preferred mechanisms. The Government should become a strategist, mobiliser and partner for local stakeholders.

49. Government officials must understand that many factors besides incentives and tax abatements determine whether an industry will locate in the state. Some of these include:

- Proximity to customers.
- Access to four lane highways.
- Availability of local labour.
- Availability of skilled labour.
- Availability of local shopping.
- Support services for the new plant.
- Local transportation.
- Availability of technical training.
- Quality education.
- Quality health care.
- Safety.
- Pro-business attitude among officials and residents of the state.

50. The government's support for any emergent entrepreneurial activity should ideally be commensurated with its relevance to the region's natural competitive advantages and the likelihood of the activity's commercial success in neighbouring markets and export markets.

Infrastructure

51. The Goa Industrial Development Corporation has established 20 industrial estates in Goa covering all the *talukas*. All the industrial estates are located in rural areas. Medium and large industries are encouraged in villages and rural areas with a view to achieve dispersal of industries and to reduce unemployment in rural areas. As per the Industrial Policy, major thrust is given for infrastructure development.

52. Goa-IDC has so far constructed more than 700 industrial sheds and developed more than 2200 industrial plots. Infrastructure facilities provided at the industrial estates include water supply system, asphalted roads, street light, drainage, besides common facilities like canteen, ESI, housing tenements, post offices, telephone exchange, public pay phone, banking facilities, warehousing facilities and other need-based requirements including police outpost. Location of industrial estates and number of plots, sheds and units functioning in each are given below. The Goa-IDC creates capacity in the industrial estates to support the following:

- Set-up of new industrial venture in small, medium or large scale sector.
- Expansion or diversification of the existing industrial unit.
- Shifting of existing industrial unit.
- Service industry/commercial venture like industrial/ warehousing/logistics, canteen, shop, health service which would support the industrial units.

The present capacity in the industrial estates is detailed in Table 5.1.

53. The Corporation is in the process of acquiring land admeasuring 13.95 hectares at Dhargal village in Pernem *taluka* to implement Integrated Infrastructure Development (IID), a Central Government Assisted Scheme of the Ministry of Industry. The government has also announced earmarking of land in South Goa for setting up Food Processing Park.

54. The existing land in industrial estates alongwith the proposed plans are sufficient for meeting the land requirement for industrial development for the next five years.

55. The Corporation has also taken steps for upgradation of ITIs at Vasco and Kakoda.

56. It is evident from Table 5.1 that the industrial estate at Verna has been the most developed. It also has the best facilities and connectivity among all the industrial estates in Goa.

57. Kundaim industrial estate has also received good response from the industry.

58. Corlim industrial estate, one of the oldest, is suitable for SSI units but lacks basic facilities. Similar is the state of Sancoale industrial estate.

59. Kakoda industrial estate which was developed at a later stage, has not received expected response due to poor facilities and connectivity issues.

60. Shiroda and Sanguem industrial estates are in the early stages of development.

61. Some of the common gaps existing in the capacity of industrial estates with respect to physical infrastructure are given below.

62. The quality of power is a major issue even in the industrial estates at Verna and Kundaim. The situation at other industrial estates is not only of the quality of power but also the regular supply of the same. Frequent power surges has severely affected electronic equipments, and irregular power supply situation has forced the industry to invest in DG sets.

63. Lack of regular water supply is another major issue. Even units in Verna have a cause to worry about shortage of public water supply.

64. Condition of internal roads in almost all the industrial estates is pathetic, except Verna and Kundaim.

65. Movement of containers is severely constrained in Goa since there is no road exclusively dedicated for movement of containers. Presently the movement takes place only at night hours. Besides, in a number of industrial estates, the roads are not built to ply container trailers.

66. Telecom facilities need total revamp in all the industrial estates. Verna and Kundaim, which have a large number of industries will need the highest level of telecom connectivity.

Existing Infrastructure Facilities

Water

67. Water supply and sewerage facilities are currently provided by Public Works Department in Goa and treated as public services. The non-market framework of providing these services has brought in substantial inefficiencies in the system such as high leakage rates, tampered and non-working metres, theft of water and poor billing and collection. The total revenues generated from the water and sewerage charges do not even cover operations and maintenance (O&M) costs. This has led to significant degradation of existing assets due to poor maintenance.

68. The service levels of water supply are very poor and every commercial establishment and industrial unit has to provide adequate capacity sump tanks, overhead tanks and pumps to mitigate this problem resulting in huge unnecessary investments to the consumer.

69. During summer months, the situation is worst since the water level of some of the reservoirs at the source of the water treatment plants go below drawing limits. It is ironic that a state like Goa, which is blessed with over 3000 mm of rainfall per annum, should have perennial water shortages.

70. Bore wells are not very successful in Goa and hence some industries are surviving on water supplied by water tankers.

71. The actual industrial demand for 2001 is as per the figures estimated by the PWD, Government of Goa.

TABLE 5.10

Industrial Water Demand

Taluka	*Industrial Water Demand (MLD)*		
	2001 (Actual)	*Additional (2011)*	*Total (2011)*
North Goa			
Ponda	9.000	1.935	10.935
Tiswadi	3.500	0.225	3.725
Bardez	5.640	7.754	13.394
Pernem	0.870	46.607	47.477
Bicholim	1.140	19.175	20.315
Satari	0.720	10.229	10.949
South Goa			
Canacona	0.760	13.950	14.710
Sanguem	0.510	3.600	4.110
Quepem	0.950	0.567	1.517
Salcete	15.000	35.109	50.109
Mormugao	20.000	2.813	22.813
Total	58.090	141.962	200.052

Source: Regional Plan, 2011.

72. Industrial water requirements have been estimated for proposed industrial estates that are to be developed by GIDC by the year 2011 at Bethora (Phase-II) and Madkai (Phase-II) in Ponda *taluka*; Sal and Nanora in Bicholim *taluka*; Salvador do Mundo and Pilerne (Phase-II) in Bardez *taluka*; Dhargal in Pernem *taluka*; Bordem, Latambarcem, Ladphi and Dumacem in Bicholim *taluka*; Honda (Phase-III), Pissurlem and Buimpal in Satari *taluka*; Poinguinim in Canacona *taluka*; Pilliem in Sanguem *taluka*; Kakoda (Phase-III) in Quepem *taluka* and Cuncolim (Phase-II), St. Jose de Areal, Raia and Verna Electronic City in Salcete *taluka*.

73. Besides industrial water requirements for the proposed SEZ's at Verna and Pernem, the proposed airport at Mopa in Pernem *taluka* have been projected.

74. As per conventional norms, an average requirement of 45,000 litres per hectare per day for industrial use has been assumed.

75. The actual industrial demand for the year 2001 is 58 MLD. Based on the above assumptions and norms it has been estimated that the unrestricted industrial demand for the year 2011 is expected to go up to 200 MLD.

76. Following are the proposed/current augmentation works that will improve the current availability of water:

- Selaulim Water Works—II

- Proposed Khandepar Water Works
- Water Works on Tillari Right Bank Canal
- Augmentation of Assnora Water Works
- Augmentation of Sanquelim Water Works
- Augmentation of Dabos Water Works
- Aumentation of Chandel Water Works

77. The following industrial estates need special attention with respect to water supply:

- Kundaim
- Marcaim
- Bethora
- Corlim
- Pilerne
- Tuem

Power

78. The power sector is the heart of the State's economy. Be it in mining or tourism or industry or agriculture or any other priority sector; "Power is the primary catalyst for growth"—neglect power and the whole economy suffers.

79. The current power allocation to Goa from central stations is 320 MW besides generation from the 48 MW combined cycle plant of REL.

80. Seventy-four MW share of Goa's share in western and southern region has been surrendered and has already been re-allocated by the power ministry.

81. The current power availability from national grid and local generation is given below.

TABLE 5.11

Source of Power in Goa

Generating Station	*Goa's Allocated Capacity*
Korba STPS, Chhattisgarh	210 MW
Vindhyanchal STPS, Chhattisgarh	35 MW
Ramagundam STPS, Andhra Pradesh	75 MW
Total allocation from central stations	320 MW
Less : 8% capacity (due to scheduled maintenance, interstate losses, etc.)	26 MW
Power availability from Central Stations	294 MW
Power availability from REL	46 MW
Total power availability in Goa	340 MW
Total peak demand	354 MW
Current peak hour deficit	14 MW

Source: Electricity Dept., Goa.

82. Hence, the common belief that Goa has a lot of excess power is a fallacy. As seen in Table 5.11, in the last financial year (2004-05), Goa has been overdrawing during peak hours for a duration of 3 to 4 hours a day.

Supply Outlook

83. Over the past few years, Goa has witnessed a substantial growth in the industrial and tourism sectors. Consequently, the unrestricted demand for power has grown at the rate of 8 to 10 per cent per annum.

84. There is a huge suppressed demand in the area due to regular load restrictions imposed on existing units and poor voltage conditions which is met through captive generation.

85. Considering that Goa's proposal for an SEZ is approved in the current financial year, the annual growth rate of Goa's power requirements over five years from the year 2007-08 is expected to be at least 15 per cent per annum.

86. There is a huge growth potential in the tourism belt, since a number of large hotels and resorts are in need of quality power.

87. Allocations finalised from the Central sector in the next five years are as follows:

Power Allocation to Goa

Project	*Goa's Future Allocation (MW)*	*Probable Date of Future Allocation (MW)*
Tarapur Atomic Power Station	11	11 MW by April '06
Vindhyanchal	24	12 MW by Feb. '07 12 MW by Aug. '07
Sipat	36	24 MW by Jun. '07 12 MW by Feb. '09
Neyveli Lignite Corporation	21	21 MW between FY 2009 and 2011
Total additional allocation	92	

Demand and Supply of Power in Goa

Year	*2004-05*	*2005-06*	*2006-07*	*2007-08*	*2008-09*	*2009-10*
Projected peak demand (MW)	354	389	447	514	591	591
Estimated demand growth rate (%)		8%	10%	15%	15%	15%
Central allocation MW)	320	320	343	379	391	412
Availability from Central stations (MW)	294	294	316	349	360	379
Availability from Goa (MW)	46	46	46	46	46	46
Total availability (MW)	340	340	362	395	406	425
Projected peak surplus/ deficit (MW)	-14	-49	-85	-119	-185	-166

Additional Sources of Power

88. Even with the additional allocations from central power plants to the tune of 92 MW in the next five years and the proposed initiatives in the demand side management, Goa is still going to face a peak hour deficit of between 50 MW to 150 MW over the next five years.

89. Power generation potential within Goa at economical cost is not feasible due to the following factors:

- Non-availability of coal in close and it is uneconomical to transport coal from Indian coal fields.
- Non-availability of gas for power generation.

90. Goa is an environmentally sensitive state because of its small size, fragile ecology, tourism dependence and a high level of environmental consciousness. Hence any thermal, nuclear or large hydro plant is ruled out.

91. Liquid fuel plants are subject to highly volatile international petroleum prices, which in recent year have fluctuated between $20 to $55 per barrel of crude oil.

Transportation

92. Transportation is one of the key infrastructure needs in a developing economy. Transportation caters to the movement of people and goods, both within the State and other parts of the country as well as overseas.

93. In Goa, the transportation network consists of airways, railways, waterways and roadways.

Airways

94. Presently Goa has an international airport at Dabolim, which caters to domestic fights connecting major cities like Mumbai, Delhi, Ahmedabad, Pune, Hyderabad, Bangalore, Thiruvananthapuram and Cochin. Besides it caters to scheduled international flights to the Middle East as well as international charter flights from United Kingdom, Sweden, Denmark, Finland, Holland, Germany and Russia.

95. Amongst all the airports in India, Dabolim International Airport is rated 9th in terms of passenger traffic. The total passenger traffic handled by Dabolim International Airport in 2004-05 was 1,266,588 out of which the share of domestic traffic was 72 per cent. The mix of passengers consisted of leisure (69%) followed by business (19%) and international connections (12%). Besides, the airport handled 5,156 tonnes of cargo, out of which the share of domestic traffic was 70 per cent. The total aircraft movements for the year 2004-05 were 13,485 nos; out of which the share of domestic aircraft movements was nearly 80 per cent.

96. Over the last four years, the aircraft movement to and from Dabolim airport has shown a compounded growth rate of 14.33 per cent per annum. The international passenger traffic has shown a compounded growth rate of 10 per cent per annum, while the domestic passenger traffic has showed a compounded growth rate of 11.02 per cent per annum. The Dabolim airport is under the control of the Indian Navy, which uses the airport for their training activities, besides handling civilian flights. Perhaps the most constraining aspect of the civilian operations at airport is the limitations associated with the military operation, as this precludes access by domestic as well as foreign carriers for operation between 8:30 and 13:00 Monday-Friday. The morning embargo on civilian flight operations provides only a very narrow window for flights during the peak departure bank. The other factors that affect flight operation are that the airport is not open for night operation. Besides, the airport offers no overnight parking capability and as such the, domestic carriers do not offer early morning departures.

97. Cargo movement through this airport has shown a low growth rate of only 5.46 per cent, primarily because cargo handling facilities is currently not available, especially for handling perishable goods.

98. The Dabolim airport is over-congested and still at a primitive state in comparison to modern international airports.

99. At present there is only one runway which handles a wide range of aircrafts from Turbo props (ATR32) to narrow bodied jet aircraft like B737-800 and A320 to wide bodied jet aircraft like A300 and MD-11. However, while the current airfield has more than adequate capacity, there is effectively no room to expand other necessary components. The apron area is limited and can only accommodate a maximum of five narrow bodied aircraft. If two of the aircraft are wide bodies, then two other parking locations become inaccessible or unusable.

100. The Dabolim terminal has no contact stands (parking bays), it only has remote stands and as such does not possess boarding bridges and fixed bridges allowing direct access to aircrafts.

101. The airport has a CAT-I Instrument Landing System and other navigational aids, which needs to be upgraded to facilitate night operations besides landing in poor weather conditions.

102. The Dabolim terminal is composed of two distinctive parts for domestic and international traffic and as such does not benefit from a synergy of capacities. The international terminal is designed for 250 arrivals and 250

departures simultaneously, while the domestic terminal is designed for 350 arrivals and 350 departures simultaneously. The total gross area of Dabolim terminal is around 12000 m^2, which is quite small, and does not have the capacity to handle more that two overlapping wide body aircraft departures. The terminal building for domestic as well as international arrivals and departures lack adequate counters for check-ins, customs, security and immigration. The waiting lounges, baggage collection areas as well as facilities for restaurants, shops and cloakrooms are inadequate and not to international standards.

Railways

103. With the commissioning of the Konkan Railway and the conversion of the South Central Railway line from Vasco-Miraj into broadguage, Goa has developed excellent railway connectivity to the rest of the country.

104. The Konkan railway which runs along the entire west coast of India, enters Goa from Maharashtra border at Pernem and cuts the State from the north to south exiting Goa into Karnataka at Pollem. The total length of the railway in Goa is 129 kms. Presently, there are stations at Pernem, Tivim, Karmali, Margao and Chaudi along this line. Besides the goods traffic, there are direct north bound passenger trains to Mumbai and Delhi and southbound passenger trains to Mangalore and Thiruvananthapuram from Goa.

105. The South Central Railway line from Vasco-Londa-Hospet-Miraj provides a major linkage of the Mormugao Port to the hinterland of the country. Besides the goods traffic, there are direct passenger trains to Miraj, Pune, Delhi, Bangalore, Hyderabad and Chennai.

106. In many other places, the railways constitute the backbone of the public mass transportation system as its operating cost per passenger (km) is much lower as compared to road transport, besides reducing pollution.

107. The local passenger traffic on the South Central Railway is fairly good because it connects three major population centres of Vasco, Margao and Sanvordem, besides smaller stations at Cansaulim, Majorda, Seraulim, Chandor, Collem, Dudhsagar, etc.

108. The local passenger traffic on the Konkan railway is not high primarily because with the exception of Margao, this route bypasses the major population centres and traffic generation points.

109. However, with the addition of a couple of spur lines and building of additional stations on the existing Konkan railway stations, the Konkan railway has the potential of becoming a major part of the public transportation in Goa.

110. All the proposed railway stations can be integrated with the public bus transport to form a convenient, efficient and cost effective rail-road public transportation system, thus relieving the growing pressure on roads due to the reduction of private vehicles, currently used as the primary means of commuting.

111. Transportation of cargo by rail is not at a high volume due to lack of easy availability of wagons.

Inland Waterways

112. Currently the Mandovi and Zuari rivers are used for transportation of around 15 million tonnes of iron ore from the mines in the Bicholim, Satari and Sanguem *talukas* to the Mormugao Port. The Cumbarjua canal, which links the rivers Mandovi and Zuari is also used for iron ore transportation in the monsoon months, since the mouth of the river Mandovi is not navigable during the monsoon due to the formation of sand bars during this period. However, due to limited draft of the canal, only smaller sized barges can navigate at high tide through the canal. Besides iron ore, imported coal is also transported from the port to a coking plant at Amona.

Port

113. Mormugao port, one of the oldest ports on the west coast of India, enjoys an enviable position amongst the major ports in India.

114. During the financial year 2003-04, the port handled traffic of 27.87 million tonnes which accounted for 8 per cent of the total traffic of 344.55 million tonnes handled by all the 12 major ports of India.

115. Mormugao port is the premier iron ore exporting port of India with an annual through-put of around 23 million tonnes of iron ore traffic. The port accounts for about 39 per cent of India's iron ore export. Though iron ore is the predominant cargo, there has been a steady increase in liquid bulk and general cargo traffic consisting of 1.32 million tonnes of petroleum products, phosphoric acid, manganese ore, coke, coal, fertiliser, iron and steel, alumina containerised cargo, etc. A quantity of 1,03,014 tonnes of containerised cargo was also handled at the port during the period.

116. The current facilities available at Mormugao port:

- Approach channel,
- Moorings and anchorage,
- Berths,

- Stream loading and transshippers,
- Ship repair facilities,
- Inter-linkages,
- Vessel traffic management system (VTMS), and
- Navigational aids and communication.

117. Mormugao port today stands on the threshold of exciting new times. With the saturation of Mumbai and Nhava Sheva ports, Mormugao port, commanding a strategic position on the coastline of the region and offering a much quicker turn around time, is poised to become a major transit point for trade in goods originating from or destined for Central and North Central India.

118. Mormugao port strives continuously to improve operations and make them more productive and efficient. To this end, a number of projects have been drawn up so as to provide facilities that will cater to the requirements of the anticipated growth in traffic.

Roadways

119. The development of a strong road network is essential to stimulate the economy and sustain a higher growth rate. In India, during the last 50 years, freight and passenger traffic have grown at an annual rate of approximately 10 per cent. In comparison, overall road length has grown at less than 5 per cent per annum. As a result, there is an urgent need to strengthen road infrastructure in the country.

120. Goa has the highest surfaced road density in the country. But even so, the smooth flow of traffic is hindered due to:

- Narrow and winding roads with poor geometrics.
- Potholes due to heavy monsoons and poor construction quality.
- Difficulty in road widening due to construction of housing on the periphery of the roads.

121. The state of Goa faces severe and worsening, strain on capacity as annual growth in road capacity has been less than half the growth in traffic. What is worse is that the national and state highways, which are just 10 per cent of the State's road network but carry 75 per cent of the traffic, have grown at an even lower rate. The emphasis, so far, has been on providing connectivity rather than ensuring mobility on the high-density corridors.

122. One reason for slow growth in road capacity is that access to funds is restricted to inadequate budgetary allocations.

123. The total length of roads in Goa is 9672 kms out of which nearly 71 per cent are surfaced. The density of roads is 2245 kms per 1000 sq. kms of area and 720 kms per lakh population, which is higher than the national average of 730 kms per 1000 sq. kms of area and 284 kms per lakh population.

124. The roads in Goa are classified as national highways, state highways and district roads besides the roads in towns and villages.

125. There are 269 kms of national highways comprising of:

- NH 17 which is part of the west coast highway from Mumbai to Thiruvananthapuram and in Goa runs from the north to south from Patradevi—Mapusa—Panjim—Margao—Cuncolim—Polem for a total distance of 138 kms in the State.
- NH 17A which runs from Vasco to Cortalim for a total distance of 25 kms.
- NH 17B with a proposed four lane configuration runs from Mormugao port to Verna and has been partly completed.
- NH 4A which runs from Panjim to Belgaum to join NH4, which forms a part of the Mumbai—Chennai arm of the 'Golden Quadrilateral' project. In Goa, it runs from west to east from Panjim—Ponda—Dharbandora—Mollem for a total distance of 70 kms in the State.

126. Only around 50 per cent of the national highways in Goa comply with standard two lane highway specifications. There are bottlenecks on many sections of the national highways since they pass through thickly populated areas where there is no scope for widening the existing road besides being accident prone zones. These areas have to be by-passed besides the highway geometrics need to be re-designed to improve traffic flow and ensure safety.

127. The road traffic on national highways is growing at a rate of 9 to 11 per cent, while on the State highways the growth rate is estimated to be 7 to 10 per cent.

Development and Growth Areas

128. Goa being a small state, it can't seek to achieve growth in all areas. Selecting strategic areas will gain a competitive edge in certain fields which will put Goa ahead for 15 or 20 years to come. That will be long enough to have a stable growth and work out the next step forward. During this period it is essential to choose a path that will create jobs and prosperity for Goans.

There is a need to identify key economic activities to focus on and to identify key capabilities that need to be built.

129. Growth areas to be selected should consist of economic activities which:

- Draw on the inherent strengths of the state.
- Can drive future growth.

130. Historically, Goa has been a literate and civil society with exceptional norms of behaviour and relationships which has led to a high quality of life. Therefore, the next logical step is to provide such occupations and technological orientations which would not tear apart the societal fabric established over the last six centuries.

131. Incentives provided by the government have played a significant role in the past in attracting investment to the state. This is understandable since local availability of raw materials or the size of the local market cannot be considered as significant factors in case of Goa for most industries.

132. Large scale conventional manufacturing in Goa will be restricted by a number of factors that render Goa uncompetitive. Such factors include the distance from established sources of raw materials and supplies as well as the distance from major markets, the availability of low cost industrial labour within the state as well as the level of environmental awareness and activism. Given these factors, it is necessary to focus on those manufacturing activities where transportation cost forms a small proportion of the total cost of production and where the environmental impact can be easily controlled by available technology. At the same time, it is necessary to develop household industry as a long term strategy to counter the limitations on conventional manufacturing.

133. The following identified areas of economic activity can be the growth engines of the economy:

Knowledge Economy

134. Rather than remain a traditional manufacturing and labour-oriented state, Goa needs to integrate into the mainstream of the knowledge economy. This will mean the development of educational and training complexes, R&D centres, conference and meeting facilities and a rich cyber network.

IT and ITES

135. Traditional economic activities will continue to play a significant role in the Goan economy. However, it is also necessary to diversify the economy, especially into services. Goa, with its high level of literacy and good quality of life offers a perfect location for emerging areas like IT, ITES and research activities.

136. The quality of life that Goa has to offer to professionals combined with the high number of graduates joining the job market in Goa creates the right foundation for IT-enabled services in Goa. The IT sector should cover not only IT software development but also broader IT-enabled services like back-office processing, medical transcription and multimedia based work. These areas will absorb local youth as well as lay the foundation for movements up the value chain of IT services over a period of time.

137. IT has been hailed as the industry of the future as it is expected to completely revolutionise almost every aspect of our daily life. It is an industry which has almost unlimited opportunities, is not affected by physical barriers, involves great application of human mind, gives the highest value in terms of revenues, exploits hardly any natural resources and does not pollute the environment.

138. Focus can also be made on R&D projects. Goa could aim to develop a niche in R&D activities over a period of time.

139. Development of a reliable broadband connectivity will be a critical success factor. The issue of connectivity must be linked to existing and potential initiatives for laying optical fibre cables (OFC) links within Goa or to the setting up of international gateways in the State.

Marine Products

140. Goa, with its coastline of more than 100 kms, 250 kms of inland waterways and a total area of 100 h.a. of water bodies in the form of tanks, provides a good resource base for developing this industry. The share of marine products in the NSDP in 2002-03 was 1.8 per cent. Majority of the fish catch in Goa is exported. There is tremendous potential for export of shrimps, squid, cuttlefish, etc.

Electronic Hardware

141. Electronic hardware is another sector that is suitable for Goa owing to its requirement of skilled manpower, high value addition, sophisticated manufacturing processes and minimal environment pollution. India is receiving more attention as a hub for manufacture of components and equipment sub-assemblies. The equipment market is expected to grow alongwith the massive expansion of the telecom network and higher penetration of computers. The consumer electronics segment has also started showing a major demand revival.

This creates multiple opportunities in the sector. This highly technology driven industry can also be a major foreign exchange earner in the hardware sector.

Shopping Destination and Trading Hub

142. The feature of Goa as a leisure destination can be further supplemented by developing world class shopping malls for the tourists. Duty free goods should be made available to foreigners under the bonded warehouse concept. High spending tourists who are now travelling to Dubai and Singapore can be attracted to Goa.

143. Since Goa lacks local availability of raw materials and a developed market, it is most suited as a trading hub for wholesale trade under automatic route. The free trade and warehousing zones proposed in the Foreign Trade Policy seeks to establish veritable trading hubs like Dubai, which had emerged as the world's biggest warehousing/ trading centre.

Agro-based and Food Processing

144. Goa presents immense scope for development of horticultural crops such as cashew, banana, coconut, mango, arecanut, red oil palm, spices like pepper, nutmeg, vanilla, cinnamon, cocoa, vegetables, mushrooms, flowers etc. Local cultivation of food grains, pulses and horticultural products will reduce the dependence on neighbouring states and provide gainful employment and higher earnings to a wider section of locals.

145. Cold storages, food processing units and canning and bottling plants are value multipliers in the agricultural value chain. Besides the general incentives offered to industries, in order to attract investment in this sector, food processing parks need to be set up wherein adequate water and power, besides common solid and liquid waste disposal facilities are available. A good logistic facility with connections to highways, ports and air freight stations in these parks will greatly help.

Pharmaceutical Industries

146. Many foreign companies want to make India as a base for establishing their future R&D operations as the cost of drug development is lower compared to advanced countries. Preference should be given to formulation companies as these do not generate harmful effluents. Development of herbal medicines can also be considered by encouraging plantation of medicinal herbs and plants. Biotechnology could also emerge as a big sector with increasing pressure to create more food using lesser resources. Today, the country is the second-largest producer of food after China.

Household Industries

147. Support to the growth of household industries will encourage entrepreneurship in the State. It will also provide industry with a shadow economy that will make manufacturing costs competitive with other states. Household industries will include handicrafts, cottage and rural industries. The village and small industries may cover wood carving, metal craft, bamboo craft, dolls and toys, embroidery handloom and *khadi* products. Household industries can also help in augmenting income during agricultural lean season.

Carrying Capacity and Sustainable Activity

148. Goa has a robust industrial base contributing to the gross state domestic product (GSDP). The value addition from manufacturing sector in the year 2002-03 (Q) stands at Rs. 2455.57 crore which forms 29.08 per cent of GSDP. The share of secondary sector of GSDP comprising manufacturing (registered), manufacturing (unregistered), electricity, gas and water supply and construction was 37.56 per cent in 2002-03(Q).

Several attempts to bolster industrial growth in Goa in the near past have come unstuck. The new Industrial Policy was unveiled in the year 2003, but the same is not yet adopted. The policy announced various schemes like capital contribution scheme, share capital to local entrepreneurs and self-employed, preferential purchase incentives for SSIs, interest subsidy scheme etc. There is an urgent need to ensure that the pace of industrial development including IT-based industries is accelerated.

149. The share of the manufacturing sector over the last decade has remained steady. Although there is tremendous scope to improve the contribution of this sector, the future growth is dependent on several measures that are required to be undertaken on a fast track basis.

Industrial Estates

150. All the 20 industrial estates have adequate spare land still available. Some of the areas are already developed and other identified areas can be developed for expansion. There is ample choice for a new investor to decide upon location of a new unit. However, the government needs to pay closer attention to these industrial estates with respect to upgradation of the various infrastructure and other facilities. This will greatly attract the new investors and improve the capacity of the industry to add value.

Workforce

151. The workforce in Goa is well-known for the following attributes—productivity, work attitude, technical skills, English proficiency, dedication, hardworking, keen to upgrade skills and knowledge. These are valuable workforce attributes for any industry.

152. Due to the present level of globalisation, every industry needs to operate at the optimum level of cost and efficiency. In achieving these high levels, the quality of the workforce is a crucial factor. This is amply evident from the fact that the calculation of Economic Value Added (EVA) has become a common practice in the industry. EVA tracks the quality of the workforce alongwith other important factors.

153. The above-mentioned attributes can only be enhanced by adding new skills required by the industry and by improving the existing skills. The Government can ensure this by putting more stress on worker training and scholarship programmes. Private initiative in the field of education will ensure a steady stream of graduates required by the industry.

Logistics

154. Having a port in Goa has been a great boon for the local industry. Industries that are dependent on imports and exports have locational advantage by setting up in Goa. The availability of port facilities is one of the big factors for prospective investors.

155. The rail network and the road network linkages have also been facilitating the industry to add value. Bulk carriage of goods by rail needs improvement to improve the capacity and frequency. De-congestion on the highways and the internal roads will also be greatly beneficial.

Technology

156. Goa has a fairly broadbased coverage of OFC network that caters to the communication needs. The telecom density in the state is one of the highest in the country. With the Government stress to further improve broadband connectivity, Goa can become one of the best technology savvy states in the country.

157. Use of technology has immense advantages for the industry. It is the ability to develop and exploit knowledge that will set apart industries in the future. Since Goa has great potential in this area, the ability for the local industry to exploit the situation cannot be doubted.

Socio-Political Stability

158. The social infrastructure in Goa is among the best in the country. A high social index is indicative of the stage of development of the state. Low crime rate, good health care facilities, excellent education system, good quality of life, etc., are positive signs for the industry.

159. Goa does not rank very high on political stability. This may explain the stagnant growth of industries during the last 7-8 years. Improvement on the political front can unleash the hidden potential in Goa.

Administrative Reforms

160. The Industrial Policy announced by the government in 2003 needs to be adopted in letter and spirit. This will spell out the direction for the industry and the commitment of the government for economic reforms and creation of industry-friendly atmosphere in the State.

161. The State needs to improve upon the approval procedure for new set-ups. It needs to move up in line with the countries like China and Singapore.

162. The bureaucracy needs to realise the importance of speedier clearances. Investors do not like to get tangled in nerve-wrecking procedural hassles.

Strengths, Weaknesses, Opportunities and Threats

Strengths

- High "top-of-the-mind" recall on account of its strong presence in the world tourism circuit—this has given tourism the status of an industry in Goa.
- Good social infrastructure—higher literacy rates, good birth rate, infant mortality rate etc. All plus points for high value added industrial development.
- Good law and order situation—reduces the ill effects of trade union activism.
- Availability of English speaking workforce—boon for IT and ITES industries as well as MNCs.
- High per capita income and urbanisation—makes it easier to push through economic agenda and to build on strong foundation.
- Proximity to fast growing metros—Mumbai, Bangalore, Pune.

Weaknesses

- Limited local availability of raw materials and supplies.

- Relatively small local market.
- Limited skill base of workforce.
- Fragile eco-system.
- Transportation networks are not adequate.
- Infrastructure bottlenecks.
- Insignificant share of FDI or exports.
- Being a smaller state, the state capacity is weak.
- Higher unit cost of public services.
- State government has not yet approved the industrial policy.

Opportunities

- Strong base of high per capita income to built up on.
- Congestion at ports at Mumbai creates a good opportunity for MPT to be developed as a backup.
- The IT capital of India—Bangalore seems saturated. Big IT firms are looking to move to other places.
- Comparative/competitive advantages in select areas.
- Potential for economic diversification—has been identified by various magazine surveys as a new growth area amongst the different states in the country.

Threats

- High dependence on tourism and mining.
- Political flux can potentially dissuade serious investors from outside the State.

Outlook: Possible Scenarios in the Short, Medium and Long Term

Short Term

163. The future growth of the manufacturing sector in Goa will be determined by the measures taken in the short term. On the government policy front, there has not been much activity. The Industrial Policy, which was formulated in 2003, has remained more on paper as a statement of intent. Going by the business as usual scenario, this trend will continue in the short term. A number of policy decisions are likely to be taken as a measure to emulate other states. Ground level implementation measures may lack the focus that is essential in today's competitive world. The age-old dependence on mining and tourism is likely to prolong the absence of aggressive focus on the industrial front. The existing industries in Goa are likely to face stiff competition from industries located in other states. In the absence of financial assistance and other serious incentives, the survival of some of the SSI units will be threatened. Existing large and medium scale units will face the effect of strains on the infrastructure, particularly in the areas of power and logistics. Delays in the approval mechanism and pressures on the environment front are likely to keep away the big investors. The tourism sector will continue to bring in the big bucks. However, the mining sector is likely to face the downturn of the cycle in the next few years.

164. The worst-case scenario will be characterised by political instability. This scenario envisages the creation of fear and uncertainty among the existing business community. Future expansion plans or new investment plans will be put on the backburner. The realisation will dawn that Goa has already missed the bus on the manufacturing front. Increasing revenues from tourism will create a dangerous sense of complacency in other sectors. The worst-case scenario for manufacturing sector will be the further stagnation of the sector, absence of fresh initiatives on the part of the government in the short term and a declining value added of the sector.

165. The best-case scenario in the short term will be highlighted by active involvement of the government in facilitation of industrial development through provision of required infrastructure, other incentives and financial assistance. The short-term measures taken by the government will be vital for sustainable growth of manufacturing sector in the medium to long term. Near term actions will signal the commitment of the government to the investor community as well as build consensus within the State. The high impact near term actions will include a high profile marketing campaign to promote Goa as an investment destination. There will be a stress on administrative reforms that will ensure sustainable development of the sector over a longer term. The Government will be a facilitator in major projects with the actual investment being taken up by private sector investors. The projects will be chosen so as to enable a shift towards areas with higher value addition. Policies will be made to encourage household industries. The Industrial Policy 2003 will be amended and made more broad-based as well as more relevant to the times. A detailed plan will be made to upgrade the infrastructure facilities like power, water, port, airport, rail linkages, roads, telecom, warehouse facilities, effluent treatment, etc. Education system will be overhauled and training institutes will be upgraded and diversified.

Medium Term

166. Under the business as usual scenario, in the medium term the manufacturing sector will get added attention to revive it out of stagnation. The Government involves the industry and trade associations to suggest measures to improve the growth of the manufacturing sector. The trigger for this action will be the declining tax and non-tax revenues of the government. The period will be marked by a reduction in the contribution of the mining sector and stagnation in the growth of the tourism sector. Strong public opinion will ensure political stability. Industry will feel the earnest need to compete with its counterparts in other industrially developed states. The Government will be forced to seek out big Indian industrial houses to convince them to invest in Goa.

167. The worst-case scenario in the medium term will be marked by the pressure on survival of the SSI units and receding bottom lines of a lot of other industries. A number of SSI units will be forced to close down as their products will not be competitive in the market. Lack of incentives and other financial incentives from the government will result in mounting losses. Large-scale retrenchment will put severe pressure on the employment front. Reduction in the value added of the manufacturing sector will affect the overall performance of the state. The local government will need to depend on Central grants for its capital expenditure.

168. In the best-case scenario in the medium term, the manufacturing sector, alongwith tourism sector will play a pivotal role in the growth of the economy. Industrial estates will get a good response in booking of plots for setting up new industries. Exports will surge. Goan industry will be integrated well with the global economy. The living conditions of the local population will be among the best in the country and comparable with the advanced economies. Completion of infrastructure upgradation will improve the delivery efficiencies of the manufacturing industries. Consequent reduction in cost will help the local industries to improve their market share.

Long Term

169. In the business as usual scenario in the long term, Goa will be known more as a prominent tourist destination. Manufacturing sector, although playing an important role in the economy, will not be a high impact sector in the Goan economy. It will grow at a modest 3-4 per cent. The undeveloped and underdeveloped areas are not feeling the positive impact of industrial growth. Lack of human resource development initiatives by the government in the short-term results in shortage of manpower in some areas and excess supply in some other areas in the long term.

170. In the worst-case scenario in the long term, the manufacturing sector is prospering only in a few industries. In most of the areas, they are either closed down or turned sick and on the verge of closing down. Due to its reduced contribution to GDP, the government pays scant attention to the sector. Manufacturing sector becomes the white elephant in the local economy and the tourism and services sector gets the most favoured status. Majority of the population seek their livelihood in tourism and other services related sectors. Investment in some specialised industries is not made due to non-availability of skilled labour.

171. In the best-case scenario in the long term, Goa emerges as an advanced economy with a robust manufacturing sector. All the hitherto undeveloped and underdeveloped areas are covered by large-scale industries. The physical, legal and social infrastructure is of the highest standard. Revamping of the education system and human resource development in the short term has resulted in highly skilled local labour force. The Government runs a lot of investor-friendly schemes like development and expansion incentives, initiatives in new technology, local industry upgrading programme, training and attachment programme, etc.

172. Robust growth of the manufacturing sector will be marked by the following features of the local economy:

- Socio-political stability
- Modern amenities and self-sufficient services including utilities (water and electricity), waste disposal and telecommunication
- Low crime rate
- Excellent education system
- World-class health care system
- Competitive costs
- Skilled and affordable labour
- Housing and recreational facilities.

Chapter 6

Infrastructure, Transportation, Logistics and Integrated Development

Issues and Fiscal Implications

Growth Plans

1. Growth is important for maintaining the high material standard of living currently enjoyed in Goa. Growth generates additional jobs and stimulates new business.

2. Within the next 25 years, about four million new residents will come to Goa. About 90 per cent of those people will settle in Panaji, Margao and Vasco. We have to plan so we can accommodate these new people without adding to urban sprawl, and without undermining existing communities. We must also prepare to handle growth pressures in other parts of the State that are growing quickly.

3. In the past, there has been an ad hoc approach to growth planning, allowing sprawling development and then trying to catch up with the costs of servicing it. Without a long-term plan for supporting and managing growth, Goans will have to experience the negative effects of urban sprawl: traffic congestion, gridlock, worsening air quality, loss of valuable farmlands and green spaces and infrastructure that is worn out or inadequate.

4. Growth planning is vital to building strong communities. Planning for growth will help achieve compact, attractive, transit-oriented communities that are economically successful and maintain a high quality of life for their residents.

5. A growth plan is a tool to help accommodate future population growth in ways that safeguard a high quality of life and ensure economic prosperity. The plan provides direction on how specific geographic areas should grow to provide jobs and homes. The plan also directs the type of infrastructure that will be needed to support that growth, while at the same time protecting valuable water resources, natural heritage, green spaces and agricultural lands.

6. Goa does not have a growth plan and its development plan is not focused on integrated development of different sectors.

Creating Public Infrastructure

7. Public infrastructure is the key driving force for growth. Commonly recognised public infrastructures are roads, railways, ports, hospitals, markets, telecom, water and electricity delivery systems, sewage and waste removal and recycling systems.

8. Amongst emerging public infrastructure are broadband services, educational and sport parks, urban parks, industrial parks, residential parks, entertainment and tourism parks and energy parks.

9. Traditionally different departments have focused on the creation of public infrastructure on an ad hoc basis. However, with the concept of growth plans and integrated development emerges a natural plan for infrastructure for the State's 20-30 year needs. When integrated planning is in place, many simultaneous infrastructure projects emerge as the priority for stimulating growth of the economy. One of the recognised problems of creating such infrastructure is the public financing of the huge sums for such infrastructure.

10. The route of PPP (public-private partnership) in various forms is often regarded as a means to attract private investment into public purpose.

Renewal, Upgradation of Public Infrastructure

11. Infrastructure renewal, maintenance and upgradation is as much a problem in Goa as elsewhere. Although

tourist destinations have their maintenance cycles, the railways, public transport, water, sewage, waste removal all exhibit decay, deterioration and breakdown before renewal or maintenance projects are considered.

12. Again, the PPP route is often regarded as a means to get renewal into the private commercial initiative to resolve the problems associated with public systems' ability to maintain such systems. Public infrastructure often meets the tragedy of the commons as it is owned by no one and used by everyone. The PPP route creates ownership and therefore, a maintenance motive.

Decommissioning Public Infrastructure

13. Old, outdated or decayed infrastructure is not easily identified, classified and decommissioned in Goa as in the rest of India. Naturally there is a long gestation before new infrastructure is created.

14. There is no decommissioning policy as there have been no growth plans; a growth plan should incorporate a decommissioning policy itself.

Growth of Transportation and Logistics

15. The transport, storage and communications industry contributed 7.55 per cent in real terms to the NSDP (Net State Domestic Product) in 2002-03. In the five years between 1998-99 and 2002-03, the industry's economic output has grown 6.22 per cent in real terms. Between 2000-01 and 2002-03, it shows a faster expansion of output with a CAGR (cumulative annual growth rate) of 12.82 per cent. However, over a ten-year period the increase in output of the sector has been more modest, having grown 42.38 per cent over the 1993-94 output.

Transportation and Logistics Strategy

16. While effective transport and logistics ensures the development of single economic space, speeds up the flow of goods, increases the mobility and tourism, allows the transport affordability level that would guarantee social stability, and provides for the development of inter-*taluka* relations and the State labour market, there is no State level integrated strategy for addressing this key sector.

17. Different stakeholders, as users or regulators of this industry sector, view the sector from their point of interaction. Currently there is no focus to integrate this industry sector to create a single economic space and a single labour market in the State.

18. Goa is on the midpoint of the western coast and approximately equidistant from Mumbai, Pune, Bangalore and Hyderabad. Goa's strategic location as a Gateway to India, was used by Vasco da Gama and the Portuguese, but remains unutilised for this advantage today.

Transportation Modes

19. By virtue of its location and geography, Goa is in a position to integrate air, sea, rail and road travel and therefore, present a series of logistic advantages to inter-state and international travel of passengers and cargo. It is in a position to become the hub of people and material movements on the western coast and even take on the traffic that Mumbai cannot handle. As the international hub, it can then create domestic linkages to points of vantage.

20. Goa's multi-modal possibilities have not been exploited and currently there is no integration of passenger or goods movements on different modes.

Interstate Traffic

Passenger Traffic

21. Interstate traffic has grown in Goa and almost 2.5 million people arrived in Goa from different states and countries in 2004.

TABLE 6.1

People Travelling to Goa from 2000 to 2004

Year	*2000*	*2001*	*2002*	*2003*	*2004*
Domestic	976,804	1120,242	1,325,296	1,725,140	2,085,729
Foreign	291,709	260,071	271,645	314,357	363,230
Total	1,268,513	1,380,313	1,596,941	2,039,497	2,448,959
Percentage change	1.9	8.8	15.7	27.7	20.1

Source: Tourist Statistics, Government of Goa, 2004.

22. Specifically the bulk of the people (more than 61 per cent) travel to North Goa *talukas* of Tiswadi and Bardez (more than 55 per cent). In South Goa, which attracts about 38 per cent people, Salcete attracts the bulk of the people (26 per cent).

23. The modal choice of people is not known, however, airline data indicates 1,58,993 passengers, which is 6 per cent of all people travelling to Goa, travelled through the 690 flights that landed in Goa in 2004-05.

24. The balance bulk of people (2,289,966) travelled to Goa by rail or road. Assuming about 50 to 100 interstate buses running full capacity throughout the year from all Goan towns, between 912,500 to 1,825,000 people or 37 to 74 per cent travel to Goa by road. That leaves an approximate 56 to 18 per cent or 1,377,466 to 464,966 persons travelling to Goa by rail.

TABLE 6.2

People Travelling to Various *Talukas* of Goa in 2004

	Domestic	*Foreign*	*Total*
Tiswadi	639,177	75,456	714,633
Salcete	537,736	115,905	653,641
Bardez	511,766	127,110	638,876
Mormugao	233,915	25,389	259,304
Ponda	104,646	533	105,179
Bicholim	16,923	109	17,032
Sanguem	9,959	359	10,318
Canacona	13,910	13,783	27,693
Pernem	17,697	4,586	22,283
Quepem	0	0	0
Satari	0	0	0
Total	2,085,729	363,230	2,448,959

Source: Tourist Statistics, Government of Goa, 2004.

Cargo

25. Volumes and modes of the interstate cargo are not available at the time of writing. In 1998-99, the Goa airport handled 525 tonnes, a mere 0.11 per cent of the country's air cargo. However, the MPT has been handling 30 million tonnes of traffic, a bulk of which is iron ore. The air cargo and the rail cargo could not be ascertained.

Intra-State Traffic

Passenger Traffic

26. There is a high intra-State mobility in Goa. People commute on a daily basis between different towns in each *taluka*. People from the villages move not only to the nearest *taluka* town, but also to towns in other *talukas*. There are 44 towns, a hundred km long coastline of beaches, dozens of churches and temples, apart from 20 industrial estates scattered across the State that are attractors of traffic.

27. The modal choice of people is not known, but the growing ownership of private vehicles suggests a preference to private rather than public transportation.[1] Currently there is no integrated plan to service attractor routes through optimal modes and networks.

TABLE 6.3

Million Tonnes of Traffic at Mormugao Port Trust

Million Tonnes	*2002-03*	*2003-04*	*2004-05*
Exports	19.27	23.4	25.03
Imports	4.38	4.47	5.63
Total traffic	23.65	27.87	30.66

Source: MPT *http://www.mptgoa.com/traffic7.htm*

28. The State owned, Kadamba Transport Corporation (KTC) that runs the public transport network does not currently have any aggressive promotion or policy for increasing use of public transport.

29. Within towns, where distances typically take less than 15 minutes, there is no route optimisation or shuttle or round rail service, resulting in regular traffic congestions.

Cargo

30. The movement of large volumes of cargo between industrial estates, towns and within towns can be significantly reduced by consolidating industrial estates, creating storage hubs and bypass roads to towns. Currently, the major State and National Highways pass through towns.

TABLE 6.4

Growth Vehicles Registered in Goa

	1966	*1971*	*1977*	*1981*	*1987*	*1991*	*1997*	*2001*
Motor cars	329	552	440	633	1,659	17,475	6,936	54,964
Jeeps	71							
Tractors	6		13	15	9	370	15	440
Buses/Mini buses	34	53	65	179	66	2,216	170	3,458
Trucks/Goods vehicles	134	393	533	862	749	14,145	2,110	24,363
Motorcycles/Scooters	419	943	1,934	3,649	11,536	99,572	17,206	239,263
Motorcycles on hire				503	265	3,864	324	4,952
Autorickshaws	0	11	55	67	117	1,513	146	3,110
Motor cabs (taxis)	NA	NA	57	104	254	2,817	378	6,970
Government vehicles	NA	NA	66	113	172	2,301	124	3,410
KTC buses	0	0	0	0	0		0	423
Others	22	0	NA	NA		NA	NA	NA
Total	1,015	1,952	2,417	6,125	14,827	144,273	27,409	341,353

Source: Department of Planning and Statistics.

1. Public transportation includes all vehicle services designed to transport customers on local and regional routes. These services include: private and public buses; trolleybuses; vanpools; heavy and light rail; commuter rail; cable cars; monorails; and ferryboats.

The tremendous growth in registered trucks suggests the large increase in volume of cargo traffic in Goa.

Coordination

31. Currently there is no coordination between different modes of passenger transport: air, water, road and rail to enable passengers to switch the mode easily and inexpensively. More often than not mode switching has a premium due to this absence of coordination.

32. Similarly cargo movements across the State are circuitous and modal shift is both time consuming and expensive.

Tariffs and Rates

33. Rates of intra-state travel are decided in the national/international market for both passenger and cargo. The Government, the RTO and the KTC decide the tariffs and rates of passenger and cargo transportation within the State.

Fiscal Issues for Transportation

34. Subsidy to KTC should shift from covering operators' losses to transport service procurement or a targeted compensation of users' expenses. It is necessary to move away from full-scale funding of commercially viable projects, and concentrate budget resources on the implementation of projects that are most efficient in the socio-economic terms.

35. Budget planning and execution by line item should be based on a programme-and-target approach, and emphasis shall be made on targeted funding of transport projects.

Institutions and Governance

Institutions

36. In Goa as in other states, the PWD is usually the agency for conceptualising, commissioning, operating, maintaining, decommissioning public infrastructures. The Town and Country Planning Department plays some role in conceptualising the region where infrastructure happens. The local urban or rural government authorities are involved in some infrastructure development. The Industrial Development Corporation, the Infotech Corporation, the Economic Development Corporation are some of the government corporations responsible for building various parks. The Housing Board is responsible for housing infrastructure along with the PDAs.

37. Recently Goa created the Goa State Infrastructure Development Corporation for conceptualising, commissioning, operating, maintaining, decommissioning public infrastructures. This corporation has actually initiated PPP for developing public infrastructure, however, it does not have its own growth plan as yet but develops infrastructure on need or ad hoc basis.

Institutions Governing Transportation and Logistics

38. This is one industry sector that has many authorities who play some role in the logistic and mobility advantage of the State. The Transport Ministry and Department, the Home Ministry, the RTO, the police, Town and Country Planning, Kadamba Transport Corporation, private buses and their association, private taxis and their associations, river navigation and captain of ports, railways, MPT, AAI (Airport Authority of India), warehousing corporations etc., are all involved in the governance of the sector.

Role of the State in Transportation

39. Public regulation of transport operations and public financing of individual transport sector components and activities in a market environment remain an objective necessity. In doing that, the State shall proceed from need to reduce its currently excessive involvement in transport operations.

40. The underlying principle of the public transport policy is the separation of transport sector governance from business functions. While restricting its functions as a business entity, the state enhances the efficiency of transport sector regulation using it to improve the quality of transport services and reduce transport-related public costs.

41. Some of the issues that need to be considered in such a policy are:

- The development of transport operations within a unified legal framework;
- The development of all modes on the basis of unified regulatory principles;
- A balanced distribution of budget funds between various modes;
- A coordinated development of the infrastructure of various modes, first and foremost, in transport junctions and accesses to them;
- The development of intermodal operations based on unified engineering and information standards and technologies, and standardised operational documents;

- The coordination of the interests and integration of the efforts of various executive authorities in respect of transport sector development and "matching" of *taluka*-wide transport networks;
- The regulation of intermodal competition;
- The establishment of a common information space in the transport sector;
- The coordination of public and private interests and integration of public and private efforts in transport sector development.

Needs

42. There is obviously a requirement for an overall board or body that can conceptualise and commission public infrastructures. Such a board would comprise stakeholders who develop as well as use such infrastructure and would be appointed on a fixed non-renewable tenure. Such boards would develop and approve the infrastructure plan to match a growth plan.

Infrastructure

43. Transport infrastructure development plays the key role in the success of the transport and logistics sector, as well as the economy.

Transport Corridors

44. Transport corridors form the basis of a spatial model of baseline transport network development. Goa needs to define a set of intra-State corridors for cargo movements as distinct from corridors for passenger movements.

Railways

45. Goa is connected to the Southern and Konkan Railway network. It can therefore, become a hub for traffic across these two distinct networks. The potential for using the MPT to Southern Railways link exists from 1954 but has been inadequately exploited to move goods across from the port as well as to get them to the port.

46. The railways in both these network need renewal and modernisation as well as the development of management information systems. Currently there is no data on the traffic to or from Goa.

47. The modernisation and introduction of remote-diagnosis and low-maintenance automatic, signalling, telemetric, communication and energy equipment as well as the development of comprehensive railway safety systems is necessary. There needs to be a capacity enhancement of major railway lines including a possible "local" service track.

48. The extension of existing lines and the construction of new railway accesses to integrate the industrial areas, mineral deposits, ports and airports needs to be undertaken. The safe development of high-speed (160-200 km/h) and super high-speed (250-350 km/h) passenger traffic to Mumbai, Pune, Hyderabad and Bangalore needs to be explored.

Road Infrastructure

49. There is an urgent need to increasing the carrying capacity of the key national highways to build transport corridors and create bypass to towns. The State highways' capacity may also be expanded through the construction of multilane highways in the existing directions.

50. It is also important to ensure that there is no growth opening onto National/State highways and improvements in traffic management like the construction of interchanges and the reduction of intersections in low-traffic roads. There is urgent need for modernisation and reconstruction of access roads leading to and from railway stations, river and sea ports.

51. New vehicle routes need to be planned to facilitate the optimal distribution of traffic flows bypassing the congested nodes and towns of access.

52. Municipal roads and road networks as well as pedestrian zones should be developed in towns and settlements with due regard for their needs.

53. There is need to establish large terminal facilities, first and foremost, in regions adjacent to the international and national transport corridors. There is also need to introduce an electronic logistic support system for vehicles and freight at major state vehicle control points.

Air Transport

54. Goa needs to look beyond just an international airport to the development of major modern international multimodal transport junction and a hub for passenger and cargo movement in India.

Sea Transport

55. The port industry in Goa needs to diversify in line with the long-term foreign trade development scenarios and the relevant freight traffic structure. It needs capacity enhancement to ensure liquid bulk cargo, coal and fertiliser exports and container processing with a view to increasing the share of domestic ports in foreign trade freight processing.

Inland Water Transport

56. Steps need to be initiated to re-enabling a sustainable and safe navigation in the inland waterways and along the coast.

Pipeline Transport

57. The development of the pipeline transport infrastructure for reliable gas and oil supply is required with due regard for legally established environmental protection requirements.

Town Mobility

58. It is necessary to explore the development of circular and lateral thorough fares in towns with intervening areas as pedestrian zones. Most of Goa's towns are small enough to have a transportation hub outside the city and have shuttle services or a ring train to service people within the city.

59. There is need for the introduction of some charges for the use of the urban road network and restriction of traffic within the urban area. The use of modern traffic management schemes, means and technologies, including the organisation of one-way and reversible should be explored.

60. Goa needs to create a comprehensive advance development of public transport systems as an alternative to car and scooter ownership growth. The development of rapid and off-street transit systems will enable to ease the burden on the roads.

Development and Growth Areas

61. While each of the infrastructure areas need vital attention, their treatment will be left to the infrastructure sections in various chapters. This section will focus on the air and sea ports, given the urgent need to develop multi-modal logistic transportation infrastructure in Goa.

Removal of Gaps

62. The first development area is to establish a baseline transport network without any gaps or "bottlenecks". This will ensure the development of single economic space, speed up the flow of goods, allow the transport affordability level that would guarantee social stability, and provide for the development of inter-*taluka* labour market.

63. At the same time, Goa must reduce the gap between the growing motorisation of within the State and the level of road network development.

64. The state should seek to reduce the freight intensity of the economy and unit transport costs by creating economic conditions for the use of rational goods delivery and distribution schemes and modern passenger service systems.

Diversification

65. There is a need to diversify export and import-related transport infrastructure with a view to enhancing Goa's global competitiveness, strengthening its positions in the traditional markets, and giving it an independent access to new markets.

66. The efforts should not focus on improved reliability of the transport but also increased security and anti-terrorist safety of the transport system.

Transport Hub

67. An accelerated development of the road network would facilitate the growth of the road transport share in the transport balance, which is required for market development. It would also enhance the mobility of the population and transport accessibility of different areas; improve the living standard due to a better accessibility of educational, medical and cultural services; improve the efficiency of small and medium businesses; and increase the value of land and real estate.

68. The better transport facilities can enable Goa to become a transport and logistics hub, making significant value addition to the economic growth. Goa must therefore, increase the export of transport services, enhance the competitiveness of domestic transporters, and ensure a better utilisation of the transit potential with a view to making the transport sector a GDP growth point.

69. The State should therefore, encourage the process by supporting the establishment of multi-modal logistic centres in the transport infrastructure and multi-modal transport operators in the transport service market, which would facilitate a comprehensive computerisation of the transportation process.

70. The development of multi-modal operations needs to be based, first and foremost, on the best possible use of the capacity for freight traffic containerisation, which requires:

- Increasing the capacity of the existing and establishing new container terminals. In doing that, it would be expedient to combine a few terminals in sea transport hubs with numerous smaller inland facilities within major transport corridors and in the railway network.

- Goa should establish a free economic zone in ports to attract major container traffic in the foreign trade, transit and transshipment sectors.
- Goa should encourage the establishment of container operators in Goa who would specialise in container transit across India along major transport corridors and actively position themselves in the global market of container operations.
- Goa will naturally have to improve customs technologies used in international container operations and create an enabling environment to enhance the production of containers, specialised rolling stock for container operations and equipment for container processing at terminals, taking into account the global trend towards a wider use of larger 40 ft containers, as well as special-purpose containers for chemicals, liquefied gases and refrigerated cargos.

Through-put and Cycle Time

71. Cycle time is critical for building advantage in the logistic business. The through-put should also not be limiting to make the hub uninteresting. With this in mind, modern information and telecommunication technologies should be integrated into the transportation infrastructure.

72. For this there needs to be a harmony between mode-specific information standards that ensure the interaction between and integration of mode-specific information systems that will establish a single information space. This information space should also be common with the authorities engaged in transport sector regulation.

73. The information system should further enable monitoring systems to track container operations and transportation of dangerous cargos and make satellite communication and navigation systems accessible to all transport process participants.

Mormugao Port Trust (MPT) Strengths

74. Mormugao Port is situated in the west of India, at a latitude of 15°25' N and longitude 73°48' E at the mouth of the river Zuari. The port is approximately 370 kms south of Mumbai and 575 kms north of Cochin. It is an open type harbour protected by a breakwater and has an entrance channel with a depth of -14.40 m and width of 250 m.

75. Mormugao Port is one of the oldest ports on the west coast and was developed during the Portuguese regime in Goa, by the West of India Portuguese Guaranteed Railway Company (WIPG). The company owed its origin to the Treaty of Lisbon between the British and Portuguese Governments aimed at union of commercial interests between the then British India and Goa.

76. WIPG constructed the port and associated facilities, which initially comprised quay wall corresponding to the length upto Berth No. 3, a 1176 feet breakwater and metre gauge railway line from Mormugao to Sanvordem. Since then, the port has been adding new structures/ facilities regularly. A Mechanical Ore Handling Plant (MOHP) owned by M/s Chowgule & Co. and with a rated capacity of 600 TPH was commissioned at Berth No. 6 in 1959. After the liberation of Goa and re-union with India in 1962, the administration of the port and connected railway was taken over by the Government of India and the main railway line from Vasco Da Gama was handed over to the South Central Railway. In 1963, the port was declared as a major port under the Indian Ports Act, 1908.

77. Major developments at Mormugao Port was sanctioned by the Government in 1970. Subsequently, an oil berth (Berth No. 8) was commissioned in 1976 and a dedicated berth for handling iron ore (Berth No. 9) equipped with MOHP was commissioned in 1979. Large-scale dredging and reclamation works were also taken up as part of this project.

78. Further, in 1985, a multipurpose general cargo berth (Berth No. 10) was commissioned. Berth Nos. 1, 2 and 3 were decommissioned in 1992 and this area was handed over to M/s Western India Shipyard Ltd. for constructing a modern ship repair facility with a floating dry dock. This facility was commissioned in 1994. The MOHP built by M/s Chowgule and Co. at Berth No. 6, was decommissioned in 1992 after nearly 33 years of service and the area was taken over by the port. In 1994, the port added another multipurpose general cargo berth (Berth No. 11).

79. In 1999, berths 4, 5 and 6 were decommissioned, in the same year; the port signed a concession agreement with M/s ABG Goa Port Ltd. for constructing and operating two modern bulk cargo berths (5A & 6A) in lieu of berths 4, 5 and 6. This facility was made operational in 2004.

80. In addition to the above, the port has also constructed three mooring dolphins, which were commissioned in 2003 for handling bulk cargo. There are also four transshippers which are privately owned, operating in the port's water which compliments berth No. 9. A shallow drafted berth (Berth No. 7) is also

available which primarily caters to shipment of coastal cargo.

Traffic at MPT

81. It can be seen that there is a steady rise in the cargo handled during the last five years. Iron ore is the prime cargo handled through the port accounting to about 80 per cent of the total traffic. Mormugao Port continues to be the premier iron ore handling port of India with a share of about 38 per cent of the total iron ore exported through all the major ports.

TABLE 6.5

Cargo Traffic at MPT

Cargo	*1999-2000*	*2000-01*	*2001-02*	*2002-03*	*2003-04*
Iron ore	14.83	15.66	17.97	18.67	22.94
Coal/Coke	01.22	01.93	02.73	02.52	02.40
Liquid cargo	01.33	01.30	01.49	01.53	01.78
General cargo	00.80	00.70	00.68	00.84	00.65
Containers	00.05	00.04	00.06	00.09	00.10
Total	18.23	19.63	22.93	23.65	27.87

Source: http://www.mptgoa.com

82. The other cargo, the through-put of which is likely to increase is coal/coke. This is primarily due to the requirement of the steel plants situated in the Toranagallu area. Berths 5A and 6A, which have been primarily developed to handle coal/coke traffic has been declared operational w.e.f. 19/6/2004. Full mechanisation of these berths will be achieved by February 2005. Subsequently these berths will have a combined capacity of five million tonnes per annum.

83. Liquid cargo is handled through a dedicated berth *viz.*, Berth No. 8. M/s Indian Oil Corporation acts as a nodal agency for the receipt storage and distribution of POL products through MPT and represents the interests of the oil industry as a whole including HPCL and BPCL. Phosphoric acid is also imported by M/s Zuari Industries Ltd. for their fertiliser plant in Goa. The import volume was 0.31 million tonnes in 2003-04 which they have plans to increase.

84. Containerised cargo which is, handled at Berths 10 and 11 has a very insignificant share (less than one per cent) of the total traffic handled at the port though it has increased in absolute terms from 6635 TEUs in 1999-2000 to 10180 TEUs in 2003-04.

85. The export cargo mainly comprises reefer cargo, metal, metal products and machinery whereas import cargo mainly comprises photographic materials, metal products, chemicals, plastics, pharmaceuticals, foodstuff etc. The port is likely to witness continued increase in the containerised cargo traffic due to improved railway and road connectivity.

86. The other commodities that are handled through the port are cement, H.R. coils, manganese ore, bauxite, pig iron etc. All these cargo are handled through Berths 10 and 11.

Cruise Traffic

87. Apart from the cargo mentioned above, the port also receives cruise vessels. Details of cruise vessels received during the last five years are given below:

TABLE 6.6

Cruise Traffic at MPT

Year	*1999-2000*	*2000-01*	*2001-02*	*2002-03*	*2003-04*
No. of vessels	19	25	11	10	12

Source: http://www.mptgoa.com

88. In the absence of dedicated facilities for handling these vessels, presently Berths 10 and 11 and of late Berth No. 8 are being utilised for berthing of these vessels. Goa has tremendous scope to attract cruise vessels to its shore provided adequate facilities are made available for these vessels. The port intends to create dedicated facilities at Baina for this purpose.

MPT Focus

89. Mormugao Port has been primarily catering to the iron ore trade over the years. With the demand in iron ore on the increase, the port needs to have additional facilities for iron ore handling. The port has to prepare itself to meet this demand and plan the facilities with adequate capacity. Besides, the port also should plan to develop into a multi-commodity port from the status of mono-commodity. The goals and objectives are then set with these underlying plans as follows:

- Retaining its position as the No.1 iron ore handling port of India.
- Developing Mormugao Port as a hub for iron ore export, with mechanised handling from barge mode, rail mode, and midstream handling and handling at moorings. Also, modernising the existing mechanical ore handling plant to increase through-put.
- Creating facilities to attract other general cargo.
- Develop a world-class cruise terminal with integrated facilities to handle containers also.

TABLE 6.7

Capacity of MPT

Facility	*Rated Capacity (Mn Tonnes)*	*Remarks*
Berth No. 9 (Iron ore berth)	10.50	
Berth No. 8 (Liquid cargo berth)	01.50	
Berth No. 10 and 11 (Multipurpose general cargo berths)	2.00	
Berth 5A and 6A (Bulk cargo berths)	05.00	Full capacity will be achieved after total mechanisation by February 2005
Mooring dolphins – 3 nos.	02.50	
Transshippers - 4 nos.	07.50	For handling iron ore
	29.00	

Source: http://www.mptgoa.com

- To achieve the above goals and objectives, various projects have been planned to be taken up which are discussed in subsequent chapters.

Existing Facilities at MPT

90. The capacity of the port at present is shown in Table 6.7.

91. From the above table, the capacity available for various types of cargo can be summarised as follows:

TABLE 6.8

Cargo Capacity at MPT

Type of Cargo	*Capacity (MT)*
Iron ore	20.50
Coal	05.00
POL	01.50
Gen. cargo	02.00
Total	29.00

Source: http://www.mptgoa.com

Projections of Traffic at MPT

92. As per the Vision 2020 report prepared by M/s RITES, the traffic projection for Mormugao Port will be as follows:

93. Looking at the traffic projections and the capacity available at present, the following conclusions can be made with regard to the need for modernisation over the next 10-year period:

94. The projections for coal are about six million tonnes. Berths 5A and 6A, which are mainly meant for handling coal, have a combined capacity of five million tonnes. These berths are operated on BOT basis. It will not be a problem for the BOT operator to suitably augment the capacity as and when the traffic picks up. Hence, there will not be a requirement to create any additional facilities for handling coal.

95. The projection for iron is indicated as 20.00 million tonnes by the year 2016-17. This figure needs to be reviewed. During the year 2003-04, the total iron ore handled through this port is 22.94 million tonnes. During the same year the nearby Panjim Port, which has been declared a minor port, handled 8.09 million tonnes of iron ore. Considering the requirement of growing economies, this increasing trend will continue for some more years. At present there exist a capacity of 20.50 million tonnes in this port exclusively for handling iron ore. The port plans to augment the capacity to 27.50 million tonnes by the year 2006-07 to cater to the increased through-put by

TABLE 6.9

Projections by Rites for MPT

(In million tonnes)

Year	*Liquid Bulk*			*Dry Bulk*			*General Cargo*			*Total*
	POL	*Cok.Coal*	*Iron Ore*	*Fertilisers*	*Other Dry Bulk*	*Other Liquid Bulk*	*Container*	*Cant. (m TEU)*	*Break Bulk*	
2006-07	0.93	6	20	0.13	1.89	0.35	0.10	0.01	0.56	29.96
2011-12	0.87	6	20	0.16	2.44	0.47	0.17	0.01	0.75	30.86
2016-17	0.95	6	20	0.18	2.97	0.55	0.28	0.02	0.97	31.90
2021-22	0.97	6	20	0.20	3.61	0.59	0.41	0.03	1.40	33.18

Source: http://www.mptgoa.com

taking up projects, which are mentioned in the subsequent chapters. Beyond the year 2008, another three million tonnes capacity will be added.

96. The general cargo traffic (excluding liquid bulk and containers) indicated for Mormugao Port by the year 2016-17 is 4.12 million tonnes. The capacity for handling general cargo is 2 million tonnes, which will have to be suitably augmented by creating additional facilities.

97. The projections for container traffic through this port by the year 2016-17 are indicated as 20,000 TEUs. The pace of the growth of container movement through Indian ports has been around 10-12 per cent and is poised for further growth. The growth in container traffic is also being experienced in ports where traditionally container volumes have remained low. Hence, there is a need to create facilities for container handling in such ports. At Mormugao Port the new four lane road connecting the port to NH 17 at Verna is in progress. Once this is completed, the traffic from the port will be able to bypass the Vasco city. With container traffic volumes showing a positive trend, facilities for handling the same will be created. The railways will also have to take up laying a second line to bypass the Braganza Ghat region. These measures will see the container traffic going up at Mormugao Port.

98. Goa being a major tourist destination, there is a big scope for development of cruise tourism. Hence, apart from creating facilities for cargo, it has also been planned to create dedicated facilities for cruise vessels calling at this port. A consultant was appointed to carry out detailed feasibility studies for creating facilities for handling cruise and container vessels at Baina.

99. The above developments, much depends, not only in the creation of the facilities within the port but also providing the other infrastructure, mainly the connectivity.

Connectivity to the Port

Existing Connectivity

100. Good transport linkages between the port and the hinterland and economic development, especially development of port-based industries in the hinterland is crucial for the future growth of any port. Mormugao Port is connected to the hinterland by road, rail and inland waterways.

Road Network

101. Goa is connected to all major towns of not only Maharashtra and Karnataka, but also of the rest of India through the National Highway network: NH 4A, NH 17 and NH 17A. There are 13 National Highways in the hinterland of Mormugao Port passing through the three states of Goa, Maharashtra and Karnataka. Out of the 13 National Highways passing through the hinterland states of Goa, Maharashtra and Karnataka, only 3 National Highways pass through the state of Goa. The important National Highways which connect Goa are:

- NH 4A Belgaum-Anmod-Ponda-Panaji.
- NH 17 Panvel-Mahad-Panaji-Karwar-Mangalore-Cannanore-Calicut-Ferokhkuttipuram-Pudu, Ponnani-Chowghat-Cranganur-Junction with NH 47 at Edapally.
- NH 17A Junction with NH 17 near Cortalim-Mormugao.

102. Thus, it can be seen that the main road connectivity to the port is through NH 17A, which joins the main highway NH 17. The highway NH 17A passes through the congested Vasco city before reaching the port, which is a bottleneck for smooth flow of traffic.

Railway Linkages

103. Goa is connected with Bangalore, Mumbai, Delhi, Mysore and Pune via Londa junction on the Miraj Bangalore sector of the South Western Railways. The current length of this railway network in Goa is only 79 kms. The railway station at Vasco in Goa is situated at about 4 kilometres distance from Mormugao Port.

104. Apart from this, the Konkan Railway with a 105 km stretch in Goa merges with the South Western Railways at Majorda. The Konkan Railway has been a catalyst for the increased tourist influx into Goa, however, the port has not been able to fully exploit this rail network for increasing its throughput.

Inland Waterways

105. Goa is blessed with a good navigable river system throughout the state. These river networks are primarily used for transporting ore. About 80 per cent of the cargo through-put through Mormugao Port is moved through, these river networks. Goa has a total of 353 kms of navigable waterways, of which 253 kms are navigable by large crafts.

106. The river system in Goa consists of the rivers Mandovi, Zuari, Tiracol, Chapora, Talpona, Sal and Galgibaba rivers. The main rivers which are used for transportation of ore to Mormugao Port are the Mandovi and Zuari. There is also a link between these two rivers by means of the Cumberjua canal which allows the diversion of traffic from the Mandovi towards Mormugao Port.

107. The Mandovi and Zuari rivers alongwith the Cumberjua canal offer a good transportation system for iron ore export. A large number of privately owned self-propelled barges of capacities varying from 200 to 2,000 tonnes ply on this river system. The iron ore handled at the port is shipped through barges on waterways. There are more than 30 loading jetties located along the river in mining areas. The ores are transported from the mines to the loading points by road.

Developments Required for Improved Connectivity

108. As mentioned earlier, the existing highway leading to the port passes through the Vasco City, which is already congested. Due to this, certain restrictions have been imposed on the trucks plying in and out of this port. In order to remove this impediment, the National Highways Authority of India has taken up the construction of new highway connectivity to the port, which bypasses the Vasco city. This highway NH 17B of about 18 kms will connect the port to the existing highway NH 17 at Verna.

109. The railway capacity particularly in the South Western Railway sector needs to be augmented. There are severe limitations of transporting cargo in the Vasco-Hospet sections as mentioned below:

- The Kulem-Londa section of about 26 kms comprises the Braganza Ghat which imposes severe restrictions for haulage of cargo.
- The Londa-Dharwar section is saturated with existing level of traffic reaching 134 per cent.

110. To overcome these problems there is an immediate need to construct a new railway line from Kulem to Gunji to double the track capacity at the Ghat section. The Londa Dharwar line and the Hubli-Hospet also needs to be doubled. The railways have taken up the work of laying the Hubli-Ankola line. This work needs to be completed expeditiously. A similar line can also be laid connecting Belgaum to a suitable point on the Konkan network. If this is done, the port will have easy access to the hinterland through the South Western as well as the Konkan Network which will mutually benefit the port as well as the railways.

111. Apart from developing the road and rail networks, the inland water transport system also needs to be fully tapped. At present these rivers are only utilised for transporting iron ore. However, there is a huge potential for making use of these river networks for transporting all types of cargo. A task force has already been formed comprising of Mormugao Port, the State government and Inland Waterways Authority of India to draw out a plan for tapping these river systems.

Airport Location

112. Goa has one airport situated on the Dabolim plateau, which precipitously drops in the Arabian Sea. Its location is excellent. It is near the midpoint of the North and South Goa axis, thus providing equal access to passengers and cargo traffic wanting to get to North Goa and South Goa, and for passengers and cargo traffic from North Goa and South Goa wanting to get to the airport. Verna, Goa's leading industrial estate, is only 14 kms, and other second-rung industrial estates are 30-60 kms away. Momugao Port is 12 kms away. The beach resorts of South Goa are 5-40 kms away, and the beach resorts of North Goa are 30-45 kms. Panaji, the capital of Goa, is around 30 kms away from the airport. The railway station is 10 kms away. Thus, most of the major centres are within a radius of 60 km of the airport.

Airport History

113. The airport at Dabolim was built in 1954 during the Portuguese rule. The first aircraft landed in 1956. Soon after, in the same year, the Portuguese national airlines started flights to Karachi, Daman and Diu. When Goa was liberated from the Portuguese in 1961, the small airport was taken over by the Indian Navy establishing INS Hansa. During the period 1962-1978, civil flights to Goa operated from INS Hansa. In 1978, the civil aviation ministry established a separate terminal at the Dabolim airport for civilian use. This terminal is under the control and management of Airports Authority of India, though the airport is under the control of the Indian Navy.

114. Since then, the growth of the 'civilian' airport has been a story of incremental and ad hoc additions. In 1982-1983 a new terminal was built to receive the heads of states attending the commonwealth head of government meeting (CHOGM) retreat in Goa. In 1984-1986, the runway was extended to 11,500 feet to accommodate bigger aircrafts. Around this time, the tourist traffic to Goa had been growing, and charter planes from Europe started flying to Dabolim airport. In 1986, Air India started international flights to Kuwait, followed by Indian Airlines in 1995. To keep pace with growing domestic and international traffic, including charter flights, two new terminals were constructed, subsuming the terminal built in 1982-83 for the CHOGM retreat. These two new terminals were constructed during the period 1995-1999. In addition, the apron was extended and modern navigation systems installed. In 2000, Dabolim airport was designated an international airport.

Current Status of Airport

115. Despite being a small state with a population of 13 lakhs (0.16 per cent share of India's population), the airport in Goa is the 9th largest in the country accounting for 2 per cent of the air traffic in India (see Table 6.10). It handles more traffic than airports in much larger cities such as Ahmedabad and Pune.

TABLE 6.10

Ranking of Airports in India

Rank	*Airport*	*% Share*
1	Mumbai	27.3
2	Delhi	21.3
3	Chennai	9.4
4	Bangalore	6.5
5	Kolkata	6.3
6	Hyderabad	4.5
7	Cochin	2.7
8	Thiruvananthapuram	2.2
9	Goa	2.0
10	Ahmedabad	2.0
11	Calicut	1.3
12	Guwahati	1.1
13	Pune	1.0
14	Lucknow	0.8
15	Vadodara	0.6
16	Jaipur	0.6
17	Coimbatore	0.6
18	Srinagar	0.5
19	Nagpur	0.5
20	Indore	0.5

Source: Goa Airport.

116. In September 2005, the airport operated 151 regular, weekly flights to 8 domestic and 3 international sectors (see Table 6.11).

TABLE 6.11

Domestic Flights Operating in Goa

Airlines	*Frequency*
Indian Airlines	48
Air Sahara	18
Jet Airways	34
Air Deccan	21
Spice Jet	14
Air India	2
Kingfisher	14
Total	151

Source: Goa Airport.

117. In 2004-05, 714 charter flights landed in Goa from 15 countries (see Table 6.12).

TABLE 6.12

International Flights Operating in Goa

From	*Frequency*
London Gatwick (England)	226
Moscow (Russia)	93
Manchester (England)	125
Brussels (Belgium)	22
Frankfurt (Germany)	26
Zurich (Switzerland)	26
Amsterdam (Holland)	20
Helsinki (Finland)	32
Arlenda (Sweden)	10
Copenhagen (Denmark)	11
Munich (Germany)	25
Ektainburg (Russia)	3
Vienna (Austria)	21
Stockholm (Sweden)	12
Phuket (Thailand)	3
Others	59
Total charter flights	655

Source: Goa Airport.

TABLE 6.13

Growth of Air Traffic in Goa

Year	*1996-97*	*1997-98*	*1998-99*	*1999-2000*	*2000-01*	*2001-02*	*2002-03*	*2003-04*	*2004-05*	*CAGR-1 (Last 8 years)*	*CAGR-2 (Last 4 years)*	*CAGR-3 (Last 1 year)*
Aircrafts												
Number	6,682	6,914	6,774	7,584	7,957	8,112	9,698	11,390	13,485			
% Growth		3.47	-20.2	11.96	4.92	1.95	19.55	17.45	18.39	9.46	14.33	18.39
Passengers												
Domestic	5,57,292	5,08,061	5,14,636	5,46,744	6,08,831	5,91,085	6,29,313	7,10,605	9,06,722			
% Growth		-8.83	1.29	6.24	11.36	-2.91	6.47	12.92	27.6	6.77	11.02	27.6
International	1,60,669	1,87,188	1,93,923	2,12,170	2,67,400	2,00,543	2,29,224	2,79,183	3,59,866			
% Growth		16.51	3.6	9.41	26.03	-25	14.3	21.79	28.9	11.94	10	28.9
Total	7,17,961	6,95,249	7,08,559	7,58,914	8,76,231	7,91,628	8,58,537	9,89,788	12,66,588			
% Growth		-3.16	1.91	7.11	15.46	-9.66	8.45	15.29	27.97	7.92	10.51	27.97

Source: Goa Airport.

Size and Growth of Air Traffic

118. Over the period 1996-97 to 2004-05, the passenger traffic has grown from 7.17 lakhs to 12.66 lakhs registering cumulative annual growth rate (CAGR) of about 8 per cent (see Table 6.13). For the same period, aircraft movements have grown from 6,682 to 13,485 showing a CAGR of about 9.50 per cent. More importantly, during the last one year period 2003-04 to 2004-05, passenger traffic has grown by a stupendous 28 per cent and aircraft movement by about 18 per cent.

119. By the year 2014 the annual passenger traffic is predicted to grow to 41 lakhs, and annual aircraft movement to 39,000 (for projected annual growth rate see Table 6.14).

TABLE 6.14

Growth Forecast for Air Traffic in Goa

	2004-05	*2005-07*	*2007-14*
Aircraft Movements			
Intl. %	11.4	10	10
Dom. %	17.6	12	12
Total %	16.3	11.6	10.5
Passengers			
Intl. %	35	20	12
Dom. %	27	15	10
Total %	30	16.5	11
Cargo (in Mts)			
Intl. %	6	6	6
Dom. %	38	7	7
Total %	28.4	6.8	6.8

Source: Goa Airport.

Capacity of Airport

120. In April 2004, a survey was carried out for the airport traffic. The survey reported that the airport is fully saturated (see Table 6.15).

Problems of the Airport

121. The major problem is that the airport is primarily a naval base of the Indian Navy, and secondarily, it is a civilian airport. This has two effects. First, the navy allows only a few time slots for the use of civilian aircrafts since it has to carry out its own daily naval operations. As a result, 75 per cent of the civilian flights arrive and take-off between 1 pm to 5 pm. This is going to be a major constraint on the growth of the airport. Second, the land required for physical expansion of infrastructure is with the navy, and not with Airport Authority of India.

TABLE 6.15

Capacity of Dabolim Airport in Goa

Facilities	*Area in Sq m*	*Existing Capacity*	*Year of Saturation*
Domestic:		450	Saturated
Arrival	1174		
Departure	1476		
SHA	739		
International :		300	Saturated
Arrival	1962		
Departure	872		
SHA	889		
Car park area	5250	Car : 84	Saturated
		Coaches : 6	
Apron	141.00x90.00	B767 :1	Saturated
	114.20x90.00	A320 : 2	
	140.00x75.00	A330 : 1	
		B737-400 : 1	
		MD11/DC10 : 1	
		6 aircrafts	

Source: Goa Airport.

122. The second problem is that the airport infrastructure is saturated. The terminal building, car park and apron are woefully inadequate to cope with current situation and traffic.

123. The third problem is that every expansion of the airport infrastructure has been done on an ad hoc basis; as a result, the expanded infrastructure has reached a saturation point within 5-10 years.

New International Airport

124. For many years the Goa state government has been considering building a new airport in Mopa in North Goa on the border of Maharashtra. It is only now that it has appointed a French consultancy to prepare a feasibility report of a new international airport at Mopa.

125. There is urgent need to build the infrastructure for the next 25-50 years, instead of planning for 5-10 years as has been the case during the last 25 years.

126. In the 21st century, airports are important gateways to modern cities or modern countries. India is regarded as a rising economic power. Goa, regarded as the most successful small state in India, should plan the airport keeping this in perspective.

127. Opinion in the country is slowly veering to the idea that large infrastructure projects should be done by private sector. The time is propitious to engage the private sector in planning, investing, executing and managing this important airport project.

Roads

128. Goa has the highest surfaced road density in the country. But even so, the smooth flow of traffic is hindered due to:

- Narrow and winding roads with poor geometrics.
- Potholes due to heavy monsoons and poor construction quality.
- Difficulty in road widening due to housing on the periphery of the roads.

129. The State of Goa faces severe, and worsening, strain on capacity as the annual growth in road capacity has been less than half the growth in traffic. What is worse is that the national and state highways, which are just 10 per cent of the State's road network but carry 75 per cent of the traffic, have grown at an even lower rate. The emphasis, so far, has been on providing connectivity rather than ensuring mobility on the high-density corridors and access to funds is restricted to inadequate budgetary allocations.

Augmentation of National and State Highways

130. Just about half of the highways in Goa barely comply with the recommended two lane standards, while the remaining half of the highways can be classified as intermediate lane highways. The current highway capacity has already exceeded at most places. Over 70 per cent of the road traffic in Goa by the year 2011 is projected to be handled on the National Highways and some state highways.

131. It is proposed that the section of NH 17 from Pernem to Bali, NH 4A from Panjim to Ponda and the section of NH 17B from Margao to Ponda be converted to four lane. In addition to the section of NH 4B from Mormugao Port to Verna, the section from Verna to Borim should also be a four lane highway. The current bridges on the rivers Mandovi and Zuari have already reached their peak traffic capacity. Four lane bridges over these two rivers have to be taken up on priority basis. It is also proposed to upgrade the State Highways (SH) and tourism boulevards (TB). A schematic diagram of these recommendations is enclosed.

Public Transportation Systems

132. Inadequate public transportation leads directly to additional private vehicles on the roads, and these roads then become overloaded and chaos prevails. Parking facilities cannot cope with the additional cars, pollution goes up dramatically and accidents take place, leading to unnecessary loss of life. Alternatively, a good public transportation system can ease road congestion, alleviate parking problems, reduce pollution and save lives. At the present stage of development of Goa, a mass transit system is fairly easy to implement, as corridors can be made available and work can progress with disruption to existing traffic. There are a total of 4,82,736 vehicles registered in Goa as on 31st March 2005. This indicates that Goa has one vehicle for every 2.8 people living in the State, which is the highest index in the country. It is imperative to improve the public transportation system in Goa since it is impossible to build enough urban roads and parking capacity to satisfy potential demand.

Pollution Control

133. Buses as well as other modes of public transport like taxis, *rickshaws* and motorcycle use liquid fuels which are highly polluting in terms of SPM, carbon monoxide and nitrous oxides. To reduce pollution levels, it is proposed to make it mandatory for all transport vehicles to switch over to compressed natural gas (CNG), which is more environment friendly and cost effective.

The Inland Water Sector

134. Immediate needs of the inland water sector:

- Comprehensive dredging programme of rivers.
- Provision of navigation aids and channel marking.
- Bunkering and berthing facilities along the river.
- Facilitate private investment in jetties and storage facilities.

Carrying Capacity and Sustainable Activity

135. Unless new infrastructure happens with an integrated growth and development plan, Goa's ability to support its 1.3 million people and 2.5 million people who visit it every year will erode.

136. Given a 20-30 year perspective, Goa will need to support at least 3 million residents and 6-8 million visitors. To enable this to be sustainable, Goa will need to focus on upgrading and adding to its infrastructure.

Interstate

137. The airport is a limiting factor for passenger arrivals from outside the country. While domestic passengers have grown by 20 per cent, foreign passengers have not grown in proportion. This is due to the limited capacity for international flights to land into the existing airport at Dabolim. The carrying capacity for foreign

FIGURE 6.1

Key Inland Waterway Developments

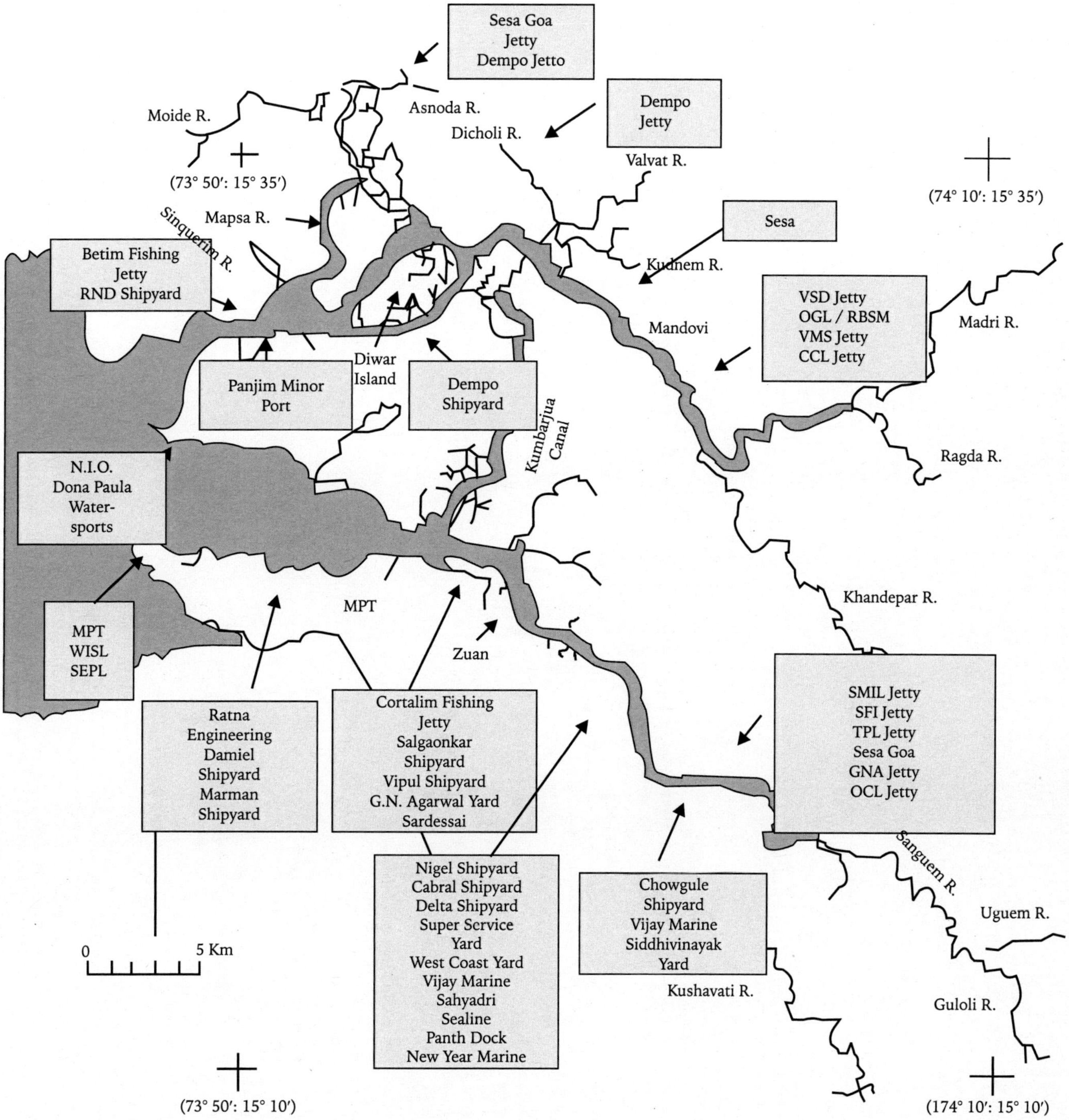

FIGURE 6.2

Goa's Roads: Schematic Diagram of Recommendations

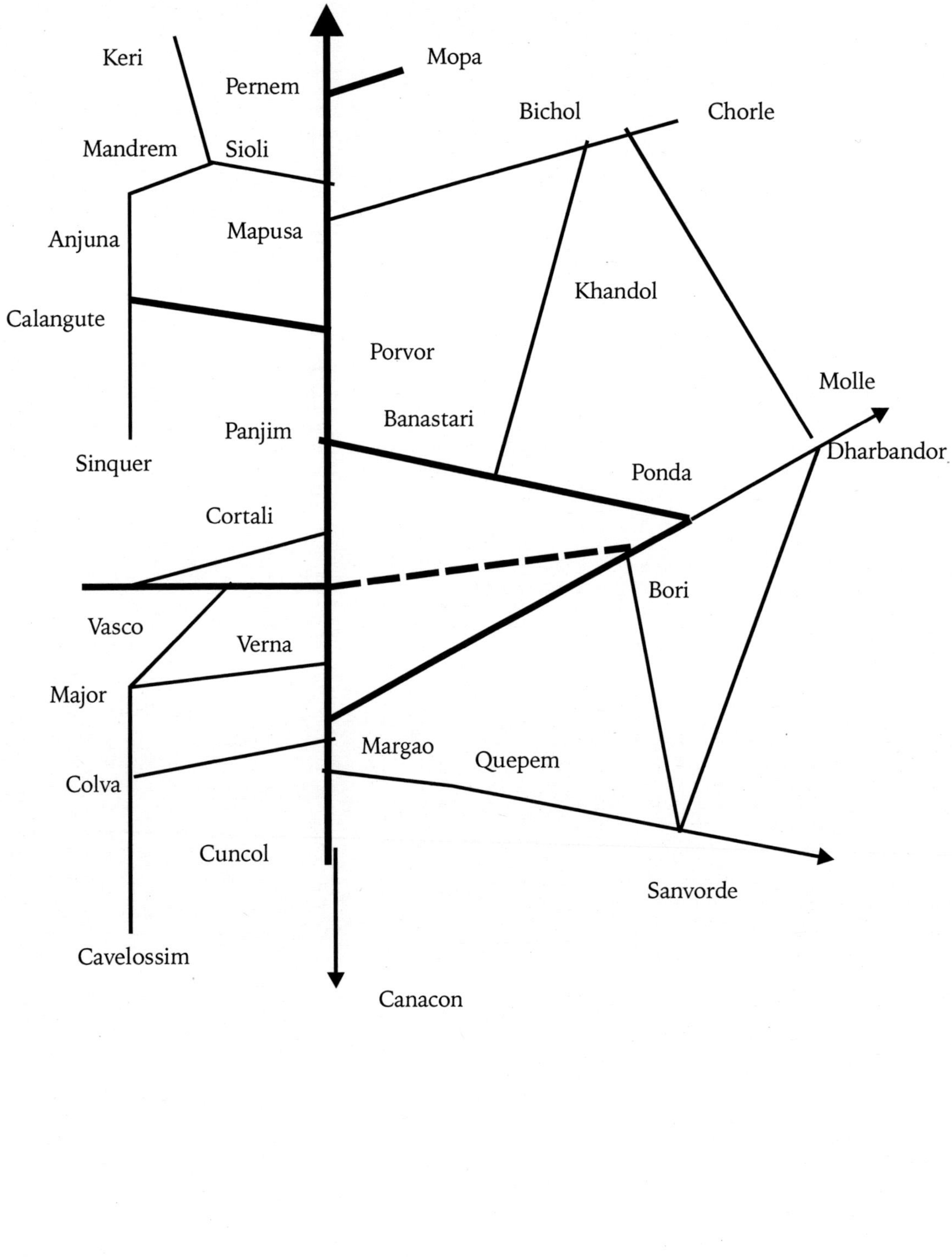

passengers will increase on creation of new infrastructure at the new international airport.

138. Passengers from other states are limited by the limited interstate busses and the limited trains ending or beginning in Goa. Although many trains pass through Goa, they carry a small proportion of people whose destination is Goa.

Inter-town within State

139. The carrying capacity of inter-town traffic is limited by the high volume of private vehicles plying on two lane roads. Many points along the road stretch that narrow down and slow the traffic also limit the carrying capacity. High speed convenient public transport links will increase the carrying capacity between towns.

Intra-town

140. Within a town, carrying capacity is exceeded due to the high volume of private vehicles and a huge volume of daily influx from other locations.

141. While pedestrian zones bring down the carrying capacity, shuttle services that facilitate movement of passengers through town actually increase the carrying capacity.

Strengths, Weaknesses, Opportunities and Threats

Strengths

142. Goa's key strength in infrastructure is the small size of the state. This can facilitate a clear and achievable growth and integrated development. It can build large infrastructure in a coordinated manner.

143. Goa's location approximately in the middle on the western coast with an approximate equidistance from Mumbai, Hyderabad, Pune and Bangalore make it an ideal gateway to India. This is its greatest strength that has been highly underutilised.

Weaknesses

144. The absence of growth and integrated development plans to serve as a basis for infrastructure development over the next 20-50 years is likely to make such projects ad hoc and even controversial.

145. Although boasting a high density of roads, Goa's road network poorly integrates with centres of attraction; rather several centres of attraction have been created (for example 20 industrial estates) without regard to the ability of the road network to cope with the resulting traffic.

Opportunities

146. Goa has a tremendous opportunity to develop in an integrated fashion and to create a infrastructure development plan for the next 50 years. This will ensure adequate economic growth without compromising the sustainable development.

147. A tremendous opportunity to convert Goa into the new gateway to India and a logistic hub is waiting to build a common economic space for Goa and its trade allies. It is capable to facilitate the economy's growth and sustain the high standard of living in the State.

Threats

148. The biggest threat to Goa's infrastructure and integrated development is real estate speculation. With properties caught in real estate interests, key infrastructure may not happen in time scales and at locations which make real economic sense to the State as a whole.

Outlook

Business-As-Usual

149. There will be a lot of political debate on new infrastructure. Renewal and maintenance of existing infrastructure will take a back seat. The infrastructure will run down and the economy will be unable to perform as it did in the past.

150. Under a business-as-usual scenario the State will saturate the people and material throughputs within the economic space. This will naturally stagnate economic growth and the economy will therefore, decline.

Utopia

151. Goa will develop an integrated development and growth plan. Key infrastructure projects will be identified over a 50-year time scale. Projects will be undertaken on innovative PPP ideas irrespective of political changes and purely on the merits of economic sustainability of the State.

152. Goa will emerge as the urban State with state-of-the-art infrastructure and the first developed region in the country. Its economy will boom and the material standard of living of its people will rise.

153. In an utopian scenario, in the medium to long term Goa will have developed multi-modal logistic centres in the transport infrastructure and have many multi-modal transport operators in the transport service market.

154. Given its excellent through-put and cycle-time Goa would be the choice destination for value-added exporting, manufacturing and trading. Due to the excellent connectivity Goa would have attracted premier educational and research centres across the world to create their Asian campus in Goa. Being well connected it allows people to make it their destination of choice for economic activities.

Dystopia

155. There will be a breakdown of existing infrastructure with no renewal. New projects will be ad hoc and create un-coordinated growth of the infrastructure. As a consequence Goa will become a urban slum and the local economy will not be able to sustain the material-standard that exists today.

156. Due to heavy load, the existing Dabolim Airport becomes overburdened and service level falls. With increase in road traffic, congestions are a routine. The sea port declines as iron ore export declines in the world market. The transportation and logistics sector provides poor throughput and cycle time.

157. Companies prefer to move out of Goa as connections are poor. Both the contribution of the sector to NSDP and the NSDP decline.

Recommendations and Development Strategies

158. Goa should create an integrated development and growth plan. Based on such a plan the State should create a master plan of infrastructure development projects for the next 50 years. Such projects should have a timeline, irrespective of changes in the government.

159. Goa should focus in key infrastructure for:

- Airports and seaports and integrated multi-modal logistic hubs.
- Renewable energy generation.
- Waste management.
- Urban housing.
- Water storage and delivery.
- Sewage collection and recycling.
- A hub and spoke system needs to be adopted for the inter city linkages, and a central area such as Verna should be considered for the establishment of a Central Mass Transit Terminus.
- Combinations of: (1) Super Bus (articulated bus) on dedicated High Capacity Bus Corridors for inter city travel, and (2) Light Rail Systems for within city travel can be adopted, integrating the two for maximum efficiency.
- Linkages of the Airport with the Central Mass Transit Terminus and with the main tourist boulevards should be a priority.
- Integrated Road—IWT terminals should be developed on each of the main inland water rivers. These should have adequate equipment for integration of road—water traffic and for transfer of goods from road to water and vice versa.

160. Create a Transport and Logistics Board with representation of all stakeholders to formulate transportation policy and oversee the various bodies involved in the management of the sector.

161. Create an integrated transportation master plan with multi-modal logistic centres, alongwith an international airport.

162. Reduce the number of transportation attractors and create multi-modal logistic centres at each location to enable mode switch.

163. Create a common information space for all transportation sectors.

164. Use the transportation sector as a means to create a common economic space and a state-wide common labour pool.

Chapter 7

Health and Wellness

Issues

1. Goa's basic health indicators are very favourable, with the crude birth and death rates being better than the national average, and not very different from the rates for Kerala, which again has recorded the best performance in the country.

TABLE 7.1

Comparative Health Status Indicators of Goa, 2001

Indicator	*Goa*	*Kerala*	*India*
Crude birth rate	14.3	17.9	25.8
Crude death rate	7.6	6.4	8.5
Infant mortality rate (deaths per 1000 live births).	16	14	68
Maternal mortality rate (deaths per 1000 deliveries)	0.4	1.3	5.4
Children between 12-23 months, who receive all vaccinations (%) (1998-99)	83	89	42
Malnourishment among children (%) (1998-99)	29	37	47

Source: Ministry of Health & Family Welfare, Yearbook, 2001.

By the end of the Eleventh Plan, the Government hopes to bring the IMR down further to eight.

Family Welfare

2. The lower birth rates in the State can be attributed to several factors including higher mean age at marriage for females (25 years), greater female literacy, lower infant mortality, low levels of poverty and overall higher living standards.

3. Nine per cent of births occur within 18 months of a previous birth and 23 per cent occur within 24 months. Forty-six per cent of births occur after an interval of 3 years or more. This is a good indicator, since short birth intervals could adversely affect a mother's health and her children's chances of survival.

TABLE 7.2

Family Welfare Programme

	2002-03			*2004-05*		
Programme	*North*	*South*	*Total*	*North*	*South*	*Total*
I. Family Welfare Programme						
Family Planning Methods						
(i) Sterilisations						
Targets	2929	2316	5245	3156	2344	5500
Achievements	2843	2407	5250	3190	2066	5256
% of Target Achieved	97.06	103.93	100.10	101.08	88.14	95.56
% of Total	20.15	25.36	22.25	24.00	27.13	25.14
(ii) IUD Insertions						
Targets	1745	1305	3050	1815	1260	3075
Achievements	1503	1274	2777	1841	1106	2947
% of Target Achieved	86.13	97.62	91.05	101.43	87.78	95.84
% of Total	10.65	13.42	11.77	13.85	14.52	14.09
(iii) C.C. Users						
Targets	9510	5480	14990	6129	3171	9300
Achievements	6023	3337	9360	6098	2834	8932
% of Target Achieved	63.33	60.89	62.44	99.49	89.37	96.04
% of Total	42.70	35.15	39.66	45.87	37.21	42.72
(iv) Oral Contraceptive Users						
Targets	2235	1465	3700	2290	1910	4200
Achievements	3738	2475	6213	2164	1610	3774
% of Target Achieved	167.25	168.94	167.92	94.50	84.29	89.86
% of Total	26.50	26.07	26.33	16.28	21.14	18.05
Total						
Targets	16419	10566	26985	13390	8685	22075
Achievements	14107	9493	23600	13293	7616	20909
% of Target Achieved	85.92	89.84	87.46	99.28	87.69	94.72

Source: Health Profile Goa, Directorate of Health Services, Government of Goa.

4. However, gender discrimination surfaces here, with the median birth interval being two and half months longer if the previous birth was a boy than if it was a girl, a pattern that may be indicative of son preference.

5. The contraceptive prevalence rate is approximately 48 per cent—roughly the same as the national average. As per NFHS-2, despite the increased emphasis on contraceptive choice and on modern spacing methods in the Family Welfare Programme, and Goan women's increasing knowledge of these methods, female sterilisation continues to dominate the method mix in Goa (59 per cent of total current contraceptive prevalence). However, DHS data indicate that within the public health domain, the use of condoms is the most dominant family planning method (42 per cent).

6. The Directorate of Health Services (2007) also points out that 17 per cent of currently married women in Goa have an unmet need for family planning. In other words, if all of the women who want to space or limit their births were to use family planning, the contraceptive prevalence rate would increase from 48 per cent to 65 per cent.

Maternal Health

7. NFHS-2 findings show that almost all mothers in Goa (96 per cent) have received the minimum recommended antenatal check-ups at the right time (i.e., not later than the second trimester). Tetanus toxoid injections are an essential component of antenatal care, and approximately 86 per cent of all pregnant women receive at least two such injections. Although this figure has not shown any major improvement over NFHS-1, it is heartening to note that the proportion of pregnant women receiving no tetanus toxoid injections declined from 5 per cent to 1 per cent between the two surveys. Iron and folic acid (IFA) supplements to combat nutritional deficiencies in pregnant women are the second major component of antenatal care. Mothers in Goa receive IFA supplements for 95 per cent of births, way above the national average of 58 per cent.

TABLE 7.3

Maternal and Child Health Activities, 2002-03

	2002-03			2004-05		
Programme	*North*	*South*	*Total*	*North*	*South*	*Total*
Maternal health activities						
1 Tetanus for expectant mothers						
TT1	11037	6825	17862	14309	7393	21702
TT2	12466	8384	20850	13918	7357	21275
2 Prophylaxis against nutritional anaemia for expectant mothers						
Targets	13265	13196	26461	15630	11870	27500
Achievements	17417	13739	31156	17131	12347	29478
% of target achieved	131.30	104.11	117.74	109.60	104.02	107.19

Source: Health Profile of Goa, 2004, Directorate of Health Services, Government of Goa, 2004.

8. In Goa, 88 per cent of deliveries take place in health facilities and are attended by health professionals. The corresponding all-India figure is just 42 per cent. A worrisome development noted by the NFHS-2 is that the proportion of babies delivered by caesarean section is 20 per cent, which is firstly, significantly higher than the rest of India (7 per cent) and secondly, higher than was recorded during NFHS-1 (14 per cent). An increase of 6 basis points in the space of six years is much too high.

9. The proportion of babies with low birth weight is an important maternal health indicator, and among births where birth weights are reported, approximately one in four babies weighs less than 2.5 kg. Considering the higher standard of living in the State and the higher use of IFA supplements as compared to the rest of the country, the incidence of low birth weight is unacceptably high.

Reproductive Health

10. Thirty-nine per cent of married women in Goa experience at least one reproductive health problem, and this is one area where Goa is on par with the rest of India (39 per cent). Reproductive health problems are more common among younger married women and women in rural areas. More than half of these women do not seek professional advice or treatment, which is surprising considering the high female literacy and the generally high status of women in the State. The NFHS-2 stresses the need for educating women about these problems and recommends an expansion of counselling and reproductive health services.

11. Within the purview of reproductive health, women are mostly targeted only during their childbearing years, and only from the viewpoint of population control. Women's reproductive health care needs that fall outside the limits of family planning and childcare must be treated by a routinely accessible and efficient system, so as to have a healthy population. Older women need counselling about menopause and its side effects. Services are also needed for occupational health problems, domestic abuse and mental health (Centre for Enquiry into Health and Allied Themes, 1997).

Child Health

Infant and Child Mortality Rates

12. As stated earlier, the IMR in Goa is among the lowest in the country. The child mortality rate is 10.5 deaths per thousand children in the age group 0-5 years.

Immunisation

13. The Universal Immunisation Programme (UIP) was introduced by the Government of India in 1985-86 with the objective to cover at least 85 per cent of all infants against vaccine preventable diseases by 1990. The target now is to achieve 100 per cent immunisation coverage.

TABLE 7.4

Maternal and Child Health Activities, 2002-03

Programme	2002-03 North	2002-03 South	2002-03 Total	2004-05 North	2004-05 South	2004-05 Total
Child health activities						
1 Immunisation						
(i) DPT for children						
Targets	13235	13196	26431	14950	10310	25260
Achievements	13024	12250	25274	12964	11810	24774
% of target achieved	98.41	92.83	95.62	86.72	114.55	98.08
(ii) Polio						
Targets	13235	13196	26431	14750	10310	25060
Achievements	12999	12357	25356	13078	11814	24892
% of target achieved	98.22	93.64	95.93	88.66	114.59	99.33
(iii) B.C.G.						
Targets	13235	13196	26431	14750	10310	25060
Achievements	14872	12168	27040	12057	9933	21990
% of target achieved	112.37	92.21	102.30	81.74	96.34	87.75
(iv) D.T. for children						
Targets	11827	10415	22242	11935	10742	22677
Achievements	11061	9291	20352	12483	11047	23530
% of target achieved	93.52	89.21	91.50	104.59	102.84	103.76
(v) T.T. (10 years)						
Targets	13174	11880	25054	13944	11723	25667
Achievements	12641	10970	23611	15789	11436	27225
% of target achieved	95.95	92.34	94.24	113.23	97.55	106.07
(vi) T.T. (16 years)						
Targets	11754	10385	22139	10144	8270	18414
Achievements	8595	7742	16337	11264	7754	19018
% of target achieved	73.12	74.55	73.79	111.04	93.76	103.28
2 Prophylaxis against nutritional anaemia						
Targets	31200	28800	60000	32500	30000	62500
Achievements	32216	29118	61334	33514	30158	63672
% of target achieved	103.26	101.10	102.22	103.12	100.53	101.88
3 Prophylaxis against blindness due to vitamin A deficiency						
Targets	39630	34550	74180	24936	17229	42165
Achievements	26364	15858	42222	26924	20366	47290
% of target achieved	66.53	45.90	53.24	107.97	118.21	112.15

Source: Health Profile of Goa, 2004, Directorate of Health Services, Government of Goa, 2004.

14. Goa is among the few states where less than 20 per cent of the children in the relevant age groups are not fully immunised, and there are no children who have received no vaccinations at all. Immunisation coverage in Goa is almost double than for India as a whole. The immunisation rate of 83 per cent is higher than the 75 per cent that was recorded during NFHS-1 and the proportion of children who received no vaccination also declined sharply from 5 per cent to 0 per cent.

15. However, immunisation rate of 83 per cent is not good enough in a State that boasts of literacy rates as high as 83 per cent and 91 per cent institutional deliveries.

16. The Pulse Polio Programme was launched all over the country in 1995, in addition to the routine immunisation for polio under the Universal Immunisation Programme so as to achieve zero polio incidence by 2000. Goa has been polio-free since October 1998 (Enterovirus Research Centre, 2004).

17. Table 7.4 above indicates that Goa lags behind on target achievement in two areas—the booster tetanus toxoid dose at 16 years and prophylaxis against blindness due to Vitamin A deficiency. The latter is particularly disturbing considering that a lifelong disability can be averted by the simple administration of this vitamin. As per WHO estimates, with more than 270,000 blind children, India is home to the largest number of blind children in the world. Subsequent data for 2004-05 show a huge improvement in target achievement in this area, but this achievement is more the result of scaling down of target.

Child Morbidity

18. Presented below is child morbidity data for the age group 0-3 years.

19. Acute Respiratory Infection (ARI) is a major cause of illness among infants and children and the leading cause of childhood mortality in the world. NFHS-2 found that 17 per cent of Goan children in the age group of 0-3 years suffer from ARI.

20. Fever is the most common illness among young children, and Goa is no exception.

21. After ARI, diarrhoea is the second most important cause of child mortality in the world. At any given time, 19 per cent of children below the age of 3 years are likely to be suffering from this illness. NFHS-2 indicates that mothers in Goa need to be educated about home management of diarrhoea and recognition of when diarrhoea needs medical attention. Also disturbing is the

fact that 42 per cent of children with diarrhoea are treated with antibiotics and other antidiarrhoeal drugs despite the fact that the use of such medicines is not recommended in the treatment of childhood diarrhoea.

22. All these three childhood illnesses peak at the age of 6 to 11 months.

Morbidity and Mortality

23. Based on the cases treated in the public sector, we can get an idea of the major illnesses that bring people in Goa to government hospitals.

24. Asthma cases are on the rise in Goa, with close to 2 per cent of the total population suffering from this respiratory illness. This prevalence rate is not very different from the all-India level of 2.47 per cent. Expectedly, incidence is higher in the oldest age group, but a greater cause of concern is the relatively high prevalence in the youngest age group of 0-14 years.

25. According to NFHS-2 prevalence of tuberculosis in Goa (0.47%) is lower than in the rest of the country (0.54%). What is alarming, however, is that the incidence of tuberculosis has increased more than two times in the space of just five years (0.18% in 1992-93). It is the population age of 60 and above (1%) where this disease is most widespread.

26. As per Directorate of Health Services (DHS) statistics, under the National Tuberculosis Programme, in 2002-03, there were 2241 patients on treatment, i.e., 0.17 per cent of the population. It is likely that a large number of patients seek treatment within the private sector.

27. Whatever the case, with the increasing migration into this tiny State and the consequent emergence of slums, the incidence is likely to increase. There are at least two factors that require tuberculosis control to be an essential part of Goa's health policy in the coming years:

1) Goa's population is going to age faster than the population in the rest of India.
2) In India, it is the HIV-Tuberculosis co-infection that is responsible for most AIDS-related deaths, and Goa is a State where the HIV-AIDS problem has reached dangerous proportions.

28. The National Tuberculosis Programme needs to be implemented more vigorously in the interests of long-term public health.

29. Malaria is an urban disease, linked to sanitation and waste management, and NFHS-2 reports that malaria incidence is much higher among the urban population (1.27%) than among people living in villages (0.69%). The incidence of malaria decreases with age, children being most susceptible to this debilitating disease.

30. The National Malaria Eradication Programme data for 2003 indicate a total of 11370 cases in that year alone. In subsequent years the number has declined and in 2004-05, the number was 7839. An overwhelming 76 per cent of these cases are among the non-local, i.e., immigrant population. For the civic, sanitation and health authorities of Goa, dealing with this class of immigrants is a matter of immediate concern.

31. Jaundice, which is a water-borne disease, affects approximately 2.2 per cent of the population. People living in rural areas are more prone to this illness (2.4%) than are people from urban areas (2%), an indication of the lower quality of drinking water available in rural areas.

32. HIV/AIDS: This is one of the biggest health challenges facing the entire country and Goa as well. That the HIV/AIDS problem is going to be Goa's most pressing health issue in the coming years can be gauged from the following facts:

i. AIDS is affecting mainly young people in the sexually active age group. The majority of HIV infections (87.7%) are in the age group of 15-44 years. More than half (52.71%) of Goa's population is in this age group.

ii. Most HIV cases in Goa are a result of heterosexual, unprotected sex. The influx of tourists and migrants, and high alcohol consumption are considered to be the major factors leading to sexual promiscuity. Goa is best known as a tourism destination, and tourism is so important that the number of tourists almost equals the population of the State. South Goa (one of the two districts in the State) has been identified as one among the 49 high prevalence districts in the country (UNDP).

iii. Goa has already entered the danger zone of high HIV prevalence (HIV prevalence exceeding 5 per cent among high-risk groups and 1 per cent among antenatal women as per the norms laid down by the National AIDS Control Organisation).

33. The surveillance at STD (Sexually Transmitted Diseases) clinics and MSM (Men having Sex with Men) clinics indicates very high prevalence among these high-risk groups. What is extremely worrisome is that HIV prevalence among antenatal women is above 1 per cent (this low-risk group is taken as proxy for the entire population).

TABLE 7.5

HIV Prevalence, 1998-2004

State	*Sites*	*1998*	*1999*	*2000*	*2001*	*2002*	*2003*	*2004*
Goa	STD 2	19.4	13.5	12.02	15	11.29	14.3	15.77
	ANC 2	1.2	0.8	1.17	0.5	1.38	0.5	1.13
	MSM 1			53.2	50.79	24	30.1	17.0
Maharashtra	STD 9	16	20	18.4	9.2	7.6	10	10.4
	ANC 35	2	2.1	1.12	1.38	1.25	1.25	1.25
Mumbai	STD 3			33.33	21.06	14.84	18.4	15.65
	ANC 6			2	2.25	0.75	1.25	1.12
	IDU 1			23.68	41.37	39.42	24.8	28
	MSM 1			23.94	23.6	16.8	18.8	9.6
	CSW 1			58.67	52.26	54.5	54.29	44.7
Andhra Pradesh	STD 8	24.9	29.5	30	26.6	30.4	19.6	16.4
	ANC 23	2.25	2.6	2	1.5	1.25	1.25	2.25
Karnataka	STD 7	16.7	15.5	12.8	16.4	13.6	10.4	12
	ANC 27	1.75	1	1.68	1.13	1.75	1.25	1.25
	IDU 1	-	1.3	4.23	2	2.26	2.8	0

Note: STD: Sexually Transmitted Diseases; ANC: Antenatal Clinic; IDU: Intravenous Drug Use; MSM: Men having Sex with Men; CSW: Commercial Sex Workers.

Source: National AIDS Control Organisation, 2005.

34. On the basis of the data reported by the Department of Health Services in respect of the number of cases treated in the government hospitals and dispensaries, the following table presents the relative incidence of the communicable diseases.

TABLE 7.6

Incidence of Communicable Diseases, 2003

Disease	*No. of Patients*	*% of Total Patients*
Tuberculosis	2241	11
Leprosy	428	2
Malaria	11370	55
Filaria	276	1
STD	147	1
HIV/AIDS	6212	30
Total	20674	100

Source: Health Profile Goa-2004, Health Intelligence Bureau, Directorate of Health Services.

35. This section presented a picture of the health profile of Goa, with respect to the various communicable diseases. However, the changing demographics of the State and in particular the growing urbanisation and affluence, the shifting age distribution, etc., have altered the epidemiological profile of the population. The increasing occurrence of diseases of affluence such as hypertension, heart disease, cancer, diabetes, mental illness, etc., signal the need for a change in the kind of health services that are available to the people. The data collected and published by the Directorate of Health Services must reflect these changes. This is a prerequisite for framing a long-term health policy for the State.

FIGURE 7.1

Relative Incidence of Communicable Diseases, 2003

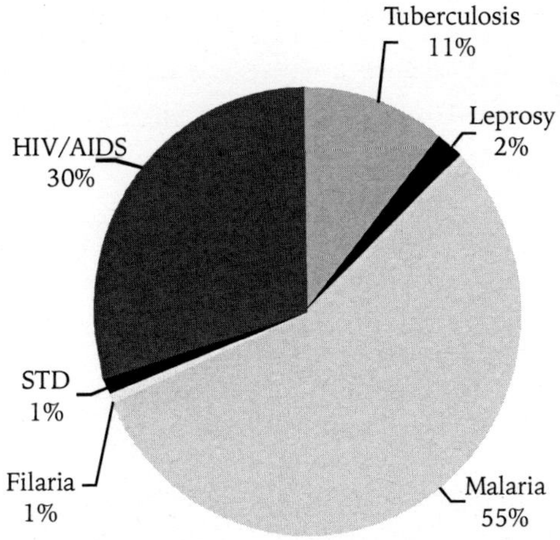

Source: Health Profile Goa-2004, Health Intelligence Bureau, Directorate of Health Services.

Areas of Concern

Malaria and Tuberculosis

36. These are the two communicable diseases that are most commonly treated within the government medical

system. While tuberculosis accounts for a lower proportion of patients, there is likely to be an underreporting of this illness, mainly because not all tuberculosis cases are medically examined and treated. The prevention aspect of the health services delivery system in respect of these diseases must be ramped up. In the case of malaria and tuberculosis, this will require close coordination between the Departments of Health, Water and Sanitation, the Planning and Development Authorities, the State Pollution Control Board and the Municipalities/*Panchayats*.

Reproductive Health Problems

37. Thirty-nine per cent of the State's married women are affected by reproductive health problems, but very few of them seek professional advice and help. It would be very appropriate for the Department of Family Welfare, which basically looks after promotion of contraception and family planning, to turn its attention to issues of women's health and well-being, and to work with the health services in respect of some other key health issues in the State, *viz.*, universal immunisation, HIV/AIDS and stress and mental health. The family planning aspect function of the Department has lost its urgency in view of the State achieving a TFR close to replacement rate.

Iodine Deficiency Diseases (IDDs)

38. The NFHS-2 has highlighted the high use of non-iodised salt (37% of those surveyed) or salt with inadequate iodine levels (20% of those surveyed). Inadequate iodine intake can cause a range of Iodine Deficiency Diseases (IDDs) such as brain disorders, cretinism and other forms of mental retardation, all of which are easily preventable. The health authorities in the State need to take cognizance of the more than 50 per cent of the population that is at risk of contracting IDDs. Collaboration with the Departments of Education, Higher Education, Social Welfare, Family Welfare, etc., would be a first step towards correcting this lacuna.

Tuberculosis Control

39. This is an area that must receive immediate attention in view of the fact that the incidence of the disease has doubled between NFHS-1 and NFHS-2, and also keeping in mind that in developing countries like India, the HIV/AIDS-Tuberculosis combination is what causes most AIDS-related deaths.

HIV/AIDS

40. HIV/AIDS is undoubtedly going to be the biggest and fiercest challenge that the State will face in the years to come; HIV prevalence in the State is already hovering around the danger mark and the conditions in the State are very conducive to the spread of this killer disease. The Goa State AIDS Control Society estimates around 12000 people in Goa living with AIDS (with 772 reported cases); the number of AIDS-related deaths has now reached 217.

41. NHFS-2 indicates a much higher level of AIDS awareness among married women in the age group of 15-49 years in Goa as compared to the rest of India. Seventy-six per cent of the women in this category have heard of AIDS as compared to: (a) 42 per cent Goan women in the same age group 5 years previously i.e., during NFHS-I in 1992-93, and (b) 40 per cent in the rest of the country.

42. However, merely having heard of AIDS cannot be interpreted as knowledge of AIDS. What is important is whether these women know how AIDS can be prevented, and this is where there is major cause for alarm.

- One in four women with knowledge of AIDS had no idea as to how it could be prevented.
- Younger women in the age group of 15-24 years, who are at greater risk of contracting AIDS, are less likely to know of ways to avoid AIDS.
- Most respondents in this age group mentioned avoiding injections and use of clean needles (41%), avoiding sex with commercial sex workers (37%) and having only one sex partner (34%) as the major means of preventing AIDS.
- Only 15 per cent mentioned the use of condoms as a means of preventing this killer disease.

43. The AIDS awareness programme in Goa needs to now focus on the following issues:

- Reaching the women who have never heard of AIDS, and
- Educating women about how AIDS can be avoided and prevented.

44. It must be remembered that this is the section of population that is considered as the general, low-risk population, primarily because of behaviour and lifestyle patterns, and education is the best way to ensure that potential low-risk translates into actual low-risk.

Sanitation

45. Sanitation is an important factor influencing improvements in health status. Data collected in Census 2001 quoted in the National Health Profile, 2005, indicates the percentage of households by toilet availability and type of drainage connectivity. The health

profile notes that in urban areas, the percentage of households not having a toilet is markedly high in the case of Goa (15.26). This statistic must occasion concern, since closed drainage and connectivity for waste water are absolutely vital for preventing the transmission of intestinal infections and spread of many other communicable diseases.

Mental Health and Well-being

46. There are red flags here, indicated by the rising incidence of suicides and self-inflicted injuries, alcoholism, drug dependence and so on. These illnesses are the outcome of stress emanating from the socio-economic changes in the State. The Institute of Psychiatry and Human Behaviour has treated 2040 indoor patients and 40365 outpatients in 2003, which is more than 3 per cent of the total population. If we consider the people visiting private practitioners and the several cases that go untreated because of the social stigma attached to these illnesses, this is clearly an area that should get the immediate attention of the authorities.

Accidents

47. The WHO has predicted that going by current trends, accidents will become the third leading cause of death in India by 2020. Goa has the highest rate of accidental deaths—71 per 100,000 population, far above the national average of 26.4, so in all probability, the WHO's prediction may come true in Goa sooner than in the rest of the country.

48. One distinct possibility here is the introduction of Emergency Medicine as a specialised branch of medicine in the Goa Medical College, to equip doctors with the necessary skills for attending to these types of medical emergencies.

49. In Goa, accidents also include deaths by drowning. In recent times such deaths have reached alarming levels. Police statistics indicate that from 2002 to date, there have been 231 drowning deaths in the State, yielding a frightening average of more than 4 deaths per month (Sudhir, 2006). Almost all these deaths are domestic tourists, many of who enter the sea ignoring signboards, and against the explicit advice of coastguards. The Tourism Department of the State Government needs to do a lot to increase awareness, demarcate danger zones, etc.

Lifestyle Diseases

50. Goa has attained a satisfactory position in respect of the basic health indicators; it is time now for the Government to widen the focus of its health policy to include non-communicable lifestyle diseases such as heart disease, cancer, diabetes, hypertension, liver cirrhosis and so on. The data collection process must also be modified to cover these illnesses, as these will soon replace the older communicable diseases (other than HIV/AIDS) as the major causes of morbidity and mortality in the years to come.

51. An examination of the claims under the Government of Goa's Mediclaim Scheme suggests that these newer diseases are on the rise and people are seeking recourse to private medical care since the requisite facilities are not available in the State. The bulk of the claims are for cardiac cases (75%), which also account for most of the money paid out by the Government under the scheme (84%).

TABLE 7.7

Claims for Compensation under the Mediclaim Scheme of Government of Goa, 2002-03

Disease	*No. of Patients*	*Patients as % of Total*	*Amount Spent (Rs. Lakhs)*	*Amount Spent as % of Total*
Cardiac	766	74.88	541.22	84.01
Cancer	48	4.69	26.2	4.07
Kidney disease	42	4.11	21.58	3.35
MRI scan	40	3.91	3.54	0.55
Ophthalmic	24	2.35	3.81	0.59
Others	103	10.07	47.89	7.43
Total	1023		644.24	

Source: Health Profile Goa-2004, Health Intelligence Bureau, Directorate of Health Services.

Geriatrics

52. The gradual ageing of the population also has implications for health and medicine—geriatrics will have to develop as a branch of medicine to deal with the physiological and mental health needs of senior citizens.

53. A study of older people in Goa by Patel (2001) indicates there is a need to raise awareness about mental disorders such as dementia and depression (which are generally not perceived to be healthy conditions) among older people, within the community and among health professionals, and to improve access to appropriate health care for the elderly with mental illness.

Institutions and Governance

54. The governance of health care provision and health care funding has emerged as an overriding concern for policymakers, health care providers and society at large. In

India this issue is drawing attention mainly because the reforms process has forced the Government of India and State governments to cut back on expenditures and control fiscal deficits. Consequently, the financing of all expenditures has come under severe strain. The rationale behind economic reforms is that governments should reduce their presence and commitment in areas that have no public good characteristics. Health and education are areas that have exceptionally large positive externalities and are recognised the world over as being merit goods. Under such circumstances, it is vital that governments continue to fund public health. However, greater accountability and efficiency is definitely needed, given the scarcity of resources, and it is here that governance can play a crucial role.

55. The recognised significant elements of health governance are multilevel government coordination, linking public and private institutions and regulation to this, we may add three more, *viz.*, inter-departmental coordination, better reporting systems and use of technology.

Multilevel Government Coordination

56. Although health and health care is a State subject, the Government of India intervenes in order to ensure a common degree of health security and standards across the country. There is consequently a need for coordination between the activities and programmes of the Central and State government, to prevent duplication and ensure that scarce resources are put to the best possible use.

Linking Public and Private Institutions

57. Partnerships between the State government, Central government and civil society organisations (NGOs) are one way of ensuring better governance of health care delivery systems and sustainable health security. With such partnerships, the public sector can continue to 'provide' public goods and services, without necessarily 'producing' them itself.

58. As a step in this direction, in January 2003, the Government of India decided to provide vouchers to households below the poverty line to allow them to avail of services from selected health care organisations run by the private sector, including NGOs. The idea was that instead of using scarce funds to set up non-viable health centres, the Government would encourage households to visit private practitioners, with the fees being paid by the Government directly to the private service provider. There is, however, no information on the implementation of the scheme.

59. The Indian Express (2005) recently carried a story about Arunachal Pradesh outsourcing its primary health care services to voluntary agencies and non-commercial hospitals, starting December 2005. Under the new initiative, the State government has announced that one primary health centre (PHC) in each of its 16 districts will now be run by a 'reputed' non-government organisation, voluntary agency or non-commercial hospital. If the pilot project is successful it could be replicated in most of the 84 primary health centres. While the infrastructure for the PHCs—buildings and equipment—will be provided by the state's health department, the agency will use its own medicines, doctors, paramedical and other staff and consumables.

60. It remains to be seen, however, whether the innovative approaches described above will improve the quality of governance. Unless widespread problems like corruption are tackled, there is every possibility that the same problems that plagued the delivery of services by the public sector could impair the functioning of public-private partnerships.

61. In Goa, such public-private partnership is restricted to the private sector providing non-medical services such as food, laundry, etc., to the government-run medical facilities. The Government of Goa has not invited private participation in the provision of medical facilities to the population through the public sector set-up. Is there scope for such partnerships in Goa, and are such partnerships feasible? The answer is a qualified yes. AIDS, mental health, use of tobacco, alcoholism—these are health-related areas where NGOs in Goa are active, and can be fruitful areas of public-private partnerships. However, the caveat mentioned above, about control of corruption, must be taken care of before the State government embarks upon this venture.

Regulation

62. A new regulatory regime is necessary to: (a) ensure quality and equity, (b) expand access and (c) incorporate technology.

Some new laws have in-built provisions to increase the scope of citizens' participation in governance. For e.g., the Electricity Act of 2003 provides for consultations to be held with citizens' groups on regulatory reform including tariff fixation. Similarly, the Consumer Protection Act of 1986 provides for the active participation of consumer groups in enforcing the provisions of the Act. Similar enactments in the area of health governance, health security and health access would go a long way in improving health governance in the State. The end objective of these legislations should be the improvement of transparency and accountability in decision-making.

Inter-Departmental Coordination

63. Health, water, sanitation and pollution are inextricably linked to one another. Goa, like all other states, has created separate departments to look after the development and management of each of these areas. The outcome has been a lack of coordination between the activities and responsibilities of all these departments, with the inevitable impact upon the health of the community. Compounding this confusion is the fact that the physical boundaries of departments and limits of municipalities do not overlap.

64. What is needed is one umbrella Board having jurisdiction over all the departments, municipality wards, and planning and development authorities. While the Chairmen and Directors of all these bodies would be members of the Board, the Board must also have other members. In fact, the Chairman of the Board must not belong to any of these departments or organisations.

Better Reporting Systems

65. Reporting systems is an area characterised by several shortcomings. For instance, there is no data regarding the incidence of new lifestyle diseases such as cancer, heart disease, hypertension, diabetes (including juvenile diabetes), obesity (including childhood obesity), liver cirrhosis, drug addiction and so on. While mental illness is recorded, its components must also find a place in the health reports of the State. Presently, these are major lacunae in the State's database on health. Despite the fact that these are becoming matters of concern, replacing older communicable diseases as the dominant causes of morbidity and mortality, the State government continues to publish data relating only to the latter. A comprehensive database would provide a realistic picture of the overall health and morbidity status of the population and help give direction and focus to the State's health policy.

Technology

66. The State government can use Information and Communication Technology (ICT) to introduce e-governance in Goa.

67. To take an example, the Government of Andhra Pradesh has taken some e-governance initiatives to improve the quality of rural health care in the State. The project involves the use of mobile devices called Personal Digital Assistants (PDAs) for recording all the information about the health conditions of the village. The information server—the PHC computer—collects this information from the PDAs and develops a database, from which the system generates reminders for immunisation, ante and postnatal care, family planning and other scheduled programmes. The system yields broad health indices of:

1. The status of health of children with specific reference to immunisation.
2. The number of immunisations of a particular kind in a particular village.
3. Health of women with specific reference to pregnant women and young women.
4. Status of infectious diseases like TB, malaria etc., as well as incidence of other diseases.

68. The system also helps to work out the requirements of vaccines and drugs of different types needed in the area, as well as the total requirement for the next six months, based on the monthly information.

69. Clearly much can be done through e-governance in the area of health and family welfare, and this is true for Goa as well.

Infrastructure

70. One factor that could be thought of as also contributing to Goa's success in achieving better health indicators is the fairly strong network of public health service facilities.

The State's infrastructure is summarised in Table 7.8.

71. Almost 80 per cent of the hospitals in Goa are in the private sector, but these are small hospitals accounting for just 45 per cent of the total beds. In addition to the hospitals mentioned above, the health infrastructure also includes 1 dental college, 1 college of pharmacy, 1 nursing school (2 private schools have just commenced operations this year), 1 homeopathy college and hospital and 1 *ayurveda* college and hospital. In 2002-2003, the government medical facilities were used to treat 1.02 lakh in-patients and 13.38 lakh outpatients.

Infrastructure Requirements

72. While it appears that the available infrastructure is adequate for the State's health needs, the changing public health needs of the people have thrown up some shortcomings that need to be addressed urgently.

73. First, there is a pressing need for special centres to address the overall health needs of adolescents and young adults. The need for such centres is indicated by the rising

incidence of HIV/AIDS among youngsters, the rise in suicides in this age group, etc. These centres should be equipped to deal with mental health and stress issues as well as physiological issues such as reproductive health, sexuality, etc.

TABLE 7.8

Infrastructure in the Public and Private Sector in Goa

Governing Authority	*No. of Hospitals*	*% to Total*	*No. of Beds*	*% to Total*
Government of Goa	49	31.61	2454	47.18
Under DHS	23	14.84	1234	23.73
Attached to CHCs/PHCS	18	11.61		
Other hospitals	5	3.23		
Goa Medical College	2	1.29	1030	19.80
Institute of Psychiatry & Human Behaviour	1	0.65	190	3.65
Central/Semi-government	6	3.87	387	7.44
Private	123	79.35	2360	45.38
Total	178	100.00	5201	100.00

Source: Health Profile Goa-2004, Health Intelligence Bureau, Directorate of Health Services.

The State's health infrastructure indicators are listed below:

TABLE 7.9

Health Infrastructure Indicators

Indicator	*Goa*	*India*
Area served per hospital (km)	23.9	292.1
Population served per hospital	9054	61810
Population served per bed	270	1412
Popoulation per doctor	636	2148

Source: Health Profile Goa-2004, Health Intelligence Bureau, Directorate of Health Services.

74. Secondly, training facilities in the State for paramedical staff are woefully inadequate, and the importance of such support staff cannot be over-emphasised. Paramedical staff includes nurses, lab technicians, X-ray technicians, multi-purpose health workers, as also emergency paramedics who are trained to respond to medical emergencies including accidents. The shortage of trained nurses and other support staff has led to the appointment of untrained youth in private hospitals. Even after appointment, there is very little formal training, most of the learning is 'by doing'. Two private nursing schools have been set up in 2005; similar initiatives are needed in the other areas mentioned above. At all times, however, there must be proper, strict regulation and surveillance of such institutions/courses by the concerned regulatory bodies such as the Indian Medical Council, the Indian Nursing Council, etc., to ensure adherence to established standards.

75. Third, counselling and rehabilitation centres are absolutely essential given the dangerously high rates of HIV/AIDS prevalence, alcoholism, accidents, etc., in Goa.

76. Fourth, organised approaches for prevention of road accidents and treatment of accident injuries are urgently needed. The government needs to implement a whole range of injury control activities, including surveillance, prevention and treatment for the injured. Presence of roadside first aid facilities can make a lot of difference. There are important significant deficiencies in the current trauma system, and the State lacks organised trauma care (notwithstanding the implementation of GATES—Goa Accident & Trauma Emergency Service). In fact, Goa has the highest rate of accidental deaths—71 per 100,000 population, well above the national average of

FIGURE 7.2

Hospitals and Hospital Beds

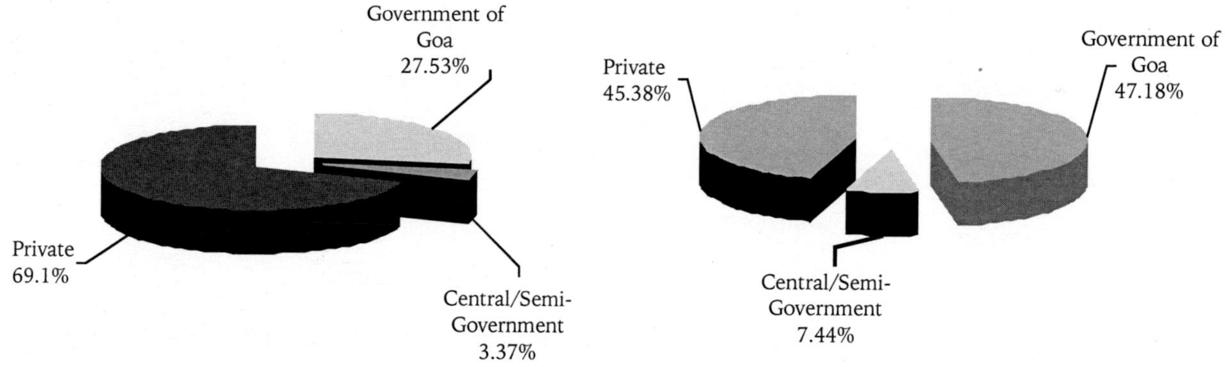

Source: Health Profile Goa-2004, Health Intelligence Bureau, Directorate of Health Services.

26.4. Clearly, although injury is a major public health problem, the Government of Goa has not yet recognised it as a priority.

77. Here the infrastructure needed is both in the nature of software as well as hardware. There is no postgraduate accredited training programme in Emergency Medicine in India and very few structured training programmes for paramedics. Consequently, most emergency rooms are manned by untrained professionals. This can be tackled right away: Goa Medical College can design and introduce postgraduate courses in the area of Emergency Medicine.

78. It is essential that the Government of Goa recognise accidents as a public health issue—and address it accordingly. Gujarat has already started work on setting up a lead EMS agency in the State comprising of a partnership between private, government and municipal hospitals (Syed, 2005). This initiative can be replicated in Goa as well. As mentioned earlier, the World Health Report, 2004, which predicts that by 2020, injury will become the third leading cause of death in the country, and if Goa does not wake up soon, the State may have the dubious distinction of being the State where injury is the most common cause of death.

79. Lastly, the Department of Family Welfare needs to refocus itself away from the traditional area of sterilisation and promotion of use of contraceptives. The term 'family welfare' suggests a holistic approach to the health and wellness of the basic social unit—the family. The Department can be reorganised to look at family welfare in this true sense, and address issues such as overall health of women, as well as the issues raised above such as problems of adolescents, mental stress among youngsters and so on.

80. Thus, the existing infrastructure can be reorganised and restructured to encompass new areas, but we also need new centres and upgradation of existing facilities.

Development and Growth Areas

Health Insurance

81. The introduction to this chapter highlighted the fact that Goa's basic health indicators are strong, particularly in comparison with the rest of the country, but HIV/AIDS, mental health, adolescent problems, lifestyle and stress-related illnesses such as alcoholism, hypertension, cardiovascular disease, diabetes, cancer and so on, are emerging as major concerns and challenges in the area of health and wellness. In the light of these developments, there is need for a fresh look at the subject of health care delivery and the related issue of financing of health care.

82. Health insurance has a crucial role to play in the area of cost constraints and financing of health care. If good health care is to be made accessible to all, health insurance is absolutely essential. The Government of Goa has taken the initiative in this direction through the mediclaim scheme: in 2002-03 alone, the Government settled claims worth Rs. 644 lakh, 80 per cent of which were claims on account of cardiac cases. There is scope for greater progress, which is possible through the public-private partnership model.

83. The growth of health insurance in the State requires certain preconditions (Mahapatra, 2004), the most important being reform and regulation of the health care industry, and the building up of a strong database. A set of common clear-cut ground rules in the areas of quality, pricing of services, accreditation norms, administration, etc., would facilitate the entry of insurers. For example, even a very simple step such as the introduction of a uniform billing format would go a long way in assisting insurance companies and reducing inconvenience to claimants. Database limitations and inadequacies have been cited as the single most important factor impeding the growth of health insurance in India (Mahapatra, 2004). This matter can be taken up on a priority basis in Goa, as the base is relatively small and building of a database would be much easier here.

84. The insurance sector in general, and health insurance in particular, is poised to grow exponentially in the coming years. Goa can participate in this growth by anticipating some of the basic requirements as outlined above, and proactively initiating the growth process of the sector in the State. The progress of this sector will benefit both, the health care industry as well as the public at large.

Health Tourism

85. The travel and tourism sector is labour-intensive, creating more jobs per million rupees of investment than any other sector of the economy. Health tourism is an area with high growth potential. Health tourism business in India is said to be growing at a rate of around 30 per cent annually, and many in the health care industry feel it has the potential to generate at least as much business as software exports. Kerala has already developed itself as a health care destination. Can Goa do the same? Should Goa aim at becoming such a destination?

86. What does Goa need to do to develop itself as a health tourism destination? Currently, Goa has no super-

specialty hospitals. Most Goans today visit either Mumbai (in Maharashtra) or Manipal (in Karnataka) for any advanced medical care for medical procedures related to cardiac cases, cancer, kidney ailments. Evidently, therefore, Goa cannot position itself as a State that can offer all medical facilities to tourists. There are, however, some areas that the State can start with.

87. One promising area is cosmetology, which is a fast-developing area in the West and also in urban India. The average length of stay in hospitals is extremely short in such cases and planned cosmetology interventions can easily be built into tourist schedules. Dermatology and cosmetology centres require less investment than other speciality areas, and can be the first step towards building up an international image.

88. Foreign tourists already visit local ophthalmologists for basic services such as lens prescriptions, which are much more expensive in their countries. The same is true for dentists, who get foreign patients visiting them for routine dental work such as fillings, etc. Presently such visits are sporadic, but this base can be built up.

89. Goa must also go all out to offer the holistic medicinal service for which India enjoys unique recognition in the West. With yoga, meditation, *ayurveda*, allopathy and other medical facilities, the State can offer foreigners an unmatched package of medical services, combined with a salubrious recuperative environment.

90. In order to position Goa as a favourable health destination even in selected areas, it is necessary to set high standards in health care. The government, the Indian Medical Council and private parties should work together to see to it that hospitals attain and adhere to high quality standards. Hospitals have to work towards getting accreditation to build up the perception of quality among foreign tourists.

91. Another major problem is that there are no regular, direct international flights into and out of Goa. To promote health care tourism, Goa needs better international connectivity.

92. Further, the health care industry also needs to find a place in the promotion of Brand Goa. The industry needs to work more closely with Goa Chamber of Commerce & Industry (GCCI) and the concerned government departments to spread awareness and remove administrative and other hurdles.

93. Some small, sporadic beginnings have already been made in the area of health tourism in the State. One resort has tied up with a famed hospital group to provide "lifestyle management holidays" to its guests (*expresstravelandtourism.com*).

Wellness Development

94. Good overall health and fitness are the only preventive steps that can be taken to combat diseases of affluence like diabetes, cardiovascular disease, obesity, etc. Regular exercise and proper diet hold the key to such fitness. The exercise habit can be inculcated at an early age in schools by ensuring that the curricula for physical education and yoga are fully and completely followed, in letter and in spirit. The importance of the correct diet cannot be emphasised enough. Here again, educational institutions, from primary schools right through to the university level, have a vital role to play in terms of creating awareness as well as providing the right facilities on campuses. Too often, the physical education period is used by subject teachers to catch up on missed classes; even where the period is not so used, children are asked to keep themselves occupied. There is very little organised physical education activity in most schools today.

95. The State is already seeing the growth of gymnasiums and fitness centres. This sector needs regulation in terms of equipment standards, trainer qualifications, etc., in order to ensure that customers' health interests are protected. Here again there is scope for private-public partnership in the area of constructing and managing jogging tracks/parks, gymnasiums, swimming pools, etc. As incomes grow and lifestyles become more sedentary, and as cities grow more crowded, there will be an increasing demand for such services and the State should be ready to meet the challenge.

Counselling and Rehabilitation Centres

96. The alarming levels of HIV/AIDS prevalence in the State point to the need for effective counselling centres. These centres are needed firstly to raise awareness, which is the best preventive measure for adolescents and youngsters. In addition, as has been mentioned earlier, too many married women are unaware of their susceptibility to AIDS and how to protect themselves. Counselling centres will meet this felt need among the people of the State. Counselling is also needed at the post-infection stage for the infected person as well as his/her family and friends.

97. The State government has, in the Tenth Plan, made provision for the setting up of counselling centres for lifestyle diseases, but these are yet to be set up.

98. The higher incidence of alcohol consumption in the State is another factor giving rise to the need for both

counselling as well as rehabilitation centres. The need becomes stronger in light of the fact that driving after drinking is a fairly common occurrence.

99. The high incidence of motor accidents in the State (Table 7.10) calls for physical rehabilitation centres for accident survivors, i.e., 90 to 95 per cent of those involved in accidents. These rehabilitation and physiotherapy centres could also cater to the needs of children born with physical disabilities.

TABLE 7.10

Incidence of Road Accidents in Goa

Year	*1970*	*1975*	*1980*	*1985*	*1997-98*	*2000-01*
Reported accidents	817	784	1055	1606	2507	2868
Deaths	56	47	86	142	238	222
Fatal accidents %	6.85	5.99	8.15	8.84	9.49	7.74

Source: Health Profile Goa-2004, Health Intelligence Bureau, Directorate of Health Services.

Community Participation

100. Internationally, research studies on the sexual behaviour patterns of truckers point to a high vulnerability to HIV/AIDS. In India, a 1994 study on Highway No. 5 at the Andhra-Orissa border by the AIDS prevention division of Child Foundation of India, Vizag (Andhra Pradesh) revealed that of 5,709 truckers surveyed, 4,949 were sexually promiscuous. Of these, only 11 per cent admitted to the use of condoms.

101. Such a situation can lead to the rapid transmission of AIDS across the country, along trucking routes.

102. To slow down the spread of HIV, the Healthy Highways Project (HHP) is being implemented by 32 NGOs throughout the country under a bilateral agreement between the Government of India and DfID-I (Department for International Development-India). The project aims at educating truck drivers on the use of condoms, motivating them to seek early and complete treatment for STDs, HIV/AIDS and getting their partner/s treated for the same.

103. The Directorate of Transport estimates 50,000 trucks enter Goa annually. The HHP in Goa is being handled by Positive People, a local NGO working in the area of HIV/AIDS.

104. Positive People's outreach targets were 10,000 truckers per year. The NGO has organised a referral network of doctors for the treatment of STDs around halt points. Truckers identified with STDs are accompanied to a network doctor. Treatment is subsidised for the poor helpers of the drivers and communication material is designed in Hindi, Kannada, Marathi, Tamil and Telugu.

105. Over a period of two years, 1999-2000, Positive People managed to speak to 14,183 truckers on STD, HIV/AIDS. More than 20,000 condoms were distributed free of cost after demonstrating their correct use. The Project in Goa identified, appointed and trained 12 peer educators, 8 from the trucker community and 4 among the sex workers (*www.infochangeindia.com*).

Indian Systems of Medicine and Homeopathy

106. Goa has one college and hospital for *ayurveda* and one for homeopathy, both within the private sector. However, the Directorate of Health Services does have dispensaries and doctors from these two alternative systems of medicines.

107. Although more people are taking recourse to these systems, ISM&H is yet to become a part of the mainstream of medicine and public health in the State.

Sustainable Activity

108. The present health infrastructure in Goa in terms of number of hospitals, beds and doctors is adequate and can sustain the population, particularly in light of the fact that the fertility rate has reached replacement level.

109. However, the facilities in the hospitals need urgent upgradation and augmentation in order to cope with the new pressures and demands on health services delivery in the State. As has been described elsewhere, these pressures are the outcome of the changing epidemiological profile of Goa. The addition of new equipment and facilities are mandatory in order to sustain the health of the population.

Strengths, Weaknesses, Opportunities and Threats

Strengths

110. Most of Goa's strengths in the area of health have been discussed at different points in this chapter. To reiterate, Goa's strengths are:

111. High literacy rates, which have probably been at the root of all developments and achievements in the area of demographics and public health.

112. Stabilisation of the population growth rate, which will allow the State to concentrate on emerging areas of concern, growth and development.

113. Very good basic public health indicators.

114. High rates of child immunisation resulting in low levels of child and infant mortality.

115. Good maternal and reproductive health, pointing to the favourable status of women in Goan society.

116. A widespread network of hospitals and urban and rural health centres, ensuring easy physical access to all people.

117. Enviable doctor/population, hospital/population, hospital bed/population ratios, indicating quantitative adequacy of infrastructural facilities.

118. The presence of committed, active NGOs in health-related areas such as AIDS awareness and prevention, rehabilitation of alcoholics, non-formal education, etc.

119. The initiative of the Government of Goa to extend mediclaim insurance facilities to the people, which has made quality health care affordable for the Goan middle class.

Weaknesses

120. Although women's health in Goa is better than elsewhere in the country, it is still not good enough. Close to 40 per cent women have experienced at least one reproductive health problem, and most of these women have not sought professional advice.

121. Continued exclusive focus on illnesses and diseases that have been brought under control; except for HIV/AIDS, the State has not yet woken up to the gravity of the situation in respect of lifestyle-related diseases.

122. Inadequate database on newer, increasingly prominent diseases such as cancer, diabetes, hypertension, heart disease, obesity, liver cirrhosis, drug addiction, mental illness and so on.

123. Insufficient investment in infrastructure such as equipment, machinery and ICT (Information and Communication Technology).

124. Absence of a well-equipped trauma centre, trained doctors and paramedics to deal with the rapidly increasing number of injuries and accidents; adequate and appropriate emergency medical care is lacking in Goa.

125. No formal training facilities for paramedical staff such as laboratory technicians, X-ray and imaging technicians, etc.

126. Separation of the Departments of Health Services, Water Supply and Sanitation, whereas the latter are inextricably, strongly and causally linked to the former.

Opportunities

127. The opportunities in health are to be found in the following areas:

128. With tourism already fairly well-developed, and the recognition of Goa as a favoured destination of Indian and foreign tourists, there is a distinct possibility of developing Goa as a health tourism destination for selected health areas.

129. The popularisation of health insurance, which will make cashless hospitalisation a reality.

130. e-Governance in health, which will contribute towards the creation of a comprehensive, up-to-date database, which will not only help health authorities meet people's needs, but will also assist in the formulation of an appropriate health policy for the State. e-Governance will also improve health outreach services, health security and the overall health status of the population.

131. Public-private partnerships are the theme of the future. Such partnerships can go a long way in improving access to health services

132. Community participation in health is another promising area in terms of spreading knowledge and awareness about diseases, their prevention and cure, etc. Goa has one major instance of such community participation in the area of AIDS; there is scope for much more.

133. The growing popularity of health and fitness centres offers ample business opportunities as well as lays the base for improvements in the overall health levels of the urban population.

Threats

134. The declining sex ratio in the State should have set alarm bells ringing. While one contributory factor could be the migration of job seekers into the State, there is also the fact that many Goan men migrate to the Gulf for employment. There is a clear contradiction between the high levels of literacy in the State and this development. The long-term solution lies in education and social change, but the immediate solution is to prevent the misuse of modern medical technology. While the Government of Goa has banned sex determination tests, it is evident that they are still being carried out.

135. NFHS-2 has found clear evidence of over-medication in the case of childhood diarrhoea—an astounding 42 per cent of children suffering from this common childhood illness were prescribed antibiotics and

anti-diarrhoeal drugs although the accepted treatment does not involve their use.

136. NFHS-2 has also documented the sharp increase in caesarian section deliveries from 14 per cent in NFHS-1 to 20 per cent in NFHS-2, i.e., over a span of just over five years. This development could be because of the changing lifestyles of women particularly in upper income brackets. This conclusion is backed up by the fact that there is a clear difference between the incidence of Caesarian section deliveries between the public and private sectors, with the former being significantly lower. When clubbed with the development mentioned in the previous paragraph, it also points to declining ethics among members of the medical fraternity; a lowering of medical ethics has serious implications for public health in the State in the years to come.

137. HIV and AIDS pose the greatest threat to Goa's health scenario. HIV prevalence among the high-risk population is already too high and the spread among the general population has also touched the danger mark. Awareness and knowledge are still not adequate, raising the possibility of a more rapid spread of the dreaded disease. Containment and prevention will have to be the Government's focus in this danger area.

138. Another disease that could strike at any time is Japanese encephalitis, since the State has a large population of pigs, which are the carriers of the virus. The highly infectious disease is already prevalent in some parts of the country, and can easily be transmitted to Goa by tourists, truck drivers, people on business visits, etc.

139. The sizeable migration into Goa of poorer people from neighbouring States will cause health issues. Beside the possibility that they will bring disease with them, there is the danger that these immigrants being housed in slums, they are susceptible to all sorts of communicable diseases, and could even set off small epidemics in the State. Catering to their basic health needs is essential not only for their sake, but also to maintain the health security of the rest of the population.

140. Along with the physiological diseases, there are also the rising instances of suicides among adolescents and youth. This is a sign of growing stress and mental ill-health, calling for urgent, special attention.

141. Road accidents have become too frequent, resulting in death and disability. Better traffic discipline, regulation and control are the need of the hour. Drowning deaths have reached disquieting proportions—four per month over the last five years.

142. The SWOT analysis of the health situation in the State has highlighted the areas that need attention in the years to come. Building upon the strengths and taking advantage of the identified opportunities will ensure quality sustenance and enhancement. Correcting the identified weaknesses and being prepared to face the threats will put the State on the path to achieving higher levels of social development for the people.

Outlook

Business-as-Usual Scenario

143. If all factors relating to health were to continue in their present state and at their current level, the overall health situation in Goa would begin to slip almost immediately.

144. This is firstly because of the HIV/AIDS threat. The State is precariously placed in terms of susceptibility of high-risk sections of the population, and more alarmingly the general population as well. If awareness, knowledge and prevention are not ramped up, all the hard-earned gains of life expectancy and health will vanish in the space of a couple of decades.

145. The spread of HIV/AIDS will also ruin the State's social fabric, as is happening in some parts of India, where states are witnessing the emergence of a new family structure—young children and elderly grandparents, both "dependents", but with nobody to depend upon. The AIDS-related deaths of young parents are forcing children into menial labour and prostitution at an early age, since they now have to take on the role of the breadwinners in the family.

146. Census 2001 brought out the declining sex ratio in Goa, which is immediate cause for concern. If things continue as they are today, the ratio will deteriorate still further—obviously this is one trend that needs to be arrested and reversed.

147. The business-as-usual scenario will also mean that new non-communicable diseases will continue to be neglected and sidelined in the scramble to reach better basic health indicators in the State.

148. Business-as-usual will also imply the continuance of collection of inadequate, lopsided data, which will hamper the development of an effective and reliable health care policy. In the area of performance management there are two statements:

> What you measure is what you get, and
>
> If you don't measure it, you can't manage it.

149. Thus, if we continue to measure the State's progress towards achievement of the traditional health indicators, there will be slow, marginal improvements in these, but if the Government does not begin to highlight and document the growing prevalence of the emerging diseases, their control and management will be neglected. The data collection process must keep in tune with the changing epidemiological profile of the State.

150. Among other areas that cannot be allowed to continue as they are, we may include

1. the high incidence of unattended reproductive health problems among women,
2. the poor knowledge of home management of childhood diarrhoea,
3. the low levels of awareness among married women about how they can protect themselves against AIDS (this is a very vulnerable group),
4. the high rates of injuries (including self-inflicted injuries) and the inadequate emergency medical services.

Best-Case Scenario

151. The best-case scenario would be:

- The existing areas of strength such as demographic indicators, maternal and child health indicators, health infrastructure, etc., are built upon, so that Goa's performance in these vital areas continues to improve. It is clear that any improvement in these areas will be very slow, since achievements are already at commendably high levels.
- If all the weaknesses identified earlier in this chapter are overcome, the State would make tremendous strides in the areas of health, social development and human development. This would require radical reforms in infrastructure, funding, data collection and the overall health policy.
- For the best-case situation, it is also vital that the administrative barriers between health, water and sanitation be broken down, allowing the State to formulate and implement an integrated health management policy.
- The best-case scenario would necessitate a change in governance along the lines discussed in the section on Governance. All the solutions outlined in the section are possible and feasible; they only require implementation.

Worst-Case Scenario

152. The worst-case scenario could be envisaged as one where:

- The identified weaknesses are allowed to continue to grow, jeopardising the health and well-being of the entire population.
- The State government does not equip itself to face the challenges and threats mentioned above, leaving the population unprepared and vulnerable to emerging diseases.
- The incidence of water-borne diseases such as diarrhoea, hepatitis and typhoid rises on account of the inadequacies in the drinking water system in the State
- HIV/AIDS gets a grip on the population, making it difficult to dislodge. This development will have personal, social and economic implications, as health expenditures rise, families break up and the number of man-days lost keeps growing.

Recommendations and Development Strategies

Recommendations

153. The discussions about Goa's health situation in the preceding sections have laid the basis for the recommendations that this section will make.

154. Given the fact that Goa has already achieved high levels of performance on basic health indicators, future gains in these areas will accrue at a very slow pace. The Department of Health Services, however, must continue to push forward for improvements, since all these gains may be negated if complacency sets in. A foolproof system of data collection must be put in place, with periodic, random checks of the data, firstly to ensure that there is no slippage, and secondly to determine where the Department is on the road to achieving its targets. The Department should benchmark itself against the best performing State on every indicator—this would be a good starting point for planning.

155. A key issue that has emerged out of the preceding discussion is that Goa is now facing health issues that have little to do with the older communicable diseases. Before a health policy is formulated, the State government needs to have an idea of the incidence of the various lifestyle-related illnesses. This calls for a reform of the database so that all diseases are properly recorded. It is highly desirable for the State to build up a database that is truly representative of the health status of the population.

156. Another very critical recommendation is in the area of governance—the constitution of a single Board to oversee the functioning of all the concerned departments as described earlier, will ensure a coordinated, comprehensive approach to health.

157. Infrastructure in terms of better equipment and facilities, special centres and emergency services are absolutely essential.

158. All these recommendations have fiscal implications. Presently the State government allocates a little over five per cent of its total annual expenditure to Health & Family Welfare (Rs. 96 crore in the last budget). The infrastructure requirements will need added capital expenditure. However, if the Government initiates public-private partnerships, the fiscal burden will be substantially lowered. Furthermore, a comprehensive health programme that coordinates the activities of the various departments (health, water, sanitation, urban development, etc.) will be able to make better, more efficient use of the same resources.

159. In 2005, the Government of India launched the National Rural Health Mission (NRHM) with a view to provide effective health care to the rural population throughout the country. The Mission seeks to provide universal access to equitable, affordable and quality health care and aims at reduction of child and maternal deaths as well as population stabilisation, gender and demographic balance. Besides it aims at decentralised management at the district with determinants of health like sanitation and hygiene, nutrition, safe drinking water, gender and social concerns.

160. The NRHM is envisaged to operate for a seven-year period from 2005-2012. The activities to be undertaken mainly include strengthening of health infrastructure in rural areas of all the States.

161. Funds released to Goa in 2006-07 under the NRHM include Rs. 4.75 lakh as untied funds for upgradation of PHCs (@ Rs. 25,000 per PHC), Rs. 9.50 lakh as annual maintenance grant for the PHCs (@ Rs. 50,000 per PHC) and Rs. 40 lakh for ugradation of district hospitals to IPHS. Goa has also been sanctioned an amount of Rs. 327 lakh for 2007-08 as its share in the NRHM flexible pool.

162. These funds can be effectively utilised to improve and upgrade the health infrastructure in the State. However, work under the NRHM in the State has not yet gained momentum—while 4 Community Health Centres have been identified for upgradation to IPHS, they have not yet been made functional and there is as yet no action plan for the implementation of the various aspects of this flagship programme of the Government of India (*www.pib.nic.in*).

Development Strategy

163. Our development strategy with respect to health should focus on consolidating the gains, reinforcing the strengths and addressing some of the weaknesses in this sector. Any people-centred development strategy must focus on health, nutrition and education, since these are the determinants of the quality of human resources.

164. The success in respect of basic health issues such as IMR, CMR, MMR, maternal and reproductive health and child health has to be sustained and improved upon. This will require continued attention from the authorities, which must be combined with a widening of the State government's focus to include emerging diseases as well. Any strategy must pay adequate attention to the HIV/AIDS issue. A health policy aimed at promoting holistic health is an important prerequisite for an effective development strategy.

165. Issues of governance now occupy centrestage in all discourses on development on account of the increasing scarcity of resources. Therefore, an important element of the State's development strategy could be the initiation of public-private partnerships for effective governance.

166. The areas of potential growth and development could also be incorporated into the State's overall development strategy.

References

Centre for Enquiry into Health and Allied Themes (1997). *Report of the Regional Consultation on Responding to the Target Free Approach*. January 31 and February 1. Mumbai.

Directorate of Health Services (2004). *Health Profile Goa 2004*. Panaji: Government of Goa.

———. (2007). *Goa*. Panaji: Government of Goa.

Government of Goa. *Demand for Grants, Volumes I & II* (various issues).

Enterovirus Research Centre (2004). *Annual Report 2003-04*. Mumbai. *http://icmr.nic.in*

International Institute for Population Sciences and ORC Macro (2002). *National Family Health Survey (NFHS-2), India, 1998-99, Goa*. Mumbai: IIPS.

———. (2005). *National Family Health Survey (NFHS-3), India, 2005-06, Goa*. Mumbai: IIPS.

Mahapatra S.K. (2004). "Migrating from a Flawed Health Insurance Model," *Express Healthcare Management*. 15th to 31st December.

Ministry of Health & Family Welfare (2006). *Report of the Working Group on Public Health Services (including Water & Sanitation) for the Eleventh Five Year Plan (2007-12)*. New Delhi.

Patel, Vikram (2001). "Aging and Mental Health in a Developing Country: Who Cares?", *Psychological Medicine* 31(1): 29-38.

Population Research Center, J.S.S. Institute of Economic Research (PRC, Dharwad) and International Institute for Population Sciences (1995). *National Family Health Survey (NFHS-1), Goa, 1992-93*. Mumbai: PRC, Dharwad & IIPS.

Sudhir, Jonquil (2006). "Drowning Destination", *Goan Observer*: 4-5, April 29-May 5. Panaji.

Syed F. (2005). "Experts Recommend National Standards to Improve Trauma Care". *falak@expresshealthcaremgmt.com*

http://www.pib.nic.in (2006, 2007). *Rajya Sabha </BL*, Information given by the Minister of State for Health & Family Welfare in a written reply to a question in the Rajya Sabha.

Chapter 8

Employment and Security

Issues and their Fiscal Implications

Employment

1. Some of the key issues facing Goa in employment generation and human security are to be viewed as a part of interlinked deficiencies, as well as self-standing issues. Some of the issues that need to be addressed are:

2. Improving the "Delivery Mechanism" which translates as reducing or eliminating the time lag between a public policy and its execution, and as a more responsive approach towards new industries that approach Goa for setting up their enterprises. Industries that are non-polluting as well as employment-intensive needs to be welcomed through well defined public policy guarded by all governments.

3. Occasionally the national policies are inhibitive to Goa's own interest. For example, some items in the original National VAT (Value Added Tax) Policy included taxes which would have discouraged tourism and hospitality industry. Timely assertive action by the Government of Goa and various NGOs introduced the necessary preventive measures.

4. Education, training and development institutions have not succeeded in providing the types of learning experiences that are needed in the globalised and highly competitive environment. The ever changing demands of the global employment market are not adopted through the education policy.

5. The major shift in paradigm in terms of curriculum and quality of education needs to be imbibed by the educators themselves. While public policy can encourage and even provide incentives, it cannot by itself enhance the quality of education. The education policy is required to be supported by the market survey as far as relevance of any particular training is concerned.

6. The above employment-related issues have significant fiscal implication. By not investing enough attention and financial resources in education, ultimately employment opportunities suffer. By not keeping the "Delivery Mechanism" streamlined, efficient, attracting investment friendly industrial enterprises becomes difficult, thereby reducing employment opportunities. The government needs to seek the support of various stakeholders comprising at least government officials, industrialists and academicians who would frame the state's education policy taking into consideration the ever changing market dynamics.

7. The Government of Goa has been trying to popularise the various employment schemes including Chief Minister's Rojgar Yojana and Deen Dayal Rojgar Yojana through rural development agencies and *panchayats* in Goa. The schemes designed by the Government needs to be re-looked in the changing scenario of education as well as the composition of population. The youth in Goa may not be attracted to a labour-intensive scheme especially if it requires unskilled labour for various reasons. Hence, such schemes are benefited by the migrant population which certainly adds value to their quality of life.

8. The Committees formed by the Central government to implement programmes and policies in the various states should be supported by appropriate follow-up with the concerned authorities or should be given guidelines so that they form their own policies depending upon the domestic requirements of that State and may be provided with the financial support with adequate accountability clause to it. The results of any such policy should be assessed from time to time in order to continue the support by the Central government. Lack of proper and regular assessment leads to non-accountability and is followed by no or not much improvement in the State.

9. The financing of the above key factors can be approached through improvements in fiscal resource mobilisation, particularly in the following areas:

Flow of Government of India Funds for Goa State Development

TABLE 8.1

Central Assistance in Crores

Plan Period	*1992-93*	*1997-98*	*2002-03*	*2004-05 P*
Approved outlay	152.5	230.56	586	883.33
Amount	52	60.15	71.45	72.41
% of Plan size	34.1	26.09	12.19	8.19

10. The decline in central assistance to State plan, according to *Economic Survey 2004-05*, clearly demonstrates that the Central assistance has dramatically reduced over a period of time. It is understandable that the approved outlay has increased from 152.5 crore in 1992-93 to 883.33 crore in 2004-05, yet the Central assistance has increased only by 20.41 crore over a period of 12 years. Such decrease may have an effect on the overall implementation of certain schemes by the State government. And the employment schemes may be the soft target of such shortfall in implementation.

Besides this, not much progress has been achieved on the suggestion.

Public-Private Partnership

11. While we have been unable to receive dependable statistics, it is clear that a number of private organisations have received public funding such as in "Goa Agenda" organised by GCCI and the Government of Goa, some NGOs and also societies formed under Societies Registration Act such as The International Centre, Goa (ICG) and the Entertainment Society of Goa (ESG). The ICG received initial funds for infrastructure from the Planning Commission of India, Ford Foundation and the Government of Goa—which also provided the land for it. The ICG has been able to meet all its operational costs from its own activities, generated reasonable financial resources through local sponsorships and also obtained a Ford Foundation grant for a major project on South Asia together. However, more significantly it has catalysed programmes, activities and institutions that have generated employment. The entertainment society of Goa through the annual event of the International Film Festival of India is also a significant employment spinner.

12. It is important to note that in these few select examples, after the initial funding was granted by the Government of Goa, these organisations and/or initiatives taken by them became self-sufficient and very little or no continuous public funding was required to sustain them. These are but a few selected examples, only to demonstrate that this method is filled with new opportunities, and should be much further enhanced. The State can consider applying similar principle to labour intensive industries that are incentive-based as well as fairly autonomous.

13. Formation of institutions such as ICG and ESG also generates immense indirect employment opportunities for peripheral services in organised as well as unorganised sectors. Existence of many such institutions may bring up a new category of commodity or service provider which would cater to such institutions. Besides this, such institutions also generate and maintain intellect and academic demand which plays vital role in envisioning the development of the society. Secondly, the PPP approach steadily also decreases the contribution of the state which in turn reduces the burden on the tax payers.

Inflow of Funds from International Funding Sources

14. Major programmes at national level such as "Operation Flood", which generated almost 15,000 employment opportunities and brought the production of milk by India as the highest in the world, is funded by USAID and EEC. Several states are launching initiatives for new airports through significant funding from the World Bank. International funding for enhancing infrastructure and special programmes such as mentioned above should be explored.

15. The data on this critical issue with regard to Government of Goa is not available at this point.

Utilisation of Revenue Raised by Government of Goa Itself—What Per cent Available for Development and Growth of Goa

16. According to the data available, the Government of Goa undertook revenue expenditures of Rs. 683 crore compared to Rs. 603 crore in receipts in 2002-03. Compared to this the capital receipts were Rs. 243 crore and expenditure Rs. 143 crore. It is this type of expenditure that contributes to long-term growth and development.

17. The much-debated initiative of IFFI generated marginal increase in employment, substantial potential for it and contributed to increase in tourism from 20.39 lakh in 2003 to 24.48 lakh in 2004.

18. In other words, the state of Goa itself through its own revenues can undertake growth and developmental activities that contribute to increases in employment opportunities.

Retrenchment Compensation

19. In this section "retrenchment" is defined as loss of jobs by employed individuals due to cut backs. Such unemployment is usually sudden and sometimes doesn't provide enough support for the unemployed to remake his/her career. Serious consideration can be given to creating an "Unemployment Fund" administered by the State to which employed individuals—government and non-government—would make a small monthly contribution. This could be as small as 2-3 per cent of their basic salary. The funds so created can be utilised for providing a compensation of up to 20 per cent of their earlier basic salary to individuals who lose jobs due to layoffs or any other reasons (except for non-performance of duty). Such support could start as soon as the persons are affected up to any such period as the fund may allow.

Human Security: Social Security Scheme—Shelter, Food and Clothing

20. As against the prevalent ad hoc financial assistance provided to people below poverty line, a "Scheme" could be developed to which employed individuals, industries and Central assistance can financially contribute on an ongoing basis. The National Policy of Development with "Human Face" provides a unique opportunity for furthering such a scheme.

21. For example, each individual registering birth in the State from 2006 onwards could receive an annual social security to cover nutritional, shelter and medical needs for life as long as he/she is not employed. Every employed individual would contribute an amount as a percentage of earnings to be determined every year based on the burden to the State. Thus, if the number of unemployed individuals decrease, the employed will need to pay less. As the earnings increase a larger sum would be contributed to the pool.

Health Care for the Poor

22. To some extent, and to a very limited population, publicly funded health care facilities provide subsidised health care to the poor. Consideration can be given to create a public policy that would require privately owned health care facilities to provide free health care which would be equivalent to a percentage of their yearly income.

23. Besides this, instead of investing directly into building infrastructure for providing health care facilities, an allowance card can be given to individuals, which they can present at private or even public health care providers, to avail of the free health care services. The government can then reimburse such private or public health care providers based on the cards they collect. This will not only generate sufficient competition among private and public agencies to be at the top and attract maximum number of clients but this will also change the role of the government to be a supervisory or regulatory body instead of providing this service by itself. This will also create more employment opportunities as the competition will generate more clients. Such a system will be very useful for those who tend to visit other states and countries to treat themselves as well as for people from other states and countries who can visit the state to avail of the facilities.

Education for Children of Families Below Poverty Line

24. Goa is fortunate to have numerous progressive private industries along with a large Goan diaspora, which if appropriately approached in a well-organised manner, would be an excellent source for education of the poor. The gap that remains thereafter can be financed through public funding. The diaspora's contribution should be recognised by giving prominence to such support among the members of the diaspora and the local domestic population. This will encourage the members to continue and increase it support. The diaspora could be given responsibility by allowing each individual or a group of individuals to adopt a town, village or any given area and invest and guide in term of providing education. Though such an approach can be focused on the families below poverty line, it can also be expanded to include families in a particular geographical area.

Employment Generation Strategies

25. With the rapid rise of workers per thousand people, the state has demonstrated its capacity to generate jobs for the rising population in working age group cohorts. The State through its craftsman training institutes (ITIs), which are spread in different parts of Goa, provide short-term and long-term courses in traditional occupations. These courses are run in various ITIs for the benefit of the youth, especially the dropouts in the age group of 16 to 22. Such courses are also supported financially by the government through its various loan schemes which are implemented through nationalised banks.

TABLE 8.2

Distribution of Workers Per Thousand

	1961	*1971*	*1981*	*1991*	*2001*
Cultivators	111	61	58	57	50
Agricultural	39	38	31	35	47
Industries	2	15	10	9	15
Other services/works	24	141	212	283	422
Average workers per '000 population	176	254	311	384	534

26. Among the State's main workers a significant 21 per cent contribute to agriculture as cultivators or labourers. In order to retain employment in this sector various strategies to keep them remunerative must be adapted. The subsidies offered by the State government in the area of agriculture and allied employments needs to be reviewed by taking into consideration the ever changing scenario of demands of the market. Proper subsidies combined with required infrastructure and marketing platform will surely act as a boost to popularising employment opportunities in the field of agriculture. This step will lead to high productivity and generation of employment opportunities in Goa.

27. About 10 per cent of main workers are employed in industry other than household, while a 9 per cent of main workers are in trade and commerce and 5 per cent in transport, storage and communication. About 15 per cent of the main workers are employed in providing services.

28. The State needs to make it attractive for manufacturing and service-oriented industry to remain viable and competitive in Goa to sustain the large scale employment in this sector. To do so, PPP (public-private partnership) and a virtual SEZ (special economic zone) approach may provide a means of large-scale employment generation. The State may promote labour-intensive industries over capital-intensive ones to ensure that more jobs are created for every rupee of capital investment. Another important attraction for any industry would be its manpower. Availability of trained and ready to employ manpower always attracts industries that are either willing to come to Goa on their own or the state of Goa inviting a certain industry to set up their unit. Such manpower sometimes is even more attractive or at least act as a value addition to the tax holidays and other benefits offered by the State.

29. Entrepreneurship and start-ups should be promoted by setting up of incubation cells at the university, colleges and polytechnics. These incubators should provide access to venture funds, management and marketing support, the creation of bankable projects, access to loans and share capital. These initiatives should address the non-worker and marginal workers within the population. The Chief Minister's Rojgar Yojana, Deen Dayal Rojgar Yojana and other schemes should be merged to a single simple scheme to facilitate viable entrepreneurship. Awareness of such a scheme is also equally important and it should be made as popular as the campus interviews. The students who undergo training at universities and colleges should be given equal opportunity to start their own enterprise by providing additional training in managing such enterprise. Part of such training can be imparted for students of various streams and disciplines.

Institutions and Governance

30. As can be seen below there exists a multiplicity of institutions in the field of employment and human security which are responsible for implementing public policy related to them. It is important to note that many non-governmental agencies have taken the initiative to recommend policies on industry, information technology etc. Most of the "White Papers" are results of study undertaken by individual experts in association with organisations such as GCCI, SSIA etc., who play an active role in policy formulation. Goa also encourages stakeholder participation in issues affecting them.

31. Yet, it is equally true that very often, large gaps exist between announcement of policy, its adoption and its execution.

32. Some of the key associations, commissions, directorates and departments who play an active role in policy-making are as follows:

- State of Goa
- Goa Chambers of Commerce & Industries (GCCI)
- Confederation of Indian Industries (CII)
- Small Scale Industries Association (SSIA)
- Directorate of Agriculture
- Directorate of Rural Development, Art & Culture
- Directorate of Planning, Statistics & Evaluation
- Goa Handicrafts, Rural & Small Scale Industries Development Corporation
- Goa State Horticultural Corporation
- Goa State Social Welfare Board

- Goa Labour Recruitment & Employment Society
- Commission of Labour & Employment
- Directorate of Social Welfare
- Directorate of Health Services
- Associations: Pharmaceuticals, Mining, Hotels, Travel & Tourism, Verna Industrial Estate etc.

Infrastructure

33. This section does not deal with those infrastructural facilities already identified such as roads, power, water, port, airport, etc., in a separate chapter of the SDR. However, those that are unique and specially needed for employment and security are highlighted.

- Land and related infrastructure for education, R&D, etc.
- Multi-modal logistic infrastructure for the Clearing House Mission.
- Marketing outlets for sale of handicrafts and other rurally produced products.
- Broadband Internet and state-of-art facilities for the IT Mission.
- Food processing plants.
- Cold storage chain—storing, transporting and marketing of processed products.
- Laboratories and facilities with state-of-art technologies.

Development and Growth Areas

34. During the post-liberation era, first as a Union Territory and later as a State, Goa has benefited from a unique set of visionaries who placed priority on its development with emphasis on preserving all that is good for Goa and all that should be pursued for Goans. This effort has cumulatively resulted in highest levels of social indicators prevalent in India. These include the tangible ones such as per capita income, literacy, state development growth and intangible factors such as quality of life, relatively better ecology and environment and fairy low levels of pollution, deforestation etc.

35. While some of the above observations are strongly debated and often disagreed with, there really is no dispute about the way the things are up to the present. There are serious concerns, however, about the direction we are heading towards. Goa being one of the advanced states in terms of the infrastructure for development, it becomes less difficult to achieve development and growth.

36. Some fundamental issues are:

- Improvement in the quality of education in the highly competitive global scenario, which is "knowledge driven".
- Enhancement of industrial growth without compromising on environment and ecology.
- Expansion and enhancement of the service sector, with emphasis on tourism which safeguards the employment opportunities for the local population.

37. While the development schemes and growth areas should take into account the above issues, none of them singularly should govern them.

38. The mining and agriculture sector have not experienced significant expansions in employment. While both mining and agriculture has the potential to employ educated and well trained personnel who can implement the latest technology in practicing the profession. Mining even though being an labour-intensive industry, with adoption of latest technology will also change the composition the labour and make it less polluting. Similarly agriculture has the potential to employ highly educated workforce which will apply the latest technology in yielding high production and earn more than by applying traditional methods.

39. The largest growths as well as employment opportunities have been available in the service sector. Although Goa is generating number of employment opportunities in the service sector, the youth of Goa is somehow not able to benefit of this situation. One important reason for this is the type and quality of education and training that is required to prepare the youth of Goa for taking the benefit of this situation. The youth in Goa take such opportunities as a vehicle of gaining on job training and look forward to opportunities abroad.

40. Goa due to its small geographic area and limited potential for growth in the traditional sectors will need to create innovative and new approaches to growth and development. One of such approaches is to encourage people of Goa to make it a hub of transition of goods as well as services to rest of the world.

Missions

41. One such innovation can be creation of "Missions". Goa is ideally suited to become an educational mission, R&D mission, trading mission and a "Clearing House" Mission for exports and imports.

42. These missions should be so created that they produce a multiplier effect. For instance, an information

technology R&D mission by itself may produce only a few highly professional employment opportunities and yet could not only support the existing IT industries but also expand them and thereby create demand for increased number of IT professionals. Similarly, pharmaceutical R&D mission could increase the total number of pharmaceutical industries then at present.

43. The "concept" of missions is not just to create sector specific capability with related intellectual and infrastructural support, but is also to create a nucleus which emanates multiple and related growth in that specific sector.

44. One of the most dominant advantages of taking the "Mission Approach" is the special focus and attention such undertakings can provide. These would become equivalent of "Missions" at national levels, one of which revolutionised the telecom sector (DoT).

Education Missions

45. To gear Goa towards a knowledge economy and to give India Asian campuses of the world's premier educational institutes, the State needs to create an educational SEZ. This SEZ will be a means to service Asian talent and attract the best teaching skills in the region. Given Goa's peculiar age structure and a poor concentration of knowledge workers (between 0.59 and 1.8 per square kilometre), this will be the fastest way to change this to a healthy concentration of knowledge workers to integrate Goa rapidly into the knowledge economy. This single mission would create a huge number of jobs per square kilometre in Goa while ensuring a sustainable path to the knowledge economy.

46. Secondly, due to Goa's location on the western coast of India in the Indian Ocean, it adds value and generates potential to become a hub of activities on education. Goa can be treated for being an education hub which will generate several peripheral activities of generating income. Goa can become a state where the output of schools, colleges, universities or any other institute of learning can be directly employed. Although having a target like this is not impossible to achieve but it is a challenge to achieve it.

R&D Missions

47. In fields such as information technology, biotechnology, pharmacy, horticulture, etc., research and development would not only attract the best talent from the nation and the globe but will also facilitate growth of related "high-end" industry, which in turn will increase employment in geometric proportions.

48. These R&D missions would also be mandated to facilitate growth and development of such sectors and industries which are environmental friendly. Such R&D centres can also be established in the existing infrastructure of universities and colleges which run not more than 50 per cent of its capacity.

Clearing House Mission

49. Goa with its unique geographic location along with planned development of airport, port, railways and roads is ideally suited to become a clearing house for products created in western India. With the container facilities having reached international standards, wherein a large amount of product can be transported from its point of origin by road, rail, sea and air, Goa can seriously consider developing such a mission. Goa can act as an entry and exit point for international markets.

50. This approach neither requires manufacturing or producing capabilities, nor markets. Just a modern multi-modal logistic centre and facilitating public policy regarding duties can maximise the use of available infrastructure in a number of jobs along with increasing state revenue.

Performing Arts and Entertainment Mission

51. With the natural talents that Goans possess in performing arts and creativity, its God given natural beauty and with the substantial investments already made for mega events such as IFFI, such a Mission is only a small step forward. To begin with, a new Educational and Training Institute for this field along the lines of the renowned one in Pune, should be established. Considerable local talent exists which can be further developed for meeting the needs of such a Mission.

52. A public-private initiative in creating state-of-art animation laboratories and processing facilities can as easily create the critical foundation, as it has been possible to create the infrastructure for IFFI. With such cinemographic infrastructure, Bollywood as well as South Indian film and TV producers will flock to Goa. Particularly because they will be able to avoid the hurdles which exists in large metropolitan areas.

53. Career in sports could also be reviewed to generate employment opportunities for the sports persons in Goa. Not only playing any particular sport but also so many other opportunities such as officials, managers, promoters, etc., can be explored and provided proper training in Goa or in other parts of India.

Cooperatives

54. Though the agriculture sector is relatively small, it is significant enough for introducing "Cooperative Approach", such that producer is closely connected to the consumer. In this approach, production, procurement, processing and marketing would all be linked from the smallest unit (*zilla* or village) where the crop is grown, to the district where it can be processed, to the city where it would be marketed and consumed.

55. Marketing certainly need not restrict itself to the state of Goa alone, but can also capture consumers at national and international levels.

56. Operation Flood for Milk (Amul) and Operation Golden Flow (Dhara) provide ample success stories that can be replicated for Goa's agricultural produce, especially cashews and mangoes.

57. Similarly, information technology, as well as many other sectors, would also benefit from adopting the "Cooperative Approach". Individually, many entrepreneurs who have undertaken this activity are small in size, employ only a few IT professionals (especially in software development) and their yearly turnover is readably small. These phenomena make it difficult for them to "bid" for any large contract available either with the Government, or a large institution such as NIO, Goa University etc. By organising themselves as a cooperative, collectively they can offer the same advantages that a large IT undertaking can make available.

Tourism Mission

58. While Goa has become a "preferred destination", it has a long way to go before it becomes a destination for "365 days" destination. "Sun, sand and sea" are attracting a large number of tourists only during the high season. The investments in the large number of guest room capacities, both in high and low end, remain mostly unutilised during the monsoon.

59. It is unfortunate that the marketing strategy for Goa tourism has not succeeded in conveying the beauty of Goa, that is during the lush green period.

60. It is also surprising that unlike Kerala, Goa has not developed eco-tourism, interior tourism etc. One of the most important interests which high end tourist have shown is in "heritage tourism".

61. Unlike other states of the Indian union, Goa doesn't have its own tourist population who would visit different parts of Goa. The tourism policy could also include a plan to develop such interest among the domestic population of the State. All of the above aspects of tourism need to be emphasised and appropriate measures taken to encourage them.

62. It is heartening to note that the total number of tourists on an annual basis has now reached almost exactly double than its permanent population.

63. However, such large number of tourists also cause a danger caused by high-density use of limited tourist spots. Either routing these tourists to larger number of places or newer places can be of immense support to reduce the density of tourists visiting such places till sufficient infrastructure is created.

Health Mission

64. Goa would do well to enhance the existing institutions such as Goa Medical College, Goa University, many state-aided colleges and privately sponsored colleges.

65. Quality health care facilities will also attract significant number of patients from India and abroad who would utilise Goa for high-end tourism purposes during post-hospitalisation care. Thailand has placed a special emphasis on this aspect.

66. Thus, such a Mission creates interlinked opportunities of growth and resultant employment.

Private Entrepreneurial Mission

67. It is noticed that a number of "entrepreneurs" are from outside Goa. While on the one hand, there need not be any concern about such a phenomena, in a state where "service sector" is predominant, which is well known for its unique heritage and which offers substantial opportunities for entrepreneurial undertakings, on the other hand, the requisite backup support leave a lot to be desired.

68. While some polytechnic institutions do provide courses in this vital area, the most important ingredient of motivation and high quality of education and training provided are not sufficient for the individual to survive in the market place.

Food Processing Mission

69. A number of agricultural, horticultural, aqua cultural (fish and other sea foods such as crabs, lobsters, etc.) produce are consumed locally and mostly marketed in their original form. Not much "value addition" is achieved. The available advanced processing and packaging facility, including tetra pack, now available removes the criticality of a "cold chain". A number of products such as

canned fish, cream of lobster, coconut milk, canned fruits and even "cashew fruit juice" have a large market potential, nationally, in the Middle East and also the advanced countries.

Rural Small Scale Industry and Handicraft Mission

70. The most vital gap experienced in these undertakings are modern outlets and a planned well executed marketing strategy. While the Government of Goa has taken significant steps for training artisans, once they begin to create their products, very little attention and investment of resources is made in competitive outlets and marketing. It is unfortunate that tourists from across the globe purchase handicrafts from Kashmir, Rajasthan and Himachal Pradesh and very little of those that originate in Goa. In fact, most visitors are not even aware of our local handicrafts traditions. The handicrafts from outside Goa are marketed by private entrepreneurs, while the Goan handicraft outlets which are often created by the public sector leave a lot to be desired in terms of their décor, sophistication, displays and trained sales person.

71. A business like approach with maximum autonomy and subsidy linked with larger sales is important for this activity.

Diversification, Backward and Forward Linkages

72. While Goa has created a few food processing industries in the private sector, very little has been developed particularly in fishing and diversified products in cashews. The juice of cashew fruit has yet to become a product of importance. It has been observed that the small amounts that do get produced are not sufficient to meet the demand.

73. Likewise, horticulture is also filled with opportunities, which is yet to receive attention.

PPP (Public-Private Partnership)

74. Each mission can be pursued as a PPP enabling the partnership to have a clear focus of purpose and ability to create large-scale employment generation while improving the state.

75. The physical infrastructure required for the missions can be concentrated in one or a few places in the entire State (at any rate, it is a very small geographical area), enabling the resources to be pooled and provided to all the Missions simultaneously. Further, the concentration of the headquarters of the Missions at one place will enable the revenues, earned or generated, and the externalities produced by the Missions to be utilised to a great extent by the other Missions (even if not to mathematical optimality). The interactions between the Missions for education, R&D (technology) and private entrepreneurial mission; health, tourism and performing arts; R&D—horticulture—SSI—food processing—handicrafts will enable the internal forward and backward linkages to be worked out.

Carrying Capacity and Sustainable Activity

76. Employment and human security are highly dependent on strong linkage between public policies governing industry, IT, education, health care facilities and human welfare schemes.

77. Political will, generation of fiscal resources, consensus building amongst stakeholders and continuity will condition the carrying capacity and sustainability in implementation.

78. Political will at the level of State as well as Centre should firmly support the policy of the day which is usually prepared by the experts of that particular field. Due to absence of this attitude, change in government also puts back the policies of previous governments and public resources are utilised to generate a new policy.

Strengths, Weaknesses, Opportunities and Threats

Strengths

79. Goa is endowed with abundant natural beauty, unique heritage and highly hospitable, friendly and cultured population. With one of the highest social indicators, the Goan population has also developed a positive and affirmative attitude.

80. Being small in size in terms of geographic area and the permanent population, management of various schemes and programmes is comparatively easier. The general population being sensitive towards environment, ecology, social issues along with general consensus on growth and development, even numerous changes in the government have kept public policies consistent and continuous.

81. Goa is also rich in some select mineral resources such as iron ore, manganese, bauxite, etc.

82. With approximately 3,500 mm of rain per annum and more than half of the year with sunshine, Goa is ideally suited for agriculture and horticulture. Only the months of April and May require some care in irrigation for farming which can be easily overcome by rain water harvesting, drip-irrigation technologies.

83. Geographically Goa is located only one hour flying time away from the major educational, commercial and industrial Missions such as Pune, Mumbai and Bangalore. This advantage is of particular importance during the era of "Knowledge Revolution". This strategically advantageous location makes it ideally suited for backward and forward linkages for these sectors of growth. Being a part of the Konkan belt, Goa has immense regional importance.

84. Most of all for over four decades Goa has become a preferred location for tourism and is a brand by itself.

85. It can be easily envisaged that bright future awaits Goa.

Weaknesses

86. In many ways, Goa's small geographic area also works against it, since it cannot accrue benefits from economies of scale in all its undertakings.

87. Goa also faces the danger of over exploiting its mineral resources and thus the workforce dependent on it could face a bleak future.

88. The service sector also, particularly tourism could soon reach its optimum potential. Historically, Goa has not been able to place a high priority on quality education, which has resulted in "low-end" jobs for its population. This disadvantage is of particular significance when globalisation and liberalisation require manpower with cutting edge knowledge base.

Opportunities

89. In spite of the weaknesses outlined above, the national and global scenario in economic growth, higher spending power and desire for leisure and travel offers Goa the opportunity of diversifying and enhancing its tourism industry.

90. Much greater interest is now shown in eco-tourism, heritage tourism, health tourism across the globe. Goa can easily replicate examples set by Kerala, Thailand and Indonesia. In fact, Goa provides a unique cultural environment due to the Portuguese influence on its music, cuisine, architecture and traditions. This is not available in rest of India, which has monolithic British influence.

91. One of the key features of Goa is the fact that the differences between its rural and urban areas are much lesser than in rest of India. Pollution, high density of population, etc., in the urbanisation process of Goa is far better than rest of India.

92. The "younger generation" in Goa forms one of the largest segments of our population. If this generation is provided high quality education, appropriate motivation and guided to accept opportunities throughout India (outside Goa), they can form the backbone of a bright future for Goa. While many of them opt for migration to Middle East in "low end" jobs, few are receiving the opportunities of getting educated and trained for "high end" employment opportunities.

Threats

93. The largest and the most dangerous threats facing Goa, are also because of its uniquely serene beauty. One need not undertake complex analysis to observe that the beautiful hillside throughout Goa is now increasingly cluttered by concrete buildings.

94. This is even more alarming, since highly affluent individuals from Mumbai, Middle East and abroad use most of these buildings as a "second home". They have little or no stake in preserving Goa's environment and ecology.

95. The other phenomena is the fact that many of "high end" hotels bring their senior executives from else where, and Goans receive entry level positions.

96. Many other states deal with this aspect through either positive or negative incentives.

Outlook: Possible Scenarios

Short Term

97. Mindset Change: "Mission Approach" to employment and human security related public policy, financing, delivery mechanism and goa state growth and development.

98. Changing the "way" we decide and not just "what": Recognising that growth and development especially in employment-related initiatives including education, infrastructure, job creation, etc., require reasonable gestation period. Hence, some initiatives in policy and its execution need to be immediate.

Medium Term

99. Many of the proposed initiatives would reach gestation; hence the advantages produced by positive outcomes would need to be built upon.

100. Strategic adjustments as required for the ultimate objective of increased employment opportunities and assured human security should be made instantly.

101. Every initiative also produces "unintended consequences". These must immediately be either discontinued or minimised.

Long Term

102. Sustainable development and growth demands "responsible" decision-making and actions at individual and collective levels, lack thereof would produce contrary results.

103. Growth and development invariably produce inequities and disproportionate advantage to certain segments of population. These need to be studied in advanced and avoided at the outset.

104. Presently, prevalent emphasis on domicile population violates certain constitutional provisions. This needs to be worked out either through the federal system defined in the framework of Indian Constitution through the judiciary system, or the current thinking should be changed through education and awareness programme. This aspect, in the long term, could be critical if other states apply the same logic towards Goans in their state. While substantial awareness and support for protection of environment and ecology exists, ample examples are available wherein development is at the cost of sacrificing these vital natural advantages are available at present.

105. If appropriate controls are not established at the outset, development and resulting growth and increased employment opportunities will also produce air and water pollution, deforestation, shortages of critical needs such as power, water, etc. "Goan lifestyle" as we know it today, our value systems and the very unique aspects of Goa could be at risk.

Recommendations and Development Strategies

Missions

106. As outlined in the earlier sections of this chapter, some of the key growth areas need to be taken up with the same sense on urgency, focus, effective governmental incentives and investment of fiscal resources, as it was done at national level for creating a thrust in these areas. The sterling example is the telecommunication sector which was headed by Mr. Sam Pitroda. In the absence of such an approach, the policy-making would suffer from delayed or no timely action.

Knowledge Economy

107. As the knowledge economy becomes the mainstream for the global village, Goa still has a long way to go to integrate into this new-age economy. It is this huge gap that needs to be addressed—to integrate Goa into the global knowledge economy of the 21st century. An educational SEZ would be a big step to promote this integration as well as generate huge jobs in the economy. The availability and practice of cutting edge knowledge will be the defining point in today's world.

Emerging Workforce

108. Given the age structure of Goa, there will be a tremendous demand to generate jobs. Goa should promote its manpower across the country, especially in cities that are ageing and need the youth to man their services. Over the next 20 years, Goa should work towards attracting manpower, especially knowledge workers as its own age structure will result in a declined workforce and an ageing population.

Resource Mobilisation

109. Government of Goa, in partnership with dynamic NGOs should promote cooperative movements in different sectors as a novel PPP of self-help. This will create the potential for sustainable employment for all and enable Goa to tap the resources available across the world. This movement will also enable to activate critical sectors in the State's economy.

Chapter 9

Education and Human Resource Development

Introduction

1. Goa, a small coastal state with an area of 3,702 sq. km. is considered as one of the educationally developed states in terms of the spread and impact of education on overall development of the territory. Goa has seen colonial rule for more than four centuries. However, the entire territory did not experience the impact of colonialism for the same period and in the same degree. Portuguese rule continued for over four and a half centuries (early 16th C. to late 20th C.) in the four major *talukas* of today *viz.*, Tiswadi or Ilhas, Bardesh or Bardez (both in North Goa), Sasashtti or Salsete, Murgao or Mormugao (both in South Goa) and for over one and a half century (late 18th C. to late 20th C.) in the remaining seven *talukas viz.*, Pedne, Bicholim, Satari, Ponda (in North Goa), Sanguem, Kepem, Canacona (in South Goa). Before its liberation in December 1961, Goa along with Daman and Diu (two small pockets along the West Coast near Gujarat, quite distanced from Goa) formed the Portuguese State of India or *Estado da India*.

2. For the first 25 years after its liberation from the Portuguese rule, these erstwhile Portuguese holdings formed a Union Territory in the Indian federation and received sizeable central aid and assistance for its development. Education also benefited by this. Expansion of educational facilities from school level to university education and other areas of education including art and culture witnessed a steady progress which made Goa a well-covered territory educationally.

Literacy

3. In terms of literacy, Goa has maintained a good record right from the time of its integration with India and has been able to keep ahead of the nation as a whole as can be seen from the following table indicating percentage of literacy sex-wise since liberation:

TABLE 9.1

Literacy Rate Over the Years

Year	*1961*	*1971*	*1981*	*1991*	*2001*
Male	39.28	54.65	76.01	83.64	88.42
Female	23.58	35.79	55.17	67.09	75.37
Goa (overall)	31.23	45.31	56.66	75.51	82.01
All India	24.02	29.46	36.22	52.21	64.84
All India rank	8	5	5	5	4
Decadal growth		14	11	19	6.5 (7)

Source: Directorate of Education, Goa.

4. From 31.23 per cent in 1961, literacy has moved up to over 82 per cent by 2001 in its march towards the goal of total literacy. Goa has successfully implemented the Total Literacy Campaign to cover 1,00,627 illiterates identified after a survey in mid-1990s and by 1997-98 as many as 1,00,527 (99.90 per cent) were enrolled, of which 79.33 per cent attained the first and second of achievement levels while 49.60 per cent continued at the third level. However, the external evaluation reports placed the achievement level at just 18.20 per cent. Still, the difference in literacy percentages of India as a whole and that of Goa (Goa-India in the above table) has increased over the three decades after liberation from 6.73 (1961) to 15.29 (1971) and up to 20.44 (1981) reaching the maximum of 23.30 (1991) before sliding to 16.95 (2001).

5. While figures reveal that there is scope to improve the situation, it is to be noted that a section of those who need literacy comprise immigrant workforce moving to the State from the neighbouring states and do not have regularity and consistency in stay and residence. The State has plans to start mobile schools in the two districts to address this issue and the ideal of complete literacy is within the reach of the small state.[1]

1. Official Announcement by the Director of Education: reported in *Daily Sunaparant*: 11th September 2005.

School Education

6. As a part of the Portuguese empire, on the eve of liberation and integration with the Indian Union, Goa had school education system under government control and also a parallel network of primary and secondary schools run by local associations or community organisations. Goa had the distinction of having the first medical school (*Escola Medica*) in Asia and also a school of pharmacy around a century before its liberation.

7. While the figures for schools at primary stage on the eve of liberation are available separately, in case of secondary stage they are not on record. But one can realise that people's initiative in education was evident at primary stage. Most of the private primary schools were supported by some local landlords or community leaders and were conducted in some public places such as temples or churches, chapels etc. In remote rural areas, the local leaders or landlords provided accommodation for running schools and also took care of the subsistence of teachers many of whom were from the neighbouring areas of Konkan and Belgaum in independent India, across the boundaries of Portuguese Goa. The following figures give an idea of the spread of education in Goa at the time of liberation in 1961:

TABLE 9.2

Spread of Education at Goa in 1961

Level	*Govt.*	*Non-Govt.*	*Total*	*No. of Students*
Primary	176	300	476	43654
Secondary	N.A.	N.A.	95	9511
Higher sec.	1	_	1	900

Source: Directorate of Education, Goa.

8. For further education in professional streams, Goa had a School of Medicine (*Escola Medica*), School of Pharmacy (*Escola Farmaceutica*) and School of Education (*Escola Normal*).

9. As a Union Territory, Goa achieved impressive growth in school education after liberation. The initial stress was on the spread of elementary education through government schools as a result of which the number of private-run primary schools came down. This was followed by opening of secondary schools both by the State government and private managements. Growth of post-matric institutions was slow in the first decade of introduction of the new pattern of 10+2+3 in the mid-1970s. As a result, the expansion of school education in Goa continued even after its attaining the statehood in 1987, as can be seen from the following figures:

TABLE 9.3

Spread of Literacy in Goa since 1970s

Year	*1971*	*1981*	*1991*	*2001*	*2004*
Schools					
Primary	1,048	1,218	1,285	1,268	1003
Middle	371	488	441	442	73
Secondary	209	267	338	365	364
Hr.Sec.	1	7	41	80	81
Teachers					
Primary	1,878	2,823	4,078	4,067	
Middle	1,080	1,156	2,307	2,368	
Secondary	2,482	2,183	3,633	3,594	
Hr.Sec.	N.A.	142	746	1,316	
Students					
Primary	104,677	129,415	104,623	97,457	106828 (classes I-V)
Middle	38,960	69,810	82,327	72,726	73446 (classes VI-VIII)
Secondary	30,447	43,116	69,054	64,178	38046 (classes IX-X)
Hr.Sec.	N.A.	7,392	19,493	21,803	23820
Teacher:Students					
Primary	1:56	1:46	1:26	1:24	
Middle	1:36	1:60	1:36	1:31	
Secondary	1:12	1:20	1:19	1:18	
Hr.Sec.	N.A.	1:52	1:26	1:17	
SC					
Primary		3,015	1,026	2,853	
Middle		1,218	1,153	1,728	
Secondary					
Hr.Sec.					
ST					
Primary		1,43	144	1,39	
Middle		172	95	92	
Secondary					
Hr.Sec.					

Source: Directorate of Education, Goa.

10. The enrolment figures in the table above indicate downward trend in the number of students attending primary and middle schools after 1981. The average annual decline in enrolment in the decade 1981-1991 (2.4 per cent) and further between 1991-2001 (0.72 per cent), accompanied by the rise in number of teachers from 2,823 (1981) to 4,078 (1991) and 4,067 (2001) has helped in bringing teacher-pupil ratio to 1:24 at the primary stage. In spite of the decline in enrolments at primary stage, expansion continued at the secondary and higher secondary school level, bringing teacher-pupil ratio at the higher secondary stage to 1:17, which is the most ideal when compared with the all India figures.

11. In the course of this expansion in the 25 years after liberation, certain other critical issues were also to be handled. The three different units in the Union Territory namely Goa, Daman and Diu being separated geographically, they also had the problems of different

languages as medium of education. Both Daman and Diu followed Portuguese and Gujarati while Goa had Marathi, Konkani and Portuguese as mediums of instruction at the elementary stage during Portuguese rule. The schools run by religious orders used Portuguese and Konkani in education but after liberation they replaced Portuguese with English as it was the language used in administrative and commercial fields all over India. Goa administration adopted Marathi at the elementary stage, allowing Daman and Diu to continue with Gujarati. Some people started schools with Konkani as medium of instruction, using Devanagari script instead of the Roman script used by the parish schools of the Roman Catholic religious orders in the past.

12. At the secondary stage there were schools running in Portuguese, English and Marathi. At the time of liberation, secondary schools prepared students for different examinations depending upon their affiliations to examining bodies. Soon after liberation it was decided that all the schools in Goa would be affiliated to the Delhi Board of school education but subsequently they were affiliated to the Maharashtra Board. The only higher secondary school functioning in Goa during the first decade of liberation was affiliated to the Central Board of Secondary Education. Goa established its own Board of Education (Goa, Daman and Diu Board of Secondary and Higher Secondary Education) in 1974. All the local schools were affiliated to this Board, with the exception of some Kendriya Vidyalayas affiliated to Central Board of Secondary Education (CBSE) and some other schools following the system of the Indian Council of Secondary Education (ICSE).

Current Status

13. In terms of access, Goa has created a network of schools at all the stages of education. In this State comprising 192 *gram panchayats* and a dozen municipalities, as of 2001, there were as many as 1,268 primary schools, 436 middle schools i.e., upper primary schools, 367 secondary schools and 81 higher secondary schools, all totalling up to 2,152 institutions for school education run, by and large, out of State funds. In terms of area served by a school the figures are as follows:

TABLE 9.4

Area Covered by Schools

Stage	*Average Area Covered*
Primary	2.92 sq. km.
Middle	8.49 sq. km.
Sec.	8.26 sq. km.
Hr. sec.	46.27 sq. km.

Source: Directorate of Education, Goa.

14. These figures show the extent of spread of education in the State and the facilities of education available. In comparison with all India figures they arc quite impressive. This is true also in terms of the average population served by a school stage and average number of schools per lakh of population.

15. In addition to these regular schools imparting general education, there are institutions of technical, vocational and professional education catering to children of school going age. In 1993-94, there were 28 such institutions serving around 7,000 students. In 2004, the number of students served by 29 such institutions remained at 7,305. Six of these institutions are polytechnics.

Gender Issue

16. This spread has benefited male and female population evenly as can be seen from the enrolment figures and employment figures in education system. Generally it is believed that female population has a lowering share of access to higher stages of education in overall Indian scenario. But in Goa enrolment figures at all levels show almost equal or considerably large participation of females with males in the system. Right from the inception of state-promoted education in Goa, number of female students and teachers has been considerable. Enrolment particulars at higher secondary level between the years 1986-87 and 1994-95 (period of major expansion at this stage) given below show these trends:

TABLE 9.5

Enrolment Particulars at Higher Secondary Level between the Years 1986-87 and 1994-95 and in 2004-05

Year	*1986-87*	*1987-88*	*1988-89*	*1989-90*	*1990-91*	*1991-92*	*1992-93*	*1993-94*	*1994-95*	*2004-05*
Total enrolment	13184	14513	14943	16812	18025	19493	20793	22483	23710	23820
Boys	7126	7863	8201	9303	9983	10808	11239	11872	12417	12072
%	54.05	54.18	54.88	55.34	55.38	55.45	54.05	52.8	52.37	50.68
Girls	6058	6650	6742	7509	8042	8685	9554	10711	11293	11748
%	45.95	45.82	45.12	44.66	44.62	44.55	45.95	47.2	47.63	49.32

Source: Directorate of Education, Goa.

17. Table 9.5 shows a very positive and favourable participation of females as students in school education. Same is true in case of teachers. In 1995, female teachers comprised 45 per cent of total teaching faculty at the higher secondary stage. In 1981 this was 28.15 per cent (40 out of 102 teachers), while in 1991 they were 43.94 per cent (316 of 719). In 2001 there were 641 female teachers against 675 males making 48.70 per cent of the total at this stage.

18. At secondary stage they formed 46 per cent of the teachers in 1995. Their figures over decades have shown changes in terms of relative percentages. In 1971, they were 1,079 out of 2,482 i.e., 43.47 per cent, in 1981 only 37.70 per cent, which rose to 45.17 in 1991 and further to 51.09 per cent in 2001.

Higher Education

19. As regards higher education, Goa has a university of its own to which all the colleges of general and professional education are affiliated. The University was established in 1985 and became functional just before Goa gained statehood. Presently Goa has 24 colleges of general education and 21 providing professional education.

20. The first college of undergraduate studies started in Goa in 1963 and at the time of attaining statehood there were 14 of them. Professional education in Medicine and Pharmacy was available in Portuguese Goa through the two schools which were upgraded and converted to colleges soon after liberation and affiliated to Bombay University before they came under Goa University in late 1980s. Now this small territory has three colleges of Engineering, one run by the State govenment and two under private managements. Recently Birla Institute of Technology (BIT) has established its Goa campus. Higher education in medicine is provided through a college each in the three systems of medicine, *viz.*, Allopathy, *Ayurveda* and Homeopathy, the first being a State government establishment and the other two under private managements. A college each in Dentistry, Pharmacy, Architecture, Home Science, Music and Fine Arts are also run by the State government. The Government of India has one of its Institutes of Hotel Management and Catering Technology in Goa. Colleges of Law, Management, and Education run by private managements receive government assistance along with others. A College of Nursing under a private management opened in August 2005 is the latest addition to institutions of higher education. Also there are the study centres of Indira Gandhi National Open University (IGNOU) serving students of general as well as select professional courses. ICFAI and other universities are also having their colleges in Goa. Goa does not have, and perhaps does not need an open university of its own. But Yashwantrao Chavan Maharashtra Open University (YCMOU) has its study centres just across the boundary of the State. Many other Indian universities cater to the needs of higher and continuing education of Goa through their Distance Education Programmes.

21. In terms of out-turn of graduates per lakh of population, Goa surpasses all the major states though immediately after its liberation, it lagged behind with its figures at 35.6 as against the national figure of 49.8. By 1970-71, it rose to 90.4 and further to 122 in 1981-82, reaching 140 in 1990-91. In the subsequent period that saw the establishment of Goa University along with a number of degree colleges and enrolments (for general, professional and university education), growing from 5,772 in 1970-71 to 14,458 in 1980-81 and 21,862 in 2003-04.

Pre-School Education

22. Schooling in Goa used to start at the age of five however in 2003, the age for school entry was fixed at six years. Early Childhood Care and Education (ECCE) is the area in which Goa has no clear cut policy or guidelines and control mechanism. As per the 2001 census, there are 1,03,823 children in the age group of 0-4 which forms 31.34 per cent of the total number of children below 14 years of age. In the year 1995-96, this figure was 28.90 per cent (1,16,816 in the age group of 0-4).

23. NCERT in its publication *School Education in Goa: Status, Issues and Perspectives* (2004) speaks of "varied set-up of pre-primary education in the state." The main agency working in this sphere is Integrated Child Development Scheme (ICDS) through its *anganwadis/balwadis* which numbered 949 in 1993 and had 21,043 children enrolled in them. The latest estimates show this figure at 1,012 *anganwadis* with around 14,000 children.[2]

24. Another arrangement is the pre-primary sections attached to the government primary schools. There were 97 such sections that provided schooling programme for the children above the age of four. Pre-primary classes (kindergartens) attached to schools, mostly in English medium, numbered 213 in 1993 and they served 13,099 children below the age of 5. As of 1993 for which the figures are available, the pre-primary schools including

2. Inputs provided by Dr. Nandita D'Souza, a stakeholder.

anganwadis/balwadis covered 34,142 children. This is not a realistic figure as a large number of independent pre-primary schools/kindergartens are neither registered nor regulated in any manner.

25. With the State government's policy decision in the mid-1990s to provide government grants to primary schools conducted in Indian languages only, there have been certain developments in the area of pre-primary education. As the upper primary (middle) and secondary education is, by and large, in English medium, parents prefer to admit children in English medium pre-primary schools or kindergartens. This demand has led to mushrooming of kindergartens in both urban as well as rural areas. But there is no official registration of such schools and no reliable figures are available. General observation is that there are some English medium kindergartens that claim Konkani/Marathi as their medium only for the purpose of government grants, while conducting routine affairs in English. Goa Children's Act (2003) provides for regulation and control of pre-primary schools but no steps have been taken in this direction so far.[3]

26. With pre-primary education in English medium, children in the age group of 4 years and above are subjected to dependence on others for their learning and not trained to acquire knowledge through experience and exposure to situations. As the entire process revolves around rote memory, individual growth through development of learning skills does not occur. As a result, bookish education starts at the age of 3 or 4 and the same is continued throughout the educational cycle of a student. Parents' preference for English medium kindergartens has resulted in mushrooming of urban institutions and closure of Government primary schools in Marathi medium. This arrangement does not function on the established universal pedagogic principles of learning from the surroundings in child's mother tongue. With no government control and regulation, pre-primary schools in English medium are run on business lines, but they do not provide education on scientific lines.

27. In some rural pockets there are Bal Vikas Mandirs in Marathi/Konkani, run by socially conscious voluntary organisations with a limited success in terms of response but the government is worried about the adverse effect they may have on government primary schools in terms of enrolment, as and when these pre-school institutions seek government permission for upgradation to primary stage. The situation is worsened by falling birth rates and growing urbanisation leading to migration of rural population to urban centres in search of jobs. With uncontrolled pre-primary sector, educational scenario in the later stages is confusing and disturbing due to high incidence of wastage and high drop-out rates.

28. The overall picture of spread of education in Goa in quantitative terms is quite positive. Education system has been able to cater to everyone willing to get education, with very favourable institutional density in the State. Both general and professional education is available within the state up to postgraduate level.

29. The figures of enrolment at different stages of education for the year 2004 are given in Table 9.6.

30. A total of 2,69,589 students were in the education system in 2004 as per government records. These are the beneficiaries of state-supported education. There are other avenues of education such as distance education and open education, figures for which are not covered here. Rate of participation in education within the State is good as can be seen from Table 9.6.

TABLE 9.6

Enrolment at Different Stages of Education

Level	*Institutions*	*Enrolment*	*Enrolment 2004-05*	*Male-Female*
Primary I-IV	1,241	82,802	106828 (I-V)	55713-51115
Middle V-VII	435	73,096	73446 (VI-VIII)	38830-34616
Secondary VIII-X	363	63,084	38046 (IX-X)	19457-18589
Hr. Sec. XI-XII	81	23,743	23820 (XI-XII)	12072-11748
College (Gen.)	24	15,721	21643 (Higher Ed.)	9074-12569
College (Prof.)	21	6,141		
Technical/Vocational	30	5,002		
Total	**2,195**	**269,589**	**263783**	**135146-128637**

Source: Directorate of Education, Goa.

3. Inputs provided by Dr. Nandita D'Souza, a stakeholder.

31. By all India standards, Goa has always done well, thanks to the small size and level of development as well as awareness in the society. Student enrolment per thousand at school level (from primary to higher secondary) in the State has grown from 205 (as against all India figure of 133) in 1971-72 to 240 (all India-142) in 1981-82 and in the year 1991 it was 232 as against the all India figure of 173.68. Gross enrolment ratios in school system (till age 14) for the three decades of growth after liberation are given in Table 9.7.

32. In keeping with the national thrust on universalisation of elementary education, the State has attained the stage of universal elementary education, though there are around 3,000 children out of school. They have been surveyed and subjected to enquiry regarding factors responsible for this situation. Recent announcement by the State government, of the proposed mobile schools (schools on wheels) is a step envisaged to tackle the out-of-school children. There is also a scheme of residential schooling for six months on the lines of traditional *gurukul*, to cater to drop-outs and re-admit them into the system.[4]

33. Growing urbanisation and widespread anxiety about changing employment scenario have combined to generate rising demand for introduction of English at the pre-primary level, leaving the foundations of education to forces outside the State purview. This has direct impact on the wastage and drop-out rates in the secondary stage of education. State government has no agency or mechanism to enumerate such schools, validate their methods or evaluate the functioning of these pre-primary schools and also no provisions to regulate, monitor and control them. No studies or statistics are available for reference.

Issues

34. Considering the size and population of Goa, the rate of expansion and financial provision for education is noteworthy. The annual expenditure on education for the past four decades since liberation has shown steady rise from Rs. 174.65 lakh (1964-65) to Rs. 25219.34 lakh (2004-05). The Plan provision for education for the Third Five Year Plan (1961-1966) was Rs. 279.71 lakh which grew to Rs. 9,500 lakh in the Eighth Plan (1992-1997).

Expenditure

35. Soon after liberation, the per capita expenditure on education in the territory of Goa, Daman and Diu was Rs. 25.78 (1967-68) and Rs. 27.73 (1968-69) as against the all India average of Rs. 10.08. This rose to Rs. 61.78 for Goa as against national average of Rs. 27.00 (1973-74) and further to Rs. 184.43 against the all India figure of Rs. 78.97 (1983-84). In comparison to per capita expenditures in some of the other states during the early years of liberation, Goa spent between 2 and 5 times more on education.

36. In the beginning of the Ninth Plan i.e., in 1998-99 the cost per student at school level in the State was Rs. 3,221 for primary, Rs.11,539 for secondary and Rs. 12,102 for higher secondary stage. Teachers' compensation consumed 95.28 per cent of the expenditure allotted for education, leaving only 4.72 per cent for administrative and supervisory expenditure.

37. In terms of percentages, expenditure on education accounted for 4.82 per cent of state income in 1973-74 and 4.34 per cent in 1983-84. Further expansion of education in the years after attaining statehood (1987) has led to lowering of this share though marginally.

TABLE 9.7

Gross Enrolment Ratios in School System (till age 14) for the three Decades of Growth after Liberation

Age Group	*Category*	*1971*			*1981*			*1991*			*2004-05*		
		M	*F*	*T*	*M*	*F*	*T*	*M*	*F*	*T*	*M*	*F*	*T*
11	Gen	125	103.7	114.35	131.9	112.2	122.05	90.6	0.5	95.55	111.43	108.76	110.13
	S.C.				132.8	107.4	120.1	69.5	55.33	62.41			
	S.T.				150.3	88.5	119.4	90.73	62.82	76.77			
14	Gen.	77.8	50.1	63.95	87.4	64	75.7	95.1	84.1	89.6			
	S.C.				113	53.4	83.2	105.31	116.77	111.4			
	S.T.				43	10.8	26.9	35.53	20.81	28.07			

Source: Directorate of Education, Goa.

4. Under the Sarva Shiksha Abhiyan (Campaign for Universal Education) of Government of India, state government has sought funds, a part of which will be utilised for this purpose, according to a Press Report on September 11, 2005.

TABLE 9.8

Budgeted Expenditure on Education Budget: Revenue A/c

Year	*1973-74*	*1983-84*	*1991-92*
Goa	29.40%	16.40%	18.40%
India	17.10%	10.80%	10.00%

Source: Directorate of Education, Goa.

Plan expenditure on education as percentage of total budget has also come down from 29.4 in 1973-74 to 16.4 in 1983-84 with a slight rise to 18.4 in 1991-92.

38. In 1992-93, the actual expenditure was Rs.7,469.64 lakh on general and Rs. 445.36 lakh for technical education. In the Annual Plan of 1993-94, budget estimate stood at Rs. 7,905.84 lakh and Rs. 397 lakh which were then revised to Rs. 8,301.64 lakh and Rs. 426.19 lakh respectively. Budget estimates for the year 1994-95 were Rs. 8,651.44 lakh for general and Rs. 520 lakh for technical education. In 1997 budgetary allocation for education stood at 19 per cent. The trend continues even today with almost 36 per cent (Rs. 30,128.33 lakh) marked for education in the State budget 2004-05. Over the last 10 years, there has been a quantum jump in expenditure on education as can be seen from the following figures for the past three years.

39. In the State budget for the year 2004-05, school education received Rs. 21,939.19 lakh. The actual expenditure on general education in the year 2002-03 was Rs. 24,237.99 lakh and on technical education the State spent Rs. 1,523.65 lakh. Budget for 2003-04 provided for Rs. 23,811.90 lakh for general education and Rs. 1,777.01 lakh for technical education, which was revised to Rs. 24,651.27 lakhs and Rs. 1,779.84 lakh respectively. The budget estimate for 2004-05 was Rs. 25,219.34 lakh and Rs. 1,963.94 lakh respectively.

40. Other areas of education such as sports and youth services, art and culture had the estimate of Rs. 1,734.18 lakh and Rs. 1,210.87 lakh respectively.

41. Sectoral expenditure in education as percentage of annual education budget for the years on completion of successive decades after liberation (against the all India figures shown in brackets) is shown in Table 9.9.

42. In primary sector, the percentage expenditure was lower than all India average as the area and population to be covered were relatively small. Number of primary schools in Goa at the time of liberation and also the literacy status were higher than the national figures. Secondary education got a big boost all along the four decades since liberation, whereas higher education caught up only after the establishment of Goa University and attainment of statehood.

TABLE 9.9

Sectoral Expenditure in Education as Percentage of Annual Education Budget

Sector	*1973-74*	*1983-84*	*1991-92*
Primary	32.3 (48.7)	34.3 (48.6)	28.8 (46.8)
Secondary	52.9 (32.1)	49.5 (32.4)	49.5 (31.1)
Adult/Spl.	0.3 (0.9)	0.7 (1.2)	0.9 (1.0)
Hr. edn.	5.2 (10.5)	6.1 (12.6)	12.4 (11.7)
Tech. edn.	5.4 (3.3)	5.1 (2.6)	5.8 (3.3)
Other prog.	3.9 (4.5)	4.3 (2.1)	2.6 (6.1)

Source: Directorate of Education, Goa.

43. Special education did not receive due attention till late and it was only in 2004 that the scheme of assistance for the special schools was approved by the State government. In the first two decades there was little awareness about special education i.e., education for children with special needs. In the early 1980s there were attempts by some local groups to start schools for hearing impaired, mentally challenged, spastics etc., without substantial support from the State. Today there are a few such schools. There are also some schools for the distressed and disadvantaged children in urban areas. Adult education was given prominence and a separate Directorate of Adult Education was established in the early 1990s which was later disbanded.

Education and Employment

44. With major emphasis on regular school education, State government spent around 85 per cent of its education outlay on school education during its Union Territory days. While attending to higher education after attaining the statehood, changing economic ambience was not really comprehended, as a result of which general education was promoted without preparing for specific skills in demand from employment market. The State government had emerged as the major employer and education did not bring in changes desired by business and industry. The figures on live registers of employment exchanges showed that more and more degree holders were added to the list of unemployed year after year.

45. In the mid-1980s, a wave of government employment was seen especially between 1985-86 (26,337 employees in the State government) and 1986-87 (32,201 employees in State government) effecting an addition of 22.26 per cent government workforce in a year. The number of government employees rose to 34,796 in 1990-91 bringing the government servant-citizen ratio to 1:30 approximately, perhaps one of the highest in the world. The overall growth in employment provided by the State

within five years of attaining statehood was to the tune of 32 per cent.

46. Education sector employed 3,260 persons i.e., 30.39 per cent of the government employees in 1966, with mass opening of primary schools in the territory in the first five years after liberation. This proportion declined with time but the rise in numbers from 4,274 (28.58 per cent of government employees) to 4,786 (21.20 per cent) in 1980-81 and further to 6,923 (19.90 per cent) in 1990-91 continued. The decline in birth rates and the resultant fall in enrolments in schools has not shown similar fall in numbers of employment figures in education. While teacher-pupil ratio has improved, the number of schools has remained the same or increased marginally. The cost-benefit ratio in education particularly at school level has not been very impressive as the schools continue to function with smaller number of students making them unviable units. With little or no reforms in education, it is the survival of institutions that remains a major concern and this has its direct impact on the quality. Security of tenure combined with complete salary grants to educational institutions continues to culminate in complacency and underperformance in the system.

Quantity versus Quality

47. With steady expansion of the school system and promotion of general education at higher levels, maintaining the numbers in the education system has become a priority to sustain the institutions of undergraduate education. This has partially affected the quality of technical education too, because the intake capacity of the existing engineering colleges requires them to admit students with percentages much lower than the minimum that are needed to enable students to complete the courses of study.

48. With protectionist view and State funded educational process, examination-centric and self-contented approach is developed throughout the education system. With introduction of reservations in state-run institutions and entrance tests for admission to professional courses, Goan students are finding themselves in a tight corner. Recent conduct of Goa Common Entrance Test (G-CET) has invited severe criticism from the educated sections anxious about the educational future of their wards. In the courses conducted/institutions based in Goa, where admissions are based on competitive examinations/tests, Goan students seldom find a place. Generally they do not attempt such examinations. There is lack of enterprise, competitive spirit and risk-taking attitude. This is due to absence of mechanism to ensure quality and skill building apparatus in education. The newly developed BITS campus in Goa has very few Goans.

49. In the changing scenario, Goan students in large numbers are finding openings in BPO sector in IT hubs in India and also in management sector. But the overall development picture of Goa is not very bright with more and more numbers waiting for employment with the type of education they acquire. The real challenge is to alter the education system and design programmes that will make Goan students suitable for emerging jobs and employment opportunities. Multinationals are entering the region with new projects for which education has to prepare for switchover in order to train and empower their students to avail of the rising opportunities.

50. Goa as a tourist destination and a centre of hospitality industry in western India has to gear up for the task of providing skilled manpower. There has been gradual decline in dependence on agriculture over the period of four decades after liberation. Even in the decade before liberation, proportion of agricultural earners had declined from 70.7 per cent (1950) to 63.9 per cent (1960). Of the total workforce only 38.83 per cent was engaged in agriculture in 1971, 28.7 per cent in 1981 and 23.94 per cent in 1991. In the decade 1991-2001, agricultural land got converted for non-agricultural uses and the trend continues.

51. Education has contributed to this partly, as education in rural areas and spread of higher education in the State as a whole has weaned away the younger generation from agriculture and ancillary jobs to industry or white collar jobs. Dependence of Goa on the neighbouring states for daily requirements of vegetables, flowers, fruits and milk is a matter of concern for government and non-government sectors. But education has not been able to address this critical issue. An attempt in this direction was made in the year 1997 by starting vocational courses *viz.*, Horticulture and Floriculture at +2 (higher secondary) stage in select schools in the peripheral *talukas* but they could not be sustained due to administrative indifference and public apathy.

Vocationalisation of Education

52. Vocationalisation of higher secondary education in the year 1988 also did not work towards genuine solution to the problem of unemployment of the educated youth. Expansion without rational basis was taken up in the form of duplication of courses, that too, mostly of commerce-based ones, till Central assistance was

available. The pass-outs from these courses, which were essentially terminal in nature, were allowed upward mobility in colleges of general education, thereby defeating the very spirit of vocational education. After five years all these courses were to be financed entirely by the State government. The significant component of 'training-cum-production unit' (which exposed trainees to actual production/service and marketing, and thereby involved them in generating revenue to meet the recurring costs for running the course) as a part of the course was missing, as a result of which all the courses became an item of expenditure for the State. Staff that was to be employed on contract for these courses was later proposed to be absorbed in the regular staff due to which the vocational/professional orientation to education was lost. Some secondary schools were allowed to offer certain subjects of practical nature under pre-vocational category, but there is no effective linkage or upward continuity in the same subjects in most of the cases.

53. Indiscriminate opening of institutions, continuing of schools with very low enrolments, neglect of vocationalisation in the right spirit, lopsided growth with academic bias against practical/skill-oriented training were responsible for not only raising the costs, burdening the State but also affecting the quality adversely. It also entailed underutilisation of facilities at the higher levels of education, with lower strengths and over-staffing in the sector.

Wastage in Education

54. In Goa, school education is for 12 years and with pre-primary school, it becomes 14 years. Drop-out rate at the primary stage is 6.26 per cent and at the upper primary stage it is 9.69 per cent. Considering the figure of 38.52 per cent of drop-outs at the secondary stage, the percentage of students reaching Standard X is around 48 per cent. Those taking the benefit of the education system for 12 years or more are expected to become active contributors to the development of the State. But in reality, the skills are not acquired in a desirable degree by majority of pass outs in the system.

55. That raises the critical question of the purpose of education. It is necessary to see whether our education aims at literacy or is designed for developing responsible citizenship or it works towards providing skills. Going by the quality of pass outs from the system as a whole, overall impression is that the system as a whole is geared for literacy, may be at different levels. If education is not able to shape attitude, inculcate habits and develop skills in the period of 12 or 15 years, fundamental questions on the relevance of education arise. Goa has a good spread of educational institutions, reasonably easy access to the system for everyone, moderately high per capita expenditure. Still the quality of academic output does not meet the requirements of the job market and its presence in the society does not seem to bring about qualitative difference in the socio-political institutions. With burgeoning of numbers of educated unemployed, doubts are raised about the efficacy of education. What drives the system is the question. If the system does not provide manpower to traditional economic activities and cannot find acceptance in modern sectors of economy, more probing is needed.

56. In the emerging scenario, Goa will have to decide its priorities. Being ecologically sensitive and technologically sidelined, Goa cannot attract heavy industries or activities that harm its serenity. Non-polluting activities are ideal. Even with ideas such as Special Economic Zone, Goa has certain risks, as the area is too small. Considering certain cultural advantages, Goa can think of developing itself into an Education Export Zone. Education Development Corporation established in the State and its proposed educational estates hold promise in this direction. Provision of infrastructure and simplified procedures for inviting investments will open opportunities to local educated manpower.

Institutions and Governance

57. While considering the possibilities of developing Goa as education export zone, the main area of focus should be governance. Goa, in the past 40-odd years has been served by the educational administrative set-up that has its roots in the erstwhile Portuguese structure. In fact mere change of name and language of the administrative structure at the time of liberation gave birth to Directorate of Education of today. There have been a number of suggestions to reorganise the set-up but nothing much has changed on the ground.[5] Of late, a separate Directorate of Higher Education has been created but there has been no independent academic expert or educational luminary to manage it. Nor does the Directorate of Education have an educationist or academician of proven ability in pedagogy or educational research as its Head.

5. Some ex-officers from the Directorate of Education point out that structure and designations have remained the same. Different stages of education such as primary, secondary, hr. sec. are under the officers managing different aspects of education e.g., hr. sec. is with an officer handling planning, secondary with the one in charge of Academics, primary stage does not figure in the work distribution at the Directorate level.

Administrative Set-Up

58. As of September 2005, the Department of Education has a Secretary, and with the Department of Higher Education, there is a Secretary, Higher Education. At the Directorate level there are separate establishments for technical education, higher education and school education. Last of these is the oldest and has to handle the optimum number of people in the education system, as also the basic issues of educational planning. The State of the Directorate as of September 2005 is that the Director is a civil servant without any past experience in managing education, who is assisted by two Deputy Directors out of eight posts existing, the remaining six being vacant. At the level of Assistant Director, there are nine vacancies, with only one incumbent in place. Vacancies in other supervisory positions at district, zone and *taluka* levels are more or less in the same range. With so many persons not appointed in sanctioned posts, there is no qualified manpower to run the day-to-day affairs of the Directorate.

59. At the level of educational institutions—schools at secondary and higher secondary stages of education—a large number of posts of heads of institutions in government schools are lying vacant. Teachers' appointments and promotions are often made without paying attention to their individual qualifications or subject competencies, making the whole curriculum transaction meaningless. This is in case of government schools, which at the secondary and higher secondary stage taken together, number around 50, and are mostly located in non-urban *talukas*. Current practice of appointing teachers on contract basis and lecture basis is also adding more problems to this situation.

60. As a result, both administrative as well as academic work suffer from lack of due and timely attention. Supervisory and monitoring activities become ritualistic. Planning too gets a raw deal, as regular assessment of practical performance in the system is not carried out and future projections are lacking. Academic leadership and pedagogic discipline is not promoted in the absence of an academician leading the system. Academic issues are made subservient to administration in managing education. Research and studies on the functioning and outcomes of different sectors in education are not in the priority list of the Directorate. Up-to-date official statistics on different aspects of the school system are not readily available for study, scrutiny and analysis. Community education with regard to changes and developments in the field of education in the country and worldwide is not organised. Mandatory training and orientation of teachers at periodic intervals for adequately long durations at a stretch is not provided for. Hence, the whole functioning is directed towards fire-fighting on day-to-day or year-to-year basis. Updating the rules and regulations for streamlining the work is not possible as there are no sufficient trained functionaries occupying the existing positions in the hierarchy. The most essential requisite is a properly qualified eligible person to head the Department for a reasonable period on continuous basis, with freedom to organise the set-up in tune with the demands of the time. Ad hoc approach to educational planning, administration, research and development has been the mainstay of the system at state level, which needs immediate change.

61. The other two bodies under the regulation/control of the State Department of Education are the Goa Board of Secondary and Higher Secondary Education, an autonomous body and the State Institute of Education (SIE), a part of the Directorate, created in 1974 and 1976 respectively, and having their distinct academic functions. The Board is representative in nature with categories such as people from educational managements, teachers, school heads etc., getting their representatives elected. Though an affiliating and certifying body, the Board has also to look after the curriculum of the secondary schools, as there is no independent agency for the task. In case of primary stage and secondary stage, State Institute of Education (SIE) is involved in curriculum development, curricular reforms, design and development of evaluation strategies etc. But for the secondary and higher secondary, there is no State Council of Educational Research and Training (SCERT) on the lines of National Council of Educational Research and Training (NCERT) at the Union level. Recommendation in the national policy for creating such Council in each state has remained unattended in Goa though every new government coming to power in the state in the last decade or more has announced its desire and plan to give it a shape. In absence of such an academic body made up of educational experts, all curricular issues fall prey to populist designs born out of the electoral system that shapes different organs and bodies of the Goa Board.

Board of Secondary Education

62. In the area of examination reforms, the Board has recently taken some progressive and forward-looking steps with a view to bring transparency in the functioning of the Board, but the past experience is that with change in guard a spate of changes takes place, often with little relevance or insights. Consequently, the Board remains in a state of flux, with very little in the nature of definite

direction and specific vision. As the examining body for school-end examination at secondary and higher secondary stages, the Board is also involved in the work of producing text-books particularly in languages. Text-books in other subjects are adopted from the neighbouring Maharashtra or the NCERT publications are prescribed. With changes in popular government, the system is uncertain about the choice of text-books or study material. This has been the case for the past five years, before which there was no major review or revision in syllabus or change of text-books for almost a decade.

63. As the Secretary of the Goa Board and some other officers are deputed from the Directorate of Education, functioning of the Board too often acquires a bureaucratic pattern. The Chairperson is appointed by the government and if the person happens to be from the Directorate, autonomy of the Board remains only nominal. There are instances of questioning by the Directorate officials in case of allotment of teaching load prescribed by the Board in some subjects involving practical work or group activities. All this accounts for functioning of the Board more as an appendage of the government and Directorate than as an autonomous body planning and executing steps to improve the quality of education and raise credibility of the system in the State. Neither SIE nor the Board being free to revise, revamp the curriculum and reform the set-up from time to time as required by the changing larger scenario, syllabus, text-books and curricular transaction/evaluation strategies continue for long years with nominal/superficial alterations or no changes.

State Institute of Education

64. Many of the programmes undertaken by the SIE are statutory exercises initiated by the central directives. The Director of the SIE is normally an officer of the level of Deputy Director in the Directorate of Education, mostly holding an additional charge along with departmental responsibilities, which leaves little time and energy of the incumbent for the Institute. Consistency in academic research is rarely visible. Funding for the Institute is through the Directorate and not much work of long term consequence is seen except as a part of the National Policy Directives or Programmes of teacher training/orientation as a one time affair. Over the period of eight years between 1993-94 and 2000-01, SIE conducted 413 courses for 12,244 teachers with an average participation of 30 teachers. Frequency and number of such courses seem reasonable, but follow-up programmes are missing. Ongoing projects or action research are not seen quite frequently, possibly due to paucity of appropriate manpower or absence of incentive.

65. District Institute of Education and Training (DIET) is functioning as a training institute for teachers from pre-primary to upper primary (middle) levels. It conducts a diploma course for teachers of primary schools, and has also covered 12,812 teachers under different training programmes during the last decade (1990-2000).

66. Most of the work at SIE and DIET is of routine nature and in terms of quality there is scope for improvement. Experimentation and innovations in pedagogic practices need to be initiated at these institutes, so that their training programmes become meaningful and enriching.

67. Educational design and delivery at school level is totally under the State control as almost all the secondary and higher secondary schools affiliated to the State board of education are state funded. Any modifications or transformation require financial investments which the State government is unable to comply with, because of the existing burden of running the unviable units without any plans of reorganisation or restructuring. Delivery system needs adequate human resource allocation and continuous orientation. Control of the entire educational set-up is centralised and with inadequate, ill-equipped staff in the field, reporting and communication is not very effective. Response and action time is also an issue. There is need to establish a working mechanism to ensure accountability and timely resolution of problems, along with periodic review of operational aspects.

68. School Education Advisory Board is a consultative and advisory body which is supposed to discuss and deliberate on the issues of far reaching consequences. Constitution of the Board from time to time and its functioning in proper way can help the State government to plan for healthy development of education sector. But there is utter neglect of this important mechanism and even the decisions taken at this forum two or three years ago have not been implemented.

Higher Education

69. At the level of higher education there are similar problems. Goa University has been craving for funds which the State has not been able to provide in a regular and sustained manner. State government has no specific agency effectively monitoring the growth and expansion of higher education through the entry of private players. Because of this, neither up-to-date information of the system is easily available nor is there a mechanism to upgrade/modify the existing set-up in order to make it competitive. Bureaucratic controls, volatile political situation and widespread lack of awareness in the

community about the speed and nature of changes, in spite of high literacy rate and ideal size of the territory, make the system static.

70. The overall performance of the institutions created for operating the education system continues to be on conventional mode. In the face of swift changes taking place in other sectors, more practical and efficient performance is desirable. This is possible through effective partnership with private sector. Though a large number of institutions are under the private managements, representing industry, commerce and other productive economic sectors, their role in design and development of education is minimal. Recent initiative in the form of restructuring of School Complex Scheme has provided scope and opportunity for such partnership in monitoring and management of school education as a whole through continuous coordination, collaboration and cooperation between the government and non-government functionaries in education. Smooth functioning of Education Advisory Board and positive state response to its suggestions/ recommendations through timely appropriate administrative actions is sure to encourage better participation of the community in education.

71. Higher education in Goa has not really braced itself to take the challenges. Undergraduate courses are long due for revision and updating, but in spite of the UGC guidelines to that effect ground situation has not changed. Introduction of UGC pattern in colleges has not got off the ground even after repeated annual directives from the University. The teaching community, by and large, seems to be complacent with the existing outdated syllabus. Extension and research activities in colleges are not worth mentioning; as a result, colleges have remained instruction houses and examination centres. Their social role is at best minimal. Even in the area of examination and evaluation, the attitude is conservative and protectionist. The size of examinee population at the graduation level is generally small. University examinations are conducted in individual colleges with as few as three and five students in a subject. All this reflects poor delivery and lack of concern for quality through open competition.

72. In higher education, there is scope for partnership with community at every level. Tie-ups with industry, involvement of business leaders and corporate thinkers in designing curriculum framework that is time tested and future-oriented, is the need of the hour. Quality development efforts can be very productive, if industry-education interface is promoted on consistent basis.

73. Undergraduate courses do have a component of field projects, which can be used for drawing on the resources and enterprise from the industrial sector to enhance the effectiveness of education. This in turn will provide access to industry and community in evolving educational design suitable for the State.

Infrastructure

74. Educational infrastructure in the State has seen steady growth. There were community schools functioning in the private buildings or religious places such as temples, churches, chapels since pre-liberation days. In the first two decades after liberation, the Union Territory administration provided buildings to schools on a large scale even in the rural areas. Considering the average number of students, majority of these were designed as a single room or two room buildings for the four classes of primary stage. By the mid-1980s, the enrolment figures in government primary schools had already started declining and there was no question of addition to such buildings, though in some cases existing accommodation was insufficient.

School Buildings

75. In the year 2000, at primary stage 994 schools out of 1,037 i.e., 96.59 per cent had *pucca* buildings while 39 had partly *pucca* or *kachcha* ones. Only 4 schools were functioning in thatched huts. The number of school buildings with single room were 244 i.e., 24 per cent, those with two rooms were 408 or 40 per cent and 154 buildings or 15 per cent had three rooms. Around 15 per cent of the buildings had more than five rooms each. Generally accommodation is not a serious problem; however, the condition of school buildings is a matter of concern in a few cases. There is no regular maintenance even after the repeated requests from teachers and parents. There are a few instances of initiative on the part of the Parent-Teacher Associations in this work. A select few village *panchayats* too have taken interest in repairs of urgent nature but recent incidents of collapse of roof of a school building located in a major village on the highway, or complaints of severe leakages during monsoon show that a planned programme of repairs and maintenance of school buildings is a must. As reported in the latest official survey, as many as 500 primary school buildings need immediate repairs.[6]

76. As regards ancillary facilities, drinking water is available in 60 per cent of these schools, but other

6. Report in local daily newspapers on 24th September 2005.

facilities such as urinals (19 per cent), lavatories (15 per cent), separate urinals or lavatories for girls (10 per cent and 7 per cent) are lacking. In some cases there are structures for these facilities which have remained unused and become unusable in course of time, due to lack of maintenance. At upper primary schools, the conditions are little better with 75 per cent having drinking water facility, 45 per cent having urinals and 38 per cent lavatories but separate provision for girls is made only in 20-25 per cent of them.

77. In case of secondary schools *pucca* or partly *pucca* buildings are available to all except one school. Over 85 per cent of these have adequate accommodation with 10 or more rooms each. But there are schools without proper playground or activity rooms and hall. Cases of school laboratories and libraries being unused or unattended are also sizeable. In all, 269 secondary schools or around 75 per cent are the ones aided by the State and managed by private managements. Some of them work in two shifts and conduct classes for not more than four and half hours every day, which is around 30 per cent than the school hours considered necessary under the National Curriculum Framework. The school system functions as a half day enterprise and looks at minimum essential requirements of students, that too in purely curricular part. Co-curricular activities, if conducted, encroach on the regular class timings, thereby causing loss to students. A part of this problem lies in inadequate infrastructure and lenient approach taken by the authorities. The State government has been extending financial assistance for developing essential infrastructure based on set criteria and approved pattern of assistance. But the problem still persists.

Government Support

78. In the early years of liberation, the Government had its Grant-in Aid Code which provided for norms of granting financial assistance to educational institutions. This was replaced by the Goa, Daman and Diu Education Act, 1984, under which the Education Rules were framed and implemented in November 1986. Under these rules building grant of Rs. 2 lakh could be availed by educational institutions for construction of their buildings. Subsequently this limit was raised to Rs. 5 lakh. The latest scheme of assistance for infrastructure development of educational institutions set this limit at Rs. 20 lakh and added 20 per cent above this for ancillary facilities. This has benefitted a large number of schools, and yet, there are schools which have no proper and adequate accommodation for running their regular classes as day schools. Many schools in urban areas are not able to make use of the scheme as they do not have land for construction.

79. But because of speedy urbanisation they are under pressure to admit the rising number of students violating the norms laid down by the Act and the Rules.[7] Often these pressures are from the controlling and regulating authorities, ostensibly under instructions from the political masters. As a result, poor infrastructure in these schools is overlooked as a trade off for 'obligation' of conceding to 'requests'. These schools, in turn, determine the school timings, by virtue of their strength, numerical and otherwise, which others in small towns or villages follow, in order to survive in the race and retain their student strengths.

80. In case of government school buildings, they are not able to cater to large numbers and have no space for activities for student development. There are buildings constructed for a lower stage but used for additional classes at higher stage without any additions, alterations, which also affects the performance of these schools with regard to overall development of students. At the same time, there are school buildings lying unutilised or underutilised due to fall in student strength.

Education Development Corporation

81. In the latest scenario, the Government has thought of projecting the State as an educational hub for which an autonomous Education Development Corporation is established. This Corporation has plans to establish education estates where educational enterprises and companies can set up their offices, production and training centres. These ideas have yet to concretise in terms of activities. Education Development Corporation is yet to have its planning and administrative set-up in place. Sites for locating educational estates are not yet finalised. Political changes have serious adverse effects on the development of these institutions.

82. Goa has a definite advantage in this regard, but there is a need to sell the idea all over the country and outside; and also make the Goan educated population aware of the opportunities available in this venture. Educational administrators, entrepreneurs, academic thinkers from the State need to be roped in for seeing the project materialise within the shortest possible time. The Corporation has to seek support and guidance of experts and resources from all over the country, and invite

7. Goa, Daman and Diu School Education Act, 1984; Goa School Education Rules, 1986.

corporate players to invest in related ventures. The Education Development Corporation is expected to contribute positively to State Domestic Product.

Higher Education

83. Infrastructure requirements at college and university level are yet to be met fully. Colleges in mofussil areas are short of adequate infrastructure. University has its ongoing projects for expanding infrastructure but financial crunch is a permanent feature. It has some centres for special areas of research and education but necessary infrastructure is not ready. Academic Staff College, Centre for Womens' Studies and Centre for Konkani Development and Studies do not have proper infrastructure or manpower.

84. Goa University has the state-of-the-art studio and satellite up-linking facility provided by ISRO for operating the Distance Education and Communication Technology Infrastructure (DEITI) with networking at 25 educational institutions all over Goa. This interactive education and communication facility is underutilised at present, though it is functional now after lying idle for over two years. The entire education system of the State can benefit by this, provided government authorities decide and act on a plan of interactive real time governance to empower the functionaries at all levels to ensure speedy delivery. Participation in decision-making on issues related to education, management and revamping of the educational set-up will be easy through this technology. Teacher training, community education and extension activities will get a boost by this. This can be of immense help in transforming the educational climate in Goa. With further augmentation of the network to include more institutions, a well organised e-governed structure can be developed within a short time.

85. The government has implemented computer education programme in all the schools under which schools will have computer laboratories set up with Internet connectivity for use by students. As a part of this, all the institutions also need to be connected to the Directorate for administrative purposes. For this, schools need to be supported by way of grants for networking along with the entire set-up for office. It is possible for the State government and can also be of advantage in terms of saving time and other resources in the matter of management of the system.

86. To encourage the school system to work towards quality, Goa needs mechanism of School Assessment and Accreditation for which a Committee on the lines of NAAC (National Assessment and Accreditation Council) can be formed. The Planning Board for Goa had recommended that "an Assessment and Accreditation Committee may be set up by the State government to evaluate the working and performance of secondary and higher secondary schools and granting them performance ratings. This would enable healthy competition among schools which in turn, can be expected to keep the education system vibrant and dynamic."

87. In this regard State government should try to insist on physical infrastructure as the basis, as it determines the viability of introducing healthy practices and progressive programmes for good performance. Rural areas in Goa have a relatively better picture on this count and they have to be supported with logistic skills and amenities such as good transport, communication facilities, library and networking, so that they can produce results. Urban institutions will have to be made accountable, and allowed to cater to students limiting the numbers to such that their infrastructure can support in the true educational spirit.

Development and Growth Areas

88. As Goa is well covered by the school and university education system it must now look at the areas where growth is possible and necessary. While Goa is ecologically and economically a fragile territory, it has to think of making the best use of what it has, in a sustainable way. Goa is already in the service providing mode. Traditional preference of a section of Goans to work away from the homeland can and should be used in the educational process.

Creative and Non-Traditional Areas

89. Hospitality industry is our niche area and training in different aspects of hospitality needs to be integrated with education at all levels. While beach tourism has come of age, Goa must decide on the limits of its expansion, as the geographical area is too small for any capital-intensive, high-end plans that require dislocation and displacement of locals. But considering the rich biodiversity of the Western Ghats, and unique ecological setting that Goa is bestowed with, education has to incorporate contents with skills that project the wealth and wisdom of our ancestors. Rich cultural heritage represented in art forms, festivals and crafts need to find place in education in a major way. Eco-tourism and agro-tourism are the areas in which Goa should specialise, for which education will have to be reshaped. This could also be used to promote Indian health care tradition through nature cure and *ayurveda*.

90. Goa is also emerging as a health destination, and health tourism can be one potential area. Caring and humane approach ingrained in the Goan psyche has to be enriched with appropriate skills required for a health worker. Speciality and super speciality health care centres are choosing Goa for their shops, where Goan youth should find place.

91. This is possible only if the school curriculum is revamped to replace examination-centric, bookish education by performance-driven activity-based one. This is possible by allowing incentives to small rural institutions to design and deliver innovative training programmes which are local-specific. Soft skills required for human relations, marketing, administration and training should form an integral part of the curriculum.[8] Evaluation system has to stress on continuous activity–oriented evaluation, coupled with field training and assessment by an external body or agency concerned with the trade or activity.

92. Secondary stage must be given greater role in deciding the area of preference of students for further practical training. Multi-track options in school education have to be made available for which individual institutions will have to be assisted in assessment of their environment *vis-à-vis* potential in terms of training and skills. Students at secondary stage must be taught additional languages to be used in their choice careers. This is to be implemented by using IT tools and ICT, which can also take care of evaluation for certification.

93. Faculty development is a major area of concern. For this, teachers in the present set-up should be identified on the basis of their skills, qualities and competencies. Pilot project of training around 100 teachers in 20 per cent of schools to design alternative courses based on their assessment of designated areas/ institutions will have to be undertaken, after which the courses will be scrutinised and finalised for implementation. This can be replicated in respect of different work areas, activities or skills over a period of five years. A thorough review of implementation, impact and outcomes after this period would help in planning further.

94. Goa is blessed with creative minds of international standing. Creativity is what Goans are known for. Arts and crafts form another aspect of the hospitality industry, wherein Goa can emerge as a centre of training, exhibition and experimentation. Developing centres of specific art education and craft training, building institutions for training in IT based art industries such as animation, film-related activities, music and other activities can be encouraged along with the mainstream educational activities for careers in business, trade, commerce, technology and industry. Entertainment industry should provide scope to educational expansion in Goa.

95. For any change in the outlook in education, Goa needs to accept the principle of work-based education which is underlined in the National Curriculum Framework, 2005 prepared by the National Council of Educational Research and Training (NCERT). It is acknowledged in the document that vocationalisation of education has not succeeded because of the prejudice against activities involving manual or physical work.

96. Vocationalisation was introduced after the secondary stage of education but traditional preference for academic courses continued to influence the ever growing first generation learners and their illiterate or semi-literate working class community members. In Goa, the choice of vocational courses introduced at +2 stage is characterised by this conventional bias and pass outs from vocational stream are allowed to enter the general stream for higher education. Admission to arts, commerce or science is allowed in case of majority of the vocational courses, without any bridge courses to make up students' knowledge base in particular subjects included in the course/s for which students are admitted. This adds to strengthening of teacher-centred education with stress on memorising for examination without any scope for meaningful evaluation of skills and knowledge.

97. Moreover, almost the entire lot that is being admitted to vocational courses is of the low scorers at the secondary school certificate examination, whose motivation for learning is not quite satisfactory. This factor goes against the credibility of vocational courses in the eyes of community. Hence vocational education in Goa has "many limitations", as pointed out by the Sub-committee of the State Planning Board, which further observes that "this programme has still to make any major impact on the educational or employment scene in Goa and utility of the programme is not clear".

98. The State government has not been able to rationally organise the higher secondary stage of education or vocational programme. It is known that the introduction of vocational courses was allowed in a number of institutions in the State without necessary groundwork or planning for providing apprenticeship training to pass outs. As a result, the programme was and

8. Inputs from Datta Damodar Naik, an industrialist, social activist and educational administrator.

is used as a by-lane to enter higher educational institutions without possessing appropriate skills or basic competencies. With vocational education having lost its focus and direction, it is time to make work an integral part of school education to make learning through work as the guiding principle, as envisaged in the National Curriculum Framework, 2005.

99. For putting the available resources to judicious use, what is needed immediately is a massive thrust on application of Information and Communication Technology (ICT) at all stages of education. Programmes such as Computer Literacy and Awareness in Secondary Schools (CLASS), Computer Literacy Programme (CLP) have been implemented in secondary and higher secondary schools in the past decade. With the latest initiative of Computer Education Programme (CEP) implemented for the period of four years from 1st September 2005 in all the secondary and higher secondary schools in the State, an intensive decentralised programme of teacher training for using the technology in classroom teaching will revolutionise the functioning of schools in classrooms.

100. Students and parents have to be made aware of the potential of the medium and suitable changes in the school timings and calendar will have to be enforced. With Internet connectivity in every secondary school, the local community as a whole will be benefited. For this, schools need to be converted into community education and information centres with information and communication centres/information windows provided in schools for community use after school hours. Connecting local self-governing institutions and other government establishments, with their higher levels through these centres (service provided on payment basis) can also help institutions generate resources to run these information and communication centres. Services can also be made available for public associations, NGOs and community as a whole. Career guidance, employment and business awareness programmes, technology transfer can empower students, teachers, educational managers and community at minimum cost. This in turn will ensure better choices by the youth in terms of training, education and careers.

101. Higher education will get the benefit of this improved school system, which will have to be supplemented by developing flexible, multi-disciplinary courses at the undergraduate and postgraduate levels. The college faculty has to be subjected to performance appraisal on practical criteria emphasising research and extension components. Rigorous orientation for college functionaries within two years is possible in Goa, which should aim at participatory approach for redesigning the curriculum to bring it on par with national level, while giving it a dimension of greater field application. Off-campus work by students has to be encouraged by involving other research and study institutes functioning in Goa, so as to introduce the element of external evaluation and public recognition to university curriculum. University can explore new avenues of partnership and exchanges with industrial and academic organisations to enhance its credibility and financial viability.

Special Education Sector

102. Special education sector in the country as a whole is suffering due to lack of trained manpower. Goa can design a programme of regular training of manpower required for special education and also develop a centre for in-service training of functionaries in this sector. This will help in utilising the health, education and communication infrastructure developed in the State, and also designing a nucleus for addressing a major national problem in the field of education. For this purpose, monetary support can come from corporate world, international organisations, social associations working for the disadvantaged sections with special needs and also Government of India.

103. Goa has not been able to make the best of its coastal location, except for beach tourism and fishing activity. Water sports are one area in which there is scope to create trained manpower with available natural advantage and ease. This has to be explored by incorporating certain basic aspects in education, augmenting them further into specialised courses with the help of different associations working for the development of such sports.

104. In short, health, hospitality, arts, special education and crafts education can be the growth areas for Goa. Training institutes and centres of continuous learning in these spheres should be promoted, giving priority to their location away from urban and suburban areas. For other sectors, existing facilities can be reorganised suitably and supported adequately. Private and corporate initiatives are already on the scene and they should be regulated to see that local manpower requirements are fulfilled while responding to larger market demands. Biodiversity conservation and environmental monitoring need to be integrated with all the educational programmes in the State as future developments will make sustainability a crucial determinant.

Knowledge Society

105. In the knowledge era we need to have knowledge workers; people who will be able to deal with knowledge work, not just skilled labour. Naturally this requires a high density of knowledge workers.

106. Currently only 8.33 per cent Goan workers are graduates and only 0.57 per cent of Goan workers have university education. There are fewer knowledge workers per square kilometre in Goa (between 0.59 to 1.8 per square kilometre) in comparison to urban centres in other states. Naturally the tertiary economic sector, the less polluting knowledge sector, requiring greater knowledge and skills are disadvantaged in Goa in comparison to Bangalore, Mumbai or Pune. If greater knowledge processing were to happen per square kilometre to grow the economy, Goa will need greater knowledge workers.

107. This obviously means that university education will need to receive greater attention than it does today.

Educational SEZ

108. With the WTO opening up the mobility of institutions, curricula, teachers and students, there will be several regional campuses of international institutions that will emerge. Under these circumstances it makes sense to look at the growth of the Asian campuses of these institutes in India, and especially Goa.

109. An excellent strategy would be to serve as the Asian campus for premier educational institutions, in primary, secondary and higher education, from across the globe in an educational SEZ. This will itself build a high value for education in the State and help a greater proportion of the population to be highly skilled or knowledge workers.

Carrying Capacity/Sustainability

110. Goa has seen growth of the educational system in numerical terms, which creates a feeling of healthy development. But as can be seen from the figures on live registers of local employment exchanges and the statistics of industrial workers, there is a glaring mismatch between education and employment. The live registers showed major growth in numbers of job seekers after 1983, which was at an annual average of somewhere between 15 and 20 per cent. From 32,082 in 1983 the figure on live registers reached 1,16,319 in 1993. Even if one considers the tendency of people in private employment to wait for government job and to retain name in employment exchange for that purpose, it cannot ignore the reality of more than three-fold rise in these numbers. This also covers a large influx of immigrants from neighbouring states, who manned growing construction activity.

111. While education and employment registers have grown in size over the last two decades, traditional occupational activities and economic areas show lesser and lesser presence and involvement of local manpower. Specialised occupations such as fishing, toddy-tapping have very small number of locals engaged in them. Agriculture is neglected. Hence, the issue of relevance and performance of our education system becomes important. With falling enrolment figures in elementary and secondary stages of education over the last decade (1991-2000), the sustainability aspect is under scrutiny.

Student Strength

112. As of 2005, there are 1003 primary schools, of which 89 have less than 10 students each in all the four classes at primary stage. All 89 primary schools have mother tongue (Marathi/Konkani) as their medium of instruction. There are 704 government primary schools and 11 aided ones that do not fulfil the criteria of minimum enrolment and are considered unviable. More than 150 schools have become single teacher schools because of enrolment below 20 students each (in all the four classes taken together). At middle and secondary stage, enrolment rates are so low, rendering teachers surplus and still being in employment, receiving salary from state treasury. The total enrolment in 81 institutions at higher secondary stage is 23,743 (2004) at an average of 293. But looking at the distribution of students there are around 25 per cent institutions with student strength in the range of 100 and another 30 per cent with less than 200 each. That over 60 per cent of these institutions being concentrated in four *talukas*, constantly struggle for survival in terms of minimum student strength is an acknowledged fact.

113. The State's concern for quality in education has to be judged with reference to resource utilisation *vis-a-vis* quantitative growth. With an ideal teacher-pupil ratio, good infrastructure and liberal state assistance, Goa has not done enough to keep pace with time as regards curricular reforms, administrative reorganisation and linkage with employment markets. Education delivery system in the State has remained trapped in the politico-administrative labyrinth. There is need to create alternatives.

114. One way is to involve Panchayati Raj Institutions at the grassroot level in planning, monitoring and administering the affairs at the elementary level of education, adopting the provisions of the 73rd Amendment of the Constitution. This will also enable community to

determine the possibilities and potentials of the system in the context of its specific socio-economic requirements. At the secondary stage, state machinery has very little to offer in the area of capacity building for the functionaries overseeing the system at present. Here it is necessary to offer active role to private management, teacher education institutions, management institutions and other professional associations to contribute by way of outlining the process of developing infrastructure and physical resources, suggesting academic inputs, evaluating the functioning of the system and presenting emerging sets of priorities respectively. This can be tried out in a period of five years.

115. The higher secondary stage needs more careful handling for which an expert committee has to be assigned the task of studying different alternatives and recommending the restructuring strategy to give credence to content and processes in the system. Higher education will need a major revamping with a view to raise the percentage of student population going through the system and also providing the beneficiaries of higher education with marketable skills. The university will have to equip itself with capabilities to export education using ICT and satellite technology. Rather than expanding conventional mode of delivery, virtual classroom should be the priority of the university. The idea of catering to international students on its campus in increasing numbers should pay good dividends. This will have to be supplemented with programmes of value added and specialised training for Indians to check the outflow of Indian students to foreign lands for education. Infrastructure is to be upgraded and there is scope to expand the activities in order to make education create skilled manpower able to support the economic system and also attract students from other lands, thereby generating resources for the State through education.

Strengths, Weaknesses, Opportunities and Threats

116. Goa, with better literacy rates and better coverage of school going age group, at the time of joining the Indian Union in December 1961, has maintained the edge all through. As a Union Territory, expansion of school education system continued for two decades (1967-1987). Even after acquiring statehood (1987), there has been some growth.

Strengths

117. All this expansion has resulted in easy access to education for masses. Even Scheduled Castes and Schedules Tribes' students in school system are in moderate numbers. Participation in education at all stages is reasonably high. Basic requirement of accommodation i.e., proper school buildings are provided to almost 90 per cent educational institutions even at primary stage. Higher education is supported by the State in the form of financial assistance. Gender equity is observed in student strength as well as teachers at different stages of school and also higher education.

118. Goa has good communication network and media presence. Technology needed for growth and development of education system also exists in a good measure. State government has always considered expenditure on education as a priority. A direction in the form of scheme of soft loans to Goan students for higher studies in India or abroad, also the 'Cyber age' scheme that has provided personal computers to all students at +2 stage at nominal contribution (ranging between Rs. 500 and Rs. 1,500 per student), is available as the basis for further advances in education and ICT orientation to education.

119. With a university—not too burdened with large numbers—the State has scope to design programmes, reforms that can make education move ahead. Adequate number of colleges of general education spread throughout the small state, each having student strength small enough to introduce and monitor reforms, so as to ensure better bridges between the world of knowledge and world of work, also stand as strength of the existing system.

120. Goa has certain historical and cultural advantages. Having experienced European impact much before the rest of India and being exposed to constant intensive interaction with the western culture for a few centuries, socio-cultural environment in Goa has evolved in a manner conducive to the global regime that has arrived. More open and receptive approach to outside influences and practices is present in Goan psyche. Presence of Goan diaspora all over the globe is equally a positive factor in the emerging order of things especially with regard to education.

121. Organised educational management at community level is a part of Goan tradition. Moreover, active involvement of those representing business and industry in the field of education is not new to Goa. Adequate spare physical infrastructure in places with easy access from the urban concentrations, and presence of functionally organised IT network in the entire State strengthen the potential for educational enterprises and services in the State.

122. Literacy rate of high order and gender equity in education also acquire significance. Relatively more forward-looking social mindset and a quality of life better in relation to that in many other large states provide good opportunity for the state to consider education as a growing field of economic significance. Implementation of IT education on a mass scale in school system is a major advantage. With 'Cyber age' scheme implemented at higher secondary level, availability of PCs in as many as 35,000 households in Goa marks a beginning of IT revolution with its direct influence on education. Equally important is the advantage provided by the presence of English language in education at all levels.

Weaknesses

123. However, the static administrative set-up managing the education system leaves much to be desired. Evaluation mechanism for different elements of the education system is missing. Appropriate system to develop alternative strategies to ensure optimum use of resources, functioning on the strength of recorded and analysed trends, outputs, processes and practices is conspicuous by its absence. Overgrowth in the sense of disproportionate expansion motivated by short sighted approach followed for immediate political gains without concern for academic priorities and resource management still continues to guide government decisions. Often, factors other than socio-economic demands and assessment of future requirements, or sustainability and efficacy of the plans and programmes, determine decisions and consequent actions. Ad hoc approach to issues of change management and laxity in reorientation of the system are the real hurdles. The State has overdone in school and college education ignoring the scope for diversification and skipping reinforcement for quality performance.

124. Complacency and general outlook of seeking security in traditional areas of education, found even in the educated sections, stand out as a major weakness. Priority is to be closer to Goa, if not in Goa, whether for education or for employment. The change, in this respect, is evident in the past four or five years.

125. A large majority of those opting for migration to the Middle East countries or other regions in search of livelihood have been the unskilled ones with educational standards below school finals or just above that level. The potential for producing skilled manpower from the existing set-up is under explored. In fact, the most salient weakness in the present educational system is the high wastage and drop-out rates. For the year 2004-05, the drop-out rate at primary stage was 2.43, -1.1 and 6.26 (I-V) per cent, at upper primary it was 6.90, 4.28 and 9.69 (I-VIII) per cent whereas at secondary it was as high as 43 per cent. At the level of Standard X, the drop-out rate in general category was 40.65, 42.66 and 38.52 (I-X) per cent, for Scheduled Castes it was 72 per cent and for Scheduled Tribes it was 96 per cent. This wastage in education also means that the practices and processes in the system need a rethinking. Assessment and redesigning require immediate attention.

126. While Goa has to opt for education as a major knowledge industry with IT, biotechnology, conservation, hospitality, art and entertainment as core areas, its manpower training as of now is not truly geared for it. Research is a major element of all the above areas but Goan youth hardly enter the institutes of general science to continue with research. In arts and humanities, students' strength is poor and among those who pursue the stream, awareness regarding the emerging careers is low. No proper and adequate research base has evolved in the State, as over 80 per cent of those entering science education land in technical and other professional education and those opting for pure sciences are mostly those least motivated and unwilling to explore for pleasure. So also in hospitality, art, entertainment, demand will be for good communicators, for which Goa has no training facilities or plans worth mention.

127. Using the available physical and technical infrastructure opens immense opportunities for the State. India's emergence as knowledge processing outsourcing destination can be utilised to project socio-cultural and technological edge Goa possesses. Goa Education Development Corporation and its proposed educational estates are the avenues to explore the market at both national and international levels. Educated youth ready to move out in search of better pastures for careers in IT, hospitality, health, tourism, management are the ambassadors of the brand of Goa.

Opportunities

128. Education as an industry in knowledge economy has scope in Goa because of its geographical location, cultural ethos, social milieu and techno-friendly ambience. With a very compact area, well laid road network, ecologically rich terrain and peaceful social life, one needs to focus on education as an area for economic gains. Coastal land strip offers both wide vision and tranquil seclusion essential for creative pursuits and quiet intellectual activities. Productive activities in crafts should not be subjected to wholesale mechanisation but should

be based on the traditional skills and ethnic talent that can be complemented with appropriate technology for enhancing efficiency.

Threats

129. While Goa has a number of advantages and opportunities at hand, the real serious threat is the volatile political climate that affects plans, projects and programmes in education. The small size of population being represented by 40 members and existence of multiple state agencies and institutions addressing the same issues and problems complicate the situation, giving rise to competing claims by political leaders to spin out populist decisions of short term benefits to small areas or a section of constituents in electoral system. Any attempt at academic treatment and application of established rules, any proposal for review and rearrangement by civil society groups or concerned institutions are perceived as a challenge and threat to authority.

130. As plans to expand the education system unfold, another cultural threat is likely. As Goa has graduated to be a much-sought spot for beach tourism, coastal areas have lost their original, peaceful cultural fabric. With rising export of trained skilled manpower through education export plans, the sense of community is likely to get weaker. At the same time establishment of training and orientation, design and production zones for educational material, entertainment centres and health hubs, growing numbers of people will look forward to settle in Goa and become a part of Goan population. This is likely to dilute the cultural essence of Goan and Konkani identity. Over the past two decades working population in Goa has seen a shift in its composition, due to waves of immigration, as a result of which some of the traditional occupations face extinction, while others have been transformed to the extent of losing their local flavour. This has also made demand on the natural, political and economic resources of Goa. Cultural essence of Goan and Konkani community is losing its lustre. This cultural loss is the price Goans may pay for development. With this change, the civic and political demands of ethnic locals may not have the strength because of which their sense of belonging and Goan pride will suffer. Goa may turn into a market place belonging to those who have only a remote idea of Goa.

131. Entry of international institutions will lead to privatisation of education. Affordability will become a major issue. Access to quality education will be determined by financial worth. This is sure to fragment the society further. New private institutions, schools opened with religious leanings and prescriptions will develop rifts and divisive tendencies will grow through education. This is a serious threat to Goan society, in which communal harmony has always been a way of life. State initiative for quality education is a possible solution.

Outlook

132. With opening of education sector to international players under the WTO and GATS provisions, the changes are expected to be speedy and drastic. In its present form, education system in Goa will continue to produce manpower that relies on the State and refuses to face competition. This will lead to unrest and disturbance as more and more educated youth find themselves unable to make a living out of what they have acquired in the course of their education. To avoid this, certain immediate steps are a must.

133. If restructuring of the school system is effected immediately, its functioning can improve. Ever growing demands in terms of new subjects such as value education, environment education, peace education etc., can be met only by making schools full day institutions. By making provisions for adequate and proper teachers in schools, reducing the number of schools by amalgamating them wherever necessary and possible and making use of connectivity established through Computer Education Plan, the system can be tuned to face the changing demands. Within two years, it is possible to train teachers online and also through interactive system that exists in a limited measure in the form of DEITI at Goa University, for more efficient delivery. There should be an exercise of assessment of manpower needs and relevant educational programmes are to be designed by the locals involving Panchayati Raj Institutions, educational institutions, corporate and business sectors.

134. The State government can also put in place its machinery with the required number of supervisory functionaries and assign the task of long term educational planning to them, through the process of consultation, dialogue and deliberations with industry, community. Within two years the system should be ready to take off. Goa University and its constituent colleges will have to complete the restructuring exercise on a war footing.

135. By adopting the policy of re-orientation of the entire system within five years, with periodic reviews and assessment, the State will develop young entrepreneurs to venture into activities promoting institutions of research and training. The State will have its education estates ready with necessary infrastructure facilities. Educational enterprises coming from all over India and outside will

offer opportunities to young Goan entrepreneurs to man units to cater to the market. Goa University will have international students attending different courses on the lines of Study India Programme. Research and study programmes on Western Ghats, ocean studies, sustainable development, culture and communication, nature cure, organic farming etc., will begin through the university and other institutions. Goan expertise in different fields of industry currently engaged outside the region and the nation will be involved on a regular basis in the planning and preparatory processes.

136. Local educational institutions will be encouraged to use the given ICT set-up to invite Goan diaspora to contribute to the local development through their ideas, projects and resources. Scheme for such partnerships has to be introduced. Offering incentives and support to institutions taking up such linkage programmes will add to the efforts of upgradation and diversification. This can also help in evolving schemes of sponsoring promising talent from Goa by Goans living in advanced countries for state of the art training in new areas of knowledge.

137. Nature, health, art and entertainment will form the focal areas of education. Regular education will introduce these activities as part of the curriculum and develop modules for specific art forms, health aspects as activity options for students pursuing regular education. Apprenticeship in these areas of work will be an integral part of educational process. Goa University will have students' exchange programmes based on agreements with different universities, cultural and other institutions from India and abroad. Teacher education in Goa will get revolutionised to cater to e-tutoring and online teaching, distance learning and virtual classroom.

Recommendations

138. For effective education, certain immediate measures are required. State-run educational institutions at all levels need proper and adequate manpower. Administrative structure also needs reforms.

139. Schools at all stages should be assessed for their location, carrying capacity, performance and viability in order to reduce their number and enhance their performance. School timings have to change to allow them to handle all the educational activities as required. Regular assessment of schools and their functioning should be done through local committees involving school complex structure and Panchayati Raj Institutions. Arrangement such as School Assessment and Accreditation Council (SAAC) on the lines of National Assessment and Accreditation Council (NAAC) may not be necessary, considering the size of the State and small number of institutions, though there have been suggestions to that effect.

140. State needs its own Council of Educational Research and Training (SCERT) as recommended by the National Education Policy. SCERT can work towards improvements in the system based on research. It can also propose reforms and prepare manpower to introduce the desirable changes. Curriculum Design and Development Centre is essential for continuous curricular reforms in the light of speedy global changes in all spheres of life.

141. Every village *panchayat* should be asked to form Education and Employment Committee, which should assess and estimate the manpower requirements within its area and suggest practical components to be added to school activities, to train local manpower. Local industries should be invited to identify youth who can be trained for their use. Educational institutions should have career guidance and counselling cell that will categorise students by their skills and provide further orientation to them in groups through training support from industry/local expertise to make them fit for work. Work activities should be given more weightage in school assessment. Continuous comprehensive evaluation should be based on work, output and skill advancement. Each school should have a community workshop or training centre for specific skills necessary for providing manpower as suggested by the Education and Employment Committee in the village. Similar committees at the *taluka*, district and state levels should include representatives of local skills and occupations, educationists, entrepreneurs that will identify and suggest areas of growth.

142. The potential of Western Ghats as a hotspot of biodiversity throws up immense opportunities for education. Germ Plasma Conservation is a rich area. Health, medicine, agriculture, floriculture and such other aspects can be linked to biological wealth and greater use of information technology to ensure sustainable development of the region. In the UN Decade for Education for Sustainable Development (2005-2014), Goa has a good opportunity to design its education system to promote and enhance sustainability. With the projected urban population of Goa moving up from 76 per cent (2006) to 88 per cent (2011) to reach 95.75 per cent at the end of the decade i.e., in 2016[9], Goa has to look at its resource base, lifestyle for maintaining its traditional peace.

9. Population Projections 1996-2016, Census of India, 1991.

"Empowerment of all people, according to the principles of equity and social justice", requires "action-oriented education" which has to be "participatory and life long".

143. Goa is ideally suited to create a model for such education. Involving community, empowering people, making education creative and productive is possible with planned, sustained efforts. Goa has been a home of rich biodiversity, which is disappearing fast. Varieties of rice, mushrooms, number of food items, members of plant and animal kingdoms in the region are facing extinction. Education has to stall this through institutional intervention. While exporting trained and skilled manpower, the State should rejuvenate its innate strength and wealth through research and action projects. Education has to be the catalyst in this. The State-civil society-corporate community combine has to join forces to prevent gross privatisation of and mass exploitation through education. By the end of the Decade for Education for Sustainable Development (DESD) in 2014, Goa should emerge as a world model for education for equity, justice and peace.

144. University and college education has to undergo transformation keeping this in mind. Goa can be a virtual classroom. Emphasis on local knowledge along with skills to use global knowledge should form a part of the vision and mission of the institutions of higher education. Professional education also should think of appropriate technologies that will help sustainable development in the region. Coastal stretches of Maharashtra and Karnataka have much in common with Goa. Educational activities that attend to this region and its socio-economic life have to be promoted through the University and extended to the region as a whole, making itself a Centre of Excellence in the area of 'Western Coast and Western Ghats Studies'.

145. Reforms have to be introduced right from the school level. Periodic review and revision to introduce new need based courses and curricula from time to time, plans and schemes to generate and allocate resources, adopt approach of neighbourhood and community schools along with educational export promotion, as a roadmap, is to be prepared and presented for implementation.

146. For this to happen, State Education Board/ Council should be established as an autonomous body to guide the State government on education. This should have experts in different aspects concerned with education, coming from the State, region, nation and even beyond. Policy-making should be left to this body and its recommendations should be followed and implemented by the State irrespective of political party or dispensation in power. Financing of education is to be rationalised through community planning, linkage with industry and marginalisation of political forces in educational process.

Chapter 10

Tourism and Entertainment

Issues and their Fiscal Implications

Growth

1. The tourism industry has seen significant increase in tourist arrivals in the last three years. This is particularly true of domestic tourism that has grown phenomenally by actually doubling in just five years. In the same period, foreign tourist arrivals have also increased by 24 per cent but are largely limited by the limited arrivals the Dabolim International Airport can cater to.

TABLE 10.1

Inflow of Domestic and Foreign Tourists

Year	*2000*	*2001*	*2002*	*2003*	*2004*
Domestic	976,804	1120,242	1,325,296	1,725,140	2,085,729
Foreign	291,709	260,071	271,645	314,357	363,230
Total	1,268,513	1,380,313	1,596,941	2,039,497	2,448,959
%age change	1.9	8.8	15.7	27.7	20.1

Source: Tourist Statistics, Government of Goa, 2004.

2. Naturally the market share of domestic tourists in the pie of tourism has increased from 77 per cent to 85 per cent. The impact of entertainment events like IFFI are attributed to have pushed this huge growth in tourist arrivals.

Stakeholders' Perspectives

3. The various stakeholders in the tourism industry would be large. According to Pearce (1989), "Attention is frequently drawn to the larger and more visible developers and BYD operators, the multinational hotel chains and the airlines, but these are complemented by a multitude of small and medium scale operators and businesses, particularly in the attractions and supporting services sectors." Generally the perspective of these larger players is viewed as a "majority" view due to the large presence of these players in the tourism industry. The Goa Tourism Master Plan has captured the views of the business community. Some of the issues raised by TTAG (Travel and Tourism Association of Goa) and GCCI (Goa Chamber of Commerce and Industry) are:

1. Apex body like a Tourism Promotion Board for Goa.
2. Conservation of all kinds of assets of Goa including natural and historical.

FIGURE 10.1

Share of Tourism Segments

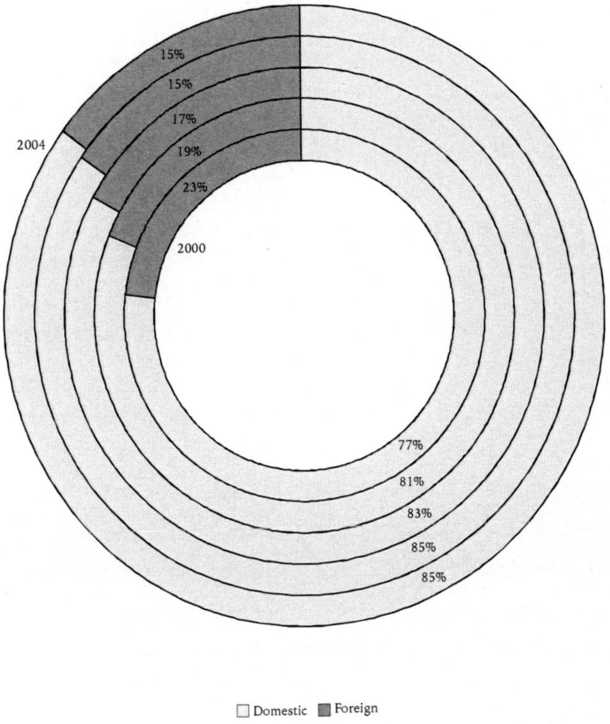

Source: Tourist Statistics, Government of Goa, 2004.

3. Control of pollution especially on the beaches.
4. Giving a fillip to the cottage industry.
5. Enforcement of legal action to stop child abuse and drug peddling.
6. Infrastructure and development issues.
7. Better human resource development to cater to the tourism industry.
8. Tourism product development.

4. The stakeholders are not limited to ones mentioned above but also include the Government, the local bodies (*panchayats* and municipalities), the local population and last but not the least, the tourists themselves. Perspectives of these entities are not available in the secondary data and primary data needs to be generated to have a better understanding of the entire phenomenon of tourism.

5. Though the TTAG indicated the identification of high spending tourists as one of the issues, there needs to be a proper segmentation of the market based on existing resources and planned resource mobilisation/development in Goa. Due to the constant change in the tourist market profile there are constant changes in what the tourist wants from a destination. Due to this the destination managers need to ensure a good "product-market fit" in order to ensure that the tourism growth is on the right track.

6. Attractions and other resources form the "pull factor" necessary for a destination to entice tourists to enjoy those attractions and resources. Some of the attractions that could have the pull factors are:

- The quality of beach experience (sun, sand and sea).
- Adventure sports (those that are resource active using the sea, mountains, rivers etc.).
- Cultural events (like the carnival, Christmas and new year eve, film festivals, folk festivals etc.).
- Eco-tourism and farm tourism or rural tourism (hinterland tourism).

Theme Parks

7. Due to the unplanned resource development in the State, certain sectors get pushed on to the tourists creating a problem for the tourists as well as for the resource. An example of this is the internal transport sector. Inadequate public transport system and more than adequate private transport system (tourist taxis) result in sub-optimal resource utilisation. Lack of adequate implementation of the regulations in this sector (hardly few tourist taxis charge the rate prescribed by the government) results in a poor tourist experience of the resource. This in turn has an impact on the image of the destination.

8. The pull factors need to be worked upon for the benefit of targeting the various segments. The quality of the resource that is used as a pull factor needs to be monitored constantly in order to see that the resource utilisation does not result in resource depletion. The carrying capacity of different resources is different. This has to be determined and monitored constantly as Goa is a coastal region and natural resource depletion is slow and almost unnoticed.

9. Secondly, the manmade resources in terms of attractions need to be developed according to a plan. The nature and types of manmade attractions that are beneficial and complementary to the natural attractions of Goa needs to be determined. An analysis of the attraction/development potential available in Goa is to be made prior to the development of manmade attractions in Goa.

10. Most attractions have some or the other interactive base wherein the tourist interacts with the resource. These resources are called activity resources which include the interactive nature of the transaction between the tourist and the resource. Mapping such resources, both, natural and manmade is an immediate requirement to enable the destination to plan the resource utilisation and development path.

Fiscal Issues

11. Financing the developmental process along with a feasible fiscal system is a developmental need and tool. The taxation policy, the number of taxes and their impact on the industry need to be studied. Some of the taxes applicable to the tourism industry are:

- Value added tax.
- Expenditure tax.
- Entry tax (for goods procured from outside the state).
- Central sales tax (for goods procured from outside).
- Luxury tax.
- Service tax.

Entertainment Tax

12. While there is a need to look at the industry from a viewpoint of revenue, there also is the need for looking at the industry from the viewpoint of utilisation of the revenue for developmental purposes. The earlier the industry uses the tourism satellite account system of defining the tourism system, the better it will be for the

entire regional and national development of the tourist destination.

Institutions and Governance

13. Tourism development in any destination is the responsibility of the society in which it is located. Specific responsibility rests with the governing system prevalent at that destination. In a state like Goa it is the primary responsibility of the Government of Goa to develop tourism in the state to further its various objectives.

The Current Institutional Framework for Tourism Development

14. The institutional framework existing for the development of tourism in Goa includes the Department of Tourism, Government of Goa and Goa Tourism Development Corporation (GTDC). GTDC was incorporated in 1982 under the Companies Act, 1956, as a Public Limited Company. The responsibility of policy-making, planning, infrastructure development and other developmental aspects rests with the Department of Tourism, Government of Goa while GTDC undertakes the commercial activities of tourism like accommodation, package tourism, etc.

15. GTDC has currently 14 tourist complexes catering to various socio-economic segments of the society with a capacity of 550 rooms and 1,307 beds. It also provides for sightseeing and river cruises through their fleet of transport vehicles and launches.

16. The Department of Tourism is also involved in the development of the tourism scene of Goa and is instrumental in promoting the State at various national and international fora across the world.

Drivers

17. Tourism being an all encompassing activity at a destination, the role of institutions participating in this activity is of paramount importance. What public institutions are and can be involved? What private institutions are and can be involved? How should their involvement be organised and channelled by the state? Should it be a market driven approach or a regulated approach? These are some of the issues that need to be addressed by the society in general and by the State government in particular.

Regulation

18. Goa has two districts (North Goa and South Goa), eleven *talukas* (Tiswadi, Bardez, Pernem, Bicholim, Satari, Ponda (NG) and Sanguem, Cancona, Quepem, Salcete and Mormugao (SG)) and 189 *panchayats*. There is a strong governance system prevailing in the State through the district administration, Panchayati Raj system and the municipal system in the cities. The existing governance system has to be dovetailed into the tourism governance system by inter- and intra-institutional bodies. All attractions are located in geographical areas that come under these *panchayats*. There can be a three-tier system at the *taluka*, district and State levels which govern the developmental process of tourism in a regulated manner. Within this regulated system the market forces for private investment in terms of identification of attraction development can be encouraged as a part of diversification of tourism product portfolio.

19. Private investors in the accommodation and food industry, attraction sector and entertainment sector should also be involved in the institutional framework apart from the local industry bodies like the Goa Chamber of Commerce and Industries (GCCI), Travel and Tourism Association of Goa (TTAG).

Accommodation

20. Additional bed requirement due to an increase (spurt) in the tourism sector is definitely felt both in the star and non-star categories. The Tourism Master Plan calculates bed requirement of 16.20 beds for every 1,000 tourists. The tourist arrivals have increased at a high rate in 2002-03, 2003-04 and 2004-05 indicating a need for greater bed requirement.

21. At the current level of tourist arrivals in 2004 of 24,48,959, the total bed requirement is 39,183 beds. If we fit a trend to the tourist arrivals then the tourist arrivals for the year 2016 are projected at 42,80,000 which needs a phenomenal increase in bed requirement of 69,400, which is almost twice the amount for 2004. This additional bed capacity needs to be integrated into the planning for development of Goa both on the physical space plan as well as the resource utilisation plan. Though a break up of this bed requirement can be given using the existing tourism spread in South and North Goa, the upcoming airport at Mopa and its impact may create a different picture for the increased bed requirement in Goa.

Education (Human Resource Development in Hospitality Sector)

22. The educational sector caters to the educational needs of the society in Goa and also for purposes of employment elsewhere. Pursuing this objective,

institutions of primary, secondary, higher secondary and higher education are engaged in developing employable citizens in all sectors of the society. The tourism sector is no exception.

23. The Hotel Management and Catering Technology institute and other such institutions have been in the forefront of creating skilled workforce in the tourism sector. Courses for tour operators and travel agents have been started by various institutions. However, there is a need for a nodal agency like the Goa University to look at tourism-related educational inputs from a tourism perspective to enable a policy-oriented movement in education for tourism purposes. Part time courses for people already employed is one of the thrust areas needed if tourism needs a boost in the short run.

24. The time taken to educate and get a person gainfully employed in the tourism sector is large if the person has to deliver productive work. This is best done by giving training inputs for the already employed workforce to get a better output in the short run and also have institutions educating the potential workforce. Given the current intake capacity of these institutions at a maximum of 500 students each year, it may not be able to sustain the employment opportunities in all the sectors. This is primarily because all sectors of the tourism industry are not covered by the educational institutions. Private infrastructure is necessary for the development of these institutions to enable the industry to have a good workforce giving a fillip to the value addition process in tourism.

Employment

25. According to the Report on Tourism Satellite Account by the Government of India, tourism-related employment (both direct and indirect) is to the tune of 8.27 per cent of the total employment in 2002-03. Given the increase in the tourism activity in the state of Goa, one can safely assume that the increased level of activity will increase the total employment level. The 8.27 per cent of total employment corresponds to 38.6 million gainful employment jobs. Given this scenario, the total employment in Goa related to tourism is about 1,47,000 in 2003 (Tourism Master Plan) and this may increase to more than 3,27,000 (Based on a tourist arrival growth rate of about 12 per cent average) by 2016.

Environmental and Social Concerns

26. North Goa's most scenic spot is being squeezed of its water resources, choked by sewage, swamped by population pressures, and its skyline and vegetation are undergoing a drastic change; Goa's tourism belt is getting overcrowded and losing the ethnic touch so loved by the tourists.

27. Candolim, a former fishing village now turned tourist destination, with the once world famous Calangute beach, has a density of 1,021 persons per kilometre, compared to Bardez *taluka's* 624 persons.

28. Male in-migration into the tourism areas of Goa has reversed the earlier favourable men-to-women sex ratio here. Calangute, notes another essay here, was the first village to be "visited by tourism"—which came in the shape of hippies in the sixties, went on to soon gain international recognition.

29. Tourism is highly seasonal in Goa. Since it is concentrated in the non-monsoon month of October-March, it causes some problems of its own. One of the fallouts is that Goa has to "scale up" its infrastructure to be able to meet the demands that arise in the peak season. So, facilities are underutilised in off-season, and the tourist population outnumbers the local host population in season. This places additional stress on coastal areas of North Goa, which have stakes in tourism—and whose population was found to be not neglecting their agricultural land.

30. Estimates also show that some 65 per cent of rent-backs are owned by non-resident Goans, 20-25 per cent by Goans from India's metropolises and 10-15 per cent by natives residing in Goa itself. Qualitative research indicates a feeling among local people that the gains from tourism are not substantial. There is a growing feeling that large hotels and external groups are cornering the economic benefits, while the local population has to bear the social and environmental burden.

31. In the Baga-Nerul watershed, covering villages again in the North Goa coast, it was found that sewage was hardly being treated. In 99 per cent of low-budget, 100 per cent of middle-budget, 89 per cent of high-budget and 33 per cent of luxury hotels, sewage is being disposed in soak-pits or tanks. Only 11 per cent of high-budget and 67 per cent of luxury hotels treat their sewage, as they had treatment plants.

32. Low-budget hotels needed 573 litres of per room per day, in terms of their water requirement. Luxury hotels, in contrast, needed 1,335 liters per room per day as they have huge landscaped areas, swimming pools, two or three restaurants and other facilities. The beaches of Goa were reported to be very clean with dense vegetation and magnificent dunes three decades ago. Overexploitation of the beaches, for tourism-related activities have severely

degraded the sand dune habitats, according to researchers T.G. Jagtap, K. Desai and R. Rodrigues.

33. According to a TERI study, it is estimated that the groundwater in coastal Bardez (*taluka*) is stressed due to tourism-related activities. Moreover, groundwater quality has deteriorated due to indiscriminate disposal of human-generated waste, including disposal from septic tanks and cesspools. The bacterial and nitrate concentrations are quite high in almost all the coastal stretches of Bardez *taluka*.

34. On the positive side, tourism has enabled a section of the people to "reduce their dependency on activities such as fishing and agriculture". Women were also found to have a "high involvement" as owners and managers in the low-budget hotels, especially guest houses. This suggests that the tourism trade can support the "evolution of women as entrepreneurs".

35. However, there is a mushrooming of casinos, body-shopping and narcotics that is a cause for alarm about both the impact on the local socio-economics as well as the kind of tourism that is growing.

Governance

36. The Government of Goa enacted a legislation to regulate the tourism-related activities in the State. This was enacted in 1982 as the Goa Registration of Tourist Trade Act and has been in force since April 1985. The Goa Registration of Tourist Trade Rules were also formulated in 1985 for registration of the hotels, tour operators and for regulating their businesses. It is mandatory for all hotels, travel agents, tour operators, tourist guides, tourist taxi operators and dealers of notified articles and other persons engaged in tourist activities to register themselves under the Act. Registration is to be annually renewed. The regulatory control exercised by the Department of Tourism gives it the needed strength to oversee the tourism growth in the state.

37. However, most of the tourism-related activities are also governed by different provisions and rules of the Government of Goa. The tourist taxi operators and tour operators are also governed by the Road Transport Authority under the Department of Transport. The hotels and restaurants are also governed by the concerned hunicipal laws as well as by the State laws on health and sanitation. Due to this multiplicity of control there is a need for an apex body in tourism that oversees the tourism sector of the State.

38. Countries like France and Portugal have a nodal body that oversees the development of the tourism sector of their respective countries. Designated as the tourism observatory, its functions include planning and analysis of the investment that is needed in the sector to achieve the pre-determined goals. This is apart from the tourism regulatory bodies at local levels and also at different regional levels.

Proposed Three-Tier System for Governance of the Tourism Sector

39. A three-tier system for governance of the tourism sector is proposed here. This system will be at the *taluka* level, district level and at the State level.

The First-Tier

40. This will comprise representatives of different village *panchayats*, private entrepreneurs in the tourism field, government at the *taluka* level and academicians/educators/tourism activists (NGOs). The function of this *taluka* level body would be to identify the level of development in their *taluka vis-à-vis* tourism. This would include identification of tourism attraction potential, infrastructure needs, educational needs related to tourism and also employment generation potential through tourism. This tier would also function as the facilitating agency for clearance of projects related to tourism in their area.

The Second-Tier

41. This would comprise the representatives of the First-tier from each *taluka* for the district as a whole. The representative would represent the interests of the *taluka* at the district level. The body would also comprise of the representatives of the district administration from various departments connected with tourism. The functions of this body would include coordinating the various resources available at the *taluka* level to ensure smooth and proper development of the tourism industry in the region (district).

The Third-Tier

42. This would be the apex body comprising the members of the various organisations involved in tourism including industry representatives, representatives of NGOs associated with tourism, academicians, planning authorities of the State etc. The body would formulate the vision, mission, strategies and policies and developmental plans for the entire State, and the breakup of this would be made available to the Second-tier and thence, on to the First-tier.

43. Most industry players would be covered under this governance system and as such the implementation of tourism projects can be focused and smooth as it involves people at the grassroot level in the State. It would also help to develop the quality of life for the residents of the State apart from giving a better tourism experience to the visitors.

Infrastructure

44. The role of infrastructure is to extend strong skeletal support to the flesh and muscle of the economy. In short, it is the backbone which supports the revenue generation activities of an economy. Without adequate infrastructure the development of the economy will retard and grow at a slow pace making it unable to keep pace with development of competing economies.

45. Major infrastructure aspects of a tourism economy like the one in Goa deal with the following:

- Transport (air, railways, road, waterways.
- Water resources.
- Power (fuel and energy).
- Sanitation (sewerage and waste disposal).
- Health systems (hospitals and other supporting services).
- Financial markets (banks, foreign exchange dealers etc.).
- Education.

Transport

46. Air transport is currently serviced by the Dabolim Navy Airport at Dabolim, Vasco. This caters to the domestic and the international charter flights operating to Goa during the season. The airport is still not a full fledged international airport and scheduled international carriers are not allowed to operate from here due to lack of facilities for such operations. With the increase in the domestic air service players there is an increased traffic of domestic airlines and this is likely to increase in the near future due to the larger number of players that would be entering the market. The Government is planning an airport at Mopa in North Goa (Pernem *taluka*) to cater to the domestic and international air traffic to Goa. This would release the airport at Dabolim to the Naval authorities. Currently till the new Airport takes shape and becomes operational, the Government has announced plans to restructure the Dabolim airport to accommodate a larger number of travellers. Air transport in India is a growing phenomenon and with the competition hotting up, the sector will evidence an increased air traffic which needs to be tapped as far as Goa is concerned. This is because Goa gets about 1.1 million domestic tourists each year. In terms of mode of transport of arrival at Goa, air transport ranks the last (an assumption since the other three *viz.*, railway, road and water travel mechanisms are not mapped for tourist arrivals).

47. In terms of railways, the state is well connected in terms of tracks with both the North and the South. The commissioning of the Konkan railway is a major boost to the potential of tourist arrivals from the south and also from the west. Since Goa gets a large number of tourists from West Bengal and Gujarat apart from Karnataka and Maharashtra, railway links to the eastern part of the country need to be shored up. Currently there is a single train that runs thrice a week to Vijayawada (Andhra Pradesh) which is the gateway to the eastern railway and the north-eastern railway. With the advent of Konkan railway the platforms also have been extended to accommodate a larger number of trains. Further shoring up of these facilities at other stations apart from Margao will enable the State to have a convenient connection to the rest of the country and draw higher domestic tourists to the State.

48. Road networks in Goa are definitely better than most other states. The quality of roads and the level of connectivity is relatively high when compared to other states. However, there is a need to improve the connectivity in collaboration with other states as the approach roads from the two neighbouring states Karnataka and Maharashtra have deteriorated and are a dampener for tourists to come to Goa. There has been a proliferation of four wheelers in the country and due to rising incomes people prefer to travel in their own vehicles. This increases the road usage and in Goa this has been seen especially during the festivals and events organised by the State as a part of the tourism activity. Due to this increased road traffic in the recent years, there is a need to develop double or four lane traffic roads on a BOOT basis. This will be the approach roads into Goa and could be peripheral roads and support the arterial roads (State Highways 1, 5 and 6) and the major district roads. There is also a need to improve the condition of the 3,622 kilometres of village roads. National Highway length in Goa is about 270 kilometres and the State Highway length and major district roads measure 232 kilometres and 815 kilometres respectively. These roads need to be looked at critically due to the fact that widening of these roads adds to the quality of the road and would serve the population of Goa in a better manner.

49. The public transport system in Goa needs to be reviewed. Though there seems to be some semblance of public transport between the cities in Goa there is a need to review the quality of the transport system. Investments by the Government in the bus stations is a welcome move but some regulated environment should be implemented for the upkeep of the quality of the transport vehicles.

50. Waterways are also used in Goa for transportation both for public and cargo. Public transportation is undertaken by the River Navigation Department at various places in Goa for a point-to-point service across the rivers. This eases some transportation problems in Goa especially to places where bus services as a part of public transportation system is not available or is difficult and time consuming. Most of this transportation is done through "ferries". The river waterways have to be further explored for designing a safe, eco-friendly transport system both for pleasure as well as for use by local population. According to the Tourism Master Plan for Goa, 2001, there are 22 inland water routes and Goa has about 555 kilometres of waterways of which 256 kilometres are navigable for large crafts. Apart from some entertainment value designed near the Mandovi River by the Goa Tourism Development Corporation and some private entrepreneurs for taking tourists for a river cruise there is nothing specifically developed in terms of waterways. This is a good activity resource which could be developed as a good public transport system. Goa also has a harbour at Mormugao, which is utilised mainly for cargo purposes. Other jetties are used for fishing and for smaller crafts to operate in the river. Waterways development would entail development of these jetties as well.

Water Resources

51. There are a total of seven water supply plants (schemes) that irrigate entire Goa in terms of potable and safe drinking water and water for commercial and industrial purposes. The total capacity in 1997 was 314 MLD and the demand was 242 MLD. The water supply demand for the year 2011 is calculated and given in the Tourism Master Plan of Goa as 338 MLD while the capacity of the seven schemes is to be enhanced to 594 MLD by 2011. The water needs due to influx of more tourists to Goa will surely need to be satisfied apart from the local demand for water.

Power

52. The total power consumed by different sectors in Goa in 1996-97 was 9,305.27 lakh kWh. More than half of this was for industrial purposes. The power situation in Goa is entirely dependent on the Southern Grid and the Western Grid with some support from a couple of projects. As Goa does not produce power to a large extent (the Reliance Power Plant produces for the industry), there is a need to assess the actual need of the tourism sector as well as the growing industry sector. The increased tourist inflow would mean more power consumption for the hotels and apartments that house tourists and also more power consumption by the supporting services that cater to the tourists needs.

Sanitation

53. Solid waste management and waste water disposal systems have been in place in Goa for a long time. According to the Tourism Master Plan 2001 of Goa, a total of 145.50 MLD of waste water was disposed in 1997. Out of this only 7.57 was from tourism. Major problems however, are not in the area of waste water disposal but associated with the solid waste management systems. The solid waste management system should be able to deal with the waste generated by the community as the tourist is affected because he/she is a part of the community for the touring period. The current solid waste management system for the entire state is inadequate and newer sites for disposal of solid waste need to be identified for proper disposal.

Development and Growth Areas

54. Every tourism destination has resources. These resources are utilised by the destination managers to enhance the tourism experience for the tourist. The major kinds of resources are:

- Principal resources (Those that are the motivating factors for the tourist to include in his/her choice of destinations).
- Supporting resources (Those that do not create a primary demand for tourists but aid the principal resources).

55. The Principal resources are further classified into:

- Natural resources (flora, fauna, landscape, climate and water)
- Cultural resources (religious, heritage, gastronomy, ethnicity)
- Event resources (festivals, sports, business, other events)
- Activity resources (recreational, services, facilities)
- Service resources (transportation, accommodation, reception, catering services).

Natural Resources

56. Among the natural resources, Goa has the following:

a) A 105 kilometre coastline which has 34 important and pristine beaches.
b) A canyon in the hills to the northwest (Devil's Canyon).
c) Islands (Bat Island).
d) Causeway (Ribander Causeway).
e) Spice gardens.
f) Marine life forms in the sea.
g) Wildlife sanctuaries.
h) Rainy season.
i) Zuari, Mandovi, Sal and other rivers, sea, Mayem Lake, Dudhsagar Waterfalls and Kesarval Springs.

Cultural Resources

57. Among the cultural resources, Goa has the following:

a) Churches, cathedrals, temples.
b) Forts, historic buildings, heritage zones, museums.
c) Gastronomy including "Feni" and "Fish".
d) Dances—both Portuguese and Goan.
e) Handicrafts.
f) Music.

Event Resources

58. Among the event resources, Goa has the following:

a) Festivals (religious, musical, dance, food and film).
b) Sports (go-carting, cricket, football).
c) Business events (conventions, trade shows, handicraft fairs).
d) Fairs (local religious fairs held in villages).
e) Carnival.

Activity Resources

59. Among the activity resources, Goa has the following:

a) Recreational activities like parasailing, water sports, snorkeling, scuba diving, bungee jumping and hiking.
b) Services like theatres, art galleries, retail outlets, shopping malls, craft galleries and convention centre.
c) Wildlife sanctuaries, mines, harbour, botanical gardens.

Service Resources

60. Among service resources, Goa has the following:

a) Transportation (local, regional, national and international).
b) Accommodation (star and non-star categories, local hotels etc.).
c) Reception (information centres, maps, guide services etc.).
d) Catering services (restaurants, bars, coffee shops, picnic sites).
e) Medical services, currency exchangers, telephone and postal services.

61. The above mentioned resources are the ones that are being currently used and various other such resources that are not as yet developed could be done in the future. This requires a strong resource audit involving an inventory of the resources and their evaluation. Mapping these resources is an onerous task and the State government should undertake this on a war footing to enable itself to plan the introduction of various products in the years to come so that tourists can be better dispersed.

62. Goa's gastronomy, wine and local drink Feni are very popular all over the world. This is evident from the food festivals that are organised by the tourism industry in the capital city of Panaji.

63. Goa's carnival as a tourist event is highly promoted by the tourism department of the State government and is also quite heavily attended by the tourists, both domestic as well as international.

IFFI and Entertainment

64. The recently enhanced status of Goa as a permanent venue for the International Film Festival of India (IFFI) is an addition to the event resources of Goa and this being a newly acquired resource for the destination will take some time to develop to its full potential in terms of being able to give adequate returns on the monetary capital and the social capital to the society. The effects of this event will have to be monitored in order to assess its potential to be able to affect the tourist and local population involvement in a positive manner. However such festivals, be it film or business or trade give rise to an increased activity and utilisation of resources that are a part of the resource portfolio of an economy.

65. There exists a good potential for the tourism activity in developing the local festivals (*Zatras* or *Festas*) that are held in the villages. These are local festivals associated with religious activities or annual celebrations of religions. They are not only a point of cultural significance but also a point where there exists a substantial amount of trade and commercial activity. The exact cultural and economic impact of these festivals has to be examined and adequate measure should be taken so that they can be developed.

Carrying Capacity and Sustainable Activity

66. Estimating the carrying capacity of a destination is not an easy task. The World Tourism Organisation (WTO) has estimated the carrying capacity of Goa as 41 lakh tourists per year (Tourism Master Plan for Goa, 2001). The figure for year 2011 (estimated by the Tourism Master Plan for Goa) is 21.23 lakh which is about 50 per cent of the capacity calculated by WTO. The current figure of tourism arrivals in 2004 is 24.49 lakh. The average rate of growth calculated by the Tourism Master Plan is 6 per cent but the growth percentage for the years 2003 and 2004 is 27 per cent and 20 per cent respectively. Moreover the figure taken by WTO does not take into consideration the quality of tourism consumption experience as well as the local consumption experience of the infrastructure. Due to the intense consumption of the infrastructure as well as due to the migration of labour into Goa from neighbouring states, there is a greater demand on the basic infrastructure and hence the carrying capacity needs to be looked at critically. The Tourism Master Plan for Goa suggests that a fresh study of the carrying capacity for Goa has to be conducted in 2006.

67. Carrying capacity of a destination as far as tourism is concerned basically looks at the capacity of the region to absorb tourism activities and facilities. It is generally considered the upper limit of tourist activity in a destination beyond which facilities are saturated, the environment degraded and the visitor experience lessened. The carrying capacity of a destination in overall terms is different from that at each and every attraction which is visited by the tourists. The carrying capacity at an attraction can be defined as

$$CC = f(Q, T, N, U_t, DM, AB)$$

Where Q = Quantity of the attraction resources

T = Tolerance to usage of the resources

N = Number of visitors to the attraction

U_t = The type of use to which the attraction is put

DM = The design and management of the visitor attraction

AB = The attitudes and behaviour of the visitors to the attraction.

68. Given this definition of the carrying capacity it is but necessary to look at each and every attraction resource as spelt out in the development and growth section of this report in terms of understanding its threshold level so that proper planning can be done by the State government.

69. Carrying capacity of coastal regions is more complex due to the fact that some of the environmental aspects need to be considered critically. The sand dunes at the beach are one of the issues wherein little attention is paid to the denudation of the beach. The dunes form part of the beach system and are neglected due to poor understanding of the nature of beach tourism dynamics.

70. Coastal tourism which is the mainstay of tourism in Goa needs special attention with respect to the quality of sea water, the cleanliness of the beaches, the availability and maintenance of the sand dunes, the level of commercial activity permitted in the designated beach area, etc. Carrying capacity at other major attractions also needs to be carried out to identify the through-put that can be accommodated by Goa.

71. The current level of tourism activity is constrained due to lack of infrastructural facilities such as an international airport, larger railway networks and better approach roads. Once these infrastructure facilities are in place then the tourist traffic to Goa will definitely increase and that would bring a challenge that needs planning.

Strengths, Weaknesses, Opportunities and Threats

Strengths

72. The strength of any tourism destination is the quality of resources that it possesses. Goa has been in fact blessed with a number of such resources. Some of these are:

- A long stretch of coastline which is ecologically and scenically beautiful.
- Excellent landscape in the hinterlands with the Western Ghats and the rivers.
- Warm and hospitable nature of the local population.
- Good climate throughout the year.
- High levels of literacy of the local population. Peace loving nature of the people.

- Rich flora and fauna together with rich cultural heritage.
- Fairly good accessibility.
- Industry status to tourism.

Weaknesses

73. Goa as a tourism destination is also encumbered with weaknesses which need to be addressed. Some of the weaknesses are:

- Lack of a comprehensive tourism policy.
- Lack of cohesiveness amongst the players in the industry when it comes to marketing Goa.
- Lack of internal marketing of tourism to the local residents.
- Lack of infrastructure.
- Lack of proper coordination between the agencies for tourism development.

Opportunities

74. Goa also has a substantive level of opportunities in the global tourism industry. Some of those are:

- Movement form beach tourism to heritage tourism as a larger part of the international and domestic tourists are more knowledge tourists who like to experience the cultures of the destination they visit. In fact, museum visitation worldwide has increased due to the desire to know the past.
- Medical tourism is one area which is developing fast due to the world class facilities in medicine available in India. There is a good opportunity for Goa if it can set up these facilities in Goa.
- The resources available to Goa can enable it to bring about a high level of activity-based tourism such as adventure tourism, events tourism, entertainment tourism, nature tourism and eco-tourism.
- Goa is a favourite destination for makers of Hindi movies. Many such movies have been shot on locales in Goa. This market can be further explored to see that proper facilities are made available to encourage this activity.
- Most organisations tend to have their business conventions in Goa. Most dealers' meets are held in Goa as it provides them the best mixture of business and pleasure. Given that many corporate bodies look out for this kind of opportunity, the Goan government should think of moving in this direction in terms of creating adequate facilities such as a convention centre to cash in on the opportunity.

Threats

75. One of the most important threats to Goa comes out of its own weakness. The lack of adequate infrastructure and lack of comprehensive long term tourism policy coupled with lack of strong implementation of existing policies create a situation of resource abuse leading to diminished visitor experience.

76. Some of the threats are:

- Competing destinations like Kerala and Maharashtra for beach tourism (within the country). Maldives, Sri Lanka, Seychelles, Malaysia, Indonesia, Thailand etc. (internationally).
- There exists the social evil of gambling, drug trafficking, prostitution, paedophilia and corruption which create a negative image of the destination. Inability to contain this is also a weakness but this threat to the tourism industry due to these activities cannot be ignored.
- Another threat that stems from lack of long term policy on tourism is the destination getting an image of a cheap destination in the international market. Due to this image the earning potential of the industry is severely crippled though there is enough scope to promote Goa as a high spending tourist market. Creating the necessary resources for the high quality image is not seen in Goa and this could spell doom for the industry in future.

Recommendations and Development Strategies

77. The need is to develop on a priority basis infrastructure to enable more through-put of people: airport with integrated rail, sea and road links; corridor of tourism and entertainment areas with pedestrian plazas and entertainment events; event and convention infrastructure.

78. Create annual event calendar for activities in Goa by developing an online portal for event details to be posted by registered event groups well in advance.

79. Develop infrastructure of better signage and shuttle services between places of common attraction.

Chapter 11

Information, Banking and Risk Management

Issues in Banking

Penetration

1. Expectedly, the bank penetration in Goa is one of the highest in the country. The number of people who are catered on average by a scheduled commercial bank is an easy measure of this. As compared to the all-India figure of 15,828, in Goa, for every 5,423 persons there was a commercial bank in 2004.[1]

2. The total amount of deposit mobilised by the scheduled commercial banks in Goa in 2004 was Rs. 10,481 crore and the credit disbursed was Rs. 2,282 crore. This works out to a per capita deposit in the scheduled commercial banks (SCBs) at Rs. 59,282 which is the third highest in the country after Chandigarh and Delhi. Interestingly though the credit-deposit ratio looks skewed, the per capita credit disbursed by scheduled commercial banks in Goa stood at Rs. 12,907 which was the fifth highest after Chandigarh, Delhi, Maharashtra and Tamil Nadu.[2]

3. The all-India total of scheduled commercial banks (SCBs) was 69,071 of which 32,227 were in the rural sector, 15,288 in the semi-urban, 11,806 in the urban and 9,750 in the metropolitan segment.[3] As on 31st March 2004, Goa had 345 SCBs—148 in the rural segment and 197 in the semi-urban segment.[4] Goa, therefore, accounts for only 0.5 per cent of the total number of commercial banks. Strangely, despite all the foreign tourists that the state attracts it has failed to attract even a single foreign bank as of 2004. The high per capita income in the state has its impact on the financial structure.

Growth

4. The expansion of the banking infrastructure in Goa has been quite remarkable. In 1962, there were only five bank branches operational in Goa. This increased to 300 branches at the time of statehood in 1987 and stood at 456 in 2002-03. The fastest expansion over the last two decades in the banking sector has evidently been in the cooperative sector which saw a three-fold increase in the number of branches. However, in terms of absolute number of additional branches opened, it is still the commercial banking segment that dominates the scene.

TABLE 11.1

Number of Bank Branches

Year	*1980-81*	*1990-91*	*2000-01*	*2001-02*	*2002-03*
Commercial banks	217	255	313	319	323
Cooperative banks	41	51	131	132	133
Total	258	306	444	451	456

Source: GOGa (Various Years).

5. The increase in the number of banks ensured that the bank penetration measured as per bank population has gone up from 3,096 persons (catered to by a bank) in 1980-81 to 3,036 in 2002-03.

1. In fact if one were to exclude Chandigarh (5126) which is a Union Territory and a city, Goa has the highest per capita concentration of commercial banks (*Source:* Table 2.3 *http://www.rbi.org.in*).
2. This data refers to 2004 (*Source:* Table 2.3 *http://www.rbi.org.in*).
3. According to RBI classification, rural centre signifies an area with population less than 10,000 persons, semi-urban indicates a population between 10,000 persons and 1,00,000 lakh.
4. The population group classification (rural and semi-urban) is based on the 1991 census. This has therefore, meant that none of the state's urban areas like Margao, Panaji, Vasco and Mapusa qualify as urban centres as far as bank classification goes.

6. Tiswadi *taluka* has the highest frequency of banks with a population of 1824 persons on average being catered to by a bank while Satari has the lowest with 6037 being catered to by a bank. North Goa on average showed a higher bank presence than South Goa. The reason for the growth in the banking infrastructure in the state is due to increased business for them which implies either a high level of deposit base and/or credit demand in the region. As we will indicate below, it is the increase in deposits that has triggered the growth of banks in Goa which is again due to large remittance of foreign incomes from abroad.

TABLE 11.2

***Taluka*-wise Population per Branch**

	1980-81	*2002-03*
Goa	3906	3036
North Goa	3762	2847
Tiswadi	2807	1824
Bardez	2482	2411
Pernem	14838	4943
Bicholim	5699	4675
Satari	13612	6037
Ponda	4904	3670
South Goa	4110	3320
Sanguem	5082	4404
Canacona	5133	4112
Quepem	6949	4759
Salcete	3399	2817
Mormugao	4105	3315

Source: GOGa (Various Years).

Spread

7. The disaggregated data available at the time of writing indicates that in 2002-03, there were 323 branches of SCBs and 133 branches of cooperative banks operative in the state. While State Bank of India being the lead bank in the state topped the volume of deposit generated in 2002-03, the cooperative banks had a remarkable performance as far as deposit and credit generation is concerned. SBI with 52 branches and Corporation Bank with 31 branches dominated the SCB segment. Goa State Cooperative Bank (GSCB) with 56 branches and Mapusa Urban Cooperative Bank with 26 branches are the 'big' two in the Cooperative segment. Note that GSCB had more branches than SBI.

TABLE 11.3

No. of Branches of Various Banks in Goa

Name of Bank	*2002-03*	*Name of Bank*	*2002-03*
Scheduled Commercial Banks	323	Citizen's Coop Bank	4
Cooperative Banks	133	Development Credit Bank of India	4
Goa State Coop Bank	56	Karnataka Bank	4
State Bank of India	52	Punjab National Bank	4
Corporation Bank	31	ICICI Bank	3
Bank of India	28	State Bank of Mysore	3
Bank of Baroda	27	United Western Bank	3
Mapusa Urban Coop Bank	26	Federal Bank	2
Central Bank of India	22	South Indian Bank	2
Canara Bank	21	Unied Bank of India	2
Goa Urban Coop Bank	18	UTI Bank	2
Syndicate Bank	17	Vyasya Bank	2
Dena Bank	16	Women's Coop Bank	2
Indian Overseas Bank	11	Allahabad Bank	1
Union Bank of India	11	Catholic Syrian Bank	1
Bicholim Urban Coop Bank	10	Goan People's Urban Coop Bank	1
Bank of Maharashtra	9	IDBI Bank	1
Madgaum Urban Coop Bank	9	IndusInd Bank	1
Centurion Bank	6	Jammu & Kashmir Bank	1
HDFC Bank	6	North Kanara GSB Coop Bank	1
Indian Bank	6	Oriental Bank of Commerce	1
Global Trust Bank	5	Punjab & Sind Bank	1
Saraswat Coop Bank	5	Ratnakar Bank	1
United Commercial Bank	5	Sangli Bank	1
Vijaya Bank	5	Shamrao Vithal Coop Bank	1
Andhra Bank	4	State Bank of Patiala	1
All Banks			862

Source: GOGa (Various Years).

Deposits

8. The total amount of deposits received by banks went up from Rs. 9 crore in 1962 to Rs. 10,585 crore in 2002-03. In the last two decades (between 1980-81 and 2000-01), aggregate deposits have grown 22-fold and between 2000-01 to 2002-03 (in three years), the increase has been one and half times. This is remarkable as far as deposits in the State are concerned.

TABLE 11.4

Deposits in Banks in Goa

	Units	*1980-81*	*1990-91*	*2000-01*	*2001-02*	*2002-03*
Deposits	Crore Rs.	381	1637	8416	9629	12474
Deposits per branch	Crore Rs.	1	5	19	21	24
Deposits per capita	Rs.	3,779	13,993	62,618	70,592	78,437

Source: GOGa (Various Years).

9. In keeping with the growth in the banking infrastructure and the jump in deposits in the state, the deposits per branch increased from a mere Rs. 1.48 crore (in 1980-81) to Rs. 23.81 crore in (2002-03). This implies that the growth in deposits actually outstripped the growth in the number of branches catering to a given population in the state. The per capita deposit in the state thus grew from Rs. 3,779 (in 1980-81) to Rs. 78,437 (in 2002-03). This indicates a 20-fold increase in per capita deposits.

10. If one examines the *taluka*-wise situation, there is wide differentiation in terms of economic affluence in Goa. The per capita deposit rate is a good indicator of the level of economic prosperity in a region. The total deposits raised in Goa amounted to Rs. 10,858.13 crore (2002-03) of which Rs. 6,089 crore came from North Goa and Rs. 4,768 crore from South Goa.

TABLE 11.5

Deposits in Banks in *Talukas* of Goa in 2002-03

	Deposits (crores)	*Per Capita Deposits (in Rs.)*
Goa	10,858	78,437
North Goa	6,089	
Tiswadi	2,875	175,095
Bardez	2,362	101,035
Pernem	88	11,835
Bicholim	219	23,409
Satari	50	8,233
Ponda	496	32,175
South Goa	4,769	
Sanguem	91	13,733
Canacona	118	26,195
Quepem	252	33,121
Salcete	3,110	116,240
Mormugao	1,197	80,231

Source: GOGa (Various Years).

11. However, the three *talukas* of Salcete (South Goa), Tiswadi and Bardez (North Goa) together accounted for Rs. 8,347 crore which is 77 per cent of the entire deposits in the state.[5] This matches the per branch deposit rate with Salcete (Rs. 30 crore), Tiswadi (Rs. 28 crore) and Bardez (Rs. 23 crore) in the top three slots. Similarly, the per capita deposit rate is highest again in these *talukas*—Tiswadi (Rs. 1,75,095), Salcete (Rs. 1,16,240) and Bardez (Rs. 1,01,035). The average per capita deposit of Goa was Rs. 78,437.

12. In order to justify the claim that this is a remittance driven bank expansion, we need to separate the domestic and non-resident deposits. In 1992, the proportion of the Non-Resident External (NRE) deposits to total deposits in Goa's banks amounted to 25 per cent and in a span of 10 years went up to 32 per cent. This too is likely to be an underestimate because some of the remittance amount gets deposited by resident family members in their respective accounts which shows up under the domestic savings column.

TABLE 11.6

Domestic and NRE Deposits in Banks of Goa

	Units	*1992-93*	*2002-03*
Domestic	Crore Rs.	1,716	7,347
NRE	Crore Rs.	583	3,512
Total	Crore Rs.	2,300	10,858
NRE as	Proportion of Total	25	32

Source: GOGa (Various Years) and SBI (2005).

Credit

TABLE 11.7

Credit Extended by Banks of Goa

		1980-81	*1990-91*	*2000-01*	*2001-02*	*2002-03*
Credit	Crore Rs.	171	641	2,405	2,862	2,992
Credit per branch	Crore Rs.	0.7	2.1	5.4	6.4	6.6
Credit per capita	Rs.	1,698	5,479	17,896	20,981	21,613

Source: GOGa (Various Years).

13. The role of remittance becomes clearer when we look at the credit side of bank transactions. The volume of credit disbursed increased from Rs. 171.18 crore (in 1980-1981) to Rs. 2991.93 crore (in 2002-03). This implies a 17-fold increase in credit over this period. The increase in per capita credit in the same period has been 12 times and the credit per branch also increased 10 times. Both these are lower than the increase in credit for the same period therefore, credit off-take has not kept pace with increase in deposits. Therefore, the increase in banking infrastructure has largely been to secure the foreign remittances as deposits and not finance a domestic economy driven growth.

5. If one were to add Mormugao to this list, then the four *talukas* account for 88 per cent of the deposits in the state.

TABLE 11.8

Credit Extended in Different *Talukas* by Banks of Goa

Taluka	*2002-03* *Credit Per Capita*	*2001-02* *Credit Per Branch (crore Rs.)*	*2002-03* *Aggregate Credit (crore Rs.)*	*Proportion of Taluka Credit in Total Credit*
Goa	21,613	6.35	2,991.93	100.00
North Goa		6.57	1,875.27	62.67
Tiswadi	78,119	13.64	1,282.65	42.87
Bardez	13,968	3.27	326.59	10.91
Pernem	3,049	1.53	22.61	0.75
Bicholim	7,168	3.24	67.01	2.23
Sattari	2,395	1.47	14.46	0.48
Ponda	10,508	3.57	161.95	5.41
South Goa		6.01	1,116.66	37.32
Sanguem	5,395	3.24	49.11	1.64
Canacona	3,265	1.34	14.77	0.49
Quepem	3,049	2.48	41.08	1.37
Salcete	24,420	5.72	653.44	21.84
Mormugao	24,015	9.86	358.26	11.97

Source: GOGa (Various Years).

14. If we examine the distribution of the credit generated by Goa's banks a little more carefully it indicates some interesting features and is similar to the deposits as far as *taluka*-wise data is concerned. The credit per branch in 2001-02 was 6.36 crore with North Goa average being marginally more than the South Goa average. However, the amount of credit disbursed differs widely between the two districts. In fact, Tiswadi alone exceeds the credit disbursement of the entire South Goa district. North Goa accounted for 62 per cent of the credit disbursed and Tiswadi *taluka* alone accounted for 42 per cent of the total credit disbursed in the state. Obviously Tiswadi also dominates the per capita credit disbursed—Rs. 78,119, which is three times higher than the all-Goa average of Rs. 21,613.

Developmental Issues

15. Two issues will be taken up here: direction of credit, geographically and sectorally.

16. We first take up the issue of which sectors have been the recipient of the credit disbursement in the State.

TABLE 11.9

Bank-wise Disaggregated Credit Distribution

Name of Bank	*Deposits*	*Advances*	*Priority Sector*	*Weaker Sections*	*Under 20 Point Programme*	*Propn of Adv. to Priority in Total Adv.*
All Banks	10,858.13	3,818.10	1,203.76	97.82	38.64	31.50
SCBs	9,563.40	2,165.76	601.00	38.48	38.52	27.80
State Bank of India	2,128.04	454.41	131.89	4.50		29.00
Bank of India	1,238.78	400.60	146.25	14.10	0.72	36.50
Canara Bank	912.29	290.15	43.48	3.92	7.08	15.00
Corporation Bank	954.91	132.69	39.80	1.28		30.00
Syndicate Bank	521.39	118.37	31.09	2.63	11.01	26.30
Bank of Baroda	702.07	107.51	39.94	5.18	1.17	37.20
United Western Bank	68.69	79.84	0.15			0.20
Bank of Maharashtra	204.46	68.56	20.45	0.16	1.58	29.80
UTI Bank	18.18	63.05	4.54			7.20
Punjab National Bank	67.11	54.07	19.81	0.02	0.11	36.60
Union Bank of India	194.46	46.48	22.42	1.51	1.09	48.20
Central Bank of India	373.66	43.52	21.08	0.99	0.85	48.40
Centurion Bank	265.67	42.62	1.56			3.70
State Bank of Mysore	29.09	31.78	4.53	0.01		14.30
Indian Overseas Bank	207.30	31.49	10.38	0.70	0.80	33.00
Dena Bank	272.72	24.73	1.65	2.54	2.54	6.70
Oriental Bank of Commerce	27.63	23.00	10.48	0.12		45.60
Vijaya Bank	80.39	18.48	9.65	0.03		52.20
Karnataka Bank	87.83	17.60	5.49	0.03	0.29	31.20
Andhra Bank	82.62	14.37	4.33			30.10
Federal Bank	57.55	14.37	1.32		0.84	9.20

contd...

...contd...

Name of Bank	Deposits	Advances	Priority Sector	Weaker Sections	Under 20 Point Programme	Propn of Adv to Priority in Total Adv
Indian Bank	99.44	13.42	5.58	0.52		41.60
ICICI Bank	312.56	12.40	0.17			1.40
United Commercial Bank	62.66	10.03	6.79	0.19	0.56	67.70
Jammu & Kashmir Bank	13.43	9.58	8.30		9.58	86.60
Ratnakar Bank	17.20	9.55	2.29			24.00
South Indian Bank	23.99	6.85	0.91			13.30
ING Vyasya Bank	48.32	4.90	1.40	0.04		28.60
Unied Bank of India	14.80	3.30	0.59		0.29	17.90
IDBI Bank	11.13	3.15	1.60			50.80
Development Credit Bank of India	18.90	3.12	0.31			9.90
Punjab & Sind Bank	4.61	2.99	0.83			27.80
IndusInd Bank	7.18	2.51				0.00
Sangli Bank	5.69	1.48	0.55		0.01	37.20
Catholic Syrian Bank	23.81	1.41	0.31			22.00
State Bank of Patiala	11.45	1.35	0.65			48.10
Global Trust Bank	110.73	1.07				0.00
Allahabad Bank	3.86	0.96	0.43	0.01		44.80
HDFC Bank	278.80					
Cooperative Banks	1,294.73	826.17	301.38	29.67	0.06	36.50
Goa State Coop Bank	341.89	283.77	51.54	2.96		18.20
Goa Urban Coop Bank	359.10	172.27	102.22	6.33		59.30
Mapusa Urban Coop Bank	214.69	132.75	39.23	7.45		29.60
Bicholim Urban Coop Bank	104.55	72.39				0.00
Madgaum Urban Coop Bank	116.39	66.28	53.60	6.88		80.90
Saraswat Coop Bank	97.21	57.17	25.12	2.06		43.90
Shamrao Vithal Coop Bank	6.18	14.31	12.22	0.15		85.40
Citizen's Coop Bank	24.41	13.65	9.91	1.70		72.60
Women's Coop Bank	15.56	7.52	4.74	1.63		63.00
North Kanara GSB Coop Bank	11.22	5.49	2.47	0.45		45.00
Goan People's Urban Coop Bank	3.53	0.57	0.33	0.06	0.06	57.90

Source: SBI (2005).

The available data informs us of the advances that each bank group has given to the priority sector, weaker sections and advances under the 20 point programme.

17. The average proportion of deposits advanced to the priority sector is about 32 per cent. The cooperative sector (37 per cent) here has outperformed the scheduled commercial banks (28 per cent). Shamrao Vithal Coop Bank had the highest proportion being devoted to priority sector lending (85 per cent), followed by Madgaum Urban Cooperative Bank (81 per cent). Among the SCBs, Jammu & Kashmir Bank (86 per cent) and United Commercial Bank (67 per cent) were the best performers. In terms of volume of credit being advanced to the priority sector, it was Bank of India (Rs. 146 crore), State Bank of India (Rs. 131.89 crore) and Goa Urban Coop Bank (Rs. 102 crore) that were the best performers.

18. The second issue which we address here is the sectoral distribution of credit. In the last quarter of 2004-2005, Rs. 561.97 crore of credit was disbursed by all banks. Of this, the service sector got 65 per cent, industry got 27 per cent and agriculture got only 8 per cent. Interestingly, in the cooperative sector, the share of credit going to services was 92 per cent, while agriculture and industry got 8 per cent and 9 per cent respectively (SBI, 2005). The large contribution of the services sector to the economy is re-emphasised by the credit disbursement data but is obviously disproportionate to its contribution to NSDP (Net State Domestic Product).

19. Service led growth of an economy in developmental parlance is regarded as a post-industrial characteristic. It is considered to be employment-oriented unlike industrial units where there is a disproportionately large expense on

capital and it is also perceived to be environmetal friendly. In fact, citizens of the state have been vigilant to the threat of entry of polluting industries.

Self Help Groups

20. The banking system also made progress in terms of expanding the self help group (SHG) programme. At the end of the 2004-05 financial year, a total of 1,486 SHG had been formed in Goa which had a membership of 17,438 persons. The Goa State Coop Bank had the highest number of SHGs as well as members followed by the State Bank of India.

TABLE 11.10

Self Help Group Scheme as on 31.03.05

	Name of Bank	*No. of SHG*	*No. of Members*
	All Banks	1486	17438
1	State Bank of India	422	4670
2	State Bank of Mysore	1	30
3	Bank of Baroda	120	1234
4	Bank of India	183	1332
5	Bank of Maharashtra	14	140
6	Canara Bank	36	455
7	Central Bank of India	38	356
8	Corporation Bank	50	570
9	Dena Bank	14	234
10	Indian Bank	1	3
11	Indian Overseas Bank	55	805
12	Syndicate Bank	10	111
13	Oriental Bank of Commerce	2	10
14	United Commercial Bank	18	360
15	Union Bank of India	9	54
16	United Western Bank	4	0
17	Goa State Coop Bank	509	7074

Source: SBI (2005).

21. We now look at the *taluka*-wise distribution of credit. This is important to understand as far as geographical spread of development is concerned. Tiswadi cornered 43 per cent of the entire credit disbursed in 2002-03. The four *talukas* of Tiswadi, Bardez, Salcete, Mormugao cornered 88 per cent of the entire credit in the same year. In fact, Tiswadi and Salcete accounted for 65 per cent of the credit disbursed. Satari and Canacona got less than 1 per cent of the entire credit.

Credit-Deposit Ratio

22. The credit-deposit ratio is often used as a yard stick to measure the economic health of a region and bank efficiency in collecting and disbursing capital. The role of banks in a modern economy is to act as a financial intermediary—mobilise savings (by providing a safe store of value) and create credit. The concentration of banks is therefore, expected to be large in any area where either there is a high income or there is need for large credit due to expansion of economic activity. While the demand for credit and supply of savings is expected to coincide in the same region because generation of economic flows also creates in its wake larger demands for credit to fund further expansion. However, under certain conditions this convergence of credit supply and demand may not occur as in the case of Goa. The reason is that a large part of the disposable income is generated outside the state (as remittances), and therefore, does not reflect increased economic activity within the state. This is reflected in the credit off-take in comparison to the amount of deposit.

TABLE 11.11

Credit Extended in Different *Talukas* by Banks of Goa

Taluka	*2002-03* *Credit Per Capita*	*2001-02* *Credit Per Branch (crore Rs.)*	*2002-03* *Aggregate Credit (crore Rs.)*	*Proportion of Taluka Credit in Total Credit*
Goa	21,613	6.35	2,991.93	100.00
North Goa		6.57	1,875.27	62.67
Tiswadi	78,119	13.64	1,282.65	42.87
Bardez	13,968	3.27	326.59	10.91
Pernem	3,049	1.53	22.61	0.75
Bicholim	7,168	3.24	67.01	2.23
Satari	2,395	1.47	14.46	0.48
Ponda	10,508	3.57	161.95	5.41
South Goa		6.01	1,116.66	37.32
Sanguem	5,395	3.24	49.11	1.64
Canacona	3,265	1.34	14.77	0.49
Quepem	3,049	2.48	41.08	1.37
Salcete	24,420	5.72	653.44	21.84
Mormugao	24,015	9.86	358.26	11.97

Source: GOGa (Various Years).

23. The all-Goa credit-deposit average for all banks (SCB and Cooperative) was 28 per cent, the SCBs notched up an average of 26 per cent while the cooperative banks had an average of 64 per cent. Outstanding in the cooperative segment were GSCB with a CD ratio of 83 per cent and Bicholim Urban Cooperative Bank. Shamrao Vithal Cooperative Bank had a CD ratio of 232 per cent but they had only one branch and therefore, their range of operation is rather limited. The SCB have much lower CD ratios—UTI bank with 2 branches tops with 324 per cent followed by United Western Bank at 116 per cent and State Bank of Mysore at 109 per cent, both with three

branches in the state. SBI and Corporation Bank, who have the largest network as described above, however have much lower CD ratios of 21 per cent and 14 per cent, respectively.

24. An additional reason why the credit-deposit ratio looks skewed for Goa is that many companies operating in the state probably conduct their financial transaction outside the state, say for example in Mumbai, even though the final utilisation of the credit may be in Goa.

25. Is the low credit-deposit ratio a reason for concern? Is Goa's wealth being drained out? The answer is a tentative 'No'. It is well-known in financial circles that banks in India are credit rich and therefore, the low credit off-take is not due to lack of supply of credit but due to low demand. This is true for not only the primary sector but also the secondary and tertiary sector. Further, the productivity of capital in other states may be higher than Goa, therefore, providing economic reason for credit to flow out of the state.

Non-Performing Assets

26. A bigger worry for banks is the level of non-performing assets (NPAs) that they possess. In 2004-05, the average of NPAs out of the total credit disbursed for all banks in Goa was 6.95 per cent. Cooperative banks however, showed a much higher level of NPAs—15.4 per cent than the commercial banks. Amongst the worst performers was the Mapusa Urban Coop Bank which has a whopping 84 per cent NPAs as a proportion of total advances in 2004-05. In contrast, the highest NPAs in the SCBs showed up in Ratnakar Bank—21 per cent.

TABLE 11.12

Non-Performing Assets of Banks in Goa

Name of Bank	*Per cent NPA to Total Advances, 2004-05*
All Banks	6.95
SCBs	
State Bank of India	4.45
State Bank of Mysore	0.85
State Bank of Patiala	0
Allahabad Bank	17.37
Andhra Bank	0.98
Bank of Baroda	7.89
Bank of India	3.87
Bank of Maharashtra	11.64
Canara Bank	4.26
Catholic Syrian Bank	0.49
Central Bank of India	12.89
Centurion Bank	0
Corporation Bank	1.53
Dena Bank	7.46
Development Credit Bank of India	4.98
Federal Bank	0.22
Global Trust Bank	
HDFC Bank	0
ICICI Bank	0
IDBI Bank	0
Indian Bank	6.57
Indian Overseas Bank	0.21
IndusInd Bank	0
ING Vyasya Bank	0.08
Jammu & Kashmir Bank	0
Karnataka Bank	1.83
Oriental Bank of Commerce	0.7
Punjab & Sind Bank	16.01
Punjab National Bank	9.24
Ratnakar Bank	21.67
Sangli Bank	0.42
South Indian Bank	2.95
Syndicate Bank	5.75
United Bank of India	0.11
Union Bank of India	9.81
United Commercial Bank	11.43
United Western Bank	1.61
UTI Bank	0
Vijaya Bank	2.89
Cooperative Banks	15.42
Goa Urban Coop Bank	0
Goa State Coop Bank	9.47
Madgaum Urban Coop Bank	0
Mapusa Urban Coop Bank	84.2
Women's Coop Bank	11.43
Citizen's Coop Bank	7.19
Bicholim Urban Coop Bank	8.67
Saraswat Coop Bank	0
North Kanara GSB Coop Bank	
Shamrao Vithal Coop Bank	25.05
Goan People's Urban Coop Bank	

Source: SBI (2005).

27. A popular financial instrument that has expanded rapidly in the last five years is the credit card. The big players in Goa are SBI in the public sector and ICICI and HDFC in the private sector. As of 2004-05, the number of credit cards issued by SBI stood at 19,500 in comparison to 16,000 issued by ICICI and 8,000 by HDFC. The delinquency rate has been reasonable ranging from a low of 1 per cent to a high of 5 per cent.

TABLE 11.13

Credit Card Usage in Goa

Players	*SBI*	*ICICI*	*HDFC*	*Others*	*Total*
Number of cards in the market	19500	16000	8000	6500	50,000
No. of EDC machines	NA	700	500	1800	3000
Since when in the market	2000	1999	2004	NA	NA
Delinquency	3.5-4 per cent	1 per cent	4-5 per cent	NA	NA

Source: SBI (2005).

Strengths and Weaknesses of Goa's Banking System

Strengths

- High per capita income leading to high deposits and growth in banking infrastructure.
- High literacy rate leading to low crime of banks.
- Highest bank penetration in the country.

Weaknesses

- Slow Cheque Clearance: Non-availability of Magnetic Identification Character Reader (MICR) technology leads to delay and increased cost of cheque realisation. For example, a cheque from Bank A in Calangute on being deposited in Bank B in Panaji could take upto five working days to get cleared because sorting is done manually bank-wise and not branch-wise.[6] Being a small state the volume of transactions is too small for individual banks to install MICR.
- Lack of Debt Recovery Tribunal: Goa does not have a debt recovery tribunal and all disputes have to be settled in Mumbai which delays recovery of debts. Banks who have non-performing assets have to seek redressal in Mumbai for resolution of pending debt recovery cases. This increases the delay and costs of debt recovery for banks.
- Low level of priority sector lending due to declining interest in agriculture and low thrust of government to establish forward and backward linkages between sectors by developing infrastructural facilities.
- Land Ownership Entitlements: Due to intricate colonial land ownership laws, sometimes tenant farmers are unable to get loans due to lack of proper land ownership documentation.
- High NPAs of some banks.

Ameliorative Strategies

- Encourage banks to install MICR—The state could subsidise or provide fiscal incentives to banks that adopt MICR.
- Setting up of Debt Recovery Tribunal—This would facilitate the recovery of assets against non-performing assets. The state machinery needs to support debt recovery as is done in case of government sponsored schemes for cooperative banks.
- Identification of below poverty line families so that targeted central funds for the same can be disbursed easily.
- Involve banks in rural development. Rural development schemes that have any financing from the state involved should be routed through banks who have the expertise to disburse as well as monitor fund use.

Issues in Risk Management

28. We now turn our attention to the Risk Management Institutions in Goa and issues related to insurance in Goa.

Segmentation

29. The insurance sector as per regulatory guidelines in India is split into two segments—life and non-life or

TABLE 11.14

Growth of Insurance in Goa

		Pre-liberation	*1993*	*1994*	*1995*	*1996*	*1997*	*1998*	*1999*	*2000*	*2001*
Life Insurance	Sum insured on new policies	93	21,058	22,522	27,972	248,266	26,197	30,458	37,705	37,584	49,662
	Premium paid on new policies (Rs. Lakhs)	n.a	421	475	480	512	592	753	1,069	964	1,271
General Insurance	Number of Policies	4,010	87,912	78,142	86	93,690	93,690	92,421		191,272	252,174
	Premium paid (Rs. Lakhs)	15	1,414	1,454	1,355	212,712	2,127	2,214	5,313	5,312	6,499

Source: GoGb (Various Years).

6. Even though the physical distance between Calangute and Panaji would be less than 30 kms.

general insurance. Till 2001, both these segments were entirely government monopolies with life insurance sector being monopolised by the Life Insurance Corporation and the non-life sector being shared by four Public Sector Undertakings (PSUs)—National Insurance, United India Assurance, Oriental Insurance, General Insurance with with General Insurance corporation acting as the holding company for the entire non-life insurance sector. In order to induct greater coverage and penetration in the market the government allowed private players to enter the insurance sector and it has led to a dramatic increase in the size and depth the market.

Growth

30. Data available till year 2001 indicates that the general insurance segment of the market has grown rapidly in Goa with a discrete jump in the mid-1990s and then again in 1999.

31. The general insurance is classified into four sub-segments: fire, marine, automobile and miscellaneous. Automobile insurance is the biggest sub-segment in the general insurance segment—about 48 per cent. It is believed that the compulsory nature of vehicle insurance makes this a large segment.

TABLE 11.15

Disaggregated View of Insurance in Goa

Insurance in 1999-2000	*Rs. (in lakhs)*	*Proportion of General Insurance (total)*
Life (sum assured on new policies)	37,705	
Life (1st year of premium paid)	1,069	
General (premium paid)	5,312	100
Fire	1,130	21
Marine	1,009	19
Automobile	2,562	48
Miscellaneous	610	12

Source: GoGb (Various Years).

Life Insurance Sector[7]

32. The life insurance sector is dominated by the Life Insurance Corporation even though newer players like Bajaj Allianz, ICICI Lombard, Aviva, New York Max Life, etc., have seen rapid growth since private players were allowed to market their products. In Goa, out of a population of 13,87,807, the number of persons eligible for insurance is estimated at 9,20,000. The LIC is currently servicing about 6,50,000 life insurance policies indicating a life insurance penetration of 68 per cent. Of this, the number of policies owned by males is 5,07,000 and by females is 1,43,000.

33. The size of the urban population in Goa is 6,90,774 and rural population is 6,97,033. The workforce division is 53 per cent for urban and 38 per cent for rural. The number of policies in terms of the urban-rural segmentation is 3,20,000 for urban and 3,30,000 for rural. The LIC under its special schemes for the rural backward sections for provision of social security has covered 10,645 persons.

Infrastructure

Connectivity

34. Communication is an essential infrastructure input that is necessary for the smooth functioning of any financial institution. However, the leased lines often have breakdowns causing connectivity failure. Therefore, broadband lines at low cost is essential for efficient functioning for online connectivity and wide area networks (WAN) to work.

Clearing House

35. At present the state does not have separate clearing house which causes delays in the transfer of funds. Given the small size of the state, there could be one central clearing house for banks such that cheques are realised without delay.

Bancassurance

36. Banks as of now are not permitted to sell insurance in India. If however, like many other parts of the world, this was permitted then a much wider insurance coverage would be possible due to wider reach of banks and their availability of greater marketing channels.

PHCs and Health Insurance

37. The government could permit the primary health centres (PHCs) to distribute and provide health insurance policy benefits. This would increase coverage and also improve quality of health care provision.

Insurance Enumeration

38. It is difficult to ascertain the degree of insurance penetration since none of the official channels of data collection enquire about insurance policies at the time of population enumeration (for example, the Census). If a

7. This section draws on Mohapatra (2005).

question on insurance could be included in the Census then it would be easy to expand the insurance coverage.

Achievements

39. Increased prosperity of a section of the population, a declining public health delivery system and rising cost of private medical health care has led to an increasing number of persons seeking medical and health insurance products. The LIC alone has sold has 6,203 such policies of which 516 have been in 2004-05 alone.

40. The other product that has attracted significant interest are pension plans which provide a fixed annuity income from the date of retirement of a person. Higher life expectancy and reduced social security systems from the state have pushed individuals to buy pension plan products. The LIC alone has sold 17,890 such policies of which 4,040 were in 2004-05 alone.

41. The LIC has introduced a programme of housing provision under the "Care Homes & Policy Holders' Housing Scheme" and Goa has been selected as one of the states for implementation.

42. We now turn our attention to the telecom and information sector.

Issues in Telecom and IT

43. Communication services and information technology are the driving forces for the surge in export growth in India in the recent past. However, Goa has not been able to attract IT investment in tune with its technical human capital potential. The high literacy rates and the widespread use of English should have made Goa a natural destination both for call centres and IT investment.

44. The share for communication in the NSDP has been about 7.5 per cent 2002-03. Given the high per capita income it has naturally seen a high consumer demand for telecommunication services as well as Internet facilities. The rapid strides of technology in India has seen a big boom in the telecom sector. From the data available from Bharat Sanchar Nigam Limited (BSNL), 17,042 mobile phone connections were provided in 2002-03 which increased to 52,195 in 2004-05. Similarly, the number of people on the waiting list has gone down from about 10,941 (as on March 31, 2001) to 3,923 in 2005. The newer technologies and increased competition have led to a reduction in operating costs and therefore, made communication cheaper and more efficient. Even though average telephone revenues per connection have fallen from Rs. 721 in 2001 to Rs. 646 in 2005, the aggregate revenues of all telecom companies have grown due to higher volumes. The substantial increase in the number of lines supplied as well as greater frequency of use has led to higher revenue earnings.

45. Internet connectivity, too, has grown substantially in the last five years. As per BSNL data (which is one of the large players in the data connectivity segment), dial up and fixed Internet connectivity has increased from 5.9 per thousand in 2001 to 21.7 per thousand in 2005 which is a three and a half-fold increase. This is an underestimate of the actual increase in Internet penetration in Goa because in the last five years, numerous big players in the private sector have also entered as internet providers Including mobile Internet.

46. Thanks to the government's policy and the cyberage scheme to give computers to students, computer penetration is the highest in the country at 40 computers per 1000 persons as against 8 per 1000 as the national average.

Strengths, Weaknesses, Opportunities and Threats

Strengths

- The small size of the state with good supporting infrastructure has been a strength. The high literacy

TABLE 11.16

Telecom Infrastructure in Goa

Items	*31-3-2001*	*31-3-2002*	*31-3-2003*	*31-3-2004*	*31-3-2005*
Total number of mobiles connected	—	—	17,042	41,874	52,195
Telephone waiting list (thousands)	11	9	5	4	4
Average telephone revenue per line per month (Rs)	722	691	585	618	647
Average mobile revenue per line per month (Rs)	—	—	—	313	233
Dial up and fixed internet connectivity (per 1000 people)	6	8	11	13	22

Source: Office of the General Manager Telecom District Goa, Panaji.

rate and economic status has been catalytic in telecom and Internet expansion.

- National Internet backbone connectivity through optical fibre cable has been established between gateways in Mumbai and Goa.
- BSNL has 125 telephone exchanges with a near 100 per cent village coverage. Total cable network measures 8,600 kms including optical fibre cables of nearly 1,041 kms. Private players too have their own cables in the state and some have adopted wireless connectivity to avoid cable laying expenses.
- The low density of population was earlier a problem but now with wireless networking, this hurdle has been overcome.
- The existence of a large number of NRIs and their families has led to increased demand for high quality telecom services.
- The increasing inflow of tourists especially those staying for a week or more and their need to be connected with their families and friends has also boosted demand.
- The NIC provides infrastructure management support to the State government. The NIC SIO has reserved as the Director IT for the State on several occasions.
- The state has a SWAN connecting kiosks/CSC's in every taluka.
- The state has website based information for all departments and most government corporations. The state is also the first to develop a prototype of a state-wide citizen-registry for single point authentication of citizen information.
- The state has implemented IT and enabled several services at the municipal, panchayat and corporation level through kiosks and on the SWAN backbone as well as through a citizen registry. The major constraint is the absence of a clear IT governance framework and continuity.
- The government should enable citizen and business accounts as a single point of contact for all government transactions. This should serve as a basis for reengineering processes that deliver various services directly to the account through a common shared set of registries.

Weaknesses

- While the coastal areas have been beneficiaries of telecom expansion, similar quality of work has been absent from the hinterland.
- Reliable high speed connection is yet to reach international standards which has been an issue raised by prospective investors in the IT sector.
- Unreliable power supply has been a deterrent in attracting IT investment which often work round the clock.

References

GoG (Various Years). *Statistical Handbook of Goa*. Panaji: Publication Division, Directorate of Planning, Statistics and Evaluation, Government of Goa.

GoGa (Various Years). *Report on Credit-Deposit Ratio in Goa*. Panaji: Directorate of Planning, Statistics and Evaluation, Government of Goa.

GoGb (Various Years). *Socio-Economic Development Indicators*. Panaji: Directorate of Planning, Statistics and Evaluation, Government of Goa.

SBI (2005). "Level Bankers' Committee, Agenda and Background Papers". Lead Bank Department, State Bank of India, Mumbai 21, September.

RBI (2005). *Database on Indian Economy*. Mumbai: Reserve Bank of India. *http://www.rbi.org.in* and *http://www.rbi.org.in/scripts/Statistics.aspx* as on September 10, 2005.

GoG (2005). *Economic Survey 2004-05*. Panaji: Directorate of Planning, Statistics and Evaluation, Government of Goa.

Hegde, S. (2005). "SDR – Bankers Point of View, SBI", Presentation made at the SDR Stakeholders meeting held at the International Centre, Goa. August 12-13.

Mohapatra, R. (2005). "Risk Management Services — Life Insurance Corporation of India", Presentation made at the SDR Stakeholders meeting held at the International Centre. Goa. August 12-13.

Chapter 12

Governance

Public-Private Partnerships

Indicators

Government which governs least, governs best.

-Thomas Jefferson

1. Any collaboration between public bodies, such as local authorities or Central or state government, and private companies tends to be referred to a public-private partnership (PPP).

2. Public-private partnership, as part of privatisation drive in governance, is a means, not an end for a better government and a better society. It is based on a fundamental philosophy of government and its role in relation to the other essential institutions of a free and healthy society. It is not merely a management tool but a basic strategy of societal governance. It is on the rise world over even in unlikely settings.

3. Goa has only a few examples of public-private partnership since it attained liberation in 1961 and statehood in 1985. Frequent political changes and instability, populist approach of respective governments with lack of vision and adequate initiative, and absence of strong consumer resistance movement in this international tourist destination are responsible for this situation.

Infrastructure Sector

4. The state government had proposed to set up state-of-the-art, Rs. 950 crore, international airport at Mopa in North Goa, the tendering process for which would begin in December 2005 even as land had been acquired for the purpose. This is expected to ease congestion at Mumbai and Dabolim (Naval Base) airports besides promoting tourism by accommodating more wide-bodied foreign charter flights and boosting employment potential.

5. It had also proposed to make a feasibility study for running monorail project, to begin with, on Mapusa-Panaji-Margao 45 km route, to ease traffic congestion on roads and provide people with cheap as well as a faster alternative mode of transport. Expression of interest would be sought soon for the project, which runs on the pollution-free CNG fuel. It is expected to cost Rs.60 crore per km.

6. Besides contemplating to link different hinterlands to exploit the full potential of the Mormugao port through an express highway, the government is keen to set up a special economic zone (SEZ) and biotechnology, food, apparel and jewellery parks for boosting industry and trade besides employment potential.

7. A state-of-the-art institute of hotel management is in the offing in collaboration with the private sector to cater to the needs of the booming hospitality industry as a result of growth in tourism sector.

8. It had entered into an MoU with the ACC Ltd. for resurfacing, strengthening and construction of roads using ACC Marg Technology in the state. A project was launched on pilot basis in the corporation of the city of Panaji besides Margao, Mormugao, Mapusa and Ponda for a length of 20 km.

Public Works

9. The state public works department with a budget of Rs. 390 crore had to maintain water supply and sewerage systems, roads and bridges, national highways and buildings, leave alone undertaking works related to different departments which allocate funds separately for them. Thirty per cent of its budget goes for salaries and maintenance.

10. One of the finest examples of the public-private partnership in Goa is the Rs.15 crore sewerage treatment

plant of 12.50 MLD capacity installed at Tonka in the capital city, the work for which had begun on October 23, 2003.

11. The prestigious project approved under the central assistance of Union Forests and Environment Ministry was made operational and was undergoing trial run quite satisfactorily meeting all its parameters such as pH, Biological Oxygen Demand (BOD), Chemical Oxygen Demand (COD) and Total Suspended Solids (TSS).

12. While the plant had reported pH value ranging between 6.5 and 7.5, the BOD in the effluent is below 20 mg/l, the COD 100 mg/l and TSS 100 mg/l as against accepted standards of 9,30,250 and 100 under respective heads.[1]

13. The project was undertaken on a five-year construction, operation and maintenance contract basis built in collaboration with Australian technology through competitive bid. There are three more such treatment plants in Goa but maintained by the PWD department.

14. The authorities had given installation and maintenance contract to a private party in division-9 of Margao city for waster meters. There are as many as 1.8 crore water connection in Goa. The authorities have planned to give another Rs.1.32 crore six-year contract to install and maintain 12,000 water metres in North Goa district.

15. In yet another significant development, the PWD encouraged formation of a 1,700-strong PWD Labour Society which meets the workforce requirement of the department on day to day basis for the last two years so that the workers were paid minimum wages on time without the intervention of the contractor.

16. The society is autonomous in that it can recruit or remove any of its workers on its own but without affecting the work schedules allocated to it. Earlier, the department used to give out the O&M (organisation and management) to contractors for its water supply works but it resulted in problems with the contractors failing to give minimum wages.

17. The department had also contracted computerisation of water bills for a two-year period for North and South Goa with satisfactory performance. This had reduced the burden on the government apart from enhancing the efficiency.

Medical and Public Health Sector

18. In the health sector, the government had for the first time signed a contract with a specialist doctor in dialysis who erected the equipment Hospicio hospital, Margao with a payment of Rs. 599 per dialysis made.

19. It had recently, identified a Nagpur-based company for setting up a Rs.50 lakh biomedical waste disposal facility at Pissulem industrial estate in South Goa to charge the hospitals at Rs.3.50 per bed for 5200 beds in Goa.

20. It had proposed to assist voluntary and non-government organisations such as Goa Red Cross Society, Goa Medical Council, Blood Transfusion Council and Goa State Illness Assistance Society for providing the people with "state-of-the-art medicare".

21. A five-storied building for Asilo hospital under BOOT scheme at Peddem, Mapusa in North Goa is on the anvil. A new scheme involving NGOs in "Awareness about Mental Health" issues is underway this year to promote voluntary compliance of people in medical checkup of school children and general public.

22. The government had floated the Goa State Aids Control Society (GSACS) being funded by the National AIDS Control Organisation (NACO) and posted health officials to manage the affairs of the organisation in prevention, control and management of HIV/AIDS cases in Goa since its inception in April 1999 replacing the then AIDS cell for effective management of the programme involving 16 different NGOs in policy and its successful implementation at all levels through a multi-modular and disciplinary approach.

Education Sector

23. Cyberage scheme under contract system was introduced in the state in the year 2003-04 to benefit XI standard students initially. The scheme will be extended to degree level students and those of professional colleges, polytechnics and law and general education. As many as 15,081 computers costing Rs.29 crore had been disbursed to the beneficiaries so far.

24. In yet another contract scheme, the government had started Computer Literacy Scheme for teachers and students even as it had contracted out the Mid-Day Meal Scheme involving the NGOs.

25. An MoU was signed with IIT-Bombay for developing a "language highway" for users of Konkani and Marathi to have Internet access to national and international knowledge communities both for education and trading purposes now underway. It was also proposed to set up an expert group for development of lexicology in

1. *Source:* Starred LAQ No. 32 answered by environment minister Dr.Wilfred de Souza on August 18, 2005.

Konkani and Marathi for universal networking language monitored by an expert from IIT-Bombay.

26. The government had also proposed to set up Goa Education Development Corporation for developing Goa as a "higher education hub" including in research and development through orderly development of educational institutions, services, computer training and allied facilities with government assistance.

27. The IIT-Bombay campus was also envisaged in Goa for upgrading technical education including knowledge and skills so that the students got competitive edge in the global scenario. A virtually extended campus of the IIT-Bombay has been set up on the Goa University campus to develop online education facilities for general and technical education students.

28. Interest-free loans/grants and land were given to the International Centre, Goa (ICG) to promote an intellectual culture environment at the national and international level. The centre is registered under the Societies Act, 1860 and is run on no-loss, no-profit basis.

Ports and River Navigation Sector

29. The Mormugao Port Trust (MPT) had invited bids from private parties for setting up a Rs.185 crore cruise liner–cum-container terminal at Baina Bay. The State government also desired to seek expression of interest from companies for setting up cruise liner terminals at different tourist places in the State under PPP arrangement.

30. The MPT had also proposed to invite bids for a Rs.85 crore Wagon tippler unit at Mormugao Port to tackle iron ore from Ballari-Hosepet section to minimise/eliminate pollution/waste before loading into the ships for exports.

31. The state government had entrusted collection of toll fee to private contractors in 7 of the 21 river navigation routes in operation through tendering process in the year 2003-04 in a bid to reduce the administrative burden and increase the State revenues. The authorities were in the process of finalising the contracts for the remaining routes.

32. The State department of ports also proposes to run passenger cruise liners between Goa and Mumbai besides boats from Miramar and Dona Paula jetties to other areas through bids from private parties during 2005-06.

33. Eleven of the 27 ferry routes in Goa had been contracted out to private parties since March 2004 and the contract had been extended for another year even as it earned Rs.1.4 crore for transporting vehicles for the last financial year. On a monthly basis, the department collects Rs.7.54 lakh towards bids from the ferry route contractors.

34. But it was pointed out by the CAG, in its latest report that it failed to collect arrears to the tune of Rs.48 lakh as on March 31, 2004. Of it, Rs.30 lakh was pending collection for more than three years and most of it was arrears towards ferry services. Only two cases involving Rs. 2 lakh had been referred to the Revenue Recovery Court.

State Legislature

35. The department started engaging private security personnel for providing security cover to the new modern Assembly complex round the clock, particularly during the business sessions with trained people drawn from Labour Society formed at the instance of the PWD.

36. The legislature secretariat is happy with the services, which also reduced the burden on the exchequer, which, otherwise would be costlier if they recruited the police personnel.

Urban Development

37. A project is in vogue now for conversion of solid waste into compost at Sonsoddo dumping site in Margao and another site at Mapusa for fish waste run by the Goa Foundation (an NGO), which trains the municipal staff in generating wealth from the waste. A waste treatment unit in Vasco-da-Gama in contract with Chemtrols Company has been working for long to manufacture compost.

38. The State government had also proposed to set up solid waste processing and treatment plants at different *taluks* through PPP route to utilise the byproducts like the plastic and the other waste for laying tar roads and energy generation (2005-06) in the backdrop of Curchorem site imbroglio.

39. Urban development department provides financial assistance to various municipal bodies for solid waste management for collecting, segregating, storing, transporting, processing and disposal of solid waste.

40. The government had also proposed to introduce "Sky Bus Metro" in technical collaboration with the Konkan Railway Corporation Limited as eco-friendly, technologically advanced, high-speed urban transport facility for which Rs.50 lakh had been earmarked for the year 2005-06 budget.

S&T and Environment

41. Through the government initiative, compaction of PET bottles collected from different tourist spots in collaboration with the Pepsi, Coca Cola, Bisleri soft drinks manufacturers and the Goa Small Industries Association (GSIA) is underway since 2003. The association is given Rs.1.80 lakh grant for purchase and installation of a modern grinder at Sanqale for compacting the used PET bottles before dispatching the material for recycling in Mumbai.

42. The government had set up a pilot Plasma Pyrolysis biomedical waste treatment plant at Goa Medical College by the Department of Science and Technology and Environment (DSTE), Goa in association with the Goa State Council of S&T and Department of S&T, Government of India.

43. The department had also proposed a Rs.236 lakh project in 2005-06 under environmental research and ecological regeneration involving the Directorate of Education and the deserving NGOs. This includes rainwater harvesting projects in all industrial estates and government establishments.

44. Besides, it had decided to build an oceanarium in collaboration with the Department of Ocean Development through a technically competent organisation, to include proper sanitation/road/water supply/pollution control infrastructure.

45. The department had also earmarked Rs.50 lakh in the financial year 2005-06 for promoting private investments in R&D in frontier fields of biotechnology, IT, pharmaceuticals, medical sciences and nutrition contributing to industries and entrepreneurship. Land is being acquired to develop modern infrastructure with state-of-the-art facilities to attract investors.

46. At the same time, the department started promoting science popularisation activities of the State Institute of Education (SIE) and the Goa Science Centre besides NGOs such as Association of Friends of Astronomy, Botanical Society of Goa and All Goa Science Teachers' Association by extending financial assistance.

47. In a big boost to promote research and development by the academia and the industry, the DSTE set up the state-of-the-art Geographical Information System (GIS) and Digital Image Processing (DIP) at its office by acquiring the hardware and the software with the financial assistance of the Department of Space, Government of India. It is helping several research scholars including NGOs besides the industry in remote sensing applications.

48. It will be extensively used in remote sensing applications besides National Resource Inventory Scheme (NRIS) database mode to undertake projects that help mitigate specific environmental problems, recommending appropriate "cropping/plantation" patterns in newly irrigated areas, afforestation of waste lands, zoning atlas for site-location of industries in Goa, estimation of agricultural production through satellite data.

49. A project of Integrated Coastal and Marine Area Management in collaboration with the department of ocean development is underway along with the remote sensing based projects such as demarcation of watersheds and wastelands useful for various departments including the forests and town planners.

Entertainment Sector

50. A Rs.21.23 crore, four-screen state-of-the-art multiplex complex was built in an area of 40,000 square feet within a record time of 180 days—from excavation to commissioning by the Inox Company Limited adjacent to the 150-year old "Old Goa Medical College" building facing the picturesque river Mandovi. The multiplex has 1,272 seats and each auditorium features wall-to-wall, stadium-style seating to enhance viewing with reclining seats and cup-holder armrests.

51. The complex was opened on November 12, 2004 for hosting the 35th edition of the International Film Festival of India (IFFI) from November 29 to December 9, 2004. It is now ready to host successive film festivals with Goa, declared as the permanent venue of the IFFI from this year.

Forest Department

52. Plantations have been raised on barren Comunidade and temple lands under the Social Forestry including Rural Fuel Wood Fodder Project Scheme. Central government shares 50 per cent expenditure initially for first four years. After deducting expenditure, the revenue will be shared between the Comunidade and Government. Upto 2003-04, plantations have been raised on 4,732 ha.

53. As many as 6 lakh nursery seedlings were raised during the year 2002-03 with the direct involvement of the peoples/farmers under the Peoples' Nursery scheme which provides for payment of one rupee for each seedling to the farmers.

54. The forest department had planned involvement of people/locals through their participation in protecting the forests, besides deploying the SC/ST communities in plantations and forestry works.

Information Technology

55. The government had set up 13 *mahiti ghars* (information kiosks) providing the citizens with an array of e-services including revenue documents and drivers' licences for learners through an MoU with a private organisation "E-Thinkx" since the year 2001. It had proposed to expend the *mahiti ghars* to 30 besides enlisting more services on par with the e-seva centres in Andhra Pradesh including receipt of government bills.

56. The government had also proposed to set up a Software Technology Park at Verna Industrial Estate and a Cyber City at Mandrem besides an IT Habitat involving a reputed IT leader like the WIPRO at Miramar.

Social Welfare

57. The authorities proposed to involve voluntary agencies for providing 900 destitute children in 2005-06 with care and protection in their own after-care home facilities for those released from juvenile homes. The organisations could get grant-in-aid for maintenance of the homes. The government had also earmarked Rs.2 lakh as grant-in-aid to an NGO, which runs a working women's hostel in Goa.

Agriculture

58. The Department is involving NGOs and self-help groups for revitalising the infrastructure to promote soil and water conservation in villages. The work involves protecting and strengthening the notified embankments and sluice gates to prevent flooding of paddy and farm fields.

Issues and Fiscal Implications

Why Public-Private Partnership in Goa

59. Goa government is likely to spend an estimated 77 per cent of its revenue for the financial year 2005-06 as against 78 per cent in the previous financial year. The break up for the year is as follows: 25 paise out of each rupee it earns is to be spent on salary, wages, pension and gratuity; 23 paise on works, maintenance and materials; 18 paise on debt servicing and 11 paise on establishment.

60. The revised estimate of the 2004-05 Budget on expenditure front under the same heads was 25 paise, 23, 20 and 10 paise respectively. The actual expenditure Goa government incurred was 28 paise, 21 paise, 22 paise and 9 paise on the same heads respectively for the financial year 2003-04 out of each rupee it earned.[2]

61. It could be thus seen that the government had been trying its best to reduce huge expenditure on servicing debts it borrowed from different institutions including the Centre from a whooping 22 per cent in the year 2003-04 to 20 per cent in 2004-05 and 18 per cent in the year 2005-06 through various prudential fiscal measures such as reducing the interest burden on loan taken on higher interest by swapping them with fresh loans taken on lower interest.

62. Significantly, the public debt of the State had been rising rapidly from Rs.707.44 crore in the year 1997 to Rs.797.30 crore in 1998, Rs.1,010.90 crore in 1999, 1,198.31 crore in 2000, Rs.1,490.17 crore in 2001, Rs.1,825.97 crore in 2002, Rs.2,141.10 crore in 2003 and Rs.2570.17 crore in 2004.

63. Simultaneously, the debt to GSDP ratio jumped from 17.84 per cent in the year 1997 to 27.67 per cent in 2004. The public debt was mainly on nine heads—Central loan, market loans (SLR based), LIC, NCDC, NABARD, REC, PFC, HUDCO and Ways and Means Advances, the highest amount being the Central loan.

64. At the same time, according to a report on the *Census of Government Employees—2002* (as on March 31, 2002) conducted by the Directorate of Planning, Statistics and Evaluation, Goa, there are as many as 45,002 employees in the government sector. They include 40,990 regular, 847 ad hoc and 3,165 work-charged employees in government, grant-in-aid and state public sector undertakings. Men with 30,532 outnumber female with 14,470 among these employees.

65. The following table gives details of distribution of employees as against the status of the posts in different types of organisations:

TABLE 12.1

Distribution of Employees as against the Status of the Posts in Different Types of Organisations

Organisation	*Regular*	*Ad hoc*	*Work Charged*	*Total*
Government	28,447	500	2,898	31,845
Grants-in-aid	10,097	208	176	10,481
Public sector undertakings	2,446	139	91	2,676
Total	40,990	847	3,165	45,002

Source: Statistical Handbook of Goa.

66. There are in all 79 different government departments, 13 public sector enterprises and 14 grant-in-aid institutions with the highest number of 4,103 in school education, followed by 3,942 employees in the

2. *Source:* Budget at a Glance: 2004-05 presented in the Goa Legislative Assembly on August 11 by Chief Minister Pratapsingh Rane.

Electricity Department, followed by 3,767 in the PWD, 3,246 in the police, 2,446 in health services, 1,679 in Goa medical college and 1,598 in water resources.

67. Under the grants-in-aid sector, as many as 8,034 people were employed in school education and 1,474 in the higher education sector. An analysis revealed that only 7.3 per cent of the government employees had been availing of the official accommodation facility and about 60 per cent of the employees were in the basic pay scale range of Rs.4,500 and below.

68. Options for PPPs are service contracts, management contracts, operations and maintenance contract, lease, concessions/vouchers, volunteer groups, cooperatives, joint ventures, franchises, retiring from business arena, and later build, own and operate (BOO), build, own and transfer (BOT), build, own, operate and transfer (BOOT) and divestiture. There is increased need for PPP in urban infrastructure (UI) for extended resources, state-of-the-art technologies and efficient project management and maintenance.

69. If the government engages in contracting out and release of grants, it makes no difference in financial terms, as it has to make budgetary provisions for the expenditure in doing so. It is benefited only in case of other options such as BOO, BOT and BOOT wherein the selected private party bears the entire cost of the project and recovers it in instalments along with its profit margin in due course during the period agreed for.

70. In case of divestiture, the government stock is diluted with private parties including the public purchasing the shares of the company, thus earning a part or more than the capital invested in setting up the companies. The government could think of divesting the loss making companies in its fold after studying why they were incurring losses as pointed out by the CAG. Even the profit making companies could also be divested or privatised to reduce the government expenditure.

71. The process of converting the public sector company into a joint venture could also be mooted by involving the private companies to share their expertise so that the public sector enterprise goes out of the red.

Institutions and Governance

72. There is a need for evolving regular and appropriate organisational/institutional mechanisms besides legal and regulatory framework for making the PPP ventures a success. Instead of each government department working on its own for operating PPP ventures, a separate board/body for the exclusive purpose should be constituted and legally whetted to give sanctity to it so that it can be held responsible for all PPP activities.

73. The board should have its own legal and regulatory framework to tackle the issues as they emanated in triggering the PPP systems. This calls for simplification of existing legislations besides strengthening the techno-legal regime like the regulatory bodies such as the Central and State Electricity Authorities and the TRAI for the telecom and NHAI for the highways sector.

74. The regulatory body should wield powers to regulate prices, promote operating efficiency and efficient use, specify and monitor service standards, control externalities, maintain public good functions, ensure asset serviceability, development of essential infrastructure and responsiveness to final customer needs besides preventing manipulation of land values and unfair trade practices.

75. In a BOO/BOT/BOOT arrangement, the regulatory authority should identify the parties to the contract, specify the objects and scope of the arrangement, duration that might lead to early termination, obligations of the operator, the guarantor. Besides, there is a need for delineating the key regulatory provisions, and the management of the risks involved, manner of measuring and monitoring the performance, assets transfer mechanism to the operator, consents required for the purpose and factors responsible for environment liabilities.

76. The countdown begins with the process of seeking expression of intent from the private agencies, firming up the project contours/consultants, shortlisting of private parties, preparing the project description report, pre-qualification of existing bidders, issue of Request For Proposal (RFP), evaluation of bids, initiating negotiations, award of the contract (Financial Closure) and commencement of work.

77. Legislation on the lines of the Andhra Pradesh's Infrastructure Development Enabling Act (IDEA) could be enacted with specified roles for working as an infrastructure authority for various projects under the PPP system. The roles include conceptualisation and processing of projects, mobilising public opinion, advising and coordinating with the government at different stages, monitoring/approval of bidding, implementation of PPP, prioritisation of projects, preparation of schedules, approval of TOR for consultancy, budgeting/financial allocation, expedition of clearances and permits, tariff fixing, user/abuser charges and cost recovery, model contract principles, supervision over implementation and project management, adopting a "Swiss Challenge

Approach" for evaluating the single bid for projects brought by proprietary agencies.

78. Urban infrastructure financing encompasses several legal issues such as non-availability of conventional securities (government guarantees, corporate/bank guarantees).

79. While collateral securities and equipment leases are used in certain infrastructure, mortgages are not viable securities in most UI projects. There is a need for partial or non-recourse financing and legislative changes for treatment as secured loans in the Book of Accounts. Negative lien could be considered only as a transient security instrument and escrow accounts of receivables enhance transparency of the cash flows and ensure sufficient balance for immediate repayments.

80. General obligation and revenue bonds could be raised by the municipalities like in Ahmedabad, Bangalore, Vijayawada and other corporations by obtaining credit rating which was directly proportional to their performance that could be audited by professional agencies such as the ICAI and rating agencies such as the ICRA. Steps should however, be taken to ensure that the municipalities/corporations would not fall into debt trap unable to redeem the bonds in the long run after utilising the funds required for projects.

81. Alternative routes such as bond banks and other credit avenues could be explored at the national level to finance the urban local bodies in mobilising resources. The governments and even the urban credit cooperative banks could also meet credit requirements of these bodies.

82. Setting up of Special Economic Zones (SEZ) could be another route to attract investments, both domestic and foreign, to facilitate expeditious development of industrial and other services and projects in urban areas and ports. The government policy envisages treatment of SEZs as priority areas in providing infrastructure, convergence of statutory clearances, exemption from duties and levies as well as liberal regulations. SEZs as industrial townships would need priority for integrated provision of infrastructure facilities.

83. The government had to identify public sector undertaking (PSE) that are set for privatisation/divestment and establish individual objectives, gain public support and restructure the enterprises besides selecting the divestment method. Addressing the concerns of the poor and the workers should be kept in mind while designing the regulatory framework and preparing the enterprise for divestment and supportive policy environment.

84. The governance requires appraisal of enterprise and its assets before marketing them through a financial transaction to be executed. At the same time, the government had to monitor and evaluate post-privatisation phase and counter resistance as it encountered even from the politically affiliated workforce in case of an aluminium company when taken over by the Sterlite Industries Limited.

Development and Growth Areas

85. The sectors with PPP possibilities in Goa are: education, entertainment, environment, forest, industry, information and publicity, infrastructure, information technology, museums-archaeology, ports and river navigation, prisons, public health, PWD, science and technology, sports, tourism and transport.

Prisons and Correctional Services

86. In Goa, an estimated Rs.634.83 lakh had been provided in the 2005-06 budget for prisons administration as against the revised estimate of Rs.364.07 lakh in the previous fiscal year and Rs.229.55 lakh in the year 2003-2004. Allocation for the prisoners' diet however, was put at Rs.41 lakh for the current fiscal as against the revised estimate of Rs.38 lakh and Rs.35.65 lakh in the previous years respectively. It works to about 15 per cent of the total budget.

87. On the other hand, the allocation for major and minor works to be undertaken by the PWD for the prisons administration was estimated to be Rs.364 lakh for the current fiscal as against Rs.105 lakh in the year 2004-05 and Rs.18.43 lakh in the year 2003-04. As much as Rs.140 lakh goes towards construction of "B" and "C" type of residential quarters for the jailors at Vasco and a new central jail in Tiswadi *taluka* for the current fiscal. A provision of Rs.10 lakh was made for upgradation of prisons' administration at the judicial lock-ups in Mapusa, Margao, Panaji and the sub-jail-cum-judicial lockup in Sada and Vasco.

88. According to the authorities, the incumbents in Central Jail at Aguada, one of the crumbling heritage structures of Goa whose maintenance itself takes a heavy toll of the budget, and four judicial locks besides the sub-jail at Vasco never crossed 500 including the women prisoners even as their total capacity of prisoners is 356 (*Source*: *Annual Administration Report of the Government of Goa*, 2003-04).

89. All the structures were built in the pre-liberation time and the Government closed down the sub-jail at Reis Magos. A state-of-the-art modern central jail is to be built

at Curca for which the authorities acquired land measuring 98,175 square metres. An additional 50,485 square metres was also being acquired for the purpose. The Centre was ready to share 75 per cent of the estimated Rs.13.62 crore cost of the new central jail complex.

90. Here is an opportunity for public-private partnership for handing over the entire central jail project for private parties for building a modern complex on BOO or BOOT basis by handing over the land. Administration of prisons by private sector is not new to the developed countries and Goa could blaze a new trail in this task. Reasonably good facilities could be provided to the inmates and remand prisoners including women with many rehabilitation and reform packages involving the services of the voluntary organisations.

91. The prisoners could be made self-reliant after they walked out of the jails on completion of the term with the experience they gain in various trades of their choice while serving the prison term. The products made in the prison could be sold and a part of the revenue could be deposited on the name of the prisoners that could form part of their seed capital for self-help ventures in future.

92. The investors could be given a grant-in-aid to run the jails, which does not entail pension and other huge retirement payments as in the case of government servants. The perennial problem of shortage of staff for escorting the prisoners to and from jails for trial would go if the administrators introduced the video conferencing system like in Andhra Pradesh and other states by linking them with the courts online.

Public Works Department

93. Goa requires more sewerage treatment plants like the one in Tonka in the Panaji capital city built under multilateral finance scheme, now undergoing trials. The agreement envisages O&M for five years to start with. Another project under PWD sector for undertaking sewerage treatment and water supply plant at a cost of Rs.630 crore with 10 to 15-year term on build, operate and maintenance contract basis with financial assistance of the Japanese Bank of International Cooperation is now being negotiated.

94. The government had already signed a memorandum of understanding with the Japanese International Cooperation Agency (JICA) for better water supply and sanitation by installing sewerage treatment plants and preventing contamination of water bodies in the state. In the first phase of the sewerage scheme costing Rs.239 crore would begin in Margao and south coastal area, the second phase costing Rs.185 crore in Porvorim, Taleigao, Caranzalem, Santa Cruz, Meres areas and the third phase costing Rs.206 crore to meet the requirements of Bicholim, Valpoi, Ponda, Quepem, Sanvordem and Sanguem.

95. The project to be finalised by March 2006 starts implementation in November 2006 for which the Japanese Bank of International Cooperation has agreed to fund while JICA would train the personnel and assist the PWD with technical know-how. The funding is by way of 30 per cent grants and 70 per cent loan component with interest below 1 per cent rate of interest. The state government had submitted its proposal while the JICA was studying the feasibility of the project for Goa.

96. It is to be noted that the CAG, in its latest report submitted to the state legislative assembly in August 2004 budget session pointed out the "failure of the state PWD to finalise tenders within the validity period of the quotes leading to avoidable expenditure of Rs.88 lakh". It also noted that the department's failure to coordinate among its own divisions and other state agencies resulting in blockage of Rs.37.61 lakh for more than two years and denial of sufficient waster supply to the public.

97. Information is necessary even within the organisation. As part of this sector's reforms, accountability was built into the PWD's internal processes to ensure internal transparency. Benchmarking actually empowered not only the consumer but the utility as well. Significantly, the department is now engaged in drafting a vision statement, after wide consultations with NGOs and others.

Health Department

98. The lone PPP arrangement, the government had in the health sector, is a contract with a dialysis specialist who erected the unit in Hospicio, Margao with an assurance of getting Rs.599 per dialysis performed. More such PPP ventures in the health sector are needed. The processes should be very clear in this task and designed in such as way that it avoids discard with the parties involved. Exploration for alliance contracts and management contract with set systems are needed for successful PPP ventures apart from having in place a regulatory mechanism to fix responsibilities.

99. South Goa patients were deprived of intended benefits of the mental health programme, which was not implemented effectively due to inadequate medical and support staff. The health department functioned with significant manpower shortages as posts of medical practitioners, technical and support staff remained vacant

in hospitals and health centres resulting in under utilisation of infrastructure/facilities created and also adversely affecting the quality of services rendered.

100. All these facts clearly call for a PPP policy framework in the health sector with the government focusing its attention more on the primary and secondary health care by strengthening its infrastructure at the ground level instead of attempting at investing in superspeciality departments, which had already been in the private sector like the Apollo Victor Hospital, Margao.

101. Public or private, the major cause for concern is lack of central hospital waste disposal facility like the one in Hyderabad where the government had built up the infrastructure. Hospital waste could be highly hazardous if its disposal and destruction in a scientific manner is neglected at the cost of general public health.

Medical Tourism

102. The Confederation of Indian Industries (CII) had estimated that India had the potential to attract 10 lakh health tourists every year, contributing $5 billion to our economy. On the other hand, McKinsey-CII report, had put the earnings at $2.3 billion through medical tourism by 2012.

103. It is estimated that about 1.5 lakh health/medical tourists come to India in a year now even as the number of health tourists to India is growing at 15 per cent a year. Thailand attracted 10 lakh health tourists last year with good infrastructure and aggressive marketing drive.

104. The experts maintain that Goa has all the ingredients to make medical tourism a success as it had a wide range of hospitals covering a large spectrum of medical treatment, besides possessing tourist spots ideal for rest and recuperation. Additional advantage is that English language widely spoken besides having a large number of five star hotels and a network of tour operators and guides.

105. Goa could thus become a destination for health tourism if certain ground rules are observed in promoting medical tourism. They are:

- Adherence to government compliance procedures for European tourists,
- Marketing and package—appealing and correct manner in terms of treatment, after care, convalescence/holiday, promotion facilities requiring skill, time and efforts.

106. Experts favour setting up of "Medical Tourism Council of Goa" to project Goa as a synergising destination for both Medical Academia and International Medical Conferences besides promoting Goa's capability to deliver 'Value for Money' health care with a human touch, and regulating and monitoring the medical tourism sector to assist patients from abroad. The Council could be a joint institution of the Goa Chamber of Commerce and Industry, Government of Goa, tourism department, private and public enterprises engaged in delivering health care.

107. Further it could act as a nodal academy responsible for the smooth operations of the medical tourism business besides striving for instilling confidence to prospective medical tourists and serving as an 'ombudsmen' specially appointed by the Government of Goa with the active cooperation of corporate and insurance sectors.

108. The advantages India could derive by projecting as medical tourism destination include huge cost benefit advantage compared with developed countries with long waiting time for treatment and an opportunity to combine a vacation with cosmetic and non-emergency treatments. Advantages include the cost of treatments and surgeries which is a quarter of what it would cost in Europe.

Infrastructure

Ports

109. In the ports sector, there is hardly any major/ minor PPP venture in Goa earlier. It was only recently that the Mormugao port had initiated the following three steps as part of its drive to develop infrastructure involving the private sector.

110. They are: Construction and operation of Cruise Vessel-Cum-Container Berth in Mormugao port on BoT basis, off Baina Bay. This is expected to cater to the growing number of cruise liners visiting Goan shore from abroad as part of boosting international high-end and high-spend tourism in Goa; building of two multipurpose general cargo berths—5A and 6A—under the private sector initiative and development, operation and maintenance of Wagon Handling System in Mormugao with 3 million tonne cargo handling capacity.

111. River transportation needs to be improved to reduce pressure on roads by encouraging private investment in loading/unloading jetties along the Mandovi/Zuari rivers. This has to be done by striking a balance between the development and environment while addressing the infrastructure sector.

112. The miners also want an industry and ecological mining policy on the lines of the Industrial Policy delineating "Mining Zones" on par with practices abroad.

Industries

113. The number of companies registered in Goa and the Union Territory of Daman and Diu since March 30, 1963 are 4,104 while only 3,347 of them are working as on August 4, 2005. They include 3,037 in the private sector and the rest are limited in public sectors.

114. The office started functioning since December 19, 1969 on its shift from Mumbai to Panaji. The first company registered was Timble Shipping Pvt. Ltd. on February 13, 1970.

115. On the other hand, there are 14 government companies and one statutory corporation working under the Goa government as on March 31, 2004 in which Rs.606.03 crore had been invested. However, only five companies are running in profits while the rest of the eight and the statutory Economic Development Corporation (EDC) incurred an aggregate loss of Rs.31.19 crore and Rs.2.89 crore respectively till the last fiscal year end.

116. There is no joint sector venture in Goa and many industries, according to the Goa Chamber of Commerce and Industry (GCCI) started going out to newly born states such as Chhattisgarh, Uttarakhand besides Himachal Pradesh and the north-east which were luring them lucrative tax incentives besides offering other facilities for development of industries. There are however, 28 cent per cent export-oriented units (EOUs) since August 1991 in Goa with an investment of Rs.480 crore providing employment to about 3,670 people. It included hardware leader D-Link Industries Limited.

117. On the other hand, Goa had mobilised a record of Rs.12,631.07 crore deposits during the year 2004-05 as against Rs.11,843.33 crore in the previous year and Rs.380.92 crore in 1980-81, accounting for a per capita deposit of Rs.89,508 last financial year. There are as many as 445 banking offices in Goa in the year 2004-05 as against 258 in 1980-81. The private sector banks however, had a grouse with the government not preferring to keep its deposits with these banks for long-term security reasons at a time when PPP has become a buzzword and touted as synonym for development.

118. The Index of Industrial Production (Base 1993-94 = 100) touched a peak of 126 in mining during the year 2003-04 followed by 404 manufacturing index and 379 combined index, the highest recorded since 1994-95. The Central Assistance to the State Plan however, had been declining from 85.49 per cent to plan size in 1987-88 to 8.19 in 2004-05 even as its total gross state domestic product (GSDP) rose from Rs.239,68 lakh in 1993-94 to Rs.844,506 lakh in 2002-03. In this background, the suggestion of Union Finance Minister Mr. P.Chidambaram needs immediate follow up by paving for opening Special Economic Zones (SEZ) which entails various tax incentives and rebates for about 15 years in phases.

119. The announcement of introducing "contributory pension" scheme to the new government recruits on the lines of the central scheme was welcomed as pension and retirement benefits themselves were eating into the vitals of the state revenue, more than the payments of salaries and perks to the existing government employees.

120. The number of applicants on live register of the state employment exchange was 103,259 in the year 2004 including 17,882 below matriculates, 35,721 matriculates, 7,068 higher secondary school certificate holders, 16,180 graduates, 2,152 postgraduates and 4,256 diploma holders, according to the Goa regional employment exchange statistics. As many as 38,268 of them are females and the rest males.

Transport Sector

121. As is in vogue in neighbouring states of Karnataka and Tamil Nadu, the Kadamba Transport Corporation could engage eligible private buses on hire/

TABLE 12.2

District-wise Distribution of Working Companies in Goa and Union Territory of Daman and Diu between 30/03/1963 and 04/08/2005

District Name	*Govt.Companies*		*Non-Govt. Companies*		*Associations Not-for-Profit*		*Unlimited Companies*		*Total*	
	Public	*Private*	*Public*	*Private*	*Public*	*Private*	*Public*	*Private*	*Public*	*Private*
N. Goa	13	4	160	1833	1	3	0	3	174	1843
S. Goa	1	1	84	1057	2	5	3	23	90	1086
Daman	1	0	43	103	0	0	0	0	44	103
Diu	0	0	3	4	0	0	0	0	3	4
Total	15	5	290	2997	3	8	3	26	311	3036

Source: Registrar of Companies—Goa, Daman and Diu, Panaji.

lease basis for running them in different routes under a memorandum of understanding, thus providing the people with accessibility to any route at any time.

122. This eliminates huge capital expenditure on purchasing new fleet and in their maintenance and spares besides manpower, as under the agreement, maintenance and running the buses is the duty of the private operators.

123. The corporation operates as many as 433 vehicles with an average age of 5.64 years, the maximum being 24 years 8 months. It purchased 68 new vehicles during the year 2004-05 as against 39 in the year 2003-04 and 19 in the previous year. They included mini buses also. It had scrapped as many as 366 aged buses since inception in October 1987 while 10 vehicles were not in working condition in the current year. The department was to collect Rs.7 crore arrears from different parties including Rs.4.27 crore pending for more than three years.

Tourism Sector

124. Even the state tourism development corporation Limited (GTDC) with 401 employees and Rs.960.18 lakh capital employed incurred Rs.48.36 lakh loss by March 31, 2005 and accumulate loss of Rs.118.80 lakh. This is despite the fact that the state was committed to attracting high-spend tourists even as the 20-lakh tourists visiting Goa outnumbering its population every year. According to projections by the year 2011 (five years from now), the tourist influx is expected to cross 4.2 million mark and the available facility at Dabolim airport is not enough.

Information and Publicity

125. The department needs a dynamic website which could be visited by all the media personnel, both in and outside Goa so that they could download news information besides photographs and backgrounders uploaded into the website. This apart, the department could e-mail the news/press notes and photographs as and when they are ready to the media units for use instead of sending the hard copies of the handouts and pictures through a messenger late in the evening.

126. This requires construction of the interactive website which could be done through a private specialist group in a regular/contract basis. The group could also be used for sending the e-mail copies to the media. The website, as it is, needs updation on a regular basis with no experienced and professional available in the department now.

127. The website could feed all the backgrounders related to the Goa government, its projects and views besides profiles of ministers and successive governors and governments in tail for use whenever necessary. It could invite articles from specialists on specialised occasions. Now that the department has digital camera with a cameraman handling it on a regular basis, the picture shots could immediately be e-mailed with captions through the internet facility to the advantage of the daily media units which race for time. The units include news agencies.

Information Technology

128. A draft IT policy to tap the enormous potential of Goa in the sector is underway. It would be unfolded shortly after the cabinet approval. There are only two IT majors worth mentioning—Zenith Computers Limited and the D-Link. The government has to open as many *mahiti ghars* (information kiosks) in the state under the PPP umbrella besides upgrading them to become e-seva centres like in Andhra Pradesh which cover a wide range of services including issue of cinema tickets and receipt of all sorts of government bills and issue of train tickets.

129. Right away, there are 13 kiosks and there is a proposal to increase them to 30 with connectivity to GoaNet linking all the government through its wide area network for easy accessibility of the government database of its 76 departments.

130. The State has proposed to set up IT Estate (Cyber City) at Mandrem for which it had initiated land acquisition proceedings apart from setting up of a "Software Technology Park STP" at Verna with high-speed data communication facility. This is expected to generate 20,000 jobs potential in Goa.

Museums and Archaeology

131. Running and maintenance of the lone museum under the department could be handed over to an interested private company/NGO which could run it on no-loss and no-profit basis on the basis of the revenue it generates out of sale of tickets for students and other visitors. The department officials could concentrate on undertaking real time archaeological excavations and protection of monuments and their conservation of *in situ* monuments.

Carrying Capacity and Sustainable Activity

132. The PPP efforts could be successful and sustainable only if a suitable institutional mechanism backed with appropriate regulatory and legal, fiscal and financial framework is available.

133. This is possible through an integrated management approach with inter-sectoral coordination with a battery of new breed of highly trained and skilled personnel to assist the regulatory body or nodal agency. This required political will and commitment to the PPP mechanism. The incumbents assisting the nodal agency should have skills in technical inputs like civil engineering, transportation engineering, hydraulic engineering, public health and financial engineering to cater to the requirements in the process of striking a PPP venture using different routes.

134. The financial instruments for providing loans to the private partners with suitable framework should be invented so that they return reasonable returns on investments and necessary protections in case of unforeseen occurrences such as natural calamities.

135. Mindless taxing of the products generated out of the PPP ventures or services should be avoided and every aspect of the venture should be delineated in the MoU before the venture begins so that it remains sustainable without emergence of a situation forcing the closure of the unit because of a lack of appropriate financial instrument or security.

136. A separate fund in the form of a venture capital, loans from cooperative banks or budgetary provisions to promote the PPP ventures to ensure their sustainability surmounting all incumbent risks may be considered.

Strengths, Weaknesses, Opportunities and Threats

Strengths and Weaknesses

137. The main advantages/strengths of privatising infrastructure are capital saving for the government, operating savings, availability of means of financing and better service, speedier implementation, providing services otherwise not available, sharing of risks. Privatisation was necessary when there was evidently lack of enterprise with government, and an urgent need for providing the people with facilities.

138. Surveys world over revealed that 99 per cent of the countries contracted out services. Contracting works well when the work to be done is specified unambiguously, several potential producers are available and a competitive climate either exists or can be created and sustained, the government is able to monitor the contractor's performance and appropriate terms are included in the contract document and enforced.

139. Public-private partnerships (PPP) for infrastructure satisfy the needs to upgrade systems to accommodate population growth to satisfy tightened regulatory requirements or to attract investment and development; minimise the cost of new infrastructure and consequent "rate shock" among citizens; and raise capital for other desired projects by receiving an upfront for the infrastructure concession.

140. Government takes advantage of specialised skills lacking in its own workforce besides overcoming obsolete salary limitations and antiquated civil service restrictions. Contracting permits a quicker response to new needs and facilitates experimentation with new programmes.

141. It avoids large capital outlays, spreads costs over time at a relatively constant and predictable level.

142. Contracting permits economies of scale regardless of the size of the government entity.

143. Contracting a portion of the work offers a yardstick for comparing costs.

144. It fosters good management because the cost of service is highly visible in the price of the contract, whereas the cost of government is usually obscured. It can reduce dependence on a single supplier (a government monopoly) and so lessens the vulnerability of the service to strikes, slowdowns and inept leadership.

145. On the other hand, contracting/privatisation is more expensive because of possible corrupt practices in awarding contracts, outrageous and pernicious work practices among private sector unions, high profits with little or no share in it for the government. The cost of managing contract and monitoring contractor performances may be high as against the low marginal cost of expanding government service. Cost-plus-fixed fee contracts provide no incentive for efficiency in the contract system.

146. Contracting nullifies the basic principle of merit employment and subverts laws regarding veterans' preferences in government employment. It is demoralising to employees, deprives government of the skills it needs in-house, and therefore, is fundamentally debilitating of government capability.

147. Contracting limits the flexibility of government in responding to emergencies besides resulting in undesirable dependence on contractors, leaving the public vulnerable to strikes and slowdowns by the contractor's personnel leading to bankruptcy of the firm.

148. Contracting depends on the adequately written contracts, which are difficult to draw up and results in a loss of government accountability and control. It limits the opportunity to realise economies of scale. Entrusting services to private organisations increases the political power of the latter and creates a lobby for more

government spending. Contracting may cause a loss of autonomy for the contractor, for example, co-opting a private, non-profit social service agency and thereby decreasing the agency's effectiveness in the long run by muting its role as critic and social conscience.

149. After all, the objectives of privatisation are to reduce cost of government, generate revenues, both by selling assets and then by collecting taxes from them, reduce government debt by debt-equity swaps etc., supply infrastructure or other facilities that government cannot otherwise provide, bring in specialised skills needed for technologically advanced activities, initiate or expand a service quickly, lessen government interference and direct presence in the economy, reduce the role of government in society (build or strengthen civil society) and accelerate economic development.

150. Privatisation, particularly of infrastructure, presents considerable risks to the partners, but suitably rewards if both acted responsibly. Total project cost are minimised if each risk is assessed and assigned to the partners by including them in the very basic contract document of partnership.

151. The risks included cost over-runs as a result of construction delays, design changes and belated identification of problems and delayed issue of permits and the like besides some unexpected problems such as natural calamities. Associated with this is the revenue risk that includes low or higher yield of income of a project such as a toll road or collection of government bills.

152. Debt-service coverage is another under the realm of financial risk followed by the exchange rate risk following fluctuations in the foreign exchange rates. The former could be met either by the private partner or a part of it could be guaranteed by the government.

153. Political risk covers the rate of regulation risk, which could be mitigated by setting up a specific regulatory mechanism so that the government allowed reasonable rate of return on investment. Another risk is expropriation risk involving re-nationalisation of the unit or severe taxation of the enterprise without paying for compensation to the partner. The compensation package could be specified in the very agreement itself before the PPP is constituted. Other risks are repatriation risk and dispute resolution risk, technology risk, environment risk and natural calamity risk (*force majeure*) which could be suitably tackled through proper documentation in the agreement.

Outlook: Short, Medium and Long Term

Infrastructure

154. Aviation industry is poised for a very rapid growth. India in general and Goa in particular will have a very high traffic growth of 18 per cent to 20 per cent in next 5 years and 12 per cent to 15 per cent in the subsequent years. This calls for huge capital investment on improving and strengthening infrastructure that would be economically viable, yielding encouraging returns if other non-aeronautical business avenues are planned and implemented. For this, active participation of State and Central governments with private participation is a must.

155. Investment should be made to increase non-aeronautical revenue from 20 per cent to 40 per cent at the Dabolim airport in Goa. This should cover creation of large commercial area inside terminal building for new business ventures, automation of baggage handling like introduction of Bar Code Identification and RFID systems, common agency for ground handling at airport automation of passenger's check-in counters and baggage handling, integrated cargo/container handling terminal, more customs and immigration check counters to reduce queues, permission to scheduled charter flights to land, night landing facility, establishment of cold chain/perishable cargo facility and connectivity via faster means of transport like rail and expressways.

156. The airport calls for meeting the projected 20 per cent annual growth for the next five years even as the infrastructure of the existing terminal building, car parking facility and apron had already been saturated. The major constraint for expansion is non-availability of land for expanding the civil enclave and the civil flights were shared with naval operations resulting in bunching of flights in the afternoon.

Strategies for Next 2 to 5 Years

157. The airport at Dabolim operating under the control of the Indian Navy since liberation of Goa in 1991 needs capacity augmentation as it has been witnessing increased traffic trend. Short-term development within the existing area of the airport should include increase in building area and facilities like elevators and escalators are now underway.

158. The planned expansion of air side, terminal building, car park and ancillary facilities like integrated cargo complex should be undertaken. Strategies for next 5 to 10 years and beyond.

159. Major expansion of the existing terminal building and expansion of the car parking area at Dabolim International Airport is needed besides construction of a new separate International Terminal at Mopa to accommodate world's largest aircraft A-380 with a carrying capacity of 600 passengers in the PPP regime. The International Civil Aviation Organisation (ICAO) is preparing the techno-feasibility report for the purpose even as it is attracting the attention of the Middle East country with Emirates keen to invest in the project to be built under the PPP route.

River Tourism (Short and Medium Term)

160. Develop river tourism on the Mandovi and Zuari and other navigational rivers for promoting hinterland tourism, which has a lot of potential for exploitation. The Goa Tourism Development Corporation (GTDC) runs three cruise boats and the private sector four now on the Mandovi. This needs encouraging private entrepreneurs through issue of licences and interest free seed capital for promoting river tourism and brackish water tourism on boats like in J&K with inbuilt safety precautions ensured by the Government. This benefits even the fishing community in promoting hinterland tourism.

Water Supply

161. Without resting content with the existing water supply, the government should plan for realising 24×7 protected water supply. This could be achieved if measures like rainwater harvesting are undertaken, with an estimated 95 per cent of the rainwater draining into the sea during the monsoon. This required short-term and long-term investments through PPP in rainwater harvesting involving specialists like the Delhi-based Centre for Science and Environment besides various NGOs in the field.

162. The demand for water rises with rise in house buildings, commercial complexes and industries and this has to be met immediately. Water harvesting is the only solution with tourist flow expected to double by 2011.

Power

163. The government could allow cogeneration of power to meet the industry needs with the state now running short of 25 mw of power while ensuring supply of quality and uninterrupted power to all. Bad power supply tells a lot on the industry, particularly hospitality sector which affects their air cooling systems and other essential operations.

164. The hotel and respective industries could be involved in beach cleaning and waste water and garbage management, provided there are waste processing and treatment plants in neighbouring states. Villages/village groups/clusters could be involved for protection of environment and sanctuaries, heritage sites and monuments besides conservation of hinterland lifestyles. Fixing of metres to taxis and auto-*rickshaws* to check looting of the tourists to keep the errant drivers on check by involving the local area committees could be made.

Strategy for 5-10 Years (Long Term)

165. This should envisage construction of international airport at Mopa by 2010, building of expressways and rail links to connect different cities/towns of the north and the south districts from the airport, construction of a new 3000-capacity international convention centre in Panaji, building of satellite townships to ease congestion and providing housing facility to tourists while protecting villages from overdevelopment.

Sports Sector

166. There is a vast scope for PPP in the sports sector that could result in not only efficiency of operation and maintenance of infrastructure but further strengthening the infrastructure involving the community.

167. The maintenance of most of the playgrounds, gymnasia and other infrastructure like the swimming pools/stadia/pavilions could be handed over to the interested private parties who could collect a nominal fee from the user to run the show. It could be given even to the *panchayats* and local bodies even as the Sports Authority of Goa (SAG) could continue giving grants for acquiring the land for such facilities.

168. Bigger sports events could be organised with the help of sponsors so that the SAG need not spend any paisa. There are about 34 state level sports associations and 465 sports clubs promoting sports, games and cultural and social activities of the communities under the direct control of the SAG since February 9, 1988 after the dissolution of the Sports Council of Goa. Even sports festivals at different levels could be promoted by the industry without any drain on the state exchequer.

Social Welfare

169. One of the areas where public-private partnerships can be introduced in the states is in the running of care homes. Asking government employees to run such homes may not be feasible as they may not be trained in the

skills to provide care to the elderly or the disabled. Transferring such homes to the NGOs is cost-effective besides ensuring better services.

170. Some other areas where Government-NGO partnership can be effective in making administration citizen-friendly are peoples' participation in natural resource management, community health and sanitation, monitoring primary education, village development schemes, water harvesting in both rural and urban areas.

Rainwater Harvesting

171. Goa receives about 200 cm rainfall annually and 95 per cent of it drains into the Arabian Sea with no initiative taken for rainwater harvesting so that the state experiences water shortages as we witness in even the rainy season in the two districts, leave alone summer.

172. The abundance of monsoon water could be stored through proper water management mechanism evolved out of a rigid policy with people's involvement. Further deterioration of water bodies, despite huge rainfall in Goa, was due to silting following deforestation, encroachment in beds and supply channels and lack of people's participation for maintenance of water bodies.

173. This could be prevented by evolving enabling legal framework, providing incentives/rebate in house tax, insurance, loans and land tax, offering special incentives for zero discharge industries, motivating industries to adopt community programmes in adjoining area for rainwater harvesting, creating awareness among masses, developing R&D for low cost technology and involving stakeholders.

Recommendations and Development Strategies

174. If the Central and State governments want to tap the full PPP potential, they need to identify viable projects and also investors who are willing to lower their profit margin to implement projects that can be showcased for the future.

175. Despite all the talk about pursuing the public-private partnership (PPP) route to implementing infrastructure projects, neither the Central nor the State governments have been able to come up with a viable formula to encourage investment. Private as well as public sector undertakings are looking for the right formula. Unless this is worked out, the governments have to keep spending precious resources. Given the financial constraints under which the States now work, finding resources for such huge investments becomes difficult. When multilateral institutions or banks are approached for funding, the first question that arises is repayment and a toll or charge for "services".

176. For more PPPs to become a reality in different sectors, Goa should ensure political stability, develop political will, motivate bureaucrats and politicians, identify PPP potential areas, develop roadmaps with suitable policy framework, carve out short, medium and long-term strategies, evolve enabling legal and financial frameworks, involve people and NGOs more in environment and social welfare sector for successful partnerships.

177. This apart, the government should fix responsibility for roles and functions regarding ownership of assets, capital financing, working capital, additional capital investments, operation and maintenance, managerial authority, bearing commercial risk, basis of private party compensation besides duration of the arrangement.

178. The PPP arrangement thus includes private members such as consortia of firms, constellation of advisers including design engineers, construction companies, bankers, investment bankers, lawyers, operations specialists, equipment manufacturers, technology providers, real-estate developers, financial consultants, marketers and public relations specialists.

179. This needs providing an environment conducive for healthy competition through a regulatory framework and incentive structure without encouraging monopolies besides eliminating all barriers, both structural and financial.

180. The government needs to spell out the regulators and their autonomy, roles and control mechanisms with adequate provisions for appeals as in the case of SEZs or STPIs or development parks or divestments. It has to ensure that the regulatee does not regulate the regulators in due course.

181. The governments have to study all risks such as legal, political, financial and business, technical, technological, environmental, *force majeure* (circumstances beyond control of the partners such as natural calamities), rate regulation, expropriation and repatriation, debt service coverage, exchange rate risk, cost over-run risk, operating risk and revenue risk.

182. At the same time, the governments should employ suitable procedures for procuring the desired and deserving private partner through advertisement or competitive negotiation so that it resulted in labor understanding and investment protection besides future requirements including expansion. Earlier, it had to study independent financial feasibility encompassing adequate capital for construction and sufficient revenues to cover operating costs for a viable project with profit potential for the private investor.

Chapter 13

Governance

Reforms

Issues and their Fiscal Implications

1. Governance[1], the act, manner and function of governing, is the fundamental driving force to the sustainable and fulfilling existence of every state. Through the role of such cabinets, assemblies and committees, governance ensures that the state is well managed. The Constitution of India has served as the basis for India's governance since its Independence. It is this framework that is the basis for the various governmental and non-governmental bodies, their composition and role, their act, manner and function. It is this framework that has led the development of the country and the state of Goa to where it is since Independence of India and the liberation of Goa.

2. The experience of governance by those governed as well as those who have governed from time to time indicate a strong feeling of dissatisfaction with governance and a need for reform. The experiences that have emerged from the practice of the constitution have much to offer in this process of suggesting reform. Therefore, the issues of governance from the perspectives of those governed as well as those governing will form the basis for reform. Reform, therefore, is not an end in itself but a means to produce different outcomes by doing different things.

3. From the perspective of those governed the most important issue of governance is the performance and the measures used to assess performance. This chapter shall focus on the measures used to assess performance of governance itself.

4. For those who are governed, the most fundamental measure of performance of governance is trustworthiness.

5. Concerns of the governed would include composition of the governing bodies, the representation of different groups, tenure of such bodies. They would also be concerned about instruments accountability when trust breaks down, when performance is biased against certain groups and performance leaves much to be desired.

6. From the perspective of those on the governing bodies there appear to be issues of role, scope and jurisdiction.

Measures of Performance[2]

7. From the perspective of those governed, trustworthiness expresses their measure of performance of governance. People invest in what they trust, they disinvest from untrustworthy portfolios.

8. While distrust is expressed in many ways, the most common way is through the instrument of vote. The low percentage of support of the electors to the government of the day or to the candidate of the governing party indicates a low level of trust. A fractured mandate is the result. The low participation of voters in elections is another indicator of distrust in the mechanisms of governance.

9. Distrust also displays itself in the rise of economic crime. A regime of bad governance often under-registers crimes or over-registers political criminals. Longer or poor conviction rates are a possible surrogate indicator of the

1. According to the World Bank (*http://www.worldbank.org/wbi/governance/index.html*), governance can be broadly defined as the set of traditions and institutions by which authority in a country is exercised. This includes: (1) the process by which governments are selected, monitored and replaced, (2) the capacity of the government to effectively formulate and implement sound policies, and (3) the respect of citizens and the state for the institutions that govern economic and social interactions among them.

2. The World Bank uses a subjective measure they term as 'government effectiveness' which combines subjective responses on the quality of public service provision, the quality of the bureaucracy, the competence of civil servants, the independence of the civil service from political pressures, and the credibility of the government's commitment to policies obtained through surveys.

existence of such practice and possible lack of police independence. The same is true for corruption and therefore, low convictions in corruption cases is a tentative indicator for lack of trust.

TABLE 13.1

Fractured Mandate to the Government in Goa as Indicated by the Assembly Constitution

Legislative Assembly	*1st*	*2nd*	*3rd*	*4th*
Cong	20	22	15	16
GPP	6	0	0	0
MGP	2	8	2	2
Ind	11	3	1	1
BJP	0	4	10	17
UGDP	0	3	0	3
GPCP	0	0	11	0
NCP	0	0	1	1
Vacant	1	0	0	0
Total	40	40	40	40

Source: Goa Legislative Assembly.

FIGURE 13.1

Fractured Mandate to the Government in Goa as Indicated by the Assembly Constitution for the Last Four Assembly Elections

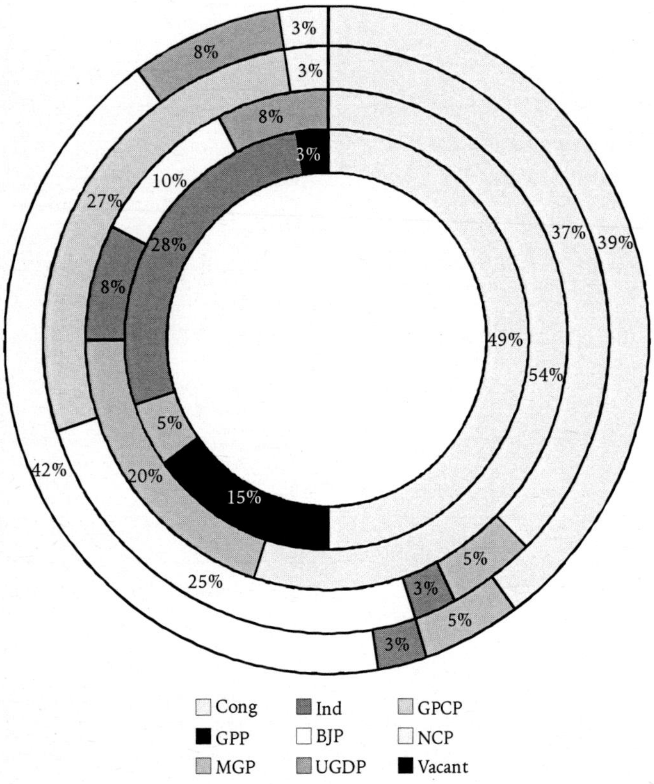

Source: Goa Legislative Assembly.

10. Good governors understand and invest in measures of governance that build long-term trust, not short-term gains.

11. However, the most common measure of performance that is put forth by those governing, are the allocation of funds and expenditure on projects, the growth rate of the economy, reduction of deficit, socio-economic indicators, infrastructure development undertaken and scheme implementation.

FIGURE 13.2

Fractured Mandate to the Government in Goa as Indicated by Per cent Votes Polled by the Winning MLA for the Fourth Assembly Elections

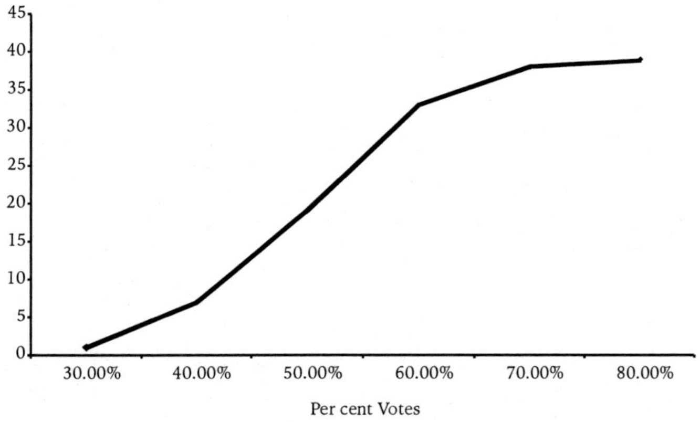

Source: GoaNews.Com

FIGURE 13.3

Reporting and Conviction of Crime in Goa

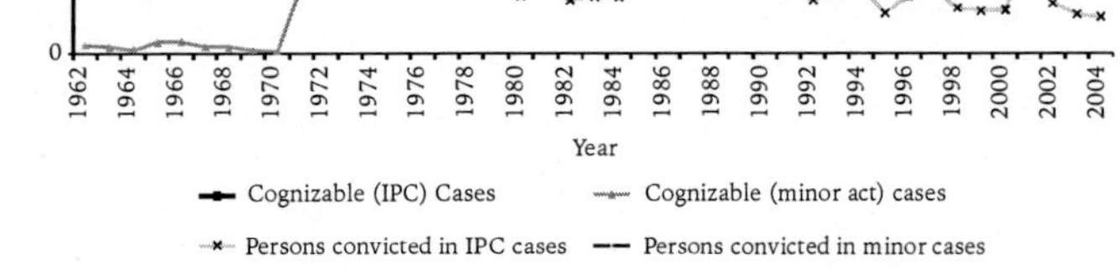

Source: Goa Police.

12. It is now widely accepted that the allocation of funds is no guarantee of utilisation. Utilisation is no guarantee of reaching the community. Consequently this is a poor measure of performance, if at all.

13. The growth of certain sectors in the economy has been recognised as resulting from the non-involvement of the government in these sectors. The most cited example is that of the IT industry. World leaders, including the Honourable Prime Minister of India have observed that it is the animal instinct of business that drives the growth of the economy.[3] Business interest fills opportunity and grows despite the government. Therefore, the growth of the economy is not the ideal measure of performance of governance.

14. The reduction of deficit is an indicator of financial prudence not of good governance; either expenditure has been curtailed or revenues have been expanded to accommodate the expenditure in comparison to the previous financial year. This however, is no guarantee of sustainable or fulfilling quality of life or resource and social security of its citizens.

15. Socio-economic indicators, often cited to conclude that Goa is amongst the top states in the country, at best reflect sectoral states, not the performance of governance.

16. Infrastructure is usually the result of projects that usually span across several governments. Rarely can it indicate the measure of performance of a particular government's ability to govern.

17. The creation and implementation of schemes and the scope of beneficiaries is also the result of several governments. This indicator also assumes the utility of the scheme, its relevance and value to the community. At their best, these are measures of performance of governance of the respective sectors, not of the performance of governance itself.

18. The Directive Principles of State Policy listed in Part IV of the Constitution, particularly the following—

- an adequate means of livelihood;
- ownership and control of the material resources of the community be so distributed as best to subserve the common good;
- the economic system does not result in the concentration of wealth and means of production to the common detriment;
- are areas where performance needs to be assessed and are therefore, an excellent basis for measuring governance in the respective sectors.

19. A measure of performance of governance cannot be a measure of operational or management indicators; it must be a measure of ability to accomplish a clear intent. To do so there are two requirements: a clear intent and accomplishment of the clear intent. It is the role of those governing to express the clear intent. The intent of an organisation is best expressed as a mission. Performance of governance, therefore, is best measured as the ability of the governors to create and accomplish clear intent. Missions are statements of clear intent. Missions build trust in the community because everyone knows and understands what is being done and why. Missions help the implementation machinery to align to a clear intent. If missions are well formulated, everyone benefits, not just a section of society. They are the best way for governors to build long-term trust.

TABLE 13.2

Directive Principles of State Policy

Article	*Outline*
36	Definition.
37	Application of the principles contained in this Part.
38	State to secure a social order for the promotion of welfare of the people.
39	Certain principles of policy to be followed by the State.
39A	Equal justice and free legal aid.
40	Organisation of village *panchayats*.
41	Right to work, to education and to public assistance in certain cases.
42	Provision for just and humane conditions of work and maternity relief.
43	Living wage, etc., for workers.
43A	Participation of workers in management of industries.
44	Uniform civil code for the citizens.
45	Provision for free and compulsory education for children.
46	Promotion of educational and economic interests of Scheduled Castes, Scheduled Tribes and other weaker sections.
47	Duty of the State to raise the level of nutrition and the standard of living and to improve public health.
48	Organisation of agriculture and animal husbandry.
48A	Protection and improvement of environment and safeguarding of forests and wild life.
49	Protection of monuments and places and objects of national importance.
50	Separation of judiciary from executive.
51	Promotion of international peace and security.

20. Since mission-oriented governance is not yet the norm, although it is the current best practice, even the mere existence of a clear mission for the government and its constituents is the first big step towards performance of governance.

3. Keynote address to India-EU Business Summit, New Delhi, September 4, 2005.

21. Where such mission statements exist, the restructuring of government machinery (departments, sections, committees, corporations, companies, etc.) to serve the mission is an indicator of greater performance of good governance.

22. When all restructured components actively align their staff towards the success of the mission, there is even greater performance of governance.

23. The final indicator of performance of governance is to accomplish mission success itself.

FIGURE 13.4

Performance Measure for Governance

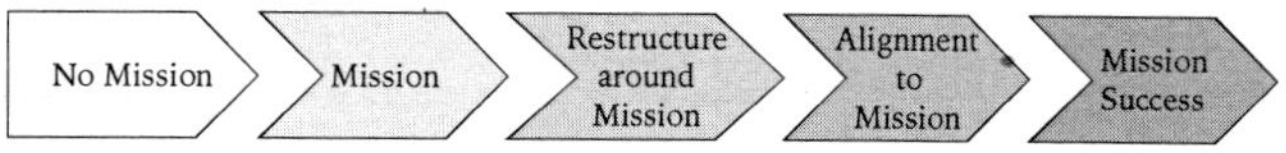

24. Goa perhaps has the distinction of being the first state to initiate mission focus with the government and its different departments. Although it is only a first step, it is ahead of Gartner's forecast[4] of mission-oriented governments by 2006.

25. Good governance reduces the time it takes for the machinery to respond to day-to-day events and crisis rapidly while bad governance actually increases the time (for example the machinery in Maharashtra has not been able to respond to the normal demand of domestic or industrial electricity consumption even after months). Therefore, good governance reduces the risk of exposing the State to scenarios where crisis and disaster strike and yet ensures ability of the machinery to handle the crisis were it to happen.

26. The increase of respite in each sector, or the time available before the breakdown of security in the sector (for example, the time available to cater to increased water demand before the inability of the current infrastructure to meet the demand), is therefore, also a measure of performance of governance. So also is the decrease in response time, or the time taken to react to needs in a sector (for example, the time taken to ensure water availability), a measure of performance of governance. However, a lot of literacy of the importance of these indicators may be required before governors understand their implications.

Composition and Representation[5]

27. If there is a breakdown of trust in governance, issues of composition and representation become important.

28. The state's legislature, the prime group responsible for the governance of the State is elected from constituencies distributed in the state on the basis of a ratio of the total population to the seats allotted to the state in accordance with Article 170 of the Constitution of India.

29. While the role of the elected representatives is the governance of the State, there is an invariable focus on the constituency. It has almost come to be assumed that the MLA represents the people of that constituency and therefore, it is expected of the MLA to develop the constituency, not the State. Therefore, rather than the State, it is the constituency that is regarded by the representative as the unit of development. As a consequence every constituency of an aggressive representative grows, at times in an unsustainable and uncoordinated manner.

FIGURE 13.5

Constituency Boundaries Bear No Correspondence to a Development Unit or Village Boundaries

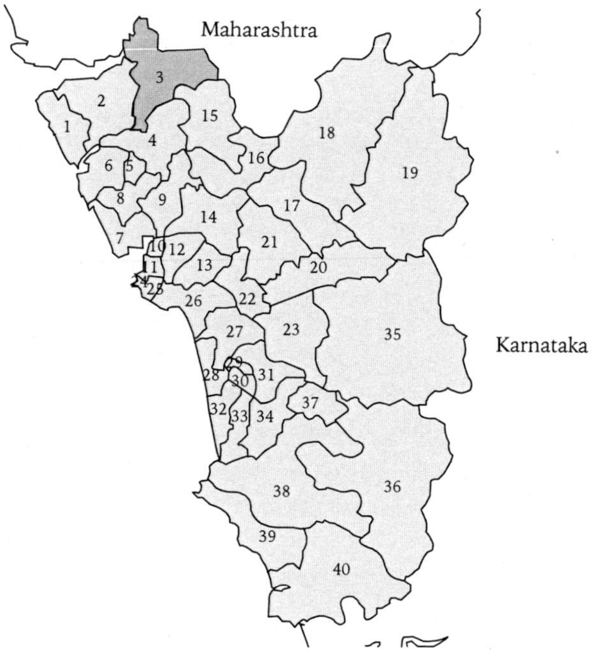

4. Gartner Report, 2003.

5. The World Bank framework uses a Voice and Accountability indicator includes in it a number of subjective indicators measuring various aspects of the political process, civil liberties, political and human rights, measuring the extent to which citizens of a country are able to participate in the selection of governments. This indicator is generated from survey of a sample of the population.

30. Since constituency boundaries get delineated as a consequence of growth of population reported in the census, there is further failure of balanced growth and planned development of the region.

31. The regional composition of people's bodies has therefore, proved to be expensive for the states development. If indeed constituencies were to be development units of which the MLA is a governor, it makes no sense to alter the physical extents of such boundaries to enable coordinated development. On the other hand, if the MLA is truly the representative of the State, in the age of computers, it is hardly necessary to manage composition by restricting geographical or gender or caste representation.

32. The electoral process selects representatives who can sustain high costs, not necessarily those with understanding of governance or with the spirit of public service. Constituency voting reinforces the advantage for those entrenched in local interest rather that with the vision of state interest. If the State is important, urgent reforms need to enable State-wide participation in nominating the 40 legislators. The selection criteria also ought to ensure that candidates selected work with a public spirit and vision, rather than those with might or with an operational focus.

33. The boards of government corporations and companies are subject to representation from the elected representatives, not professionals. Government corporations neither maintain clear records of board members nor make them public. Their composition is largely from within the government and with the exception of a very few cases no independent directors, Chairperson or Vice-Chairperson are appointed.

34. By the current process, stakeholders of different sectors find unequal representation in governance if at all. If development is to be balanced and all stakeholders interests are to be balanced, every stakeholder group including the minority stakeholder needs to find representation.[6]

Tenure[7]

35. If decades of liberation for Goa and decades of freedom for India, where thousands of people have represented the people on various bodies of governance have not yielded development or built the peoples' trust in governance, the issue of tenure of the representatives becomes relevant. Typically tenures are fixed time blocks, not based on performance or project. It is therefore, often seen that the basic agenda, projects, programmes and activities of governments oscillate like a pendulum on change of governments due to current tenure practices. Such changes also erode the credibility of the government and governance as contracts, obligations, policies and acts of previous government are negated, dishonoured or reversed. Quite often the people involved with such previous governments are also harassed and face vindictive tactics.

FIGURE 13.6

Tenure of Chief Secretaries in Goa

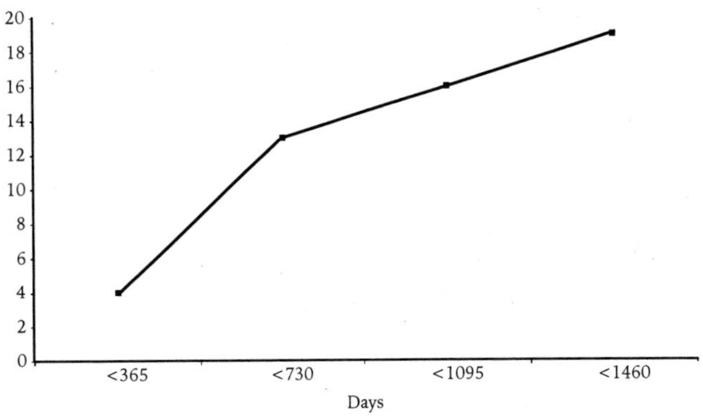

Source: Office of the Chief Secretary, Goa.

36. If development is for the people and the governments work for the people, such changes in projects are hardly justifiable. Goa has seen a particularly striking tenure effect and consequently not been able to cash on the small state advantage to the extent it should be possible.

37. While the official tenure of the MLAs is five years, the Goa Assembly has shown much volatility. The government in turn has been even more volatile. The civil services, responsible for the management of the affairs of the State, also have shown an interesting tenure. Naturally their interest in the State diminishes.

38. The boards of corporations, and the positions of chairpersons' and vice-chairpersons' have been typically regarded as "quango's" rather than as independent and professional positions and therefore, their tenures have also followed path.

6. This is the general perception shared by various stakeholders who participated at the Stakeholder Roundtable for the State Development Report on August 12th and 13th in Goa.

7. The World Bank framework uses Political Stability and Absence of Violence indicator that combines several indicators which measure perceptions of the likelihood that the government in power will be destabilised or overthrown by possibly unconstitutional and/or violent means, including domestic violence and terrorism.

39. Unless tenures are linked to missions or projects, the agenda for the State by those in charge will keep changing. Fixed time tenures make sense if the system needs to generate continuous change and reversal of priorities. Tenures based on the process of majority voting make sense if development is majority dependent and not for every citizen. If the process of development is needed for by all, the only choice is in sequencing the programmes or projects.

Accountability[8]

40. Currently the only mode of accountability is through the process of re-election. Unless the measures of performance of governance are not reported as mandatory or even optional framework on a periodic basis, accountability will be illusive or shift governance to operations where governors hold themselves accountable to individual issues, not State issues.

41. Transparency is often regarded as a mechanism for accountability. However, in the absence of a framework for measuring governance, the transparency of management decisions is simply divesting the responsibility of governance and giving the licence to ad hoc-raj.

42. The present system of Governance with too much emphasis on "controls" and rules inhibit Goa's development. Better governance will mean breaking free from the shackles of bureaucracy, using modern tools including e-governance to liberate the citizens, entrepreneurs and business. This will mean the development of a new breed of professionals with high competence and ethics to man the machinery and reforms of the Goa Government.

Role[9]

43. Governance as an act is to be understood in a strategic sense; it involves processes of vision development, strategic discussions, long-term goal formulation. Management is an act at a tactical level: processes of agenda-building, negotiating, networking, coalition building. At the operational level are the processes of experimenting, project-building, implementation.[10]

44. Governance is often mistaken as management[11] of the government function. Most forget it is not for the governors to manage but rather ensure the State is well managed without doing the management themselves.

45. Currently the management decision-making involves ministers as evidenced by file movements. Rather than create policy and review its implementation, the governors are trapped in management and operations. Consequently it is not a policy that drives decisions but the ad hoc inputs from time to time.

46. Corporate boards are expected to[12]:

1. Define the organisation's purpose, direction and priorities.
2. Develop a governance policy 'umbrella'.
3. Specify key outcomes and approve the availability of resources.
4. Appoint, support, evaluate and reward the senior executives.
5. Establish a framework for assessment and risk.
6. Regularly scan the environment beyond the organisation.
7. Gain the organisation's owners' and other stakeholders' input into determining direction and goals and maintain communication with them.
8. Ensure the board complies with statutory and contractual requirements and with the board's own policies.
9. Set standards and evaluating the board's own performance
10. Ensure there's appropriate succession planning.

47. Clearly this role is what those governing the state also need to play.

48. It is widely lamented by many a minister from different cabinets that there is a poor track record of implementation of cabinet resolutions. Many a policy has not been presented, debated or cleared by cabinet for years due to more operational pressures. This is clearly a crisis of understanding role. The cabinet meeting is governance as opposed to a management forum. Cabinets

8. The World Bank framework uses Control of Corruption indicator as a measure of the extent of corruption, conventionally defined as the exercise of public power for private gain. It is based on scores of variables from polls of experts and surveys.

9. The World Bank uses Regulatory Quality as a subjective indicator that focuses more on the policies themselves, including measures of the incidence of market-unfriendly policies such as price controls or inadequate bank supervision, as well as perceptions of the burdens imposed by excessive regulation in areas such as foreign trade and business development.

10. Loorbach Derek (2005). "Governance and Transitions: A multi-level policy-framework based on complex systems thinking", Berlin Conference on Human Dimensions of Global Environmental Change.

11. Dayton, Kenneth (1987). *Governance is Governance.* Washington, DC: Independent Sector.

12. SPARC Quick Reference Cards.

benefit from an agenda that tackles strategic issues early in the meeting, leaving monitoring and other compliance-type topics until later. Cabinet meetings should be used primarily to create the future, not to rehash or review the past.

49. A review of the management of the government and reform in the mechanics of governance has not happened across the country. This is also an indicator of the failure of the governance system to assert its role as governor.

50. Acknowledgement of conflicts of interest between the constituency and state, as well as other areas, has not happened. This has not only undermined the democratic process itself but also brought the legislator or government into disrepute and compromised the integrity of the governance process. For example, in Goa this is evidenced by a 3,700 square kilometre state having 18 industrial estates and more in the pipeline.

Scope[13]

51. The scope for the State's legislature is delimited by the State List defined in Schedule VII of the Constitution of India. The scope for the various departments is limited by the policy or more often by orders and notifications. The scope of the boards is delimited by companies act or the act of legislature that formed the corporation, or more often by respective government departments who sanction the contracts, resources and existence of the corporations irrespective of their performance.

52. While the state list is a first attempt to define scope, it does not define scope in functional terms. Further it does not imply a developmental mission but rather leaves scope for a variety of interpretations. In functional terms, for example, the list might contain economic self-reliance, food security, energy security etc.

Jurisdiction

53. The jurisdiction of ministries and departments as designed or inherited by the governors and the management machinery is non-overlapping. Consequently the zone for town and country planning does not match the water supply zone which in turn has no correlation to the electricity department.

54. It is no surprise that urban sprawls and slums result from such a plan approach. The result of such a system is that the water or electricity departments, for

TABLE 13.3

The State List

246. Subject-matter of laws made by Parliament and by the Legislatures of States.— (3) Subject to clauses (1) and (2), the Legislature of any State 1 *** has exclusive power to make laws for such State or any part thereof with respect to any of the matters enumerated in List II in the Seventh Schedule (in this Constitution referred to as the "State List").

List II—State List

1. Public order (but not including the use of any naval, military or air force or any other armed force of the Union or of any other force subject to the control of the Union or of any contingent or unit thereof in aid of the civil power).
2. Police (including railway and village police) subject to the provisions of entry 2A of List I.
3. ***Officers and servants of the High Court; procedure in rent and revenue courts; fees taken in all courts except the Supreme Court.
4. Prisons, reformatories, Borstal institutions and other institutions of a like nature, and persons detained therein; arrangements with other States for the use of prisons and other institutions.
5. Local government, that is to say, the constitution and powers of municipal corporations, improvement trusts, districts boards, mining settlement authorities and other local authorities for the purpose of local self-government or village administration.
6. Public health and sanitation; hospitals and dispensaries.
7. Pilgrimages, other than pilgrimages to places outside India.
8. Intoxicating liquors, that is to say, the production, manufacture, possession, transport, purchase and sale of intoxicating liquors.
9. Relief of the disabled and unemployable.
10. Burials and burial grounds; cremations and cremation grounds.

4 * * * * *

12. Libraries, museums and other similar institutions controlled or financed by the State; ancient and historical monuments and records other than those declared by or under law made by Parliament to be of national importance.
13. Communications, that is to say, roads, bridges, ferries, and other means of communication not specified in List I; municipal tramways; ropeways; inland waterways and traffic thereon subject to the provisions of List I and List III with regard to such waterways; vehicles other than mechanically propelled vehicles.
14. Agriculture, including agricultural education and research, protection against pests and prevention of plant diseases.
15. Preservation, protection and improvement of stock and prevention of animal diseases; veterinary training and practice.
16. Pounds and the prevention of cattle trespass.
17. Water, that is to say, water supplies, irrigation and canals, drainage and embankments, water storage and water power subject to the provisions of entry 56 of List I.
18. Land, that is to say, rights in or over land, land tenures including the relation of landlord and tenant, and the collection of rents; transfer and alienation of agricultural land; land improvement and agricultural loans; colonisation.

1 * * * * *

21. Fisheries.
22. Courts of wards subject to the provisions of entry 34 of List I; encumbered and attached estates.
23. Regulation of mines and mineral development subject to the provisions of List I with respect to regulation and development under the control of the Union.
24. Industries subject to the provisions of 2 (entries 7 and 52) of List I.

13. The World Bank framework uses Rule of Law which includes several indicators which measure the extent to which agents have confidence in and abide by the rules of society. These include perceptions of the incidence of crime, the effectiveness and predictability of the judiciary and the enforceability of contracts.

25. Gas and gas-works.

26. Trade and commerce within the State subject to the provisions of entry 33 of List III.

27. Production, supply and distribution of goods subject to the provisions of entry 33 of List III.

28. Markets and fairs.

3 * * * * *

30. Money-lending and money-lenders; relief of agricultural indebtedness.

31. Inns and inn-keepers.

32. Incorporation, regulation and winding up of corporations, other than those specified in List I, and universities; unincorporated trading, literary, scientific, religious and other societies and associations; co-operative societies.

33. Theatres and dramatic performances; cinemas subject to the provisions of entry 60 of List I; sports, entertainments and amusements.

34. Betting and gambling.

35. Works, lands and buildings vested in or in the possession of the State.

4 * * * * *

37. Elections to the Legislature of the State subject to the provisions of any law made by Parliament.

38. Salaries and allowances of members of the Legislature of the State, of the Speaker and Deputy Speaker of the Legislative Assembly and, if there is a Legislative Council, of the Chairman and Deputy Chairman thereof.

39. Powers, privileges and immunities of the Legislative Assembly and of the members and the committees thereof, and, if there is a Legislative Council, of that Council and of the members and the committees thereof; enforcement of attendance of persons for giving evidence or producing documents before committees of the Legislature of the State.

40. Salaries and allowances of ministers for the State.

41. State public services; State Public Service Commission.

42. State pensions, that is to say, pensions payable by the State or out of the Consolidated Fund of the State.

43. Public debt of the State.

44. Treasure trove.

45. Land revenue, including the assessment and collection of revenue, the maintenance of land records, survey for revenue purposes and records of rights and alienation of revenues.

46. Taxes on agricultural income.

47. Duties in respect of succession to agricultural land.

48. Estate duty in respect of agricultural land.

49. Taxes on lands and buildings.

50. Taxes on mineral rights subject to any limitations imposed by Parliament by law relating to mineral development.

51. Duties of excise on the following goods manufactured or produced in the State and countervailing duties at the same or lower rates on similar goods manufactured or produced elsewhere in India:—

(a) alcoholic liquors for human consumption;

(b) opium, Indian hemp and other narcotic drugs and narcotics, but not including medicinal and toilet preparations containing alcohol or any substance included in sub-paragraph (b) of this entry.

52. Taxes on the entry of goods into a local area for consumption, use or sale therein.

53. Taxes on the consumption or sale of electricity.

1 [54. Taxes on the sale or purchase of goods other than newspapers, subject to the provisions of entry 92A of List I.]

55. Taxes on advertisements other than advertisements published in the newspapers 2 (and advertisements broadcast by radio or television).

56. Taxes on goods and passengers carried by road or on inland waterways.

57. Taxes on vehicles, whether mechanically propelled or not, suitable for use on roads, including tramcars subject to the provisions of entry 35 of List III.

58. Taxes on animals and boats.

59. Tolls.

60. Taxes on professions, trades, callings and employments.

61. Capitation taxes.

62. Taxes on luxuries, including taxes on entertainments, amusements, betting and gambling.

63. Rates of stamp duty in respect of documents other than those specified in the provisions of List I with regard to rates of stamp duty.

64. Offences against laws with respect to any of the matters in this List.

65. Jurisdiction and powers of all courts, except the Supreme Court, with respect to any of the matters in this List.

66. Fees in respect of any of the matters in this List, but not including fees taken in any court.

1 Subs. by the Constitution (Forty-second Amendment) Act, 1976, s. 57 for certain words (w.e.f. 3-1-1977). 2 Subs. by s. 57, ibid., for entry 2 (w.e.f. 3-1-1977). 3 Certain words omitted by s. 57, ibid. (w.e.f. 3-1-1977). 4 Entry 11 omitted by s. 57, ibid. (w.e.f. 3-1-1977).

1 Entries 19, 20 and 36 omitted by the Constitution (Forty–second Amendment) Act, 1976, s. 57 (w.e.f. 3-1-1977). 2 Subs. by the Constitution (Seventh Amendment) Act, 1956, s. 28, for "entry 52". 3 Entry 29 omitted by the Constitution (Forty–second Amendment) Act, 1976, s. 57 (w.e.f. 3-1-1977). 4 Entry 36 omitted by the Constitution (Seventh Amendment) Act, 1956, s. 26.

1 Subs. by the Constitution (Sixth Amendment) Act, 1956, s. 2, for entry 54. 2 Ins. by the Constitution (Forty–second Amendment) Act, 1976, s. 57 (w.e.f. 3-1-1977).

Source: http://lawmin.nic.in/coi/SEVENTH-SCHEDULE.pdf

example, have no means to know, project or plan for the changed demand in their zone as a result of building permissions or re-zoning of a municipal or village area.

55. This also results in tight information compartments; the citizens recognised by the Electoral Officer, by the Public Delivery System or by the Chief Electrical Engineer are not common, shared or matching. The same is true of the businesses.

56. In Goa, an exercise was launched under e-government to create common shared citizen and business registries in the form of a government wide digital exchange. It is the continuity of such a common shared system that will resolve and reform the jurisdiction issues.

Institutions and Governance

57. The Legislative Assembly of the State consists of 40 MLAs and a cabinet whose average size has been 18. This is the apex governing body at whose advice the Governor institutes governance. The State government has 84 departments to deal with the state subjects defined in the Constitution. Fourteen government companies and one government corporation support various departments in the management and operational functions.

58. It is evident that the institutional structure does not correspond to the State List and there are multiple institutions dealing with the same subject. There is no clarity of mechanisms to resolve conflicts and issues that fall into the domain of several departments and institutions other than refer it to the Chief Minister. For example, the policy formulated by a department is expected to deal with matters of different departments and is therefore, circulated to all of them for clearance. Based on issues raised by different departments the Policy or many of its cross departmental implications may not be notified or implemented in even six years. A policy is an agreed basis for action, made ahead of time. If it is an agreement at management and operational levels that is sought, governors have forgotten their role or it is micro managing. Different mechanics actually create several parallel procedures through different departments by having this lack of clarity and focus.

59. There is no common shared best practice for the common functions across the machinery. Although such an exercise was launched in Goa as a part of the e-government initiatives, there has been no effort to capitalise on the success.

60. The different geographical blocks of towns and villages are governed by municipal corporation/council and *panchayats*. The 18 towns in the North District have 1 municipal corporation, 5 municipal councils and 12 *panchayats*. The 220 villages here are governed by 118 *panchayats*. The 13 towns in the South District have 7 municipal councils and 6 *panchayats*. The 140 villages here are governed by 65 *panchayats*.

61. The presidents of the *zilla panchayats* do not worry about reform, they are currently worried of the implementation of the existing reforms though the 73rd and 74th Amendments. They lament the devolution of power has not happened, nor have budgets been appropriated as per the act.

62. The Department of Municipal Administration administers the municipal bodies in the State. The Department of *Panchayats* is responsible for overseeing the *panchayat* administration.

63. The smallness of the state and the administrative structure that divides the landmass into 11 *talukas*, 12 municipal councils and 201 *panchayats*, helps to distribute the tasks and reduce the complexity of governance at each administrative level. However, the feedback between each administrative level is still inadequate as information sharing mechanisms does not exist and is not formalised. For example, the citizen and business registries are neither common nor shared. This results in poor control, collapse of planning, lack of flexibility of mechanisms and long delays.

Strengths, Weaknesses, Opportunities and Threats

Strengths

64. Being only 3,700 square kilometres and 1.3 million people, Goa's governance structure does not need to be large and can institutionalise reform and feedback rapidly. It can therefore, implement infrastructure and governance changes with the agility that could be the envy of larger states.

Weaknesses

65. Being a small state, the failures of governance can accumulate problems rapidly as there is less of a buffer in comparison to large states. This can destroy all that is sacred and valuable to the state and its citizens: the tranquil beauty, peace and sustainability. The respite time in Goa can change more rapidly than other states due to its smaller size. Growth can cross the inflexion point from economic to uneconomic as the impact of compound growth in resource and environmental problems hits faster.

Opportunities

66. Goa is the first state to have created and implemented a State-wide infrastructure for common and shared information and best practice in the form of a "Digital Exchange". This facilitates common and shared information and transactions for citizens and businesses across local, state and Central government. This will ensure good governance of different sectors as it builds greater trust between the citizens and the government. It will also ensure good governance as

governors will have in real time the trusted status of all needs and gaps of services and schemes and their beneficiaries available.

Threats

67. The failure of governors to assert their role as governor and sink into the role of management and operations is the biggest threat to governance in Goa. Due to the smallness of the state those governing are often expected to "look-after" the interests of individuals rather than create policy and ensure its implementation. This erodes good governance and loses the focus of those governing from their role as governors.

Outlook: Possible Scenarios in the Short, Medium and Long Term

68. In the short term, over the next year or so, tenure considerations will override performance. Historically tenure has become the centre of attention in Goa because of its diminishing size. Since Goa's socio-economic indicators and quality of life is generally better than the rest of India, it has tended to ignore the weaknesses and threats to its governance.

69. In the medium term, tenure is likely to retain focus unless there are reforms that enable mission and project tenures as well as a reporting of the performance of governance through the framework outlined in this chapter.

70. In the long term, scope and jurisdiction reforms are likely to help Goa to refocus on performance and good governance in different sectors.

Recommendations and Development Strategies

71. Governance is perhaps the most critical driver to development. Since existing governance mechanisms have yielded the development we see today, it is clear that reforms are necessary if we were to see a different development state.

Performance Measure Reforms

72. In order to distinguish between the management and operational performance and the performance of governance, the assessment of the performance of governance through ability of those governing to create mission, restructure the machinery around mission, align the machinery to perform the mission and mission success, will have to form part of routine governance ratings. This will help the governor to recognise their contribution as distinct from management and operational contributions in the development process.

Composition and Representation Reforms

73. In contrast to composition of legislatures through constituency, more innovative ways of representation of different stakeholders across missions need to be designed. For example, for an energy security mission a representative of the consumer, producer and distributor will be more relevant than a representative of a constituency.

74. Such a composition reform will radically alter the representation to different stakeholders and will bring the diverse informed perspectives needed for governance of that mission on to the legislature.

Tenure Reforms

75. To ensure a continuity of mission, projects and programmes, government tenure should not be based on majority support, rather on a mission or project period. This may even mean that different legislatures could have different tenures based on the missions, projects or programmes they govern.

Accountability Reforms

76. To ensure focus on governance by those governing, a reform of presenting the measures of performance of governance on a periodic basis is needed.

Role Reforms

77. The role of legislators' needs clarity and definition; if they are elected from constituencies what roles are they expected to play for the state and for the constituency. The conflict of interest of the legislator in matters relating to the constituency and the state needs to be clearly dealt with.

78. On the other hand with representation reforms, as the representative stakeholders in a specific area they bring an understanding of the issues and fair mechanisms to resolve the issues. They bring clarity of the changing governance and infrastructure needs of the sector.

Scope Reforms

79. Development needs can be more clearly defined in terms of energy security, health security, economic security etc. Allowing the legislatures the scope of defining missions to accomplish these will ensure balanced and consistent development. Leaving a state list to reflect management and operational issues focuses the

legislatures into micro management rather than macro issues.

Institutions and Jurisdiction Reforms

80. Consolidating departments and corporations and focusing on machinery to deliver missions will be as important as creating uniform development units, or common zones, for each mission area and departments that engage in the mission.

81. Common information infrastructure like the "Digital Exchange" creating a common and shared local, state and Central government wide registry for citizens, businesses, projects, budgets and assets need to be created.

Chapter 14

Urbanisation and Growth Nuclei

Issues and their Fiscal Implications

Growth

1. Since its liberation in 1961, Goa's urban population has increased by almost 670 per cent. In the last decade itself, the population has grown by 40 per cent. The number of urban centres have quadrupled in Goa since liberation. However, it is 50 per cent of the State's population that now lives in the 4 urban centres in the State.

TABLE 14.1

Urban Growth in Goa from 1961-2001

	1961	*1971*	*1981*	*1991*	*2001*
No. of towns	11	11	15	31	44
Per cent urban habitats	4.38%	2.63%	3.66%	7.75%	11.25%
Urban population	87,329	203,243	322,785	479,752	670,577
Per cent urban population	14.80%	25.56%	32.03%	41.01%	49.76%
Urban area in sq. kms.	19	122	177	385	N.A.
Urban density	4,596	1,671	1,821	1,247	N.A.

Source: Census of India (1961-2001).

2. The 44 urban centres cover a little over 385 square kilometres and are relatively low-density urban towns with a density of around 12 people per hectare. While this does mean that the pressures felt by high density are distant, it is alarming to see the proliferation of the urban centres without adequate means of governance of the nuclei of urban growth.

3. Urban population in Mormugao has grown the fastest, followed by Bardez and then Salcete. The slowest is Bicholim, followed by Pernem and Sanguem.

4. All *talukas* show growth of their urban population. Urban population in Ponda has grown the fastest, followed by Pernem, Bicholim and then Sanguem.

5. However Bardez, Bicholim, Ponda and Sanguem show a decline in rural population. Rural population in Bicholim has shrunk the fastest, followed by Ponda and Bardez.

6. This clearly calls for a look at the local attraction centres created in the *taluka* in form of towns that may have led to a relocation of the rural population from these *talukas* to the urban centres.

Age Structure

FIGURE 14.1

Urban Age Structure in Goa from 1961-2001

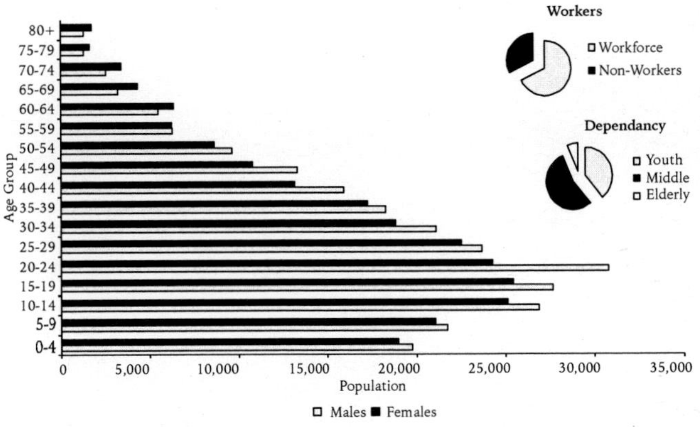

Source: Census of India (1961-2001).

7. The 0-4 age cohorts of urban Goa show a decline as the birth rates have fallen to below replacement levels in Goa. The 10-30 age groups are the largest in 1991. The urban centres therefore, need to gear to double the jobs created in the state. To cater to this highly mobile cohort, the state will need to create means of mass transport if it were to avoid congestion.

8. If the current trend continues, in the next 30 years the urban centres will see an ageing population as these

TABLE 14.2

Growth of Population from 1991 to 2001 in Different *Talukas* in Goa

		1991				2001			
		Area	*Total*	*M*	*F*	*Total*	*M*	*F*	*Growth*
Urban	Bardez	59	84,315	43,220	41,095	133,445	69,189	64,256	58.27%
	Bicholim	28	20,200	10,532	9,668	37,087	19,140	17,947	83.60%
	Canacona	19	10,447	5,381	5,066	11,901	6,196	5,705	13.92%
	Mormugao	48	96,727	52,095	44,632	120,362	64,435	55,927	24.43%
	Pernem	3	4,578	2,296	2,282	9,613	4,950	4,663	109.98%
	Ponda	5	14,661	8,149	6,512	48,615	25,675	22,940	231.59%
	Quepem	37	29,481	14,977	14,504	33,980	17,248	16,732	15.26%
	Salcete	85	111,295	55,640	55,655	151,579	76,307	75,272	36.20%
	Sanguem	5	6,198	3,181	3,017	11,006	5,558	5,448	77.57%
	Satari	12	6,825	3,486	3,339	7,917	4,031	3,886	16.00%
	Tiswadi	85	95,025	49,664	45,361	105,072	53,974	51,098	10.57%
	Urban Total	385	479,752	248,621	231,131	670,577	346,703	323,874	39.78%
Rural	Bardez	20,470	105,068	51,768	53,300	94,250	47,216	47,034	-10.30%
	Bicholim	21,073	64,332	32,912	31,420	53,647	27,567	26,080	-16.61%
	Canacona	33,335	30,269	15,241	15,028	32,096	16,080	16,016	6.04%
	Mormugao	6,124	23,776	12,070	11,706	24,587	12,135	12,452	3.41%
	Pernem	24,917	62,111	31,176	30,935	62,386	32,114	30,272	0.44%
	Ponda	28,756	113,566	58,083	55,483	100,826	51,460	49,366	-11.22%
	Quepem	28,156	35,037	17,822	17,215	40,054	20,279	19,775	14.32%
	Salcete	20,782	108,602	52,631	55,971	110,456	53,491	56,965	1.71%
	Sanguem	86,883	53,157	27,132	26,025	53,074	27,017	26,057	-0.16%
	Satari	48,341	42,705	21,567	21,138	50,696	25,849	24,847	18.71%
	Tiswadi	12,901	51,418	25,767	25,651	55,019	27,337	27,682	7.00%
	Rural total	331,737	690,041	346,169	343,872	677,091	340,545	336,546	-1.88%
State	Bardez	20,529	189,383	94,988	94,395	227,695	116,405	111,290	20.23%
	Bicholim	21,101	84,532	43,444	41,088	90,734	46,707	44,027	7.34%
	Canacona	33,354	40,716	20,622	20,094	43,997	22,276	21,721	8.06%
	Mormugao	6,172	120,503	64,165	56,338	144,949	76,570	68,379	20.29%
	Pernem	24,919	66,689	33,472	33,217	71,999	37,064	34,935	7.96%
	Ponda	28,762	128,227	66,232	61,995	149,441	77,135	72,306	16.54%
	Quepem	28,193	64,518	32,799	31,719	74,034	37,527	36,507	14.75%
	Salcete	20,867	219,897	108,271	111,626	262,035	129,798	132,237	19.16%
	Sanguem	86,888	59,355	30,313	29,042	64,080	32,575	31,505	7.96%
	Satari	48,352	49,530	25,053	24,477	58,613	29,880	28,733	18.34%
	Tiswadi	12,985	146,443	75,431	71,012	160,091	81,311	78,780	9.32%
	State Total	332,122	1,169,793	594,790	575,003	1,347,668	687,248	660,420	15.21%

Source: Census of India, 1991, 2001.

cohorts that were between 10 and 30 in 1991 age to 55 and 75. This will unleash a need for infrastructure and services that support the old. Even so the jobs created for this cohort are likely to be unfilled causing business decline unless immigrants replace the working age cohorts that have aged.

TABLE 14.3

Population of Towns in Goa from 1961-2001

Town	*1961*	*1971*	*1981*	*1991*	*2001*
Aldona	N.T.	N.T.	N.T.	N.T.	6,588
Calangute	N.T.	N.T.	9,621	11,925	15,783
Candolim	N.T.	N.T.	N.T.	7,108	8,604
Colvale	N.T.	N.T.	N.T.	N.T.	5,475
Guirim	N.T.	N.T.	N.T.	4,795	6,372
Mapusa	8,198	20,001	25,998	31,667	40,487
Penha-de-Franca	N.T.	N.T.	N.T.	11,546	15,377
Reis Magos	N.T.	N.T.	N.T.	7,504	8,708
Saligao	N.T.	N.T.	N.T.	N.T.	5,559
Siolim	N.T.	N.T.	8,892	9,770	10,318
Socorro (Serula)	N.T.	N.T.	N.T.	N.T.	10,174
Bicholim	3,969	8,550	11,233	13,743	14,913
Carapur	N.T.	N.T.	N.T.	N.T.	5,339
Pale	N.T.	N.T.	N.T.	6,457	5,641
Sanquelim	N.T.	N.T.	N.T.	N.T.	11,194
Canacona	N.T.	N.T.	N.T.	10,447	11,901
Chauri	450	1,335	1,629	N.T.	N.T.
Cortalim	N.T.	N.T.	N.T.	6,298	N.T.
Chicalim	N.T.	N.T.	N.T.	7,062	7,604
Mormugao	6,483	44,065	69,684	83,367	97,154
Sancoale	N.T.	N.T.	N.T.	N.T.	15,604
Parcem	N.T.	N.T.	N.T.	N.T.	4,324
Pernem	1,994	2,930	3,975	4,578	5,289
Bandora	N.T.	N.T.	N.T.	N.T.	12,267
Curti	N.T.	N.T.	N.T.	N.T.	13,179
Ponda	3,279	7,658	15,330	14,661	17,713
Queula	N.T.	N.T.	N.T.	N.T.	5,456
Curchorem Cacora	N.T.	N.T.	7,998	18,489	21,407
Quepem	1,142	2,925	55,593	10,992	12,573
Aquem	N.T.	N.T.	N.T.	N.T.	4,987
Benaulim	N.T.	N.T.	N.T.	9,898	10,158
Chinchinim	N.T.	N.T.	N.T.	6,173	7,033
Cuncolim	N.T.	N.T.	12,706	14,979	15,860
Davorlim	N.T.	N.T.	N.T.	N.T.	10,929
Margao	15,364	41,655	53,075	64,581	78,382
Navelim	N.T.	N.T.	N.T.	7,819	11,014
Raia	N.T.	N.T.	N.T.	7,845	N.T.
Sao Jose de Areal	N.T.	N.T.	N.T.	N.T.	8,351
Varca	N.T.	N.T.	N.T.	N.T.	4,865
Sanguem	2,440	5,006	5,977	6,198	6,173
Sanvordem	N.T.	N.T.	N.T.	N.T.	4,833
Valpoi	8,542	2,922	3,895	6,825	7,917
Bambolim	N.T.	N.T.	N.T.	4,955	5,785
Calapor	N.T.	N.T.	N.T.	9,390	11,830
Chimbel	N.T.	N.T.	N.T.	8,023	11,984
Goa Velha	N.T.	N.T.	N.T.	N.T.	5,395
Jua	N.T.	N.T.	N.T.	4,555	N.T.
Panaji	35,468	34,953	43,165	53,823	59,066
Taleigao	N.T.	N.T.	N.T.	14,279	N.T.

Note: N.T.: Not Town.

Source: Census of India (1961-2001).

9. Over the next 30 years, therefore, urban Goa is going to see a tremendous need for attracting people to man services and run the economy to support itself.

Resource Demand and Supply

10. With 44 urban centres, Goa has 44 nuclei of demand growth.

11. Forty-four demand centres will display differing patterns of resource demand: water, land, electricity, oil and food.

TABLE 14.4

Urban Resource Demand Per Capita in Goa

Per Capita Demand Per Day	*Litres of Water*	*kWh Electricity*	*Kg Food*
Domestic	104	0.14	0.625
Other	0	0.27	0
Industrial	44	0.05	0
Agricultural	100	0.12	0
Commercial	30	0.09	0
Total	278	0.68	0.625

Source: Statistical Handbook, Govt. of Goa.

Product and Service Delivery Systems

12. Urban life demands a delivery of products and services through a role taken over by public delivery systems. The common products demanded of the public delivery system are foodstuff. The common services demanded of the public delivery system are water, telecommunication, electricity, mobility, solid and liquid waste removal and treatment.

13. The role of delivery of foodstuff is taken over by the PDS (public delivery system) and rationing system, handled by the Collectorate. The electricity and water delivery systems in Goa are the responsibility of the electricity department and the PWD respectively. Telecom is delivered by the BSNL and private players. Mobility is delivered by the PWD, town and country planning, police, RTO, public transport system and the private players. Solid waste is handled by the municipal authorities. The liquid waste is the responsibility of PWD, Sewage Treatment Board and PCB.

Access and Cost

14. A comparison of property prices from nine metros in India compared with Goa indicates that Goa is as expensive as Ahmedabad. Low-end residential property in Goa is more expensive than Pune and Hyderabad, although cheaper at the higher end.

FIGURE 14.2

Urban Commercial Property Prices

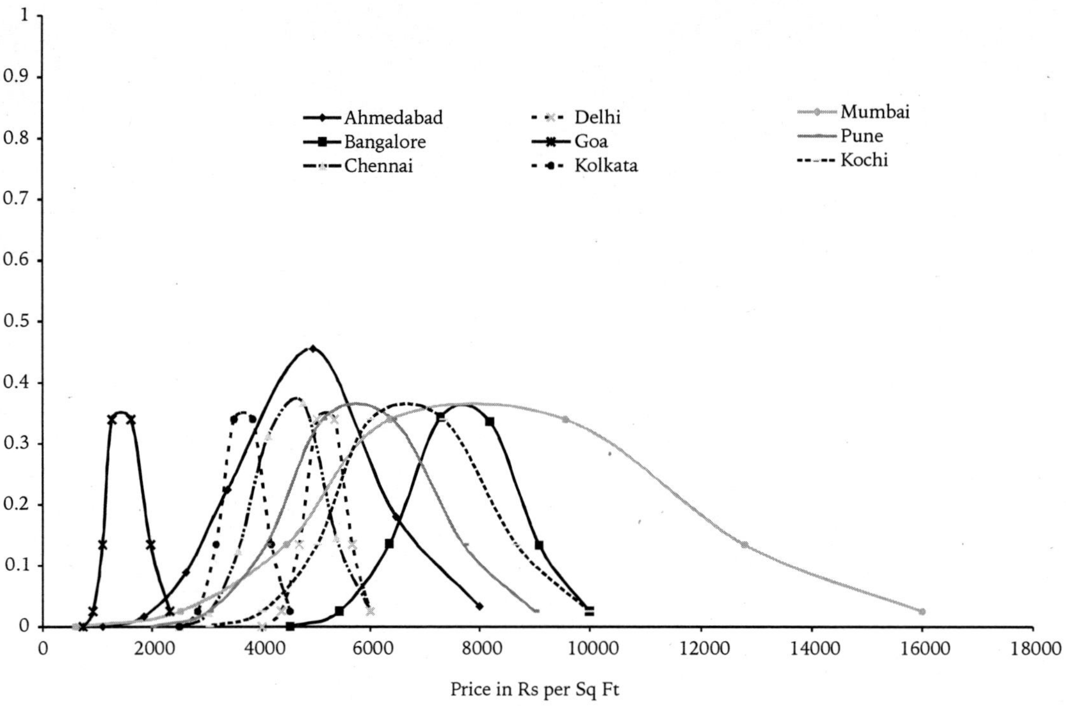

Source: Nasscom/GCCI/Real Estate Publications.

FIGURE 14.3

Probability Distribution of Residential Property

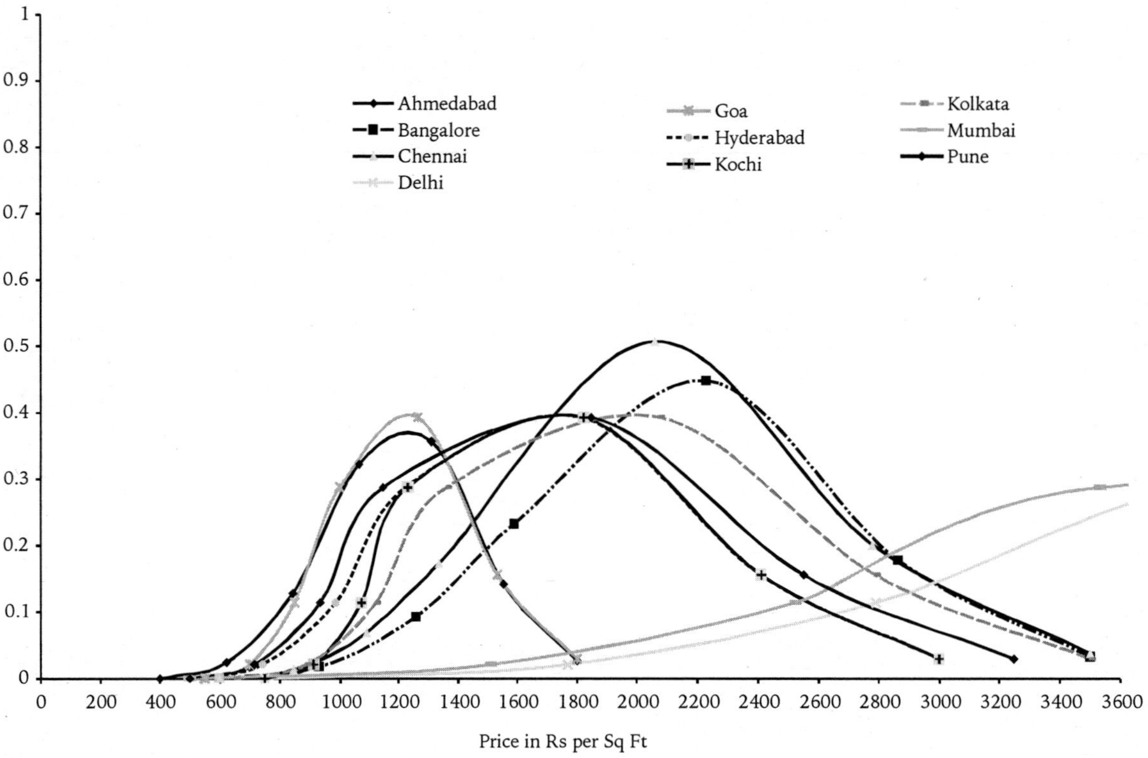

Source: NASSCOM/GCCI/Real Estate Publications.

TABLE 14.5

State Capital Area

Town/Village	*Area*	*Population*	*Households*	*Household Density*	*House Density*
Panaji	2263	43,349.00	9,097.00	4.02	3.84
Panelim (OG)	137	883.00	183.00	1.34	1.34
Morambi-O-Grande (Merces)(OG)	605	2,858.00	531.00	0.88	0.83
Renovadi(OG)	27	196.00	44.00	1.63	1.52
Morambi-O-Pequeno (Merces)(OG)	184	1,629.00	326.00	1.77	1.63
Durgavado (OG)	18	551.00	97.00	5.39	4.67
Cujira (OG)	177	769.00	147.00	0.83	0.82
Murda (OG)	188	3,588.00	700.00	3.72	3.64
Calapor (C.T)	982	9,390.00	1,913.00	1.95	1.77
Chimbel (C.T)	328	8,023.00	1,529.00	4.66	4.42
Taleigao (C.T)	1956	14,279.00	2,946.00	1.51	1.48
Penha-de-Franca (C.T)	542	11,546.00	2,534.00	4.68	4.67
Reis Magaos (C.T.)	761	7,504.00	1,487.00	1.95	1.88
Bambolim (C.T)	764	4,955.00	789.00	1.03	1.03
Jua (C.T)	827	4,555.00	1,083.00	1.31	1.30
Ambarim	14	114.00	27.00	1.95	1.80
Capao	130	176.00	43.00	0.33	0.33
Caraim	63	248.00	55.00	0.87	0.87
Nerul	985	3,912.00	678.00	0.69	0.64
Pilerne	654	2,662.00	562.00	0.86	0.80
Ella	801	2,494.00	492.00	0.61	0.58
Bainguinim	323	207.00	53.00	0.16	0.16
Salvador do Mundo	1159	4,451.00	975.00	0.84	0.80
Chorao	1983	5,577.00	1,107.00	0.56	0.53
Goltim	397	1,920.00	425.00	1.07	1.05
Malar	525	1,660.00	341.00	0.65	0.63
Naroa	139	511.00	99.00	0.71	0.60
Navelim	695	1,237.00	282.00	0.41	0.40
Marra	327	791.00	172.00	0.53	0.52
Curca	272	1,886.00	352.00	1.29	1.13
Siridao	772	2,673.00	510.00	0.66	0.62
Talaulim	532	564.00	112.00	0.21	0.19
Sangolda	339	2,542.00	529.00	1.56	1.51
Corlim	574	3,249.00	689.00	1.20	1.13
Cumbarjua	240	4,239.00	740.00	3.08	2.81
Gandaulim	135	290.00	63.00	0.47	0.47
Socorro (Serula)	1250	6,358.00	1,368.00	1.09	1.07
Olaulim	153	667.00	138.00	0.90	0.87
Pomburpa	501	3,564.00	711.00	1.42	1.26
Saligao	586	5,038.00	1,048.00	1.79	1.74
Azossim	331	1,069.00	193.00	0.58	0.55
Batim	378	1,567.00	332.00	0.88	0.85
Carambolim	1504	4,545.00	830.00	0.55	0.49
Gancim	303	494.00	102.00	0.34	0.32
Goalim Moula	320	332.00	56.00	0.18	0.15
Goa Velha	1013	5,038.00	975.00	0.96	0.91
Mandur	206	3,598.00	695.00	3.37	3.19
Mercurim	256	5,902.00	1,110.00	4.33	4.17
Neura-O-Grande	889	1,452.00	267.00	0.30	0.27
Neura-O-Pequeno	107	376.00	58.00	0.54	0.53
Total	28615	195,478.00	39,595.00	1.38	1.32

Source: Census of India, 1991.

15. In the state capital area itself there are at least six households per hectare without a house.

16. Of the essentials food, clothing and housing, access to food and clothing remain an issue in urban centres. Goa has the highest cost of living index in the country. Naturally food a major component of the basket, is expensive. The traditional fish-curry and rice in the local diet is also becoming a problem to those below the poverty line.

Land Records and Titles

17. It is known that 90 per cent of all the lands in India do not have clear titles. The ownership is unclear and hence, the land is off the market, thereby creating a scarcity of land. In Goa, the Portuguese laws of owning and inheriting property with spouse and all heirs makes titles even more complicated.

18. While land records are computerised, there is no inventory of State's assets and linkage to a single shared citizen registry. This makes it impossible to identify land holdings, as much as to ensure clean transactions.

Land Use and Planning

19. While the urban expansion is eating into the orchard and agricultural land of the hinterland, within the urban area open spaces are fast disappearing. Currently the Town and Country Planning Department, the Planning and Development Authorities and the Municipal Body have their own independent say in the land use and planning of the towns and cities. As new towns have sprung up, there have been no town plans for these regions.

20. Creating defined zones of attraction linked to the transportation network is also a crying need. The location of educational institutes, markets, institutional areas, recreational areas such that there is reduced traffic moving from one attractor to another is another need. Open spaces and their maintenance as a part of the urban fabric is going to be a challenge.

State Capital Area

21. While Panjim has been the capital city, in order to meet the growing demand the neighbouring area has grown as a State Capital Area. Naturally this entire region needs to be looked upon as the State Capital Area and planned for accordingly. The entire area then should be governed by a common authority and its infrastructure development planned and created through a common plan.

Institutions and Governance

22. Currently there are multiple institutions at different levels of hierarchy that govern urban centres in the State. The Department of Municipal Administration oversees and audits the operations of municipal bodies. The GSUDA is responsible for developing and sponsoring urban development schemes for the municipal bodies or funding the programmes proposed by municipal bodies. The municipal bodies are responsible for the upkeep of the urban centre in association with State Development agencies or bodies. The PWD Water Department is responsible for water connections and billing. The PWD Roads Department is responsible for the urban road network and its maintenance. The Electricity Department meets the electrical needs of the urban centre. The Sewage Treatment Board commissions and maintains the sewage treatment plants.

23. The Twelfth Schedule of the Constitution lists functions of the municipal bodies.

TABLE 14.6

Functions of Municipal Bodies under the Twelfth Schedule of the Constitution of India

Urban planning including town planning.
Regulation of land-use and construction of buildings.
Planning for economic and social development.
Roads and bridges.
Water supply for domestic, industrial and commercial purposes.
Public health, sanitation, conservancy and solid waste management.
Fire services.
Urban forestry, protection of the environment and promotion of ecological aspects.
Safeguarding the interests of weaker sections of society, including the handicapped and mentally retarded.
Slum improvement and upgradation.
Urban poverty alleviation.
Provision of urban amenities and facilities such as parks, gardens, playgrounds.
Promotion of cultural, educational and aesthetic aspects.
Burials and burial grounds; cremations, cremation grounds and electric crematoriums.
Cattle pounds; prevention of cruelty to animals.
Vital statistics including registration of births and deaths.
Public amenities including street lighting, parking lots, bus stops and public conveniences.
Regulation of slaughter houses and tanneries.

Source: Constitution of India, Ministry of Urban Development.

24. In practice, the State government undertakes many of these functions for municipal areas. Each authority has its own jurisdiction and geographical zones of planning

and operation. Since these geographical zones do not coincide but intersect, different regions grow at different rates with respect to different facilities and therefore, different usage patterns. Naturally there is unbalanced growth and a failure of urban development.

25. There is an urgent need for:

- Common geographical units for planning, operations and maintenance by all divisions, departments or institutions governing and maintaining urban infrastructure and service delivery.
- A single authority within each urban centre responsible to govern all urban needs;
- A single development authority comprising stakeholders of urban and rural areas to ensure urban growth is not at the cost of the rural hinterland and there is a balanced perspective of planning not just land use but the entire socio-economic fabric of the region.

Infrastructure

Integrated Development of Small and Medium Towns (IDSMT)

26. The Centrally sponsored scheme of IDSMT was initiated in the year 1979-80 in order to:

- improve the economic and physical infrastructure
- provide essential facilities and service
- slowdown the growth of large cities by developing small and medium towns through increased investments in these towns.

27. It had been visualised that with the development of small urban centres' migration to larger cities would be reduced. It was expected to create a support for the growth of surrounding rural areas as well.

28. The components for assistance under IDSMT include:

- Works as per city/town development/master plans which may have city/town wide significance.
- Strengthening of master plan road facilities including ring, arterial, bypass/link roads and small bridges.
- Sites and services.
- Development of bus/truck terminals.
- Construction/upgradation of master plan drains including storm water channels.
- Solid waste management.
- Development of market complexes/shopping centres.
- Provision of tourist facilities.
- Development of city/town parks.
- Street lighting for master plan roads.
- Slaughter houses.
- Major public amenities like gardens, playgrounds, marriage halls, pay-and-use toilets, etc.
- Cycle/*Rickshaw* stands.
- Traffic improvement and management schemes.
- Construction of retaining walls and slope stability measures in hill station towns.
- Social amenities, especially for the poorer sections.

29. Only nine towns from Goa have benefited to the extremely small extent of Rs. 2 crore from this scheme.

TABLE 14.7

Central Assistance Released and Expenditure Reported in lakhs of Rupees under IDMST Scheme Since 1979-80 till March 31, 2002

State	*Towns*	*Covered by IDMST*	*C.A.Released*	*Expenditure*
Goa	44	9	204.00	118.72

Source: Ministry of Urban Development.

30. Clearly the mechanisms for implementing this scheme need to be reviewed.

Housing

31. As already indicated, there is an acute access problem in urban housing in Goa. There is urgent need for rent control act and the release of speculation property for rental and purchase access to the residents of the region. Given that Goa will need to attract talent in large numbers to service the economy over the next 20-30 years, development of large scale new townships is needed. The Ministry of Urban Development has a scheme to provide for housing advance to Central government employees. However, there is no scheme for those with no housing but with the ability to repay the advances. Nor do such schemes actually acquire and make available land for housing.

32. With a view to ameliorating the conditions of the urban slum dwellers living below poverty line that do not possess adequate shelter, under the Valmiki-Ambedkar Malin Basti Awas Yojana (VAMBAY) the Central government provides 50 per cent subsidy towards costs prescribed both for dwelling units/community toilets. While the response from the BPL group has been moving, the procedures have been far from convenient and easy.

Again, the delivery mechanism for the scheme needs to be looked into.

Educational Institutions

33. While educational institutions for resident population have some infrastructure, this should be more contemporary and not a collection of box classes.

34. There should also be planning for potential educational SEZ that would host Asian campuses of different international institutions. This should take into account the housing and other needs of this population group.

35. Currently there are no schemes or PPP projects that will create educational infrastructure in urban environments.

Commercial Establishments

36. Commercial establishments provide the hub of economic activity in an urban area. Planned infrastructure that will promote commercial activity should also be created in urban centres. Currently there are no PPP arrangements to develop state-of-the-art commercial establishments for the urban population considering their age structure.

Health and Hospitality

37. While health is a State subject, it is also listed as a function of the municipal bodies under the Twelfth Schedule of the Constitution. However, public health and wellness centres and their infrastructure is largely left to the State government or market forces. There are no PPP arrangement nor are there schemes to seed such infrastructure in small and medium towns.

Parks and Recreation

38. Parks and recreational infrastructure is usually left to the Forest Department and the Arts and Culture Department. In Goa, urban areas have a good focus on theatre and sports facilities, though they could be augmented. However, urban forestry and parks remain a concern.

Mobility

39. Most urban centres in Goa have a poor intra-city infrastructure for transportation. The road-network planning is poor and unscientific as with most of urban India. This results in congestion and chaotic traffic from time to time. Too many authorities govern the creation, management and maintenance of urban infrastructure.

40. Intra-city public transportation is virtually non-existent. Most towns are small enough to have continuous rail/shuttle routes for free pick-up and drop-off and allow the town to be free of private vehicles.

41. Inter-city transportation can be networked in a better manner by augmenting rail, air, or ferry/boat links. Typical town routes like the beach belt also need to have planned infrastructure for greater mobility.

42. Alternate infrastructure of public transport as attractors of traffic is poor. For example, there are no buses, trains from airport, railway station, inter-state bus station or educational institutes, industrial areas, entertainment centres. Although there is a fundamental infrastructure for a set of tourist towns, this is not adequately developed.

Water Reservoirs and Distribution

43. Town alignments with water reservoirs and distribution lines are not even an afterthought. There is no plan, scheme or process that builds this major delivery channel to service urban growth of the next 20 years.

44. The Accelerated Urban Water Supply Programme was initiated in 1993-94 to provide safe and adequate water supply facilities to the entire population of the towns having population less than 20,000 as per 1991 Census. Goa has been allotted a mere 1.76 crore for 4 water supply schemes whose expected cost is 3.52 crore in 2003-04. In 2004-05, the allocation is a mere 0.9 crore. In 1994, Calangute and Reismagos benefited to the extent of 0.5 crore under this scheme.

Waste Collection and Disposal

45. Currently most of the towns are reeling under the pressure of potential groundwater contamination by septic tanks. The infrastructure to collect, pump and treat sewage is inadequate and needs urgent augmentation. However schemes to do so have not been developed.

Electricity Generation and Distribution

46. Electricity comes to the urban centres in Goa from the western and southern grid. The distribution network is mostly overhead and task for laying underground cables is underway. The transformer planning is not as per a common unit based on Town and Country Planning Plans, rather on demand driven by markets.

47. This infrastructure needs planning and also possible augmentation to do remote metering, transmission of broadband signal and transformer-based audit system.

Petrol and Diesel Distribution

48. Although traffic is an integral part of the urban ethos, there is no planning of infrastructure for delivery of petrol and diesel. The location of pumps often blocks traffic through queues. Although fuels are consumed in high volume, pipelines to pumps have not been explored and trucks still ply in and out and logistical issues often cause periods of shortages.

Development and Growth Areas

49. Goa is an opportunity to develop new eco-friendly townships. The proposed Mopa International Airport, the convention Centre and the SEZ will all build pressure on the urban fabric that does not have the buffer capacity to accommodate the growth that is proposed. New townships need to be planned for the purposes of supporting this load.

Carrying Capacity and Sustainable Activity

50. Goa literally doubles its population over the year with the tourist traffic it supports. The tourism industry projects a target of 2 million tourists for 2005-06. This may even grow to 8 million with Mopa International Airport, a seaport accommodating passengers and fast rail links with Mumbai and Bangalore. However, most of the tourist traffic may well have converted to the business visitor.

51. This kind of traffic will extend the ecological footprint of Goa beyond the 1.5 ha per capita closer to the national average of 1.8 ha per capita. With 370,000 ha that would mean Goa can support less than 250,000 people. Obviously its footprint already extends beyond its own land and it has to rely on its needs from land beyond.

Strengths, Weaknesses, Opportunities and Threats

Strengths

52. Small towns are the greatest strength of Goa. Before the number of towns increases to 50 or more, Goa needs to get into the act of managing these small towns effectively; having systems and good governance in place to ensure they do not become slums.

Weaknesses

53. The age structure that will not be able to support the Goan economy beyond 20 years is a weakness of urban Goa. This means that Goa will have to strive hard to attract talent to run the services and the economy and it must begin doing that now.

Opportunities

54. Goa has a tremendous opportunity to develop new townships and relocate people and infrastructure. It can develop eco-towns of the future. This is an almost unprecedented opportunity.

Threats

55. The greatest threat to Goa is its unwillingness to integrate with the global knowledge economy and create communal distinctions between Goan and non-Goan groups in the State. This will drive talent away, make Goa unattractive and result in the decay of the Goan economy over the next decade or two.

Outlook: Possible Scenarios

Business-As-Usual

56. Under a business-as-usual scenario, Goa will have 20-30 new towns by the next census. By then about 60 per cent of the population will be living in urban centres. The workforce will have increased by 30-40 per cent due to the age structure of urban Goa. Jobs being scarce, a greater out-migration of the workforce will occur and those remaining will continue to depend on repatriated funds. Under a Business-as-Usual scenario Goa will have 20-30 new towns by the next census. By then about 60 percent of the population will be living in the urban centers. The workforce will have increased by 30-40 percent due to the age structure of urban Goa. Jobs being scarce a greater out-migration of the workforce will occur and those remaining will continue to depend on repatriated funds. Under a utopian scenario Goa will promote 2-3 new planned towns that adapt the best practices of urban development from across the world on a BOOT basis and take the pressure off from the unplanned growth of existing towns. The new towns attract wealth and employment creators give a boost to the economy already stirred by the newly developed integrated transportation network. The Goa Educational SEZ has located premier institutes from the world at their campus. With the best brains in Asia recruited to teach at these institutes, Goa is regarded as the center of the Knowledge Economy in western India. Under a dystopian scenario Urban growth is controlled by real estate speculation. Property soars due to scarcity fueled by speculators. Goa is economically unviable for wealth and job creators. Very few jobs can be created in Goa. The youth leave Goa. Urban infrastructure becomes a ghost town, full of speculated property that is not lived in. The property values crash and yet find no takers as the

economy has lost its ability to grow and generate returns for the citizens.

Utopia

57. Goa will promote 2-3 new planned towns that adapt the best practices of urban development from across the world on a BOOT basis and take the pressure off from the unplanned growth of existing towns. The new towns attract wealth and employment creators, give a boost to the economy already stirred by the newly developed integrated transportation network. The Goa Educational SEZ has located premier institutes from the world at their campus with the best brains in Asia recruited to teach at these institutes. Goa is regarded as the centre of the knowledge economy in western India.

Dystopia

58. Urban growth is controlled by real estate speculation. Property soars due to scarcity fuelled by speculators. Goa is economically unviable for wealth and job creators. Very few jobs can be created in Goa. The youth leave Goa. Urban infrastructure becomes a ghost town, full of speculated property that is not lived in. The property values crash and yet find no takers as the economy has lost its ability to grow and generate returns for the citizens.

Recommendations and Development Strategies

59. Urban governance should ensure common and geographically identical units of planning development and maintenance by all department, divisions and institutions involved in the delivery of urban services.

60. Delivery of services, development of infrastructure and implementation of Central/State schemes should all be explored through a franchise to the Municipal Body Route, thus leaving local governance locally as intended by the 74th Amendment.

61. New township development incorporating best practices from across the world on a BOOT basis with only a governance control should be explored.

Chapter 15

Economic Growth and Fiscal Policy

Issues and their Fiscal Implications

Sustaining Growth

1. Between 1998-99 and 2002-03 Goa's economy has grown at a CAGR (Cumulative Annual Growth Rate) of 6.96 per cent. In real terms, this amounts to a growth of 3.59 per cent. The per capita terms in NSDP (Net State Domestic Product) has grown at 5.37 per cent or in real terms 2.05 per cent.

2. Clearly sustaining the growth of NSDP in real terms in relation to the growth of population will be a challenge. Balancing the need for additional people to fuel the growth of the economy and at the same time ensuring the rate of growth of the economy is faster, is a challenge even for Goa which is near replacement value for its population.

FIGURE 15.1

Real NSDP and Per Capita NSDP Growth in Goa in 1993-2003

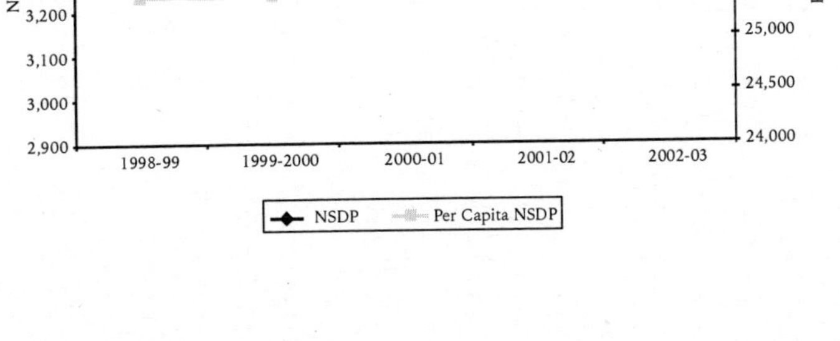

Sectoral Expansions and Contractions

3. In the five years between 1998-99 and 2002-03, the primary sector has grown at a CAGR of 4.37 per cent, the secondary sector at a CAGR of 10.32 per cent and the tertiary sector at a CAGR of 5.89 per cent. In real terms, this amounts to a CAGR of 1.21, 7.69 and 2.42 per cent in the primary, secondary and tertiary sectors (See Table 15.1).

4. In this period, the secondary sector displays a greater ability to expand its output in comparison to the other sectors. This elasticity may be due to increased capacity utilisation and productivity, the commissioning of new units or change due to changes in value of the output.

5. In real terms, during this period, in the primary sector forestry displayed a CAGR of 7.21 per cent. Agriculture displayed a slow expansion of 3.79 per cent while the output of the fishing and mining industries contracted during this period.

6. In the secondary sector, construction displayed rapid expansion in output. Electricity, water and gas displayed a CAGR of 8.58 per cent and registered manufacturing of 7.64 per cent. Unregistered manufacturing expanded more slowly at 3.16 per cent.

7. In the tertiary sector, real estate expanded at a CAGR of 9.62. Other services and transport, storage and communications showed medium expansion whereas banking, insurance and public administration expanded their output slowly. Trade, hotels and restaurants contracted their output during this period.

8. As is evidenced across different economies, different industry sectors experience different rates of economic expansion and contraction in different time periods. Expansion of output signifies the utilisation of capacity of

an industry sector and contraction the idle capacity or depreciation. Sustained capital investments ensure adequate capacity to counter depreciation or even expand capacity and therefore, sustain or expand future output.[1] Economies with lower or near zero growth rates can also sustain the economy by ensuring replacement of depreciated capital, thus accomplishing an equilibrium state.

9. The availability of capital, labour, materials and energy drive the capacity utilisation. Policies in force from time to time facilitate the access and economics of capital, labour, materials and energy altering the expansion or contraction of the industry output. Changes in policy expose different industry sectors to altered risk of capacity utilisation.

Inflationary Growth

10. The significant differences in current and real rupee distort the current growth and reduce both its value and CAGR (see Figure 15.2). Goa has consistently had amongst the highest cost of living index in the country. It has also had a rising cost of living index in the five-year period being considered.

11. The presence of high inflation is suggestive of industry sectors that produce output forming part of the basket consumed by the people which is unable to meet the states' own demand for these goods or services.

12. Economic growth under high inflation scenarios will require considerably and consistently higher rates of growth for sustained expansion of the economic output in real terms.

FIGURE 15.2

Components of NSDP by Industry of Origin in Current and Real Rupees

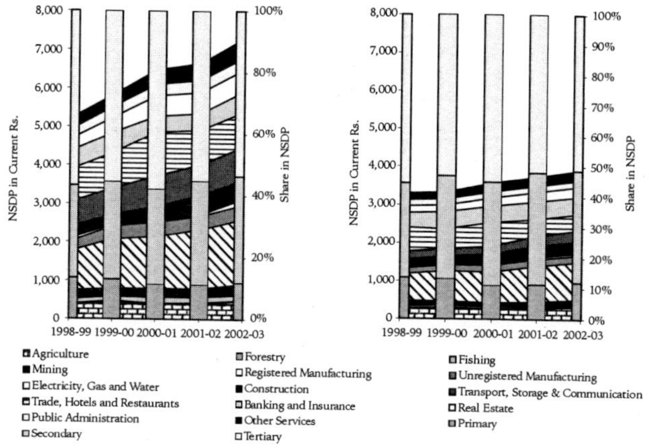

Source: Reserve Bank of India (*www.rbi.org.in*) Costs of Growth.

TABLE 15.1

CAGR of NSDP of Goa for Different Periods P1 (1998-99 to 2000-01), P2 (2000-01 to 2002-03) and P3 (1998-99 to 2002-03) in Current and Real Rupees based on NSDP in Current and Constant Rupees for Goa Published by the Reserve Bank of India (*www.rbi.org.in*)

NSDP	*CAGR Current Rs.*			*CAGR 1993-94 Constant Rs.*		
	1998-99 to 2000-01	*2000-01 to 2002-03*	*1998-99 to 2002-03*	*1998-99 to 2000-01*	*2000-01 to 2002-03*	*1998-99 to 2002-03*
Agriculture	1.87%	7.31%	5.50%	-0.68%	7.12%	3.79%
Forestry	-15.58%	20.58%	1.07%	4.91%	7.05%	7.21%
Fishing	9.00%	-7.37%	0.58%	-7.25%	-6.18%	-8.01%
Mining	-1.74%	9.28%	4.36%	-10.43%	8.45%	-1.73%
Registered manufacturing	10.31%	7.62%	10.84%	6.00%	6.67%	7.64%
Unregistered manufacturing	11.58%	-0.40%	6.54%	4.31%	0.97%	3.16%
Electricity, gas and water	-168.86%	289.48%	17.30%	1.12%	13.43%	8.58%
Construction	11.68%	4.24%	9.55%	10.18%	7.21%	10.51%
Transport, storage & communication	8.52%	2.92%	6.86%	-1.99%	12.82%	6.22%
Trade, hotels and restaurants	10.57%	-7.19%	1.57%	-0.93%	-12.05%	-7.93%
Banking and insurance	-4.80%	8.38%	1.90%	4.49%	-0.43%	2.41%
Real estate	19.07%	1.40%	11.97%	6.25%	9.68%	9.62%
Public administration	6.09%	3.18%	5.58%	1.06%	2.83%	2.33%
Other services	7.09%	8.07%	9.17%	7.73%	5.54%	8.01%
Primary	1.94%	5.35%	4.37%	-3.96%	6.23%	1.21%
Secondary	8.80%	8.26%	10.32%	6.46%	6.27%	7.69%
Tertiary	8.54%	1.35%	5.89%	2.99%	1.04%	2.42%
Total	7.55%	4.01%	6.96%	2.79%	3.17%	3.59%

1. Sometimes referred to as growth in the waiting.

13. Expansion or contraction of output of an industry sector poses an opportunity cost to the State—the opportunity of the expansion of alternate sector output, the opportunity of enjoying a quality of life that is altered by the expansion or contractions through environmental and social impacts, the opportunity of capital investment: an opportunity for future consumption. Unless understood and controlled clearly, the net costs can make growth uneconomic.

14. Growth also requires the economy to work faster; unless there are more through-puts and decreased cycle times, more cannot be accomplished in the same time. This requires more capital, material, labour and energy. Each has its own cost in addition to a social and technology cost.

15. Particularly in a small state like Goa, labour, energy and material all need to be imported for sustaining growth. For sustained growth, Goa will have to weigh the costs it is willing to pay for this growth.

Fiscal Policy

16. From an economic standpoint the government's plan for spending and taxation is considered to steer aggregate demand in a desired direction and therefore, serve as a means to balancing aggregate supply and aggregate demand in the economy. It uses this as a means to cause expansion of the economic output.

17. From this perspective the budget allocations are primarily aimed to steer demand and supply in order to stimulate the economy and not balance revenue and expenditure and balance the finances of the state. From this perspective, deficit financing is a need for economic growth in a recessionary economy as a fall in SDP shrinks the tax and non-tax receipts of the government. It can, therefore, be argued that deficit changes even when government policy does not and is a poor measure of fiscal policy.

18. Balanced budgets are regarded as contractionary fiscal policy that will retard the growth of real SDP (State Domestic Product). A zero cyclically adjusted, inflation corrected deficit is therefore, regarded as the sustainable deficit.

19. The choice between spending policy and tax policy will ultimately determine the deficit created to balance the payments resulting from these policies. Greater public spending through public services and goods requires financing through greater taxes or a greater deficit. Lower tax rates would require public spending to be reduced or deficits to mount.

FIGURE 15.3

Deficit Financing in Goa

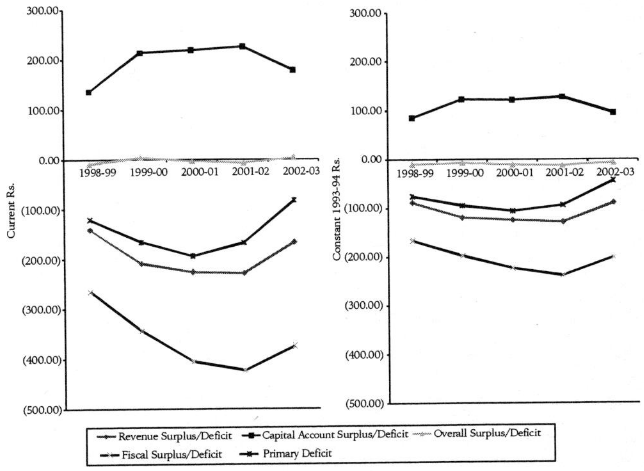

Source: Finance Department, Budget at a Glance 1998-2003.

20. Both the 11th and 12th Finance Commission, however, sets certain norms for states in exercising financial prudence (See Table 15.2). Deficits give rise to debts. As long as these debts are held within the state, it may be argued that it merely redistributes money in the state. However, debt held outside the state poses a burden to the future citizens of the State as a group. The revenue deficits of all states are expected to fall to zero. Goa has moved closer to this goal of balancing the

TABLE 15.2

Targets Set by the 11th and 12th Finance Commissions

Goal	*11th Finance Commission*	*12th Finance Commission*
Gross fiscal deficit	2.5 per cent of GSDP	3 per cent of GSDP
Revenue deficit	Falling to zero	Falling to zero
Debt to GSDP ratio		To be brought down to 28 per cent
Interest payments as percentage of revenue receipts	18-20 per cent	15 per cent
Increase in wages or salaries	5% or increase in CPI	
Increase in interest payments	Limited to 10 per cent per year	
Recruitment policy		Salary bill, relative to revenue expenditure, net of interest payments does not exceed 35 per cent
Subsidies	to be brought down by 50% and eliminated by 2009-10	
States share in central taxes	29.5 per cent	40 per cent
Grants and loans	4	Centre to do away with loans and confine support to grants

Source: Finance Department, Budget at a Glance 1998-2003.

revenue deficit. The gross fiscal deficit of states is targeted to fall to 2.5 per cent of GSDP. In Goa this has moved to 5.14 per cent of NSDP. The interest payments are to move to becoming 18-20 per cent of the revenue receipts. In Goa this has been brought down from 30 per cent in 1998-99 to 25 per cent in 2002-03.

21. In Goa the outlay has grown to 21.46 per cent of the NSDP. The revenue receipts have increased their size from 12.56 per cent of NSDP in 1998-99 to 15.39 per cent of the NSDP in 2002-03. The revenue expenditure has also increased as a proportion of NSDP in the same 5 years from 15.26 per cent to 17.68 per cent, much slower than the increase of the share of receipts (See Table 15.3).

TABLE 15.3

Budget Indicators as a Percentage of NSDP

Budget	*1998-99*	*1999-2000*	*2000-01*	*2001-02*	*2002-03*
Outlay/NSDP	18.53%	18.87%	19.56%	21.40%	21.46%
Revenue receipts/ NSDP	12.56%	12.25%	12.18%	13.98%	15.39%
Tax/NSDP	6.85%	7.87%	7.95%	8.56%	8.26%
Non-tax/NSDP	3.03%	2.05%	1.58%	2.92%	4.52%
Share in central taxes/ NSDP	1.86%	1.65%	1.62%	1.61%	1.56%
Grants-in-aid/NSDP	0.81%	0.69%	1.03%	0.89%	1.06%
Revenue expenditure/ NSDP	15.26%	15.83%	15.66%	17.41%	17.68%
Interest payment/ NSDP	2.76%	3.06%	3.27%	3.85%	4.00%
Plan/NSDP	2.03%	2.13%	2.17%	2.74%	2.99%
Non-plan/NSDP	10.47%	10.64%	10.22%	10.83%	10.69%
Overall deficit/NSDP	-0.19%	0.06%	-0.06%	-0.11%	0.04%
Fiscal deficit/NSDP	-5.08%	-5.91%	-6.25%	-6.36%	-5.14%
Revenue deficit/ NSDP	-2.70%	-3.58%	-3.48%	-3.43%	-2.29%

Source: Finance Department, *Budget at a Glance 1998-2003*.

22. In real terms, during the 5-year period from 1998-1999 to 2002-03 the revenue receipts have shown a CAGR of 7.85 per cent, two times faster than the NSDP which grew at 3.59 per cent. To sustain this rate, the economy will have to grow faster or the revenue receipts will form an increasing share of the NSDP. The State's share in central taxes has shown a decline of 0.32 per cent. The revenue expenditure has grown more modestly at 6.65 per cent bridging the revenue deficit. The non-plan expenditure showed a growth at 3.97 per cent whereas the plan expenditure has grown at 11.66 per cent.

Institutions and Governance

23. Currently, the Finance and Revenue Ministries as well as the Departments of Accounts, Sales Tax, State Excise and the Economic Development Corporation of the Finance Department are the institutions responsible for the issues concerning economic growth and fiscal policy.

24. In the absence of a single Economic Development Authority or Board, the longer-term plan and the annual budget and accounting exercises become merely administrative tasks of the multiple departments. To focus on growth strategies and evolve periodic targets, the State needs to evolve an Authority or Board consisting of economists to plan growth and investments in the State.

Development and Growth

Development

25. Goa's development requires a greater understanding of the balanced expansion of output of different industry sectors. Left to the forces of the market, development will be unplanned; sectors that see demand will expand output rapidly at the cost to the state and its coordinated and planned development.

26. The government has, therefore, a significant role of stimulating and balancing aggregate demand and supply in the economy to ensure development of diverse sectors of the economy.

Growth

27. The growth of the output requires adequate capacity to be created in different industry sectors. Unless this capacity exists, the industry sector cannot expand its outputs to meet demands.

28. Stimulating this capital investment for growth of the industry sectors is necessary to ensure the sustained growth of the economy.

Carrying Capacity

Limiting Factors

29. The biggest constraint to Goa's economic growth is its size and ability to accommodate through-put. With a small working cohort and a smaller pool of workers, it does not offer industry sectors the human resource in large quantities for expansion. The State is constrained by the Power Purchase Agreement (PPA) negotiated till 2007. The subsequent electricity security will be decided only after renegotiations with neighbouring states in an increasingly dismal power scene in the country.

30. The state has inadequate means to double or quadruple its material supplies by air, road, sea or rail. This constrains economic expansion of industry sectors that are material-intensive. The state has limited banking, insurance and risk management facilities and although there has been growth of this industry sector, it may have inadequate capacity to increase throughput significantly or reduce the cycle time.

TABLE 15.4

CAGR of Receipts and Expenditure of Goa for Different Periods P1 (1998-99 to 2000-01), P2 (2000-01 to 2002-03) and P3 (1998-99 to 2002-03) in Current and Real Rupees Based on NSDP in Current and Constant Rupees for Goa Published by the Reserve Bank of India (*www.rbi.org.in*)

Budget	*CAGR Current Rs*			*CAGR 1993-94 Constant Rs*		
	1998-99 to 2000-01	*2000-01 to 2002-03*	*1998-99 to 2002-03*	*1998-99 to 2000-01*	*2000-01 to 2002-03*	*1998-99 to 2002-03*
Revenue receipts	6.41%	12.46%	11.38%	1.68%	11.55%	7.85%
Share in central taxes	2.24%	2.83%	3.05%	-2.48%	2.00%	-0.32%
Grants-in-aid from the Central government	15.60%	4.78%	12.19%	9.99%	3.94%	8.36%
State's own tax revenue	12.89%	5.37%	10.97%	7.83%	4.52%	7.44%
State's own non-tax revenue	-13.50%	47.48%	15.73%	-17.43%	46.29%	12.00%
Revenue expenditure	8.46%	8.30%	10.14%	3.64%	7.43%	6.65%
Interest payment	13.57%	11.22%	15.04%	8.40%	10.32%	11.33%
Non-plan	6.62%	5.59%	7.37%	1.87%	4.74%	3.97%
Plan	9.76%	15.71%	15.42%	4.72%	14.77%	11.66%
Capital receipts	15.38%	-1.32%	8.09%	10.20%	-2.12%	4.65%
Internal debt	3.47%	10.34%	8.27%	-1.27%	9.45%	4.76%
Loans and advances from Central government	17.91%	-1.08%	9.68%	12.52%	-1.88%	6.12%
Non—debt capital receipts	18.18%	-16.56%	-0.84%	9.91%	-17.24%	-5.52%
Others (public account-net)	29.94%	-19.25%	2.92%	23.72%	-19.90%	-0.54%
Opening balance carried over from previous year	-198.50%	-227.23%	14.50%	10.63%	21.49%	19.41%
Capital expenditure	13.83%	2.93%	9.97%	8.67%	2.10%	6.44%
Non-plan	-243.95%	23.87%	-241.48%	-224.50%	22.87%	-229.05%
Repayment of debt	14.29%	9.41%	14.35%	8.66%	8.53%	10.40%
Lending	27.75%	-7.53%	10.51%	19.03%	-8.28%	5.41%
Plan	13.39%	4.76%	10.88%	8.21%	3.91%	7.29%
Others (Contingency fund, etc.-net)	-53.86%	-625.41%	-270.11%	-62.20%	-621.16%	-250.21%

Source: Finance Department, *Budget at a Glance 1998-2003*.

31. The significant growth of Singapore and similar small nations or states has been accomplished by facilitating a high through-put of people and material. This was made possible by expanding the air and sea ports of the nations/states. Naturally Goa will have to examine this strategy to enhance its carrying capacity.

Sustainable Development

32. The expansion of output in different industry sectors has different impact on the ability of the economy to sustain expansion. The expansion and contraction of output also results in environmental degradation that, in a place like Goa, is of considerable social and cultural value.

Strength, Weakness, Opportunity and Threat

Strength

33. From a growth perspective the greatest strength of Goa is its near replacement population. This makes the problem of dealing with compounding growth far easier than one where the growth of the economy does not pay dividends due to a faster growing population.

Weakness

34. The absence of 10-20 year policy timeline, independent of a political process, makes the different industry sectors vulnerable to expansion and contraction of their output from time to time.

Opportunity

35. The strategic location on the central western coast of India offers Goa a tremendous advantage in a global economy. It can increase its NSDP by several fold in just 10-20 years if it develops the infrastructure to accommodate through-put of the global world: people, materials, energy and capital.

Threat

36. Due to high cost of living and a high inflation rate, inflationary growth requires higher growth rates to ensure small real growth. Unless addressed this can well offset the advantages of Goa's strength and erode its per capita income and material standard and offset the opportunity offered by its strategic location.

Outlook

Business-As-Usual

37. Under a business-as-usual (BAU) scenario, if capital investment rates sustain the real NSDP CAGR at current levels, it will take 20 years to double the output of the economy. As long as the population remains at replacement value, they can expect to enjoy a doubling of their material standard in 20 years. The continuation of this trend is practicable only if the age structure will provide enough workers from amongst those cohorts in the labour pool to ensure utilisation of capacity to sustain the CAGR. The more likely scenario in a BAU case is that the population will have to grow at a faster rate to sustain the NSDP CAGR. Goa will therefore, see a significant erosion of the material standard in 5-10 years.

Aggressive Growth Scenario

38. In an aggressive growth scenario the state will focus on increased throughput of capital, material, energy and labour. It will create the necessary infrastructure, in under 3-5 years, to facilitate a 3-10 fold increase in throughput of capital, people, material and energy through the state. As a consequence over the next 10 years, the NSDP will increase between 2-5 fold while the population may have doubled. The average citizen will, therefore, enjoy better than a doubling of the material standard of living in less than 10 years.

Decline Scenario

39. The State will fail to create infrastructure to increase material, people, energy and capital through-puts in the next 3-5 years. The existing infrastructure will further depreciate and erode the ability of the industry sectors to expand output. While there has been a flight of the working cohorts from Goa, they will be replaced by those retiring into Goa. With an increased dependent population and a slower and declining economy, the State output will fall. The average individuals' material standard of living will halve in less than 5 years.

Development Strategy and Recommendations

40. Creation of infrastructure to increase the through-put of people, material, energy and capital in the state by 10-50 fold in the next 3-5 years will be a necessary step to ensure rapid growth of 7-8 per cent in the economy.

41. CAGR of real government expenditure should not exceed the CAGR of real government receipts and these in turn should match or be slower than the growth of the NSDP.

42. Fiscal policy should be used to adjust aggregate demands and PPP with public purpose and corporate accountability should be explored for public delivery systems of essential services and products.

Chapter 16

Development Strategies and Recommendations

Background

1. Since its liberation in 1961, Goa's economic output has altered radically and moved rapidly from a primary sector dominated economy to a high growth service and manufacturing economy. It was especially after the 1990s that saw a spurt in manufacturing as industries moved in to take advantage of the various tax benefits as well as favourable investment climate.

2. It was in the last five years that the power scene in Goa improved radically in terms of quality and choice with private power generation and saw an expansion of economic output from the manufacturing sector that was probably able to work to full capacity.

3. The path of transformation of Goa was set by Dayanand Bandodkar, the first Chief Minister of Goa who invested heavily in the social sectors. It is, therefore, one of the few states to have free school education and high enrolment rate. However, Goa still needs to focus on quality of school education and higher education. As the knowledge economy becomes the mainstream for the global village, Goa still has a long way to go to integrate into this new-age economy. It is this huge gap that needs to be addressed now to integrate Goa into the global knowledge economy of the 21st century.

4. In this context it is clear that the development strategy has to look forward to creating a Goa of the next 20 years and not of the next 12 months. The key objective of the development strategy should, therefore, focus on ensuring that Goa is able to rise to the challenges of a global knowledge economy in every essential respect.

Development Strategy

Infrastructure

5. Goa needs to sustain an economic growth rate of 8-10 per cent in order to sustain or increase per capita income and reach the standard of living of middle-income economies.

6. Like other smaller countries or states like Singapore, Hong Kong or Delhi, Goa's growth strategy will have to focus on increasing this through-put, decreasing the cycle time or both. Naturally the growth strategy will need to create and expand infrastructure: both land, sea and airports and have greater integration of transport links to the soft infrastructure especially in education and skill development.

Education

7. Currently only 8.33 per cent of Goan workers are graduates and only 0.57 per cent of Goan workers have university education. There are fewer knowledge workers per square kilometre in Goa (between 0.59 to 1.8 per square kilometre) in comparison to urban centres in other states. Naturally the tertiary economic sector, the less polluting knowledge sector, requiring greater knowledge and skills are disadvantaged in Goa in comparison to Bangalore, Mumbai or Pune. If greater knowledge processing were to happen per square kilometre to accelerate the growth of the economy, Goa will need greater knowledge workers.

8. In R&D, IT, ITES and other high skilled services, Goa will have to work at attracting highly skilled and knowledge-based workers and develop these services rapidly. Failing this, Goa will have to move more material, energy or capital per square kilometre or fall back to tourism of vices to sustain even an average economic growth.

9. An excellent strategy would be to serve as the Asian campus for premier educational institutions in primary, secondary and higher education, from across the globe in

educational SEZs. This will itself build a high value for education in the State and help a greater proportion of the population to be highly skilled or knowledge workers.

Governance

10. Governance is basically ensuring the management of the affairs of the state especially to improve the quality of life of the people of Goa. With high growth rate, the State will be confronted with a high risk of unfriendly or unequal governance in terms of the development objectives. Just as infrastructure is an enabler of growth, good governance is an enabler of development.

11. Not only must Goa's governance focus on clear mission areas, but it must also reduce the role of the government giving greater economic freedom to the people consistent with the security of food, water, employment, health, energy, livelihood, housing, mobility etc., of every Goan. Goa must raise the level of governance that ensures reforms and a machinery of government to manage and operate the affairs of the State well. Goa must create mechanisms that facilitate the economy to align to and address the objectives of the missions. Better governance from the shackles of bureaucracy will mean using modern tools including e-governance. This will mean the development of a new breed of professionals with high competence and ethics to man the machinery and reforms of the Goa government.

12. To ensure effective governance for the next phase of its development, the State will have to create appropriate institutions responsible for governing mission areas for the State. It will need to create a means to have common, shared information systems to facilitate better planning, coordination and responsiveness.

13. Above all, good governance in Goa must mean that the State government should do well the key functions specified on the State list of the Constitution and not do what others can do better, especially managing economic activities which need greater freedom and flexibility than the Goan bureaucracy or any other bureaucracy can handle well.

14. The Government of Goa has implemented the site *http://egov.goa.nic.in/rtipublic/start.aspx* for making available RTI related information to the public. Each department has appointed Public Information Officers and Assistant PIO and has also appointed a Chief Information Commissioner under the act. Although there is decentralization for information access the RTI has no mechanism for ensuring relevant and coordinated information. A departmental PIO can provide information from the department but require the applicant seeking information pertaining to another department be filed with other departments. This can prevent good governance.

Recommendations

15. In order to ensure the successful implementation of the development strategy, it is recommended that:

1. The State government formulates clear mission areas that will help Goa to be in the forefront of the knowledge economy. It should create appropriate institutional mechanisms that work for a fixed non-renewable tenure of three years from stakeholders affected by the mission area.
2. Each mission should formulate a clear set of objectives for each quarter and evaluate the progress of all statutory bodies, departments, corporations or bodies responsible for implementation of the objectives.
3. Immediately take steps broadly towards "Less Government" in areas not core to the constitutional mandate of the state and "to unleash the creative energies" of the people of Goa so that the Goan people and the economy moves rapidly to the standards of at least the middle income economies of the world, if not more.
4. Undertake to use IT to create government-wide common shared registry of citizen, business, project, asset, receipts and expenditure in order to create a common information space for planning, monitoring and delivery of service.